THE

PUBLICATIONS

OF THE

SURTEES SOCIETY

VOL. 215

THE

PUBLICATIONS

OF THE

SURTEES SOCIETY

ESTABLISHED IN THE YEAR
M.DCCC.XXXIV

VOL. CCXV

117.

Pall Mall. Nov. 29. 1664.

Sir, yours of the Oct. 29. with ye postscript of Nov. 18 I received. As for wt concerns mr Dyowse, my Lord knowes not yet what to answer, nor how to remedy him. [my Lo. might sequester for the K. Tenths, or for want of sufficiency, or present upon the Lapse.] It came in well (as he hath protested to me he did, though he confessed yt he gave 160l by way of gratuity, wch I understand not) the law will give him remedy, my Ld cannot. For how should he give him possession, when another takes it violently from him? The law must do it.

For what you write of ye concerning ye excommunicated persons, if you have not already determined any thing, my Ld thinks you had best to pass it by. one you say desired absolution, & so it may be the better passed over.

The clergy is not yet so firmly established as to do every thing as in former times, I think, it might more safely do.

All the friends you mention are well. Mr Thorndike is at Cambridge. The Dean of St Pauls is expected to morrow, as men say; but I have it only by report. The Commons have voted, at a Comittee, the 2500000l to be raised by a regulated subsidiary way, & are now to consider how it may be best done. wt it will mean, I know not: But I guesse it must not be called a monthly tax, because they formerly declared agt having more such, nor a subsidy, because it cannot be raised but by a great many, wch cannot be paid in a few years. My service to mrs Basire, & to all my friends in the College. yr sons I saw very well. I am

yr humble servant,
Geo. Davenport.

Durham University Library, Cosin Letter Book 1B, letter 117.
Letter 64 in this volume.
Courtesy of Durham University Library.

THE LETTERS OF GEORGE DAVENPORT 1651–1677

EDITED
BY
BRENDA M. PASK
with
Margaret Harvey

THE SURTEES SOCIETY

THE BOYDELL PRESS

First published 2011

A Surtees Society Publication
published by The Boydell Press
an imprint of Boydell & Brewer Ltd
PO Box 9, Woodbridge, Suffolk IP12 3DF, UK
and of Boydell & Brewer Inc.
Mt Hope Avenue, Rochester, NY 14620, USA
website: www.boydellandbrewer.com

ISBN 978–0-85444–070–2

ISSN 0307–5362

A CIP catalogue record for this book is available from the British Library

Details of other Surtees Society volumes are available from Boydell & Brewer Ltd

Papers used by Boydell & Brewer Ltd are natural, recyclable products made from wood grown in sustainable forests

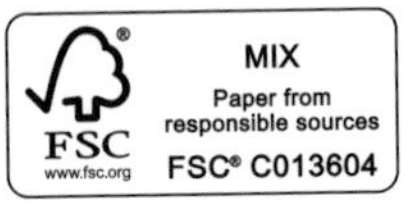

Printed and bound in Great Britain by
CPI Antony Rowe, Chippenham and Eastbourne

CONTENTS

FOREWORD AND ACKNOWLEDGEMENTS

George Davenport has long been known for his contribution to the establishment of Bishop Cosin's Library in Durham and his work, together with Miles Stapylton, in running the bishop's affairs, but little has been written about the man himself.[1] I hope that the present volume goes some way towards revealing George Davenport as an individual worthy of consideration for his own merits within his seventeenth-century context.

I am most grateful to Dr A.I. Doyle for his advice, for generously providing me with a copy of his lecture and for his help in elucidating difficult parts in the text; also to Dr Patrick Mussett for many valuable suggestions for the footnotes, to Mr Norman Emery, Cathedral Archaeologist, for his information on the prebendal houses in the College, and to Professor Emeritus C.K. Barrett for his constant encouragement.

My thanks are due to the staff of the following libraries and archives:

The Bodleian Library, Oxford
The British Library
Cambridge University Library
Durham County Record Office
Durham University Library, Palace Green
Guildhall Library, London
Lambeth Palace Library
Leicestershire Record Office
Lincolnshire Archives Office

My thanks are also due to Mr John Marlow, a member of the Davenport family, for his generous provision of genealogical material.

I am most grateful to all my friends for their help and

1 A.I. Doyle, 'The Cosin Manuscripts and George Davenport', *The Book Collector* 53/1 (Spring 2004), pp. 32–45; H. Gee, 'The Correspondence of George Davenport, sometime Rector of Houghton-le-Spring', *Archaeologia Aeliana*, 3rd ser., 9 (1913), pp. 1–10.

encouragement and especially to Brent Sowerby for computer assistance throughout the project.

Finally I wish to thank the clergy, parishioners and churchwardens of the parish church of Houghton-le-Spring, who gave me such a warm welcome to George Davenport's own church.

Brenda M. Pask

When Brenda Pask was unable to finish this edition I completed it. It would not be possible to assign authorship of the various parts between us. I thank Dr Adrian Green and Dr Anne Orde for reading through the entire final typescript and saving it from many errors.

Margaret Harvey.

We are grateful to Durham University Library for permission to reproduce the photograph of letter **64**.

A NOTE ON THE MANUSCRIPTS

Most of the papers of Archbishop Sancroft, including many of the Davenport letters printed here, were bought from his nephew and steward Thomas Sancroft by the well-known antiquary Thomas Tanner and left by him to the Bodleian Library. Some other Sancroft papers were given to the Bodleian by Bishop Richard Rawlinson. The following manuscripts have been used.

Durham University Library, Archives and Special Collections:
Cosin Letter Book 1B.

London, British Library:
  Harleian MSS (cited as H. with folio number) 3783, 3784, 3785, 3786.
  Additional MS (cited as Add.) 4292.
  Sloane MS (cited as S.) 813.

Oxford, Bodleian Library:
  Tanner MSS (cited as T. with volume and letter number) 40, 42, 43, 44, 45, 47, 48, 49, 52, 55, 92, 144, 145, 149, 150, 155, 314.
  Rawlinson MSS, Letters (cited as R.) 100, 101.

A copy of letter **31** is in the Baker Collection (Baker MSS, xxxiv, 146.) of Cambridge University Library.

Leicester Record Office:
DE 1139/2–3
A selection of Davenport letters copied into two volumes in 1893 by Francis D. Ringrose, a descendant of the Leicestershire Davenport family. Ringrose claimed to be a tenth descendant of George Davenport's grandfather, Richard. He included a number of letters written to William Sancroft by George's elder brother, John.[1]

---

1 John Davenport's letters date from 22 November 1649, 4 December 1650, 6 March 1650, 16 May 1655 and 25 May 1666.

EDITORIAL CONVENTIONS

I have integrated the letters in chronological order and numbered them 1 to 148. In general I have retained the order within the various collections. I have retained Davenport's abbreviations in a few places but have silently completed yr, yt, yn etc. Davenport's punctuation has been retained, except in a very few places where I have added punctuation to assist the reader.

When giving sums of money Davenport wrote pounds as l, in superscript. I have used £ throughout.

The following conventions are also used:

* ... *	text illegible.
/ \	word(s) inserted above the text.
< >	erasure.
</\>	inserted over erasure. Where possible the erased word(s) are noted at the foot of the letter.
// //	phrases inserted at the side.
{ }	editorial addition.

In the Introduction, the numbers in bold refer to letters in the collection.

ABBREVIATIONS

Abbott, *Writngs and Speeches*	W.C. Abbott, *The Writings and Speeches of Oliver Cromwell*, 4 vols, Cambridge (Mass.) 1937.
Acts and Ordinances	*Acts and Ordinances of the Interregnum, 1642–1660*, ed. C.H. Firth and R.S. Rait, 3 vols, London 1911.
Add.	Additional Manuscript, BL.
Al. Cant.	J.A. Venn, *Alumni Cantabrigienses*, 4 vols, Cambridge 1922–7.
Al. Ox.	J. Foster, *Alumni Oxonienses, 1500–1714*, 4 vols, Oxford 1891.
AV	Authorised version of the Bible, 1611.
BDB	F. Brown, S.R. Driver, and C.A. Briggs, *Hebrew and English Lexicon with an appendix containing Biblical Aramaic*, Peabody (Mass.) 1906.
BL	British Library, London.
CCED	The Clergy of the Church of England Database 1540–1835, www.theclergydatabase.org.uk, with individual person ID.
Cosin Corr. I	*The Correspondence of Bishop Cosin*, ed. G. Ornsby, I, SS 52 (1869/70).
Cosin Corr. II	*The Correspondence of Bishop Cosin*, ed G. Ornsby, II, SS 55 (1870).
Cosin, *Works*	*The Works of the Right Reverend Father in God John Cosin* …, 5 vols, Oxford 1893–5.
CSP, Dom.	*Calendar of State Papers, Domestic*, with date of coverage.
DCM	Durham Cathedral Muniments.
DCRO	Durham County Record Office.
Diaries, SS 118	*Six North Country Diaries*, ed. J.C. Hodgson, SS 118 (1910).
Diaries, SS 124	*North Country Diaries: Second Series*, ed. J.C. Hodgson, SS 124 (1915).
DUL	Durham University Library.
Durham Cathedral Registers	*The Baptismal, Marriage and Burial Registers of the Cathedral Church of Christ and Blessed Mary the*

	Virgin at Durham, 1609–1896, transcribed and annotated by E.A. White, Harleian Society (1897).
Durham Cathedral Statutes	*The Statutes of the Cathedral Church of Durham*, ed. J.M. Falkner, SS 143 (1929).
Durham Parish Books	*Church Wardens Accounts of Pittington and other Parishes in the Diocese of Durham from 1580–1700*, ed. J. Barmby, SS 84 (1888).
G.D.	George Davenport.
GEC, *Baronetage*	G.E. Cokayne, *Complete Baronetage*, 6 vols, London 1900–09, repr. 1983.
GEC, *Complete Peerage*	G.E. Cokayne, *The Complete Peerage of England, Scotland, Ireland, Great Britain and the United Kingdom, extant, extinct or dormant*, 14 vols in 15, London 1910–1998.
H.	Harleian Manuscript, BL, followed by folio number.
HBC	*Handbook of British Chronology*, 3rd edn, ed. E.B. Fryde, D.E. Greenway, S. Porter and I. Roy, London 1986.
Hennessy	G. Hennessy, *Novum repertorium ecclesiasticum parochialis Londinense, or, London Diocesan Clergy Succession from the Earliest Times to the Year 1898*, London 1898.
HPC	*History of Parliament. The Commons 1600–1690*, 3 vols, ed. B.D. Henning, London 1983.
Hutchinson, *Durham*	W. Hutchinson, *The History and Antiquities of the County Palatine of Durham*, 3 vols, Newcastle 1785–94.
L. (LL.)	Letter(s) of G.D. with number of letter in bold.
Le Neve, *Fasti*	J. Le Neve, *Fasti Ecclesiae Anglicanae, 1541–1857*, 12 vols, London 1969 onwards; with volume number and name of diocese.
Mussett	P. Mussett, *Lists of Deans and Major Canons of Durham, 1541–1900*, Durham 1974.
Newcourt	W. Newcourt, *London: an Exact Delineation of the Cities of London and Westminster and the Suburbs thereof, together with the Borough of Southwark*, London 1905.
Nichols, *Leicester*	J. Nichols, *The History and Antiquities of the County of Leicester*, 4 vols in 8 parts, London 1795–1811, repr. Wakefield 1971.

ODCC	*The Oxford Dictionary of the Christian Church*, ed. F.L. Cross and E.A. Livingstone, 3rd edn, Oxford 1977.
ODNB	*Oxford Dictionary of National Biography*, online edn.
OED	*Oxford English Dictionary.*
PCC Wills	Prerogative Court of Canterbury Wills, now in TNA.
PR	Parish register.
R.	Rawlinson Letter, Bodleian Library.
RO	Record Office.
S.	Sloane Manuscript, BL.
SS	Surtees Society, followed by volume number and date.
STC	A.W. Pollard and G.R. Redgrave, *A Short-Title Catalogue of Books Printed in England, Scotland and Ireland and of English Books Printed Abroad, 1475–1640*, 2nd edn, 3 vols, London 1986–91.
Stapylton Corr.	*Northumbrian Documents of the Seventeenth and Eighteenth Centuries, comprising the Register of the Estates of Roman Catholics in Northumberland and the Correspondence of Miles Stapylton*, ed. J.C. Hodgson, SS 131 (1918).
Surtees, *Durham*	R. Surtees, *The History and Antiquities of the County Palatine of Durham*, 4 vols, London 1816–40.
T.	Tanner Manuscript, Bodleian Library, followed by volume and letter number.
TNA	The National Archives, Kew.
TRHS	*Transactions of the Royal Historical Society*
VCH	*Victoria History of the Counties of England*, followed by county name and volume number.
Walker Revised	A.G. Matthews, *Walker Revised, being a Revision of John Walker's Sufferings of the Clergy during the Grand Rebellion, 1642–60*, Oxford 1948.
Wing	D. Wing, *Short Title Catalogue of Books Printed in England, Scotland, Ireland, Wales and British America, and English Books Printed in Other Countries, 1641–1700*, 4 vols (vol. I 2nd ed.), New York 1980–98.
W.S.	William Sancroft.

INTRODUCTION

This is a collection of 148 letters written by George Davenport, almost all to Dr William Sancroft, his former tutor at Cambridge.[1] They cover the years between 1651 and 1676/7 and so span the period of the Interregnum and nearly twenty years after the Restoration of the Monarchy in 1660.

George Davenport, the third son of John and Elizabeth Davenport (née Hales), of Wigston Magna, Leicestershire, was baptised on 17 January 1631. His older brothers were John (baptised 20 January 1625) and Stephen (baptised 19 April 1629). A sister Abigail was baptised in 1623 and died in 1632. His parents had been married in Exhall near Coventry in 1622.[2] His family may be traced at Wigston from 1599 when his grandfather, Richard, bought property there.[3] Richard is described in parish records of Wigston Magna as 'Gentleman'. He was also, from 1611, churchwarden. After Richard's death in 1623 the estate passed to George's father, John, and in 1655 to George's eldest brother, John.[4]

The Davenport family is thought to have taken its name from the Cheshire township beside the River Dane, about five miles west of Congleton.[5] By the end of the thirteenth century Richard de Davenport

---

In this Introduction the numbers in **bold** refer to letters in this collection.

1 Sancroft was subsequently Dean of St Paul's and, after Davenport's death, Archbishop of Canterbury from 1678 to 1690: *ODNB*.

2 George, Stephen and John: Leics. RO, Wigston Magna PR. The Davenports were often named 'Damport' in the early period. Abigail had been baptised at Exhall, Coventry (Warwickshire RO, Exhall PR), and died at Wigston (Leics. RO, Wigston PR). For the parents' marriage, 30 September 1622: Warwickshire RO, Exhall PR. The connection between Davenports and Hales is acknowledged in George's will: Appendix II, p. 263.

3 '2 messuages, 2 cottages, 4 gardens, 4 orchards and 24 acres of land': W.G. Hoskins, *The Midland Peasant, a study of a Leicestershire Village*, London 1957, pp. 198–9. Hoskins defines the Davenports as 'peasant gentry'. For an eighteenth-century account of the Davenport Wigston property: Nichols, *Leicester*, IV / I, p. 377.

4 Leics. RO, Wigston PR; TNA, PCC Wills 1654.344, L. **2**.

5 T.P. Highet, *The Early History of the Davenports of Davenport*, Chetham Society, 3rd ser., 9 (1960), p. 1.

had gained favour with the Earls of Chester and established his family as powerful landholders. George's family, the Davenports of Leicestershire, were descended from the Cheshire family; by the sixteenth century the cadet lines were settled in a number of locations in Staffordshire, Warwickshire, Lincolnshire and elsewhere and used the same arms as the Davenports of Cheshire: 'Argent a chevron between three cross-croslets fitchy sable'. The crest was 'a man's head couped at the shoulders with a halter about his neck all proper' and the motto *Tu ne cede malis*.[6]

Some members of the Warwickshire and Leicestershire Davenports gained a reputation in commerce in the sixteenth century, among them Thomas Davenport, appointed Mayor of Leicester and Merchant of the Staple of Calais, and Henry, a merchant and alderman of the city of Coventry.[7] These well-to-do Davenports employed their wealth in educating their sons, some of whom became noted clergy, among them Christopher and John Davenport of Coventry, the former a Roman Catholic priest in the service of Catherine of Braganza, wife of Charles II, and the latter a Puritan divine.[8] The Wigston family also produced

6 B. Burke, *The General Armory of England, Scotland, Ireland and Wales*, London 1884, repr. 1967, under Davenport of Davenport. The arms are on the chalice given by George Davenport to Wigston church in 1661 and on his memorial in Houghton church. They also appear on the seal of the will of his brother Stephen in 1680. The same motto is mentioned by Mr Rich in his letter (20 Nov. 1633) to W. Sancroft (BL, H. 3783, f. 31) commenting that it had been his desire for the motto of Emmannuel College.

7 Thomas Davenport of Leicester: TNA, PCC Wills, 6 July 1558. Henry Davenport of Coventry: TNA, PCC Wills, 17 Jan. 1571.

8 Christopher Davenport (c. 1595–1680), eldest child of Barnabas and Mary Davenport of Coventry. After education at Oxford and the English College, Douai, he joined the Franciscan Order at Ypres and was known as Franciscus à Sancta Clara, with various other aliases. After the Restoration he became chaplain to Catharine of Braganza, the wife of Charles II. He was buried in the Savoy Chapel in 1680: *ODNB*; L. **98**. John Davenport (1597–1670), the uncle of Christopher, was the son of Henry Davenport of Coventry. He gained a reputation as an inspiring preacher. After a period ministering to the English Church in Amsterdam, where he supported the Congregationalists, he returned to England briefly before his departure to Boston, Massachusetts, in June 1637. There he played an important part in establishing the colony later named New Haven. He wrote and preached, encouraging the colonists to hold fast to Congregationalism against Presbyterianism and sectarianism. Although he was invited to join the Westminster Assembly of Divines, convened in 1643 to reform the Church of England, he chose to remain in New England and died in Boston in 1670: *ODNB*; L. **123**.

clergy, including George, his brother John, and their nephew George, second son of Stephen. Many of the surviving Davenport letters refer to the family, with whom George kept in close and amicable contact, especially with John, who had married Sarah Thompson, daughter of Anthony Thompson, rector of West Rasen, Lincolnshire. They had eight children and John succeeded his father-in-law as rector.[9] Stephen and his wife Mary farmed the land in Wigston.[10]

*

George's youth and young manhood coincided with the Civil War with its complex political and religious quarrels. Central to these were sharp divisions about political ideas, ranging from the wholly republican to fiercely monarchical, coupled with equally bitter quarrels about religion, ranging from desire for the Church of England to become Presbyterian or Congregational, to plans for strict adherence to the Prayer Book and to episcopacy. In the bitter quarrels over these matters King Charles dispensed with Parliament for eleven years (1629–1640) and this, together with the increasing desire of some members of the House of Commons to play a greater part in government, led to armed conflict, the trial and execution of the king in 1649 and the establishment of the Protectorate under Oliver Cromwell. The shocking trial of the king horrified even many who did not agree with him and served only to deepen political and religious divisions. Davenport's home county, Leicestershire, became a thoroughfare for the forces of both the Royalists and the Parliamentarians and suffered at the hands of both. While the northern part of the county was Royalist, the south was staunchly Parliamentarian. The city of Leicester (only four miles north of the Davenport home) was besieged in 1645 during the movement of the Royalists from Oxford northwards, while the battle of Naseby, the effective defeat of the king's resistance to Parliament, on 14 June 1645, took place approximately twenty miles to the south.

Against this confused religious and political background John and George Davenport obtained their school and university education. After a grammar school education either in their village, where a schoolmaster was often provided, or in the Free School in Leicester, in

9 *Al. Cant*. He remained in West Rasen until 1693 when he became vicar of Great Wigston (1693–1706): CCED, person ID 87679; Nichols, *Leicester*, IV/1, p. 383.

10 Approximately a quarter of Davenport's surviving letters contain references to his family.

1646 George followed his brother John to Emmanuel College, Cambridge.[11] The college had been founded in 1584 by Sir Walter Mildmay, to train men for a preaching ministry.[12] In the early seventeenth century Emmanuel had become, with Christ's, a major Puritan influence in the university.[13]

The period spent by the Davenports at Cambridge was difficult both religiously and academically. The University, like the whole country, was a cauldron of opposing political and theological doctrines. In 1633 William Laud became Archbishop of Canterbury.[14] His theological position was Arminian, that is anti-Calvinist and liturgically inclined, contrary to the prevailing theology and liturgy of the English church.[15] In 1638 he aroused the hostility of the Puritans by his attempts to impose liturgical uniformity by force. In 1638 Laud's chaplain and one of his most ardent supporters, John Cosin, Master of Peterhouse, had introduced into his college chapel an elaborate altar and other similar church furnishings and ceremonies in keeping with his Arminian tendencies. The Laudian party also supported the requirement that M.A.s must swear an oath accepting 'the doctrine, discipline or government established in the Church of England'. Moves like these were denounced in January 1641 by the House of Commons and in 1643 the Solemn League and Covenant resulted in the abolition of episcopacy. In August 1643 'all monuments of superstition and idolatry' were ordered by Parliament to be removed from college chapels and parish churches. In January 1644, when those regarded by Parliament as unfit for their positions as ministers or as college heads were ejected,[16] the first group of the latter in Cambridge

---

11 J. Broughton, *All Saints, Wigston Magna*, Wigston 1999, p. 51; *Al. Cant.* for the two brothers.

12 Mildmay: *ODNB*.

13 S. Bendall, C. Brooke and P. Collinson, *A History of Emmanuel College, Cambridge*, Woodbridge 1999, chapter 6.

14 Laud: *ODNB*.

15 N. Tyacke, *Anti-Calvinists: the Rise of English Arminianism c. 1590–1640*, Oxford 1987, p. 246; M. James, *Family, Lineage and Civil Society: a Study of Society, Politics and Mentality in the Durham Region, 1500–1640*, Oxford 1974, pp. 112–13. The Arminians were followers of the Dutch Reformed theologian Jacobus Arminius (1560–1609): *ODCC*.

16 R.S. Bosher, *The Making of the Restoration Settlement: the Influence of the Laudians (1649–1662)*, London 1951, p. 5, cites an estimate that approximately 2,425 were sequestered. Those ejected from cathedrals and collegiate churches totalled 650 and those from Oxford and Cambridge 829. However, allowing for livings held in plurality a further 780 might be added to the list.

included the Arminian Cosin of Peterhouse, followed by the Calvinist Bishop Ralph Brownrigg of Catherine Hall and the moderate Puritan, Richard Holdsworth of Emmanuel, the college attended by both Davenports.[17]

In spite of some disruption to academic studies, John Davenport obtained his B.A. in 1647 and was elected a fellow of Emmanuel in 1649. He obtained his M.A. in 1650 but was ejected from his fellowship in 1654.[18] George received his B.A. in 1650 and M.A. in 1653. Though the letters do not give explicit information about their religious and political positions, it is clear that both brothers were 'Prayer Book men'. Both obtained (illegal) episcopal ordination[19] and George, as we shall see, worked for a deprived bishop, Brownrigg. The later letters, written when George had a freer hand to suit his own religious tastes, show that he believed in churches beautifully adorned, with altar and pulpit cloths and organs (**39**, **67**, **115**, **121**, **123**, **139**). We do not know what became of George Davenport immediately after he obtained his M.A. but a man of these religious views would have found it hard to obtain preferment without good friends with private patronage.

What must have altered the situation of both brothers was the death of their father in January 1655. George wrote to William Sancroft, his former tutor, to thank him for condolences on his father's death (**2**). At that time both John and George were at home in Wigston with their mother, but afterwards, by August 1656, John, illegally ordained, was preparing to take the living of West Rasen in Lincolnshire and to marry the widowed daughter of Anthony Thompson, the rector there (**16**, **17**). John was already rector in September 1656 and the marriage occurred on 24 July 1657 (**26**). Thereafter George visited his brother at his living. He continued to visit his mother at Wigston (**12**) but by early 1657 he was writing of her increasing infirmity(**19**) and in November 1658 speaks of her as 'a dying woman' (**34**). By February 1559 she was dead (**35**).

By 5 March 1655 George had been episcopally ordained (**3**). He had by then joined a group of friends in London, chief among them two brothers called Gayer, whilst some of the group were acquiring legal training. They lived first in the Temple and later in the area of Lincoln's

17 For Holdsworth at Emmanuel: Bendall, *Emmanuel*, pp. 224–6. For him and also Cosin and Brownrigg: *ODNB*, under their respective names.

18 J. Twigg, *The University of Cambridge and the English Revolution*, Woodbridge 1990, pp. 159, 304.

19 Below, p. 6.

Inn Fields (**3**, **6**, **17**, **18**). The advantages of a university education included not only training and the acquisition of knowledge, but also the accumulation of social contacts including the forging of links which would be of benefit during later life when patronage would be essential for the furtherance of careers.[20] Time spent in the Inns of Court had the same advantage, furthering contacts already made.

The most significant of George's friends and the most influential on his clerical career, however, was not in London. This was William Sancroft, who in 1642 became Fellow and Tutor of Emmanuel College, a position he held until his ejection in 1651.[21] He was tutor to both Davenports. Although much older, he became their firm friend; it is to his hoarding of letters that we owe the greater part of our knowledge of George Davenport. Sancroft spent much of the period from his ejection until the Restoration at his family estate at Fressingfield in Suffolk and on extended visits to a number of his Cambridge friends. In 1657 he visited the Netherlands and France and with John and Robert Gayer, also former pupils, embarked on a journey to Geneva, Venice, Padua and Rome, probably largely financed by the Gayers.[22]

The Gayers remained George's good friends, frequently mentioned in the letters.[23] They were the sons of Sir John Gayer or Gayre, a wealthy London merchant and Lord Mayor of London in 1646, a Royalist, who had died in 1649. They supplied many exiles with money.[24] In 1657 John Gayer bought Stoke Poges manor (now Stoke Park) in Buckinghamshire (**19**)[25] but he died later in the same year. Davenport was present at his death-bed and gave Sancroft a most touching account of his end (**27**, **28**). His young wife was pregnant at his death and eventually had a son (**30**).

The Henley family of Bramshill Park in Eversley, Hampshire, are

20 F. Heal and C. Holmes, *The Gentry in England and Wales, 1500–1700*, London 1994, p. 268.

21 For Sancroft at Emmanuel: Bendall, *Emmanuel*, pp. 248–56; *ODNB*.

22 Sancroft enrolled at the University of Padua. He returned to England in 1660: *ODNB*.

23 See index.

24 G. D'Oyley, *The Life of William Sancroft, Archbishop of Canterbury*, 2 vols, London 1821, I, pp. 95, 101, 102. For their father: *ODNB*; V. Pearl, *London and the Outbreak of the Puritan Revolution: City, Government and National Politics, 1625–43*, Oxford 1961, appendix I, pp. 301–2.

25 *VCH, Buckinghamshire*, III, pp. 306–7.

often mentioned also.[26] Andrew Henley, a barrister of the Middle Temple in 1646, married as his first wife Mary, sister of the Gayer brothers.[27] He and his wife invited Davenport to live with them in September 1656 (**17**). In February 1659 again Andrew Henley offered Davenport a permanent place in his household (probably as his chaplain) (**35**).

After the death of his brother, Robert Gayer lived for a while with Sir Robert Abdy at Albyns at Steepleford Abbots in Essex and then went abroad again (**34**). Abdy was another of the Gayer in-laws, who about 1643 had married Catherine Gayer, their eldest sister (**32**). George did not take up the Henley offer but he stayed regularly with all these friends; their circle was evidently most important to him. Throughout the period of Sancroft's exile the Davenports maintained contact with their former tutor by means of sporadic letters which show George's own refuge in the country houses of these friends and in London, and his undertaking of at least one visit to the Continent in 1655 (**13, 14, 15**).

George Davenport's first clerical appointment, by 2 June 1655, was as chaplain to Ralph Brownrigg, Bishop of Exeter, a position he almost certainly owed to the influence of Sancroft, as Brownrigg had been Sancroft's tutor.[28] A chaplain's work involved performing religious duties connected with a private chapel but also could include more 'secretarial' tasks. In 1642 Brownrigg had become Bishop of Exeter, though apparently he never visited his diocese because of the troubles. After his ejection from Cambridge in 1645 for preaching a Royalist sermon, he spent his time between London, Bury St Edmunds, Highgate and Sonning in Berkshire, the home of his friend Thomas Rich, a 'Turkey' merchant, who also supplied the king in exile with money.[29] Robert Gayer married one of Thomas Rich's daughters.[30] At Sonning Brownrigg carried out ordinations, thus helping to ensure that episcopally given orders were maintained in the Church of England.[31]

Brownrigg had ordained Davenport (**3**). George's letters contain

26 GEC, *Baronetage*, III, pp. 69–70.

27 *HPC*, II, p. 523.

28 L. **10**. Ralph Brownrigg (1592–1659) had been Master of St Catherine's Hall from 1631, and Vice Chancellor in 1637–8 and 1643–4. A Calvinist and an opponent of Arminianism, he was nevertheless an episcopalist: *ODNB*.

29 GEC, *Baronetage*, III, p. 180; *VCH, Berkshire*, III, p. 222; *HPC*, III, pp. 229–30.

30 *Al. Cant.*, under Gayer, Robert, for Mary Rich.

31 J. Spurr, *The Restoration Church of England*, New Haven 1991, p. 9.

references to 'My Lord of Exeter' during 1655, 1656 and 1658 though none survive from July 1658 to the end of Brownrigg's life. The links between these friends were close. Brownrigg would have conducted John Gayer's funeral had he been well enough (**28**) and it was he who christened Gayer's posthumous son in May 1658 (**30**). Brownrigg's last months were spent in lodgings in the Temple where he died on 7 December 1659 (**36**).

Following their eviction from their livings, many Anglican clergy took refuge abroad. These included a number of Davenport's clergy friends who had gone into exile in France and Holland. At the heart of one such group was John Cosin.[32] In 1634, after a stormy earlier career in Durham where he championed Laudian ideas against much opposition, Cosin became Master of Peterhouse and, in 1639, Vice Chancellor of Cambridge. He was ejected from Peterhouse on 13 March 1644 and took refuge in France where he was appointed by Charles I to serve as chaplain to the Protestant servants of Queen Henrietta-Maria.

After the execution of Charles I in January 1649, Henrietta-Maria was under pressure from her French hosts to convert any Protestants still in her party and John Cosin experienced great difficulty in maintaining his 'Anglican' flock, and supporting himself; by 1651 he was in dire poverty, dependent on friends in England including Sancroft and others to supply his needs.[33] When Davenport and his friends went abroad in December 1655, they may have been acting as couriers for money being dispatched to him (**13**, **14**, **15**). Such assistance was a treasonable act, for not only were sequestered clergy forbidden to teach, preach, administer sacraments or use the Prayer Book for any purpose, but others were forbidden by law to assist them financially.[34] Fortunately the visit engendered a rapport between Cosin and Davenport which was to prove of great significance for the latter's future. Already in February 1657 Cosin was telling Sancroft that Mr 'Damport' 'truly is *ad mentem meam*' and could tell Sancroft about his situation.[35]

After the death of Oliver Cromwell in 1658 and the abdication, in 1659, of his son Richard, the restoration of monarchy became a serious

32 Cosin: *ODNB*.

33 *The Diary of John Evelyn*, ed. E.S. De Beer, 6 vols, Oxford 1955, III, p. 62 n. 8, p. 636.

34 J.W. Packer, *The Transformation of Anglicanism*, Manchester 1969, pp. 38, 40.

35 *Cosin Corr.* I, pp. 286–7.

possibilty.[36] Dependent on letters and visits from friends, the exiles kept one another abreast of events in England; on 28 August 1659 John Cosin wrote to Sancroft from Paris mentioning the stirrings of revolt in favour of the monarchy: 'Wee are here assured that there is in England a considerable armie of ten thousand about Chester & divers others in severall parts of the Kingdome, that are resolv'd to put off their new masters and to call in the King, who with his brother the Duke of Yorke, is already gone that way, to attend God's good pleasure and blessing.'[37]

Negotiations for the Restoration centred not only on political issues but also on the religious settlement required. Despite a hope that a religious settlement would include moderate Presbyterians who could tolerate a form of episcopacy,[38] the Restoration government proved much more intolerant than its king, and it soon became clear that the re-instated church was to be Anglican. In 1660 the surviving bishops returned to their sees and the vacancies were filled in the autumn by new appointees. Episcopal ordination was now publicly available again to supply the deficit of clergy in the parishes; clergy and gentry returned to a parish-based episcopal church; church courts were restored. Ecclesiastical property, much of which had been sold off, was claimed back and often recovered. Only trivial concessions were made to the Prebyterians in the Prayer Book of 1662, with the result that most staunch Presbyterian ministers were deprived by the Act of Uniformity of 1662, which required their use of the Prayer Book and their assent to everything in it.[39] All of this of course also provided openings at last for episcopally ordained young men like George Davenport.

After the return of Charles II many of his loyal supporters, including many in Davenport's circle, were rewarded. Andrew Henley was knighted and made a Baronet in June and July 1660.[40] Thomas Rich was made a baronet in March 1661.[41] Robert Gayer was made a Knight of the Bath on 23 April 1661.[42] After seventeen years of exile, Cosin was restored to the Mastership of Peterhouse and the Deanery

---

36 G. Davies, *The Early Stuarts 1603–1660*, Oxford 1959, repr. 1992, pp. 254–60.
37 *Cosin Corr.* I, pp. 289–90.
38 Spurr, *Restoration Church*, pp. 30–1; R.S. Bosher, *The Making of the Restoration Settlement: the Influence of the Laudians (1649–1662)*, London 1951, p. 143.
39 Spurr, *Restoration Church*, pp. 38–40, 41.
40 GEC, *Baronetage*, III, p. 69.
41 GEC, *Baronetage*, III, p. 180.
42 W.A. Shaw and G.D. Burtchaell, *The Knights of England*, 2 vols, London 1906, p. 166.

of Peterborough. Very soon he was also appointed to the see of Durham and on 2 December 1660 was consecrated bishop. William Sancroft, newly appointed Cosin's chaplain, gave the consecration sermon, on the office of a bishop and the divine origin of the apostolic ministry. In addition to his position as chaplain, Sancroft received the rectory of Houghton-le-Spring, Durham, on 7 December 1661, and in March the following year became canon of the ninth stall in Durham cathedral. He was, however, non-resident from July 1662.[43]

George Davenport, who had continued as chaplain to Brownrigg at least until the latter was provided with lodgings in the Temple in 1658, and perhaps up to his death, obtained the rectory of St Peter's, Westcheap in 1661.[44] This he held until 1665, by the patronage of the Earl of Southampton, perhaps the result of Sancroft's influence (**41**, **43**, **46**, **51**, **62**). In addition he appears to have held some unidentified office at Westminster Abbey (**43**, **46**).[45]

St Peter's, Westcheap, also called 'St Peter & St Paul', which stood at the south-west corner of Wood Street, near Cheapside, was destroyed in the Great Fire of 1666. Although little evidence of Davenport's occupancy survives in parish records, the Visitation records of the Bishop of London, in 1664, record that the rector of St Peter's, 'Mr Georgius Davenport', was absent.[46] He was by then living elsewhere, in fact in Durham, serving the benefice with a curate. In the Letters Davenport mentions his house in London, though commenting on 18 December 1671 that it is seven years (i.e. since 1664) since he saw the capital (**46**, **134**). This date would coincide with the end of his period as rector of St Peter's.

An appointment in the diocese of Durham was the next important step in Davenport's career. By the summer of 1662 he had succeeded Sancroft as domestic chaplain to Bishop Cosin (**38**). From then until the summer of 1671 his letters frequently refer to his duties as chaplain,

43 See below, L. **37**, n. 290.

44 Hennessy, p. 438; Newcourt, p. 527.

45 It has not been possible to establish Davenport's precise relationship with the Westminster clerics at this time. He evidently did not have the status of a canon or minor canon and St Peter's, Westcheap, was not an Abbey living. I am grateful to the staff of the Muniment Room and Library, Westminster Abbey, for this information: L. **50**.

46 The parish registers were destroyed by a bombing raid in 1940. The Precinct Minute Book and the Church Warden's Accounts, which survive, do not bear the rector's signature: Guildhall Library, London.

an office which continued after his own appointment in succession to Sancroft to the rectory of Houghton-le-Spring in 1665 (**66**).

Cosin had inherited a diocese spiritually very divided and in a poor state materially. During the Interregnum the cathedral and its property had been allowed to degenerate, as had many parish churches, and church lands had been sold off. The cathedral and castle had received the attention of the Scottish prisoners after the Battle of Dunbar, 3 September 1658.[47] The cathedral had been used as a prison and the castle as a hospital.[48]

Cosin devoted much effort to regeneration of the diocese and its churches. His large-scale building operations both within the city and outside were very costly. Much of the cost was provided from the bishop's own resources and it was estimated that he had spent over £2,000 per annum on charity during his eleven-year episcopate.[49]

While the building operations were difficult enough to accomplish on such a large scale, the spiritual refreshment of the diocese was even more difficult. The cities of Durham and Newcastle had considerable groups of dissenters, including staunch Presbyterians, Quakers, Roman Catholics and varieties of Independents.[50] The bishop himself set an example to his clergy, visiting, removing recalcitrant and unsuitable clergy and ordaining others, chivying, and closely overseeing all that went on. Durham cathedral had been one of the earliest places to reveal an inclination towards Arminianism, demonstrated in a fierce quarrel between the canons Cosin and Smart from 1628 and it was this anti-predestinarian ritualistic brand of Anglicanism which was now re-introduced.[51]

If Cosin was the figure-head and leader in the campaign to restore the Anglican Church in the diocese of Durham, George Davenport was to become one of his most assiduous lieutenants. Davenport's work as Bishop's chaplain included, in addition to the regular

47 The former choir stalls were said to have been used by the Scottish prisoners for fire wood: J. Field, *Durham Cathedral: Light of the North*, London 2006, pp. 114–15.

48 S.E. Lehmberg, *Cathedrals under Siege, 1600–1700*, Philadelphia 1996, p. 37.

49 Cosin's munificence: *Cosin Corr.* II, pp. 334, 338; *ODNB*.

50 For the state of the diocese at the beginning of the episcopate of Cosin's successor, Nathaniel Crewe, see C.E. Whiting, *Nathaniel Lord Crewe, Bishop of Durham (1674–1721) and his Diocese*, London 1940, appendix, pp. 361–71.

51 M. Tillbrook, 'Arminianism and Society in County Durham, 1617–1642', in J. Marcombe, ed., *The Last Principality*, Studies in Regional and Local History 1, Nottingham 1987, pp. 202, 206–7.

preaching duties and administration of the sacraments, attendance at the Bishop's Visitations of the diocese, and at sittings of the Bishop's court, and dealing with lower clergy on Cosin's behalf, interpreting the bishop's mind to Archdeacon Basire of Northumberland in 1664, for instance (**64**).

He also deputised for the bishop in his secular duties. He was thus heavily involved in dealing with the so-called 'Derwentdale plot' (**52**), a multi-faceted but incompetent conspiracy by various disaffected groups to force the government to declare for Presbyterianism and liberty of conscience and to end the hearth tax. In 1663 Cosin and the Deputy Lieutenants informed the government of 'seditious and dangerous persons' at Muggleswick in Derwentdale and elsewhere. There was evidence of widespread discontent and anti-Royalist feeling. The local ramifications of this depended on evidence from John Elrington that preparations for a rising were being laid. Among those named was George Lilburne of Sunderland who also owned property in Offerton in Houghton parish and who appears in the Letters sharing in Davenport's hospital building (**110**, **113**). He was briefly imprisoned but then released and was probably innocent. The local plotting was nipped in the bud but elsewhere, in Yorkshire, meetings continued and the government continued to collect evidence from spies. In October 1664 most of those chiefly suspected had been arrested and in the Durham area the attempted rising came to nothing. John Joplin, former jailer in Durham and one of the central committee of plotters, was tried in Durham in August 1664 but acquitted, though not released.[52] The atmosphere of suspicion and distrust revealed in this episode was part of the background to Cosin's (and Davenport's) ecclesiastical work in the diocese.

One of Davenport's duties was to preach at the opening of the new Auckland chapel dedicated to St Peter, which replaced that destroyed by the Parliamentarian Sir Arthur Haslerigg when he purchased the castle in 1646. The chapel was to be a model for the rest of the diocese, as Davenport's sermon at its dedication service in 1665 made clear (**71**). He there urged the clergy to repair and beautify their own churches in the same way. Davenport also collected subscriptions for the building.

52 According to *VCH, Durham*, II, p. 55, 700–800 men were ready to rise in Durham but the plot collapsed on the imprisonment of the leaders: H.Gee, 'The Derwentdale Plot, 1663', *Transactions of the Royal Historical Society*, 3rd ser., 11 (1917), 125–42; C.E. Whiting, 'The Great Plot of 1663', *Durham University Journal* 22 (1920), pp. 155–67; *Cosin Corr.* II, p. xix.

In March 1662 his letter to Sancroft acknowledged a donation towards the rebuilding of the chapel and informed him that subscribers might have their armorial arms in a window if they wished (**51**).

Cosin's family were of great importance to him and therefore loomed large in the lives of his subordinates. Cosin had married Frances, daughter of Marmaduke Blakiston of Newton Hall near Durham.[53] The frequently mentioned Ralph Blakiston, prebendary of the seventh stall in Durham and rector of Ryton from 1660, was Marmaduke's son, Cosin's brother-in-law (**78, 115, 128, 136, 137, 148**). The Cosins had five children. The eldest, John, was at Peterhouse in 1649 and joined his father in France, where he became a Roman Catholic in 1651.[54] His father was furious and cut him off but did in fact supply him with money from time to time. The boy recanted and then changed his mind, calling himself by his mother's maiden name. Cosin eventually allowed him £50 per annum, adding £150 in his will. Davenport can be seen helping to administer the allowance (**111, 114, 115**), and it is clear that Sancroft was also in touch with the young man. Mary Cosin, the eldest daughter, had married before 7 March 1660 Sir Gilbert Gerrard of Fiskerton in Lincolnshire and Brafferton in Yorkshire.[55] He was created a baronet on 17 November 1666, with the title entailed on the male heirs of himself and Mary, cutting out earlier children by his first wife (**57, 69, 74, 93, 141**). The second daughter, Elizabeth, married as her second husband Sir Thomas Burton of Brampton in Westmorland (**40, 66**),[56] and as her third on 23 December 1662 Samuel Davison, Esq, of Wingate Grange, Durham, the younger brother of the High Sheriff of Durham, Sir Thomas (**49, 74**). Samuel had died by 15 April 1671.[57] The son of this marriage benefited in 1671 from the Frankland patent which caused Cosin a great deal of trouble with the Durham chapter (**49**). Elizabeth finally married Isaac Basire, son of the Archdeacon of Northumberland, Davenport's friend. Frances Cosin married as her first husband Charles Gerrard, brother of Sir Gilbert, who had died by 15 April 1665, leaving his wife pregnant

53 Pedigree: *Stapylton Corr.*, at p. 144.

54 *Cosin Corr.* II, p. 28n; P.H. Osmond, *A Life of John Cosin: Bishop of Durham 1660–72*, London 1913, pp. 126–8, 316–17.

55 GEC, *Baronetage*, IV, p. 38; *Cosin Corr.* II, p. 11n; Mary died on 5 December 1680 and her husband was buried on 24 September 1687. Pedigree: *Stapylton Corr.*, at p. 162.

56 *Cosin Corr.* II, pp. 28n, 210n.

57 Surtees, *Durham*, III, pp. 166–7, for Davison pedigree: *Stapylton Corr.*, p. 135n, and pedigree of Elizabeth, at p. 212.

(**66**, **74**).[58] In 1667 she married Mr Thomas Blakiston of Gibside. Anne, the youngest Cosin child, was of unstable temperament at least and often ill. She married on 16 September 1662 Denis Granville or Grenville, brother of Sir John Grenville, first Earl of Bath.[59] As part of the marriage settlement Cosin appointed him to the first stall in Durham cathedral and the archdeaconry of Durham, following this with several other lucrative preferments.[60] The marriage was very unhappy; the lady was volatile and Granville, though a conscientious churchman, was a spendthrift. The letters reveal some of this, showing Davenport's attempts (which failed) to achieve an exchange of benefices for Granville (**44**, **45**, **46**) but also Davenport's displeasure particularly when Granville wrote derogatory letters about Cosin, who refused to allow him as much money as he thought was his due (**92**, **98**).

Following his bishop's example, Davenport was also heavily involved in building works, both in Durham and Houghton-le-Spring. In Durham city itself he became involved in the rebuilding of the church of St Mary-le-Bow in the North Bailey of Durham, which in the seventeenth century was in a poor state.[61] The last Divine Service had taken place on 27 August 1637 and in the afternoon of 29 August the steeple fell into the street, destroying much of the west end of the church.[62] The parishioners agreed on 10 December to take down and replace the building, but nothing had happened by 1662 so Davenport set about raising money. By April 1670 he had assembled sufficient funds from the bishop and his own friends and acquaintances to begin rebuilding (**111**, **125**). He expected the operation to cost £400 but was optimistic about success. He also intended to gain sufficient money to support a curate there to provide afternoon sermons. This project, however, was not completed until after his death, though the building was begun during his lifetime as is recorded in Richard Wrench's letter to Sancroft, 24 January 1673.[63] The church was not in fact completed until 1685 and the western tower was not built until 1702.

---

58 *Cosin Corr.* II, p. 30n; Osmond, *A Life of John Cosin*, p. 318; pedigree: *Stapylton Corr.*, at p. 146.

59 *ODNB*, Denis Granville (1637–1703).

60 R. Granville, *The Life of the Honourable and Very Reverend Denis Granville, DD*, Exeter 1902, pp. 10–11.

61 *VCH, Durham*, III, p. 137.

62 This is the date given by Surtees, *Durham*, IV, pp. 38–9; E. Mackenzie and M. Ross, *An Historical Topographical and Descriptive View of the County Palatine of Durham*, Newcastle 1834, p. 389, gives 29 May.

63 T. 144.83 and 84, 24 Jan. 1672/3.

By the time he was collecting for St Mary le Bow Davenport had acquired a new post. In January 1664 William Sancroft was nominated as Dean of York, and then, in December of the same year, installed in the deanery of St Paul's, in London. Already by 26 July 1662 Sancroft had had a royal dispensation from his residence in Durham and although he held his prebend until October 1674, he was never resident again.[64] Davenport supplied some of the duties of the position. On Sancroft's resignation from the rectory of Houghton in 1665 Davenport was promoted to succeed him.[65]

Houghton-le-Spring was a rich living, one of the most sought after.[66] The parish included eighteen townships, some of which feature in the letters.[67] Houghton Hall had been built by Hutton family. Robert Hutton, prebendary of the third stall in Durham cathedral had been rector of Houghton from 1589 to 1623.[68] He had assembled considerable property in the parish. His grandson, also Robert, who inherited this, was a captain of horse-guards under Cromwell and served under General Monk. He remained a puritan and is probably the parishioner who Davenport says never comes to church (**39**). When he died in 1680 he was buried in his own orchard.[69] Other important figures, 'the gentlemen', in the parish, were Thomas Delaval of Hetton, Thomas Lambton of Biddick, Henry Smith of West Herrington, Thomas Shadforth of Eppleton, Alexander Amcots of Penshaw Wood, William Bowes of Biddick, Thomas Lilburne of Offerton, Robert Ayton of West Herrington, Francis Carr of Cocken, Francis Middleton of Offerton, Marmaduke Allison of West Rainton, and Cuthbert Scissons of West Rainton.[70] Many of these occur in the letters, some causing the

64 Dispensation: DCM, DCD/B/AA/4, ff. 59–60. Prebend: Mussett, p. 71.

65 The Dilapidation document relating to Houghton dates from 19 June 1665. See Appendix IV.

66 J. Freeman, 'The Distribution and Use of Ecclesiastical Patronage in the Diocese of Durham, 1558–1640', in Marcombe, *The Last Principality*, pp. 152–75, esp. pp. 152–3.

67 The Houghton Hearth Tax entries for Lady Day 1666 record twenty-one individuals, each taxed for one hearth, nine for two hearths, five for three hearths and the Hall and Parsonage each taxed for fifteen hearths. A further thirty-one individuals, having one hearth, were exempt and one for two hearths: A. Green, E. Parkinson and M. Spufford, *County Durham Hearth Tax Assessment, Lady Day 1666*, Index Library 119, British Record Society 2006, pp. 55, 145.

68 Mussett, p. 25.

69 James, *Family, Lineage and Civil Society*, p. 73; Surtees, *Durham*, I, pp. 147–9 (with picture of the hall); III, p. 163.

70 *Durham Parish Books*, p. 323: 'The Gentlemen in Houghton Parish in the yeare 1658'.

rector considerable problems, since not all were wholly committed to the religious settlement of 1660 and some seem simply to have begrudged the attempts to gather their tithes after the laxity during the recent upheavals (**39**, **109**).

The mixture of political and religious views in the parish can be seen from a few examples. After Hutton, Thomas Lilburne and his father George were probably the most important persons in the area. George was a leading figure in Sunderland from 1630 with considerable interests in coal, shipping and commerce.[71] He owned property including a house in Offerton in Houghton parish. The Lilburne family were Presbyterian and some became extreme religious and political radicals. In the 1640s George already found himself in trouble with the law for his religious views. He was soon involved in raising resistance against Royalists. From 1644 to 1648 George became dominant in local politics but was soon accused of helping himself to property, causing bitter local enmity, particularly in the end with Haslerig over the colliery of Harraton. Briefly the family regained influence from 1653 and under the regime of the Major Generals both George and his son Thomas enjoyed very wide powers. Thomas Lilburne became an MP, supported the offer of the Crown to Cromwell and struggled to help keep the regime in being after that was refused. At the Restoration, not surprisingly, the most radical Lilburne, Robert, a regicide, was imprisoned for life. Cosin was anxious that George and Thomas should suffer also for their support of the Protectorate and Thomas in particular for being a Protectorate MP. Cosin briefly had George arrested during the Derwentdale plot but nothing could be proved and he died peacefully, a wealthy man, in 1676. Yet Thomas seems to have lived quietly and lawfully under the new regime (**54**) Davenport's letters show him having to rub along with such men, and he seems to have had no problems sharing the foundation of Houghton hospital with Thomas and his father (**110**, **113**).

Thomas Delaval of Hetton, third son of Sir Ralph of Seaton Delaval, had been a leader of the parish during the Commonwealth, as a local JP. He seems to have lost this position at the Restoration.[72] Thomas Shadforth of Eppleton, mentioned from time to time by Davenport, was brother-in-law to Cosin, having married another of the daughters

---

71 W. Dumble, 'The Durham Lilburnes and the English Revolution', in Marcombe, *The Last Principality*, pp. 227–52, for the rest of this paragraph; G. Cookson, *Sunderland: Building a City*, London 2010, pp. 60, 70, 71.

72 *Durham Parish Books*, p. 305 n. 1.

of Marmaduke Blakiston of Newton Hall. He was also father-in-law of Robert Hutton of Houghton.[73] During the civil war he had serious quarrels with George Lilburne over Lilburne's alleged seizure of local property which Shadforth wanted, and the pair had vied with one another for local positions of power.[74]

Davenport was an exemplary pastor, following Cosin's lead. The Letters and the parish accounts reveal a dutiful parish priest caring for his parishioners and his church with energy and example, catechising and encouraging and evidently liking his flock for the most part (**69**). It is notable that he is anxious not to harrass people needlessly and expresses to Archdeacon Basire a worry that too strict an attitude does not do until the church is more securely established (**64**).

Many of the letters refer to Davenport's building activities at Houghton, the most important of which was the rebuilding of a large part of the rectory. The old rectory of Houghton-le-Spring stands to the west of the church and is now council offices. In the fifteenth century it already had an 'embattled' tower above the lower porch.[75] Sancroft had never resided and it seems that Davenport could not take up permanent residence until 1667. He still retained a room in Durham and Auckland castles to accommodate him when on the bishop's business.[76] His account of the defects of the Houghton house and how he envisaged its improvement are of considerable interest (**39, 66, 67, 72, 83, 88, 96, 97, 99, 105, 109, 132, 133, 140, 141, 145**). Building work required Davenport's constant supervision and considerable costs. When he had completed his rebuilding he 'embattled' the whole of the house in keeping with seventeenth-century taste and the Davenport arms and the date, 1664, were placed under the west window of the dining room.[77] According to the 1666 Hearth Tax records, after this rebuilding Houghton Parsonage was assessed at fifteen hearths, a sign of comparative affluence.[78] Some idea of the layout of the new parsonage may be obtained from the inventory

---

73 Surtees, *Durham*, I/2, p. 221; III, p. 163.

74 Dumble, 'The Durham Lilburnes', pp. 232, 236, 246.

75 W. Fordyce, *The History and Antiquities of the County Palatine of Durham*, 2 vols, Newcastle 1857, I, p. 554.

76 See *Cosin Corr.* II, appendix, pp. 341, 350 where the accounts for Auckland castle record the whitening of Mr Damport's chamber and the sweeping of Mr Damport's chimney in 1666 and 1667.

77 Fordyce, *History and Antiquities of Durham*, I, p. 554.

78 Green, *Hearth Tax Assessment*, pp. lxxviii–ix, 55.

taken after Davenport's death. The living accommodation consisted of Hall, Parlour, the Little Chamber, Dining Room, the Red Chamber, the Men's Chamber, the Greene Chamber, the Wainscot Chamber, and the Tower, which contained a bedroom and study. There was also the kitchen, maid's chamber and pantry. Nearby were the chapel, bakehouse, stable and barn.[79] The letters also show that Davenport built a bowling alley and had an orchard (**126**, **145**).

Although the correspondence shows little of it Davenport contributed to the restoration of Houghton church. The wainscoting and stalls on both sides of the chancel are attributed to him. On the north side they bear the arms of Cosin and on the south the arms of Davenport.[80] He almost certainly contributed new glazing.

Davenport's buildings also included one wing of a hospital at Houghton (**113**). The town was already served by a noted grammar school set up by a former rector, Bernard Gilpin, and his friend John Heath in 1574.[81] Gilpin was remembered in Protestant history for his commitment to the evangelising of his far-flung parish and his selfless devotion to the material support of the poor and of five or six students at Oxford. As well as his school he had also founded an almshouse, but this was very decayed indeed by Davenport's time. The new hospital was for six poor folk, comprising two wings linked in the middle, situated to the east of the church and to the south of Gilpin's old Kepier Grammar School. For this Davenport provided the funds for the south wing and George Lilburne the north. On that wing was placed the inscription: 'George Lilburne, Esq. built the moiety of this hospital at his own charge and endowed it with ten pounds per annum forever for the maintenance of three poor people. Anno Dom. 1668.' The south wing was known as 'Davenport's End' and bore the inscription: 'All things come of thee, O Lord, and of thine own have we given thee.'[82]

Davenport's ability to build depended on a regular income from the tithes and glebe land of his parish. The glebe land constituted the

---

79 For the full account of his house, contents and furnishings see the Inventory, Appendix III.

80 Hutchinson, *Durham*, II, pp. 541–2.

81 L. **40**, Gilpin: *ODNB*; D. Marcombe, 'Bernard Gilpin: Anatomy of an Elizabethan Legend', *Northern History* 16 (1980), pp. 20–39.

82 G.D.'s will, Appendix II. The south wing now also bears the inscription: 'The Charitable Intention of the reverend William Sharp M.A. carried into effect by Miss Dorothy Spearman his heiress by will who added to the revenues of the Almshouses £18 per Annum'.

incumbent's benefice and the endowment of his church, which he could farm himself or let out. Davenport's letters (**121**) and his probate inventory of 7 July 1677 give some evidence of his own farming activities.[83] Much of his time and energy appear to have been spent ensuring that the payments due to him were delivered (and also those still owed to Sancroft and even before him to previous rectors of Houghton). The tithes were of two kinds – the 'great' tithes which included corn, hay and wood, and the 'small' tithes which included all other produce.[84] The *Valor Ecclesiasticus* of 1535 rated Houghton at £124,[85] but by the seventeenth century the value should have increased. It has been estimated that the price of wheat had risen six times as high as at the time of the *Valor* and hay eight times. Lambs had increased five times in value and calves four times. It was not unusual to commute the tithes to a money payment. The value of the land was increasing more rapidly than the tithe commodities themselves.[86] During the Civil War, however, there was much confusion and a great deal of ecclesiastical property passed into lay hands. The Restoration theoretically ensured that lawful incumbents got back their property but a rich harvest of problems remained to be solved from 1660 onwards.

The rector of Houghton was entitled to both great and small tithes and the payment was due twice a year: at Lady Day, 25 March (to be paid at May Day – 1 May) and at Michaelmas, 29 September (paid at Martinmas – 11 November) (**58**). The tithes were let out, the 'farmer' gathering them in and paying the rector. Tithes of each township in Houghton parish were let separately (**55, 56**), for a short period of three or four years, the value being secured by land or a surety (**83**). A great deal of Davenport's energy was consumed in bargaining with his leading parishioners over tithes and their arrears. On several occasions he threatened non-payment with legal action, though he was often content to settle for some payment rather than go to law. Some Cocken tenants were particularly recalcitrant (**91**, **95**, **97**, **102**). In addition to the income from tithes and glebe, the incumbent was entitled to

83 Inventory: Appendix III.

84 Tithes: *OED*; R. O'Day, *The English Clergy: the Emergence and Consolidation of a Profession, 1558–1642*, Leicester 1979, p. 173.

85 *Valor ecclesiasticus temp. Henry VIII auctoritate regia institutus*, 6 vols, London 1810, V, p. 307.

86 O'Day, *English Clergy*, p. 173.

Surplice Fees (paid at marriages, burials and churchings),[87] which Davenport let his curate have (**69**), and Easter dues or rates which were levied on property, whether owned or leased, estimated by the amount of land held, which Davenport gave for apprenticeships (**69**).

In addition to gathering his own income from tithes and glebe (and Sancroft's arrears), Davenport had undertaken oversight of Sancroft's prebendal affairs, including the rebuilding of his prebendal house on the south-west corner of the College in Durham, which the canon was obliged to repair.[88] Many letters refer to the problems connected with this (**42, 66, 70, 72, 74, 76, 78, 80, 82, 83, 85, 87, 89, 90, 91, 93, 95, 96, 97, 99, 100, 109**). Each prebendal stall in Durham cathedral had land attached to it, referred to as 'corps lands' which might be leased out according to the choice of the holder of a particular stall.[89] The lands attached to the ninth stall, allocated to Sancroft in 1662 and held until 1674, were at Relley and Amnerbarnes (**85**).[90] The letters witness the trouble Davenport experienced with Sancroft's tenant, Pleasington, who had undertaken the 'paring and burning' of five acres of his land apparently without permission. He had also requested abatement of his dues as a result of four years' 'spoyl of winter eatage' and because of the making of a highway by the waterside (**84, 104, 107**).

Davenport was not, however, responsible for the payment of Sancroft's 'dividend', the yearly sharing out among the prebendaries of any surplus cathedral revenue. This was a 'secret of the chapter' of which, of course, Davenport was not a member. He does, however, seem to have taken responsibility for getting money to Sancroft (**58, 74, 79, 80, 82, 85**). Mention is also made of various sermons Davenport preached on behalf of the non-resident Sancroft, or for which he organised a substitute in fulfilment of the latter's prebendal duties (**37, 83, 88, 106, 108, 115, 119**).

After so much dedicated service Davenport could have expected to be made a canon and prebendary of Durham. The appointments lay

---

87 Churchings: the occasion of a woman visiting the church for the first time after the birth of a child to give thanks for its safe delivery: *OED*; see also the Book of Common Prayer, 'The Thanksgiving of Women after Child-Birth, commonly called the Churching of Women'.

88 The building no longer exists. I am indebted to the Cathedral Archaeologist, Norman Emery, for the information about it. Green, *Hearth Tax Assessment*, p. lxvii, for prebendal houses.

89 *Durham Cathedral Statutes*, pp. 120–259.

90 *Durham Cathedral Statutes*, p. 121.

with the bishop, except during a vacancy of the see or when the vacancy occurred because the holder was promoted to a bishopric by the king, when the king could appoint. The chance came in 1671 when Thomas Wood, canon of the eleventh stall, was promoted Bishop of Lichfield, potentially leaving one stall vacant (**127–131**). This would normally have been a royal appointment but the king had promised to allow it to Cosin, and Cosin had promised the next vacancy to Davenport. Already in December 1670 he alerted Davenport to the impending promotion of Wood. On 27 April 1671 the bishop wrote again, advising Davenport what support he would need to secure the soon-to-be-vacant prebend against the competition which was inevitable. Cosin had already, apparently, tried to ensure that the king kept his word by canvassing civil servants in London but he warned Davenport to seek support for himself. Davenport professed not to be ambitious, but the letters show that he asked Sancroft to alert Gilbert Sheldon, the Archbishop of Canterbury, and Richard Sterne, Archbishop of York, to support him, as well as Dr Timothy Thruscross, whom he had known in London during the Interregnum. The prebend was one of the most lucrative in Durham, so he said, and it is clear that he felt he deserved it. By 28 May, however, his hopes were dashed. Wood was indeed made a bishop but kept his prebend *in commendam*, in other words, in plurality. Cosin died in January 1672 and a long vacancy followed, after which Nathaniel Crewe became bishop. With him any hope of advancement for Davenport vanished and he ended his life still rector of Houghton.

No one would read these letters for a close commentary on politics or international affairs but they do contain much that is of interest about both. Before the Restoration Davenport supplied Sancroft with carefully circumspect information about friends who were suffering and told him a little about Anglican church life in London. We find him, for instance, listening to sermons by persons who were suspect, commenting on the execution of the leaders of the Penruddock rising in May 1655, and praying for the condemned (**4**, **8**, **21**). He clearly knew a great many Royalist and sequestred ecclesiastics. He is very careful in his remarks about the convoluted politics of the time, including the offer of kingship to Oliver Cromwell by Parliament in 1657 (**23**).

After the Restoration of course Davenport was less often in London and so he relied on his correspondents to supply him with information rather than vice versa. Thus his letters reveal the concerns of a provincial rather than of a dweller in the capital. One major concern was the plague and related illnesses. He mentions it in fourteen letters (**30**, **57**, **71 72**, **73**, **74**, **76**, **78**, **79**, **81**, **83**, **85**, **88**, **89**).

Outbreaks of 'malignant' and 'pestilential' fever, including typhus, occurred throughout the years 1661 to 1664 and in the spring of 1665 the 'pestilential' fever was succeeded by the Plague itself, said to have killed seven thousand people in London in a single week at its climax. In the provinces smaller outbreaks occurred, thought to have resulted from the introduction of the infection from London. The eastern ports of Yarmouth, Lynn, Norwich, Ipswich and Harwich all experienced smaller outbreaks in the autumn of 1665 and spring of 1666, as did some north-eastern towns such as Sunderland and Wearmouth, and, to a lesser degree, Newcastle, Gateshead and Durham. At Sunderland on 18 July seven houses were 'shut up' and one at Durham.[91]

After the Great Plague came the Great Fire of London. This was an event which no one in England could ignore, and for which, in any case, nation-wide fasts were enjoined (**83**, **100**) It raged from 2 to 6 September 1666, covering nearly 400 acres and making over 100,000 people homeless. Eighty-eight churches, including St Paul's cathedral, were destroyed, also the Royal Exchange, the Guildhall, Sion College and many other public buildings and over 13,000 homes.[92] It is clear from Davenport's correspondence that one of the sources of extreme anxiety was the lack of news about the fate of individuals (**100**).William Sancroft was made homeless by the Fire and while he found lodgings with friends, his servant, Arthur Sissons, was given a home by Sancroft's friends in Durham; indeed he may have been a kinsman of the Cuthbert Sissons mentioned in Bishop Cosin's correspondence.[93] The possibility of assistance provided by Durham Cathedral Chapter for the Choir of St Paul's cathedral, made homeless by the fire, is mentioned in a letter from Dean Sudbury of Durham to William Sancroft.[94]

If the correspondence is anything to go by Davenport was much less interested in international affairs than in his family and friends. The Dutch Wars form a background to much of this correspondence, but little detail is found here. Whilst the pre-Restoration letters were being written the effect of the First Dutch War, waged between

91 J.F.D. Shrewsbury, *A History of Bubonic Plague in the British Isles*, Cambridge 1971.

92 *Cosin Corr.* II, p. 155.

93 Arthur Scissons (Sissons) is mentioned by W.S. in T. 467.52. (20 Sept. 1665), and by G.D. in LL. **100** and **101**, concerning the obtaining of a patent for his father's property. Sisson wrote to W.S. requesting to be allowed to re-join his master on 13 October 1666: H. 3785, f. 255.

94 *Cosin Corr.* II, p. 196; T. 45.118.

September 1652 and March 1653, resulting in piracy and intermittent raids, was still being felt.[95] The Second Dutch War followed from October 1663 to July 1667, as a result of continued commercial rivalry with naval battle off the English coasts and attacks on eastern English ports.[96] The Dutch were defeated off Lowestoft in June 1665 but were aided by the French from January 1666 and were successful in destroying ships at Chatham. The war was concluded by the Treaty of Breda in July 1667.[97]

Davenport has no references to events of the First War but several times mentions news he had received of naval activities during the interim period between that and the Second War (**11**, **17**, **22**). He also refers to the Baltic War between 1656 and 1658 (**22**). During the period of the Second Dutch War Davenport comments on a Portuguese victory (probably the Battle of Ameixal, 29 May to 8 June 1663), the effect of the war on the price of lead, so important for his building activities, and the capture of a Dutch privateer, with twenty to thirty brass guns, off South Shields (**54**, **88**, **92**, **96**, **108**). Davenport's letter of 1 September 1667 describes the announcement of the peace at Durham and its effect upon his workmen at Houghton (**108**). There is no mention at all of the Third War (1672–74), which probably shows how little it impinged on the northern area.

The Letters show that the friendships forged in Davenport's early days continued for many years. The most important continued to be the Gayers and the Richs, though he evidently saw much less of them when he came to Durham. Sir Thomas Rich died on 15 October 1667 and was buried at Sonning,[98] though it was some time before the news reached Davenport, from Sancroft (**109**, **110**). He was succeeded by his son Sir William, his only son by his father's second wife. This lady subscribed to Davenport's hospital in Houghton (**115**). He mentions in July 1672 the marriage of Sir William Rich, who was eighteen, to the (twelve-year-old) daughter of Lord Aylesbury, Robert Bruce, Earl of Aylesbury and Earl of Elgin (**135**). Davenport was still enquiring about the well-being of Sir Robert Gayer and his family and Lady Rich in

95 T. Venning, *Cromwellian Foreign Policy*, Basingstoke 1995, ch. 12; hostilities mentioned in 1655: L. **10**, and in 1657: L. **21**.

96 Although war was not declared officially by Charles II until March 1665, hostilities had begun in the autumn of 1663.

97 G. Clark, *The Oxford History of England, 10: The Later Stuarts, 1660–1714*, Oxford 1955, repr. 1992, p. 65.

98 *VCH, Berkshire*, III, p. 222 for his tomb.

1675 (**140, 142, 148**). The Henleys continued to be remembered. George tried, but did not succeed apparently, to pacify a quarrel between Sir Andrew and the rector of Eversley, who seems to have criticised him for paying a French chef and therefore accused him in a sermon of gluttony (**60, 61**). He comments also on a very public quarrel between Henley and Lord St John in the very presence of the judges in Parliament (**104**). Henley was actually prosecuted in the King's Bench and not pardoned until 1668. Evidently he was both extravagant and sharp tempered. But George notes with sorrow on July 1675 that Sir Andrew is dead. He had died on 17 May (**140**).[99] In July 1676 he had heard that Sir Robert Henley, junior, the son and heir of Sir Andrew by Mary Gayer, had run his sword into a footman, though later it appears that he got away with this (**146, 147**). By then the estate at Bramshill was heavily in debt and eventually had to be sold.[100]

He also made new friendships among his many Durham acquaintances, including cathedral clergy and the staff of Bishop Cosin, notably Richard Wrench, Isaac Basire and Miles Stapylton.

Miles Staplyton served Bishop Cosin as secretary for many years and was responsible for overseeing his affairs in the north while Cosin was in London. Stapylton and Davenport worked as a team, the former dealing with legal matters and the latter with religious concerns. The two seem to have been responsible for administering the allowance that Cosin gave to his estranged son John (**111, 114, 115**). Together they were also responsible for the establishment of Cosin's library and its maintenance.[101]

Isaac Basire was Archdeacon of Northumberland, and seems to have been as conscientious in his duties and his residence as Davenport himself. Davenport attended him in his last illness (**147**), and the relationship is demonstrated in his will:

> I do give to my reverend freind, Mr George Davenport, parson of Houghton in the Spring, for his Christian and pious care and paines about me, the sume of six pounds.[102]

99 The exact date was not known to GEC, *Baronetage*, III, p. 69.

100 *HPC*, II, p. 525.

101 Miles was the third son of Brian Stapylton of Myton. He married Elizabeth, daughter of John Mynde of London. He died in 1685 and his memorial was placed in Durham cathedral: *Stapylton Corr.* for letters.

102 W.N. Darnell, *The Life and Correspondence of Dr Basire*, London 1831, pp. 314–17.

Davenport's closest friend in Durham, by his own assessment, was Richard Wrench.[103] He had been nominally canon of the sixth stall since 1646, but was not installed until 20 March 1661. His living was at Boldon and he seems to have been resident and conscientious in his fulfilment of his cathedral duties. Davenport frequently mentions meetings with him. As Treasurer of the cathedral he was responsible for Sancroft's dividend. Wrench is often mentioned in the letters to Sancroft by the nick-name 'the monk' or 'monk of Boldon' (perhaps an allusion to Uthred of Boldon, the noted member of Durham priory in the fourteenth century).[104] Wrench died in October 1675 and Davenport wrote to William Sancroft that he had 'lost the best friend I had in this countrey' (**144**).

George Davenport is particularly remembered today as a bibliophile. His responsibilities in the setting up and care of Bishop Cosin's library on Palace Green in Durham have long been known through the bishop's correspondence with Miles Stapylton (**120**, **121**, **123**). John Cosin built his library on the site of the castle stables and adjoining the Exchequer and Chancery Court on Palace Green. The book collection, previously in the library of Peterhouse, Cambridge, was to be made available to the clergy of the diocese of Durham. The main building was completed by 19 September 1668 and the books installed during 1669.[105] Many of Cosin's letters give instructions to Davenport and Stapylton on the arrangement of the books and practical advice concerning their care, especially in winter.[106]

Davenport was also an independent collector of books and manuscripts and a catalogue of the manuscripts he gave to Cosin's library remains. Some other books are known, which escaped into other hands. In addition to the books given to Cosin's library others

103 Richard Wrench, B.A., St John's College, Cambridge, 1631–2; M.A. 1635, B.D. 1642. Fellow 1636–46, when he was ejected; Prebendary of Durham 1646–75. Vicar of Heighington 1661 and rector of Boldon 1665–75. He married Ann Baddeley 16 August 1664. He died 26 October 1675 and his memorial was placed in Durham cathedral: *Al. Cant.*; Mussett, p. 52; Hutchinson, *Durham*, II, p. 192.

104 *ODNB*, under Boldon (1320–97).

105 A.I. Doyle, 'John Cosin (1595–1672) as a Library-Maker', *The Book Collector* 53/1 (Spring 2004), pp. 335–57, for the whole account. A small room adjacent to the main library was added in 1671 for the storage of maps.

106 *Cosin Corr.* II, p. 257.

were given by him to Kepier Grammar School in Houghton.[107] They are now in the Kepier Collection in Newcastle University Library. The earliest acquisitions among the Cosin manuscripts have been traced to 1651 and 1652, with the largest number of acquisitions in 1664.[108] He was evidently known as a collector. Donors of manuscripts to him included some local gentlemen mentioned in the Letters, including John Tempest (manuscript nos 37, 38,44, 54), George Barkas (no. 50) and also Timothy Thurscross (no. 11), whom he had known ever since his days in London.[109] Several of the manuscripts came originally from the library of Durham priory (nos 3, 8, 12, 24, 28, 30, 33, 62), including the mid-twelfth-century work of Lawrence of Durham (no. 46). The collection also gives ample evidence of Davenport's use of the books, with his notes and sometimes 'perlegi' inscribed in them, for instance in no. 16, a work by John Lydgate, or a work by Richard Rolle (no. 41).[110]

It is possible that Davenport himself hoped to publish. He seems to have helped William Sancroft in London in 1651 with publication of *Fur praedestinatus*, an attack on Calvinism. In 1652 he probably transcribed the Peterborough Chronicle, now Cambridge University Library MS Dd.14.28.6.[111] But for the most part he simply bought and read the latest publications and took an interest in the recent scholarship. His letters record arrangements for acquiring printed books from London booksellers (**88**, **106**, **116**, **118**, **119**, **121**, **123**). We find him enquiring about a second edition of Somner's *Saxon Lexicon*, replacing the volumes burnt in Dugdale's lodging during the Great Fire of London, for which he had supplied emendations. (**148**) He

107 R.W. Ramsey, 'Kepier Grammar School, Houghton-le-Spring and its Library', *Archaeologia Aeliana*, 3rd ser., 3 (1907), pp. 306–33, esp. pp. 323, 325–6, 328.

108 A.I. Doyle, 'The Cosin Manuscripts and George Davenport', *The Book Collector* 53/1 (Spring 2004), pp. 32–45.

109 Below, Appendix I.

110 Other works formerly owned by Davenport but now in the British Library include a volume of seventeenth-century Durham Cathedral music (Add. 30478), and a fifteenth-century prose book of vices and virtues (Add. 30944).

111 *Fur Praedestinatus, sive Dialogismus inter quendam Ordinis Praedicantium Calvinisticam et Furem ad laqueum damnatum habitus.* It was a translation from Henricus Slatius, *Den Ghepredestineerden Dief* (1619): A.I. Doyle, 'The Cosin Manuscripts and George Davenport', p. 35. The Davenport transcription formed the basis of W.T. Mellows, *The Chronicle of Hugh Candidus, a Monk of Peterborough*, Oxford 1949, p. vi. I am grateful to Mr J.L. Marlow, a descendant of the Leicestershire Davenports, for drawing my attention to the transcription.

describes a business undertaking on which he had embarked to obtain six copies of 'Great Bibles' (Walton's Polyglot Bible) and sell them on (**5**, **18**, **19**, **119**).[112]

*

On 15 January 1672 Bishop Cosin died in London after many years of suffering varieties of ill-health. His funeral cortege was unable to travel to Durham until April but then the coffin was preceded into the cathedral by five of Cosin's chaplains, almost certainly including George Davenport.[113] After that his coffin was interred in Auckland chapel. In his will, dated 11 December 1671, Cosin appointed George Davenport as one of his executors and bequeathed to him forty pounds for his 'care and pains'.[114]

Cosin was succeeded as Bishop of Durham by Nathaniel Crewe in 1674 and Davenport ceased to be a domestic chaplain. The few letters which survive from the period after Cosin's death show Davenport still taking an active interest in the affairs of the clergy and diocesan news and gossip as well as continuing his own building efforts and literary pursuits (**135–48**). There is perhaps evidence of less willingness to embark on journeys in the later letters. In July 1675 he comments that he is well and may go as far as York, for it is only a day's journey from the meeting with the bishop at the River Tees (on entry into his diocese) (**140**).[115] On 13 March 1677 (the last letter which survives) he reports that he has not been to Durham since 11 January for the weather had been cold and the ways foul (**148**).

George Davenport died unexpectedly in the summer of 1677. Surtees records that 'Mr George Davenport died of a violent feaver the 6th of July 1677, and buried Sunday the 8th. The bearers of the worthy and charitable Mr George Davenport were: Dr Grey, rector of Wearmouth; Mr Davison, Vicar of Norton; Mr Ladler, rector of Gateshead; Mr Thompson, Vicar of Pittington; Mr Johnson, rector of Washington; Mr Cock, Vicar of St Oswald's; Mr Noel, rector of Seaham; Mr Broughton, Curate of Wearmouth. The office of burial performed by his sorrowful curate, John Alcock, most of the parishioners attending in mourning.'[116] The parish records state in July

112 *Biblia sacra polyglotta*, 6 vols, London 1653–7.
113 *CSP, Dom. 1671–2*, p. 397.
114 *Cosin Corr.* II, p. 302, will of John Cosin.
115 Crewe: *ODNB*.
116 Surtees, *Durham*, I, p. 171.

1677 'Mr George Davenport, rector of the Parish of Houghton, buryed the 8th of July. Houghton.'

Davenport was buried in the chancel of Houghton church and his memorial, which now lies in the north transept, by the north wall, reads:

Here lyeth the body of the Reverend and
Charitable Mr George Davenport late
Rector of this church, who died July the
6th 1677. He rebuilt the Parsonage House,
the Chappell, and the walls about the Garden &
repaired the out houses.
He built one half of the
Hospital in the Churchyard, and bequeathed
For the maintenance of 3 poor people in it
160£; also 40£ to the poor stock & 10£ to be
given to the poor at his Funerall. He was also a
great benefactor to the Bough Church, and
gave 70 manuscripts to the Bishop's
Library in Durham.

If the soul's transmigration were believed,
you'd say good Gilpin's soul he had received,
And with as liberal hand did give or more,
His daily charity unto the poor;
For which, with him, we doubt not he's possest
Of righteous men's reward, eternal rest.
The Righteous shall be had in eternal Remembrance.
Ps. 112.6.

The memorial is a black stone, now worn away on the right-hand side. It bears in the centre the arms of Davenport of Cheshire.

George Davenport's letters are frequently hurried notes dashed off in answer to correspondence received from a respected friend, living over two hundred miles away. Their importance lies in the details they provide of the everyday life and experiences of a priest from his ordination, through the early years of his clerical career, his adjustment to the requirements and difficulties of the Interregnum and the conditions of the Restoration Church. They are important not only for the light they throw on the experiences of the writer but also for the brief glimpse they provide of the many clerics and others who crossed his path. He was well-read in the latest theological publications of his day but also had a consuming interest in the literature of earlier times – demonstrated by his avid collection of mediaeval manuscripts.

We learn something of the man himself. They show us the caring brother and uncle, mindful of his family and roots, the loyal friend, the grateful student, the appreciative master, the benevolent parson pouring his own efforts and money into the poor hospital, providing a new parsonage for the benefit of his successors as well as himself.[117] They show us a man with a sense of humour as well as a serious, spiritual side.[118] He might have been rendered bitter and disappointed not to obtain a Durham prebend but on the contrary seems to have been contented. He certainly did not seek earthly 'glory' and was ever mindful of his need to give account of himself to his Maker (**128**, **130**).

*

The assessment of George Davenport by his contemporaries is preserved on his memorial in Houghton church. There he is compared with his predecessor, the noted and scholarly Bernard Gilpin.[119] The Letters reveal George Davenport as a worthy successor, a man whose devotion, hard work and commitment were underpinned by his personal piety, wit and learning.

---

117 Nichols, *Leicester*, IV, p. 384, records the contents of the donations list which hung in All Saints' church, Wigston. For 1671 it recorded 'The Rev. George Davenport, rector of Houghton in le Spring, in the county of Durham, gave a silver cup and cover for the Sacrament.' According to W.G. Dimock Fletcher, *Leicestershire Pedigrees and Royal Descents*, Leicester 1887, the paten was inscribed 'Ecclesiae de Wigston dedit Georgius Davenport Clericus natus ibid.' The chalice bears his arms and crest. According to the donation list for 1677, 'George Davenport aforesaid gave 20£; the interest to the poor of Great Wigston for ever.'

118 Of the latter there is no doubt, as we see in the many invocations of divine assistance scattered throughout the letters.

119 Above, p. 18.

THE LETTERS OF GEORGE DAVENPORT

1 **6 September 1651**
T. 55.43
G.D. to W.S. from Emmanuel College, Cambridge

Worthy Sir,

Upon Friday last Dr Arrowsmith the new Regius Professor read his probation lecture.[1] His text was Genes.3.15.etc. After a long preface (wherein hee shewed the dignity of that place, being like Davids Michtam or St Paul's faithfull saying & as Luther sayd, containing in it the doctrine of the whole Bible) hee came to the exposition.[2] By the serpent was understood the Divell. By the woman Eva, the mother of the faithfull (wherein hee blamed the Jesuits for expounding it of the B. Virgin & others for making the history but an allegory, & consequently turning the scriptures into a fable).[3] By the seed of the serpent was understood first, the cohors diabolorum:[4] 2ly such men who are of there father the Divell: and the tares sown by the divell. I cannot remember that hee speak anything of the emnity (I suppose that was to bee explayned in the latter part of the B.[5]) At length he set down theise conclusions.[6] 1. That Eve did absolutely

---

1 John Arrowsmith (1602–59) was Regius Professor of Divinity, 1651–56. He was Master of St John's College from 1644, Vice Chancellor and a leading Presbyterian: *ODNB*; J. Twigg, *The University of Cambridge and the English Revolution: the History of the University of Cambridge*, Woodbridge 1990, pp. 103, 123–5, 129.

2 Michtam: the Hebrew term used in the superscription of Psalm 16.56–60, which deals with human suffering and evil and God's victory over it. St Paul's faithfull saying: probably I Tim. 1.15, 'This is a faithful saying: Christ came to save sinners.' M. Luther, *Works*, I: *Lectures on Genesis 1–5*, ed. J. Pelikan, St Louis 1958, esp. p. 196.

3 Jesuit interpretation: perhaps Robert Bellarmine (1542–1621), noted Jesuit theologian and controversialist: *ODCC*.

4 Cohors diabolorum = company of devils.

5 B = brief, see later in the letter.

6 'emnity': sic (enmity): Gen. 3.15.

believe. 2. That shee was the mother of the beleivers & 3ly that the scriptures doth hold out so much to us. This hee proved out of places, I think, in Isaiah /about Jerusalem\ but I can/not\ call the place to mind. When hee had done this hee thought time to give over: leaving the latter part of the text to bee disscussed aut hic aut alibi;[7] some say that hee entends to preach ad clerum[8] on the latter part of the brefs. Hee complayned much that so short a time should bee alotted to him to explicate so large a text of scripture. This is all at present I can remember of it. Hee is much commended by those with whom I converse: what abler heads say of him I am ignorant. I never thought /it\ impossible for a professore to equall the lecturer. I think hee is admitted, I am not sure. Wee have little news. There is a report that one Dell, in a sermon or at least a confermer, was blasted by the Generalls not approving of his doctrine, being the same which hee last taught in St Marys.[9]

{p. 2} I had a letter from the Mr Gayers on Satturday.[10] They are in health. Since your departure hence I have /scarce\ gone out of the college onely to church & the new professore, having been extraordinarily troubled with a cold. Your friends are all in health. My Brother & the rest (too many to reckon & more than I can remember) present there service to you.[11] I presume you will pardon my rude & abrupt stile. This with the tenders of due service to you, I< > take my leave and remain

Your devoted servitour,
George Davenport

Imman: Coll.
Sept.6.1651.

---

7 Aut hic aut alibi = either here or elsewhere.

8 ad clerum = to the clergy.

9 Probably William Dell (d. 1669), an Independent, 'intruded' Master of Gonville and Caius College, Cambridge, 1649–60 and vicar of Yelden, Beds., until his ejection in 1662: *ODNB*. In 1653 he preached in St Mary's, Cambridge (Twigg, *University of Cambridge*, pp. 153, 182–4, 221, 223–5, 239). The rumour was probably false: E.C. Walker, *William Dell, Master Puritan*, p. 94n, for the story, denied by Dell, that Cromwell disapproved of his *The Crucified and quickened Christian*, published in 1652, but first delivered before Cromwell, who is the General. St Mary's was the university church, Great St Mary's, Cambridge.

10 Gayers: Introduction, pp. 5–6, 23.

11 His brother John (1625?–1708): Introduction, pp. 1, 3, and *Al.Cant*. He remained in West Rasen until 1693 when he became vicar of Great Wigston, Leics. (1693–1706): CCED, person ID 87679; Nichols, *Leicestershire*, IV/1, p. 383.

2 **15 January 1655**[12]
H. 3783, f. 96
G.D. to W.S. from Great Wigston, Leics.

Sir;
I have received your letter : & with my friends (to whom I shewed it) give you many thanks for your seasonable expression of your affection to us in this time of sadness.____[13] Oh how good is it! He who hath put a full period to my father's misaryes, hath not left us comfortless. I shall abide but a little while longer with my mother before I take my journey towards you: which I purpose to begin the beginning of the next week. If either company or any accident at home that may happen & I cannot think of, to make me delay longer (which I have no reason to think can) I shall give you an account. In the mean while my service with my brothers to you with Mr John Gayer.

Your obliged friend & servant,
Geo. Davenport.

Wigston Jan. 15.

3 **5 March 1655**[14]
H. 3783, f.103
G.D. to W.S.

Sir;

This day fortnight I wrote to you and enclosed one from Mr Widdrington, which was brought to me by his brother.[15] I suppose it might miscarry, because you mention it not in your letters. Mr R. Gayer began to be sick so soon as he had wrote to you the last week, but nature stept in & relieved him by a sudden flux: otherwise saith Mr Battersby it had proved a violent feaver, his sisters was his continuall visitants, but since he hath visited them & was yesterday at

12 No year given in the text, but it is supplied by the date of his father's death. He was buried 8 January 1655 and his will proved 14 March 1655: TNA, PCC Wills, 1654.

13 Sic.

14 Date: below, n. 26.

15 Ralph Widdrington, younger brother of Sir Thomas (Speaker of Parliament), (1614–1688). B.A. and tutor of Christ's College, Cambridge, 1636. Made Greek Professor by Cromwell, 1654. Created D.D. by royal mandate in 1661. Many letters to Sancroft survive: *ODNB*. The Davenport letter mentioned here does not survive.

church.[16] Some physick is to be given to him this week by Mr Battersbyes advice, for he will not consult a Dr. They begin now to prepare for Lincolne-Inne fields where they were on Saturday; & the house is not so well relished as formerly, as not having the conveniences they thought it had.[17] The lowest chamber hath no study. I think a little hole belonging to the buttery or larder was mistaken for it. Mr R.G. study is very mean; & which the study above is they do not well remember, & did not then see. We long for your company, that you might settle us & settle with us, & that the morning and evening sacrifices might begin & never fayl.[18] My Lord hath made me a full minister:[19] he desired to be remembered to you, so did Mr Martin[20] & Mr Lant.[21] Mr Thusscross[22] sends his respects to you. I supped with him on Friday & last night, having read evening prayer for him. Mr Tolly died lately at Belvoir Castle, being taken with an apoplexy on a Sunday as he was reading service;[23] it killed him in a quarter of an hour. I hear that Mr Holdsworth is nominated to my Lord to succeed him, either as domestick chaplain, or to go with his

---

16 Battersby: possibly Nicholas, B.A. Exeter College, Oxford, 1615; student of Middle Temple, 1617: *Al. Ox.*; *Register of Admissions of the Honourable Society of the Middle Temple, I: 1501–1781*, compiled by H.A.C. Sturgess, London 1949, p. 106; see also L. **17**.

17 A reference to 'Gryffins', see L. **4**.

18 'morning and evening sacrifices': perhaps a reference to I Chron. 16.40 where the gathering of priests with Zadok, the high priest, at the Tabernacle of the Lord is described. Their duty was to offer the morning and evening sacrifices.

19 'My Lord' from 1654/5 to 1658 is Ralph Brownrigg: Introduction, p. 28.

20 Martin is possibly Nicholas M. of London, who was at Queen's College, Cambridge, 28 July 1658. He was admitted to Lincoln's Inn 20 December 1658 and called to the Bar 12 May 1666: *Al. Cant.*; or William M. who published Brownrigg's sermons in 1661: *ODNB* under Brownrigg, Ralph.

21 Thomas Lant of Shropshire. Jesus College, Cambridge, 1620; B.A. 1623/4; Fellow 1626–38, and rector of Harringey, Middlesex, 1637–44. Sequestered. Restored 1660–88. Prebendary of St Paul's 1662–88. Died 1688: *Al. Cant.*

22 Thrusscross: Davenport's spelling of this name varies. Timothy Thrusscross was vicar of Kirby Moorside, 1625–38, in succession to his father. Prebendary of York 1622–71. He was living in Westminster in 1657: *Al. Cant.*; Evelyn, *Diary*, III, p. 237n.

23 John Tolly, born in London. B.A. Christ's College, Cambridge, 1633. Fellow of Peterhouse 1633–44 and became rector of Tattingstone, Suffolk, 1641 and of Little Gransden, Cambs., 1643. He was ejected in 1643 and sequestered from his fellowship for his part in helping to convey college plate to the king: *Al.Cant.* In his will, dated 5 July 1654, he left his goods in trust to his patrons, the Earl and Countess of Rutland, of Belvoir castle, Leics.: TNA, PCC Wills, 18 May 1655.

son to the university, & that he stews in the business.[24] Not to trouble you any further I remain

Your obliged to serve you,

G.D.

//Mr R.G. sends his service, & had he been /very well\ he would have done it in his own letter, but his late sickness keeps him in his bed this morning.//[25]

{March 5 1654/5}[26]

4 **19 March 1655**

T. 49.59

G.D. to W.S. from London

Sir,

I thank you for your good letter & better wishes. At present we are all in health. This day some of us should take possession of the Griffons and ly there but for ought I can perceive our removall goes on so slowly that you may take us in the temple.[27] I never doubted that the המיך should cease on our part: I wish I may find but little jealousyes of it on their part.[28] That it may not fayl elsewhere, so soon as I have sealed up this I go to officiate for that reverend man to whom you directed your respects /&\ to whom I yesterday presented them & hereby return his.[29] Yesterday Sunday Dr Taylor gave us a sermon

---

24 Probably Thomas Holdsworth, B.A. Emmanuel College, 1645. After the Restoration he was Dean of Middleham, Yorks., 1660–80. He wrote a biography of Dr Richard Holdsworth, Master of Emmanuel in 1637: Introduction, p. 5.

25 A letter from Robert Gayer to Sancroft, mentioning a letter from G.D. to W.S. about Gayer's illness, survives as H. 3783, f. 116.

26 Francis Ringrose transcript, Letter 5, records the date as 5 March 1654, Leics. RO, DE 1139/2–3.

27 Temple: Evidently G.D. and his friends had previously lodged in accommodation in the Temple. They later moved to 'Gryffens' which appears to have been near Lincolns Inn Fields. The site cannot be identified precisely but a public house called 'The Gryphon' stood in Shire Lane which was later demolished to accommodate the Law Courts.

28 המיך = Heb., duration, extension, continuance: BDB. The reference is to Tamid, as a noun, meaning the daily burnt offering in the temple, whose continuance was essential. I thank Dr Robert Hayward for his help here. Davenport is covertly referring to continuing to use the Prayer Book.

29 Probably Brownrigg.

at the wharfe.[30] I know not whether I told you in my last that he is here to print his Cases of Conscience.[31] He, say some, hath again take the whole disposall of the business into his own hands. I hope your next will assure us of the time of your coming up: which earnestly desired by many here & not a little by

Yours obliged to serve you,

G.D.

Mar. 19.

Mr Beaumont is here & sends his service.[32]

5 **2 April 1655**

H. 3783, f. 107

G.D. to W.S. from London

Worthy Sir;

We are not yet at < > the Gryffins. I see that there is greater preparation for a journey than to get up & ride. I had hoped that your last would have fixed the day of your return: but it gives us so little hope, that if you come before another month be past it will be sooner than I can expect. My Lord desires to be remembered to you: & I fear may be in Essex before your return. He hath taken much physick lately. I was with him on Munday last; & he hath promised to come & dine at the Gryffins & be my curate for the morning service. Mr Thriscross sends his respects to you. He tells me that Dr Hammonds answer to Cawdrey is finished, but as yet I have not seen it.[33] I have

30 St Peter's, Paul's Wharf, on the north side of Thames Street, at the south-east corner of St Peter's Hill, in Queenhith Ward: Newcourt, p. 527. Many came here for celebration of Communion according to the liturgy of the Church of England. John Evelyn records Jeremy Taylor preaching at St Gregory by Paul's in March 1655 on Matt. 14.17: *Diary*, III, p. 148. He also preached in private houses. In December 1657 the Council of State summoned Taylor and Gunning to account for the frequent meetings of multitudes of people: *CSP, Dom. 1657–8*, p. 226.

31 *Cases of Conscience* was his *magnum opus*. Part I was complete in 1654. The complete work was published in 1660: *ODNB*.

32 Robert Beaumont (1650–78), a bookseller in whose house Sancroft lodged, 'at the sign of the Star, in Little Brittain, London': Wing, IV, p. 74.

33 Dr Henry Hammond (1605–60). Chaplain to Charles I. Cawdrey attacked ceremonies and observances of feast days. Hammond's *Answer* was *Account of Mr Daniel Cawdrey's Triplex Diatribe concerning Superstition, Will Worship and the Christmas Festival*, London 1654, 1655: J.W. Packer, *The Transformation of Anglicanism*, Manchester 1969, pp. 15–44, 169; *ODNB*.

received a letter from the undertakers[34] for the great bible to provide the 3^{d} payment against the beginning of June, at which time they hope the 2^{d} vol. will be finished.[35] Sir Theod. Mayern is lately dead, and a farr more deserving man the D{uke} of Lennox dyed on Thursday last in a cold fitt of a quartane ague, which had held him, they say, 4 years.[36] Dr Harvey I hear, was with him at his death & sayd that if he could but struggle out that fitt, it would lead ad perfectam sanitatem, & that the ague would < >no more return.[37]
Your friends here long to see you and so doth
your affectionate friend & servant,

G.D.

Apr.2.1655.
Address: To the Reverend, my worthy friend Mr William Sandcroft
At Fresshingfield in Suffolk.

6 **3 April {1655}**[38]
H. 3783, f. 111
G.D. to W.S. {no place or year}

Sir;

We are not yet in Lincoln-inn fields, but are upon our removall & on Wednesday hope to be there.[39] Mr Godolphin settled there on Saturday.[40] From thence you shall hear from us: & also what we do. On Saturday being with Mr Thriscross, he told me, that Sir Nich. Crisp having a church voyd in Bread-Street, was minded to conferr it upon

34 Undertakers = 'publishers'.

35 Great Bible: as is clear from later references (see LL. **18**, **29**), the Polyglot Bible of Brian Walton. The six volumes, containing the Bible text in Hebrew, Greek, Latin, Syriac, Ethiopic, Arabic and Persian, were published in London between 1653 and 1657: *ODNB*, under Walton, Brian.

36 Theodore Turquet de Mayerne M.D., Physician to Charles I and Charles II (1573–1655), died 22 March. James Stuart, fourth Duke of Lennox, first Duke of Richmond (1612–55) died 30 March: *ODNB*, for both.

37 William Harvey (1578–1657), noted for his discoveries concerning the circulation of the blood: *ODNB*. Ad perfectam sanitatem = to complete health.

38 A date in the spring of 1655 seems likely since Davenport and his friends had not yet moved their lodgings.

39 At Gryffins: see LL. **3**, **4**, **5** and **15**.

40 Perhaps William Godolphin, second surviving son of Sir William G. of Spargor, Cornwall. Student of the Inner Temple 1654: *HPC*, II, under Godolphin, Francis (of Godolphin, Breage, Cornwall).

you.[41] I told him, I thought I know your mind sufficiently in that poynt & that you would know how much you {are} beholden to that K{nigh}t: but wisht that you would desire him to defirr no opportunity of preferring a worthy man to it, //although it was\\ befor I heard from you. We are all in health & send our service to you.

Your affectionate friend & humble servant

G.D.

Apr.3.
Mr Chamberlain sends his service to you.[42]

7 **25 April 1655**
H. 3783, f. 112
G.D. to W.S. from London

Sir;

I wrote to you on Munday on which day I waited upon my Lord of Exeter, who enquiers much after you & desired to be remembered to you. He intends for Anstey the next month & soon after for Bury, as Mr Richart tells me.[43] I have little hope of a speedy sight of you, now I see your horse returned. I see no likelyhood of our being in the countrey, as formerly, in summer. I have little news to acquaint you with. Yesterday, I heard that the presbytery was to have their meeting on a great occasion (but I cannot learn it) at Sion College.[44] Prayers are made publickly in churches, & more boldly in houses for the

41 Sir Nicholas Crisp (1599–1666), son of Ellis Crisp, Royalist, leading London merchant operating in West Africa. He was created knight 1640, and baronet 1665. The church was probably St Mildred's, Bread Street, where he was buried in 1666: *ODNB*; Hennessy, p. 339.

42 Chamberlain: see also L. **10**. Possibly Edward, admitted to Lincoln's Inn 1650: *Al.Cant.*, p. 316.

43 Anstey: near Cuckfield, Sussex, or Ansty, Herts., south-east of Royston; perhaps the latter as it lay on Brownrigg's route between Sonning (home of Mr Thomas Rich where he frequently stayed) and Bury St Edmunds. Brownrigg was the son of an Ipswich merchant and probably took refuge with his family as did Sancroft. Mr Richard or Riccard (also L. **15**, **16**, **30**) was probably Andrew (1604–72), a merchant whose daughter, Christian, married John Geare (Gayer) at St Olave, Hart Street, March 1656: *ODNB*.

44 Sion College was founded by Thomas White, rector of St Dunstan-in-the-West, as a meeting place, in London Wall, for London clergy: Packer, *Transformation of Anglicanism*, p. 8 n. 28. It was a centre for Presbyterian clergy: Spurr, *Restoration Church of England*, p. 13.

prisoners,[45] but whilst we are thus perplext & sit down to eat up those that are killed all the day long,[46] & to drink the wine of the condemned,[47] pray let your next give us hope of seeing of you. For you may be assured you can be nowhere more wellcome than to this family & amongst the rest to
your obliged servant,

G.D.

St Mark. 1655
Wee keep our old way:[48] but I hope this holyday we shall add evening service.[49]

8 **7 May 1655**
H. 3783, f. 123
G.D. to W.S.

Worthy Sir;

I am sorry to see you so far from your journeys end. I hope your sister will < >not stay untill weddings go out.[50] I can acquaint you with /no\ good news from hence. Your last tells us that 3 prisoners suffered on Thursday at Sarisbury,[51] that they at Execeter are to suffer this day.[52] I am going to meet with some of theire friends, /and\ to perform the last Christian offices we can at this distance & to protest Deut. 21.7.8.[53] They </were\> boldly prayed for yesterday.

---

45 Prisoners: at Salisbury and Exeter in the aftermath of the 'Penruddock Rising', January to March 1655: Abbott, *Writings and Speeches*, III, pp. 584–656, esp. 648–9; below, L. **8**.

46 Ps. 44.22.

47 Ps. 60.3.

48 Old way: i.e. pre-Presbyterian way of worship, based on the Book of Common Prayer.

49 Holyday: may refer to St Mark's feast.

50 Church weddings were suspended by an Act of 24 August 1653, when they became the responsibility of the Justices of the Peace, though some were still carried out by clergy: *Acts and Ordinances*, II, pp. 715–18; Spurr, *Restoration Church of England*, p. 17.

51 The prisoners who had taken part in the 'Penruddock Rising'. Some were hanged, drawn and quartered, others only hanged (Richard Reeves and Edward Davy and six others), and John Penruddock and Hugh Grove beheaded: Abbott, *Writings and Speeches*, III, pp. 688–9 (gives 8 May for date at Salisbury), 695–6, 704; IV, pp. 32, 130.

52 Exeter: these prisoners were sent to Barbados.

53 Deut. 21.8: 'Our hands have not shed this blood, neither have our eyes seen it. Be merciful, O Lord, unto thy people Israel, whom thou hast redeemed, and lay

I have further ill news. Yesterday sevennight Mr Gervas fell sick of the small pox at Okenden at church. Mr Goldman is gone down to preach yesterday for him, & stop untill Wednesday.[54] My Lady Saltonstall tells me that she hears that the worst is past.[55] God grant it. I have acquainted his sister here, but she knows how to send word to her mother. We are all in health at present, & great talk we have of going to Tunbridge at Whitsuntide.[56] God send you your health & a prosperous journey hither. I cannot hear that the presbytery did meet, as was reported.

Your obliged servant.
G.D.

May 7.

9 **No Date**[57]
H. 3783, f. 140
G.D. to W.S.

Sir;

Mr Medes life was written by Dr Dow but Mr Worthington having the correcting of the copy expunged what hee pleased.[58] Mr Brearly (who was intimately acquainted with Mr Mede) wrote somthing concerning /him\, & sent it to Mr Worthington, but in it hee declared Mr Medes judgment concerning altars, & the favour the

---

not innocent blood unto thy people of Israel's charge. And the blood shall be forgiven them' (AV).

54 Francis Goldman (1607–1688/9) was rector of South Ockenden, Essex, 1634–44 (when he was sequestered) and 1660–88. Perhaps Mr Gervas was his curate: *ODNB*, under Gouldman.

55 Perhaps wife of Richard Saltonstall of South Ockenden, Essex: *Al. Ox.*

56 They visited Tunbridge Wells several times, perhaps for health or because the Henleys had property in Kent. Sir Robert Henley (1624–92) was left houses in Lincolns Inn Fields by his father: *HPC*, II, p. 525; Introduction, pp. 5–6.

57 The Leicester RO Ringrose transcript bears no date but the Harleian reference number is before that, dated June 25 1655.

58 Joseph Mede or Mead (1586–1638), a biblical scholar and linguist whose works were edited by John Worthington. Mede's works included *Clavis Apolyptica (On the Book of Revelation)*; *Of the Name Altar*; *The Apostasy of the Latter Times*. Mede's works were first collected in 1648 and were enlarged by Worthington and published together with an anonymous *Life*, probably by Worthington, in 1672. This contains a Latin epitaph by 'G.D. a reverend person sometime of Camebridge', perhaps to be identified with George Davenport. John Worthington (1618–71) had been educated at Emmanuel College from 1632: *ODNB* under Mede and Worthington respectively. Dow unidentified.

Archbishop bare to him, & I think, his delight in church musick &c.[59] Insomuch as touching too much on those stringes which accord not with the descant of Presbyterian harshness, it was slighted as not in consort. And after John had a while pored on it, he lookt at it at a distance (refusing to wink at it) gave a nod, & so cast it away. I marvail that Mr Worthington would not give us the best & worst of Mr Mede. Why should hee deny that to the Archb{ishop} which, I suppose, hee doth himselfe, and although hee was for altars; yet, I presume none would therefore have sacrificed to him. And his church musick (though now hissed out of doores) was not more detestable, than our daily vain-janglings, & the howlings in the temple.[60] But Mr Mede, though dead, answers for himselfe. This relation I had from Mr Smith, who presents his service to you, & so likewise doth

Your most humble servitour,

G.D.[61]

Megg Boat I was bid to buy for some of you: and I have sent her to those whom shee may concern.[62]

10 **2 June 1655**[63]

T. 52.144

G.D. to W. S. probably from London

Sir,

On Friday sennight evening I left Mr R.G. upon the sea for Diep: & the next day I came from that place to London.[64] We have not yet heard of his arrivall in France: which makes us blame either his or his messengers negligence. To morrow I purpose for Cambridg by easy journeys: & the week after for Leicestershire. Your friends here salute you. Mr Thruscross (who was here a little before you left us to take his

59 Perhaps William Brearly, Fellow of Christ's College, Cambridge, 1635–44. He was rector of Clipston, Northants, in 1654 and died 1667: *Al.Cant.* The archbishop was Laud, Archbishop of Canterbury, 1633–45: *ODNB*.

60 Church musick: possibly a comparison of church music under Laud and the contemporary style.

61 Mr Smith: unidentified.

62 Arnold Boate (1606–53) wrote a touching life of his wife Margaret née Dungan in 1651: *The Character of a trulie vertuous and pious Woman as it hath been acted by Mistris Margaret Dungan*: *ODNB* under Boate.

63 The date given by the Bodleian catalogue of the Tanner manuscripts is 1655. Bosher, *Making of the Restoration Settlement*, p. 42 has 1656.

64 R.G.: Robert Gayer.

leave but you was not told so much) Mr Samways,[65] Mr Chamberlain[66] & others. Dr Hewet continues yet silenced: but hopes (in vain tis supposed) for his restoration.[67] 1 C{ommon} praier is down at St Peter's: yet they retain the creed.[68] No Communion at St Gregorys on Whits{unday} but yesterday (being the monthly Sunday they had one without the exhortation.[69] Dr Wild is not very well:[70] I hope no dangerous relapse after so long time. My brother went from hence two days after me re infecta: twas well done.[71] T'is sayd, hence some say on the exchange, that 22 merchant ships are lately lost to the Ostenders:[72] men talk as they would have it: hearken to the end of it. I wish you a prosperous summer. I shall somtimes trouble you with a letter: R. Beaumont must be our Post master. My Lord of Exceter will be at High-gate untill the next week: & then he intends for Sonning.[73]

June 2. Your humble servant

D.G. Geo. Davenport.[74]

Mr Gayer & his Lady are your servants.

---

65 Peter Samwaies (1615–93), vicar of Cheshunt, Herts., but was ejected. He became rector of Maldon, Beds., 1657: *ODNB*.

66 Chamberlain: L. **6**.

67 John Hewet or Hewitt (1614–58), preacher at St Gregory by St Paul's, London, 1653–8 and intermittently in trouble. He became involved in a Royalist plot in late 1657, was tried for treason with Sir Henry Slingsby and others and sentenced to beheading. Executed 8 June 1658: *ODNB*; Abbott, *Writings and Speeches*, IV, p. 799; *CSP, Dom. 1658–9*, pp. 16–17. Evelyn considered him a martyr: *Diary*, III, pp. 214, 216. See also LL. **16**, **30**.

68 St Peter's: probably St Peter's, Paul's Wharf.

69 Monthly Sunday: a reference to the monthly celebration of Communion enjoined by Parliament in preference to the celebrations according to the *Prayer Book* at Easter, Whitsun and Christmas: Spurr, *Restoration Church of England*, p. 18. The Exhortations in both the First and Second Prayer Books of Edward VI demanded that the worshippers come to Communion worthily. Its use indicated fidelity to the Prayer Book.

70 George Wild (1610–65) was Fellow of St John's College, Oxford, 1631–48. He became chaplain to Archbishop Laud. During the Commonwealth he preached in Fleet Street and at Exeter House in the Strand where the principal preacher was Mr Gunning. Wild became Bishop of Derry from 1661 until his death, 29 December 1665: *ODNB*.

71 *Re infecta* = with the matter undone.

72 By action of privateers: C.H. Firth, *The Last Years of the Protectorate, 1656–8*, 2 vols, London 1909, I, pp. 42–3; Venning, *Cromwellian Foreign Policy*, pp. 177–8.

73 Sonning, Berks., since 1654 home of the Rich family: *VCH, Berks*, III, p. 222; Introduction, p. 7.

74 The name is in a heavier hand, probably added later.

11 **25 June 1655**
H. 3783, f. 144
G.D. to W.S.

Sir;

We have been here near the Wells almost a fortnight. By that time that I have sealed this we shall be taking horse and coach for Rochester where we hope to ly this night, & to morrow to dine at Canterbury, & the day following to sup at Dover: afterwards we shall make towards this place again.[75] Here we enjoy good health and aire, & ride abroad & see good houses. About a fortnight hence, I suppose, we shall think of returning to London, but I believe not /by\ the readyest /way\. I am apt to think that Lewes and Chichester & Bramsil & Pirford will be in our way thither.[76] The 16th of August draws nigh; and before that time we hope we shall see you. I would fain see my mother; if it may be, before Michaelmass.[77] My Lord, I suppose is at Dr Young's house long before this.[78] Your friends here (I need not name any) present their service to you, & amongst them

Your obliged fr{iend} & servant
Geo. Davenport.

June 25. 1655.

12 **29 July 1655**
T. 52.76
G.D. to W.S.

Worthy Sir,

I should have been glad that myne infirmity would have permitted me to /have\ waited upon Mr Gayers into your countrey

75 this place: Tunbridge Wells in Kent.

76 Bramsil: home of the Henleys: *VCH: A History of Hampshire and the Isle of Wight*, IV, pp. 36–7; Pirford = Pyrford, north-east of Woking, Surrey. The manor was held by the Parkhurst family. Robert Parkhurst married Sarah, daughter of Sir John Gayer (the Lord Mayor), and when he died in 1674 his heirs entrusted Pyrford to Sir Robert Gayer: *VCH, Surrey*, III, p. 433; O. Manning and W. Bray, *The History and Antiquities of the County of Surrey*, 3 vols, 1809–14, repr. Wakefield 1974, I, p. 167, pedigree; Introduction, pp. 6–7.

77 Michaelmas: 29 September.

78 Probably Dr Thomas Young (1587–1655), who was Master of Jesus College, Cambridge, from 1644 to 1650 when he was deprived. He retired to his house in Stowmarket, where he died 28 November 1655: *ODNB*.

& /to\ have given you a visit at Fressingfield.[79] I hope I have in some good measure recovered my strength: yet being at sometimes better than at others, I am not confident (though no other misfortunes should stay me here) that I dare adventure tomorrow towards Cambridg which I hope to see in 2 days & in the latter end of the week to see </Leicestershire.\> I purpose to wait upon my Lord; & give him some kind of assurance of the Gentlemen their waiting upon him & but hopes of your doing so likewise.[80] I hope you will be at London before my return but I know not your occasions:[81] which if they be such as will detain you longer, I think, I could easily be here again at such time as Mr Gayers return from Bramsil with Mr Godolphin.[82] My buisness is merely to see my mother. Mr Beaumont is to acquaint me with there return from you & the day that they shall appoint again to settle here. Common-Prayerbook-men (as they call them) are threatened & warrants issued out against them (say some who pretend to know much) which by document in some bodyes hands & to be executed as they shall think convenient.[83] Mr Thurscross salutes you & saith that Dr Hammond (who is now in town) mentioneth you amongst his most precious friends:[84] he bad me say so much. My service to our Gentlemen. Their & your wellfare & the safe return of all of us hither shall be the daily prayer of

Your most affectionate friend & servant.

Jul. 29. 1655. G.D.

//I wrote to Mr Godolphin on Thursday.//

</Leicestershire.\>: Cambridge erased.

---

79 Fressingfield was Sancroft's family home in Suffolk.

80 Gentlemen: former Cambridge students.

81 Occasions: opportunities.

82 Godolphin: L. **14**.

83 Common Prayerbook men: those clergy who insisted on retaining the Book of Common Prayer for services. Its use was banned at the introduction of the *Directory for the Public Worship of God* in 1645: *Acts and Ordinances*, I, p. 582. Cromwell issued orders against the use of the Prayer Book, 24 November 1655, but persecution was not actually carried out: Spurr, *Restoration Church of England*, p. 15.

84 Henry Hammond: L. **5**.

13 **22 December 1655**

T. 314.63

G.D. to W.S. from Dieppe

Worthy Sir,

After a tedious passage of 30 houres we arrived safe at Diep on Thursday night. We are all well & eat our ill-drest meat as well as we can. We have sent for a coatch to Rouen, which if it come to morrow (Sunday) we hope will bring us easily on Christmas Day (I wish we could avoyd travelling that day) to Rouen, where we purpose to stay one day, & this day sennight to be in Paris. This is new yeares day here, & I have this morning walked before 20 altars (neither much adorned nor frequented) which I did without any further respect than carrying my hatt in my hand. Afterwards I went to the Protestant church (which is about /halfe\ a mile distant from the town) & in it found as I ghess four thousand people, & the church way full of people thronging thither.[85] My humble services to Mr John Gayer, Dr Wild, Mr Thurscross, & all my worthy friends.[86] When we are settled at Paris &< >sent directions to you, we shall hope to hear from you. I long to hear what will be the fate of my brethren & companions. Pray sir, cover the inclosed to my mother with one of your own, & send it </with\> the other to Mr Beaumont before the next Monday or Thursday. My respects to Mr Beaumont.

Your affectionate servant

G.D.

Diep Dec. 22

Address: For Mr Sancroft.

14 **15 January 1656**

T. 149.82

G.D. to W.S. from Paris

Paris Jan. 15 1655.[87]

Worthy Sir;

I wrote to you from Diep & sent it in a packet which I hope came safe to London long since. We came hither this day sennight, &

85 The Huguenots had built a church at Charenton le Pont to serve their followers in Paris in 1606: *ODCC*. For Cosin's relations with the French Protestants of Charenton see *Cosin Corr.* I, p. xxxvii.

86 Dr Wild: L. **10**.

87 The date has been over-written by a later hand and now reads 1656.

missed through misinformation our first opportunity of sending to you. We stayed one day at Rouen. Dr Cosin desireth to be remembered to you.[88] He preached a good sermon the last Sunday before the D. of York, who is (as it is reported) shortly to abandon this kingdom.[89] Sir Ken. Digby is here, but how well approved you will ghess by this story.[90] So soon as he was come hither the Duke of Gimaines hasted to dine with the Q{ueen} of England, & to bring her the 1st wellcome news of his arrivall;[91] but she suddainly interrupted him, as he was commending the knight, & said openly in the < >hall, Mr K. Digby c'est un grand cochin [knave] Dr Cosin is my authour.[92] The Princess Royall is expected here about a fortnight hence, & so is her attendance.[93] We find all things very dear. Our lodgings furnished cost 50 crowns by the month.[94] Sir William Godolphin hath a lodging elswhere provided by the Duke of Espernon.[95] We enjoy our health, God be thanked. I think Mr R. Gayer meaneth very suddainly to part with his French man, for he doth not answer expectation & old Bridget is more refractory than could be expected.[96] We can find no meal provided for us without pottage, which is one of the primest dishes of France & as much approved off by gentlemen here, as a white pot in Devonshire.[97] In it they usually boil bacon & pork, cabbage, leeks, & sometimes beef, mutton & ham. We want nothing, but are very merry

88 Cosin was chaplain to Anglican members of Queen Henrietta Maria's court in exile: Introduction, p. 8.

89 Duke of York: James, son of Charles I; this kingdom: France.

90 Sir Kenelm Digby (1603–65) was brought up a Catholic and became Chancellor to Queen Henrietta Maria's court: *ODNB*.

91 Duke of Gimaines: unidentified, but perhaps Henry Jermyn (1605–1684), the Queen's Chamberlain: *ODNB*.

92 That man is a great knave (Fr. lit. 'a pig').

93 Princess Royal of England = Mary, Princess of Orange (daughter of Charles I).

94 Crowns: a crown was a gold coin first minted in 1526 (worth 4s 6d). In 1551 it was issued as a silver coin worth 5 shillings (25p) and continued until Victorian times.

95 Sir William Godolphin (1604/5–1663) of Spargor, Cornwall. Not to be confused with his third son who was admitted to the Inner Temple in November 1654: *ODNB*. The Duke of Espernon (1592–1661), Bernard de Nogaret de la Valette, duc d'Epernon; in 1639 he took refuge in England, after he and his father were disgraced in France and Bernard was about to be arrested. (He was condemned to death in France in May 1639.) Bernard returned to France rehabilitated after the death of Louis XIII and died in Paris 25 July 1661: *Dictionnaire de Biographie Française*, 18 vols, Paris 1933 onwards, XII, cols 1341–2.

96 Bridget: unidentified.

97 White pot: a Devonshire specialty, a kind of custard or milk pudding with bread.

& speak English very fluently. My humble service to Mr John Gayer, Dr Wild, Mr Thurscross & all my friends. I hope you have letters upon a journey for us. I would fayn heare what is the fate of the clergy: but then I shall be sorry to know it. If you write at any time to my Lord of Exceter, pray present my duty //Pray send the inclosed to Mr Beaumont. If he should happen to be out of town, give the 2 other according to the direction I left with you, & Mr Beaumont will repay the charge.//

Your humble servant,
G.D.

Address: For Mr. William Sandcroft. In his absence to John Gayer Esq. In Lincolns-Inne-fields.

In the < > hall: hall erased.

15 **26 January 1656**
T. 52.103
G.D. to W.S. from Paris

Paris Jan.26.1655.

Sir,

Our last letters I hope, are safely come to your hands; & yours, I hope, will be in ours before this cometh to you. We are impatient till we hear from you, absence teacheth us but to prize good company. I thank God we are all well. As for my part, I think I never had my health better than I have had since I left London. I long as old Eli did (verbo absit invidia) to hear what is become of the ark: but fear I shall not hear what I desire, and that my answer will be with the daughter in law translata est gloria Dei de-.[98] I have /in my last\ troubled you with some inclosed to my friends, & know that you will easily pardon that trouble. If any come to </your\> hands for me, pray open them, & mold them up to the fashion of the packet you send. You know that I will readily se/r\ve you in anything here that I can. Now we hear nothing from England, we tell one another what we dream of it. My

98 *verbo absit invidia*: I Sam. 4.21–2: 'dicens, Translata est gloria de Israel quia capta est arca Dei', referring to the triumph of the Philistines over the Israelites. The former had taken the Ark of the Covenant, which was in the care of Phineas and Hophni, the sons of Eli. When the news was brought to the aged Eli, he died from shock and Phineas's wife died after childbirth. She had named her child Ichabod, meaning 'the glory is not' (i.e. the glory in which Israel boasted) and she said 'The glory is departed from Israel: for the ark of God is taken' (AV).

service to Mr Chamberlain, Mr Beaumont & all my friends at Grins.[99] The Dean is well but I cannot trouble him at present so much as I would, because of his course of preaching.[100] I learnt of him the other day that the book wherein the ordination of the French Church is vindicated, was made by Bp. Overall (with whom the Dean then lived) & not by Mr Mason.[101] Mr Mason indeed added something to it, with the approbation of the Bishop & printed it in his own name at the desire of the Bishop whose chaplain (I think) he was. The Dean, I think, is of the same mind. Thus wishing you all happiness, I take my leave till this day sennight & rest < >

Your assured late fr{iend} & servant,
G.D.

Mr Gayer with Mr Godolphin /& his Lady\ present their service to you.[102] He <fane> would have written to you had not the sudden flight of post prevented him. We have not been here long enough to know there certain houres, for want of better letters, pray look favourably upon mine. Mr Gayer hath a large catalogue of trouble for some {of} you: I mean many things to buy against the time that Richard cometh: expect it the next.[103]

</your\>: 'my' erased.

16 **6 August 1656**
T. 52.152
G.D. to W.S. from London?

Sir,

Yours of July 16th I received about a week since: & deferred to trouble you with another < > till this time, because of Mr Beaumont's absence. I heard of Mr R.G.[104] wellfare at Paris < > in a letter from

99 Chamberlain: L. **6**. Perhaps Grin's = Gryffin's?
100 Dean: Cosin, Dean of Peterborough.
101 John Overall (1560–1619), Bishop of Coventry and Lichfield, then Norwich. Cosin had been his secretary and librarian. Overall's work was *Sententia ecclesiae Anglicanae praedestionibus*, 1631: *ODNB*. Francis Mason (1566–1621) wrote *Of the Consecration of Bishops*, 1613. His Latin translation, *De Ministero Anglicano*, was completed by Nathaniel Brent and an amplified version, *Vindiciae ecclesiae Anglicanae* (1625), was dedicated to Bishop de Gondy of Paris: *ODNB*.
102 Mr Godolphin: L. **6**.
103 Richard: perhaps Mr Rickard or Riccard, LL. **7**, **16**, **30**.
104 Robert Gayer.

</Dr Cosin\>he is gone from thence with Sir Ed. Mansell towards Lion & God go with him.[105] I have received 2 letters from the Dr. Not much which may be < > communicated. But I must undeceive you about the additionalls to Mr Mason: for he saith, he said, that the Bishop was the chiefe composer of the 1st draught of the book (De Minist. Anglic.)[106] in English, which was printed at London by Bill the King's printer.[107] He is very angry at Mr Fuller, & will let him know how much he is injured by him: for he purposeth to print his answer to the articles against him in the Lords House.[108] My brother came not hither as I expected : but I was lately with him. I think he proceeds fairly on in his design, the parsonage< > & widow are disposed off to Batch. of Arts –[109] till it shall please God to bring us together again) you say. I would have had /it\ to be understood < > as if we should live together again: & if you mean less I am sorry. I am very courteously invited by Mr Henley & his lady to live with them, untill Mr R.G. return:[110] if I may have rope enough & live in London in

105 Lion = Lyons. Sir Ed. Mansell is probably Edward (died by 10 March 1690/91), son of Sir Anthony of Muddlecombe, Carmarthen, succeeded as fourth baronet to his uncle Francis (died 1654): GEC, *Baronetage*, I, p. 184, but see also ibid., I, p. 4, Edward Mansell of Margam.

106 L. **15**.

107 John Bill, king's printer in Shrewsbury, Bristol and London, where his printing house was in Blackfriars: Wing, IV, under Bill.

108 Thomas Fuller (1607/8–1661) included references in his *Church History* (1655) to Cosin's quarrel with Peter Smart during the Laudian crisis over the liturgy and furnishings of Durham cathedral when Cosin was a prebendary. After Cosin's appointment as Dean of Peterborough in 1640, Smart petitioned the House of Commons concerning Cosin's 'superstitious and popish innovations'. Cosin rejected the charges that he had spoken scandalously of the reformers or that he had denied the Royal Supremacy. The Commons Committee found him guilty and articles of impeachment were taken to the House of Lords in March 1641. As a result Cosin was sequestered from all his ecclesiastical benefices: *Cosin Corr.* I, pp. 144–52; *ODNB* for both Fuller and Cosin; P.H. Osmond, *A Life of John Cosin, Bishop of Durham, 1660–1672*, London and Oxford 1913, pp. 90–102. Fuller's comments might have been interpreted as evidence of 'Romanism': Cosin, *Works*, IV, pp. 390–9, for Cosin's reply. Fuller carried out his promise to clarify his earlier comments in his *Worthies of England*, London 1662, pp. 295–6; Osmond, *Life of John Cosin*, pp. 77–8.

109 Batch of Arts = John Davenport, George's elder brother. The reference is to John Davenport's intention of obtaining the rectory of West Rasen and a wife, the widowed daughter of the rector: Introduction, p. 5.

110 Andrew Henley: L. **8** and Introduction, p. 7.

winter, I shall not decline the proffer. When I take my journey into the west I shall know /more.\ I purpose to be at Bramsil September. 3. & the day before with my Ld., who is well, as Mr Rickard lately informed me in a letter.[111] My mother presents her respects & service to you, & on all occasions expresseth a great desire to see you hear: which I cannot hope, but I hope to see you either at London, or Fressing-field, when God shall give leave. I wish your health & much happiness & that we /may\ meet again with joy & not with sorrow for the churches sake. Dr Wild tells me in a letter, that Dr Hewet preacheth again: but questions whether his license be any more than a confidence of others winking hard.[112]

Your affectionate friend & servant
Aug. 6. 1656 D.G. Geo. Davenport

Address: For Mr Sandcroft

</Dr Cosin\>: 'DC' erased; another < > till: 'before' erased; Paris < > in: 'by' erased; understood < > as if: 'that you' erased.

17 **15 September 1656**
T. 52.164
G.D. to W.S. from Lincolns Inn Fields, London

Lincolns-inne fields Sept 15 1656.

Worthy Sir,
I came hither on Saturday night last, & tomorrow or the day following am for Bramsil: whither I am invited on myne own terms, to stay till Mr Gayers return. I know not yet whether I shall stay there: but I will make good my promise of seeing you there. My brother was lately here & dispatcht his buisiness in one hour (I think) & hath since taken possession of his living.[113] He presents his service to you: I came by Cambridge to this place. His other buisiness I think proceeds fairly. I hear that many souldiers are listed here very lately: & some say a </fort\> is to be built at Charing Cross. Some say we are in great perplexity about the fleet, which is very refractory & the banished malignants do not hast away.[114] Sir R.Shirley & manye others are put

---

111 Rickard: L. **7**.
112 Hewet: L. **10**.
113 West Rasen, Lincs.: Introduction, p. 5; L.**16**; Nichols, *Leicestershire*, IV/1, p. 383.
114 Malignants, i.e. supporters of Charles I against Parliament.

into the tower.[115] Mr Hinton of the Old Baily & Mr Nevil the draper were sent to Lameth (some letters found in their chambers caused it) but are both at liberty again.[116] Mr Chamberlane, Mr Holdsworth, Mr Batersby & Mr Thruscross, send their service to you.[117] The last was told by Mr Holbeach that you intend to travail.[118] Not having further at present to trouble you withall, I rest
Your humble servant
G.D.

Mr Beaumont is not in town.

18 **9 November 1656**
T. 52.178
G.D. to W.S. from Lincolns Inn Fields, London

Lincoln Inn fields Nov. 9 1656.

Sir; I came hither with Mr Henley & Mistress Henley & Mistress Godolphin on Thursday last and here we unexpectedly (though by letter he said he would hasten into England) found Mr Rob{ert} Gayer who landed at Dover the Sunday before. All these with Mr Jo. Gayer & his Lady present their service to you. Mistress Godolphin landed with her husband at Rye 3 weeks since: they came to Bramsil and stayd there till Mr Henley came to London, and then Mistress Godolphin came to see her brother & sisters here, & Mr Godolphin (who by act must not come within 20 miles of London) went to Salisbury where he intends to live, & whither Mistress Godolphin intends to follow on Thursday next.[119] You are earnestly expected here. I desire to know when I may expect you here, in your next; unless you purpose to

---

115 Sir Robert Shirley (1629–56), Royalist conspirator, and shelterer of sequestrated clergy. About thirty Royalists, including himself, were imprisoned about 12 September, suspected of plotting. There was considerable unease before Parliament. Shirley died in the Tower, November 1656: *ODNB*; Abbott, *Writings and Speeches*, IV, pp. 248, 256; Firth, *Last Years of the Protectorate*, I, p. 32.

116 Possibly Samuel Hinton, Archdeacon of Coventry. He was educated at Trinity College, Cambridge. He died at Lichfield 5 January 1668: *Al. Cant.* Mr Nevil: unidentified. Lambeth Palace was used as a prison at this time.

117 Batersby: see L. **3**.

118 Thomas Holbeach (1606–80), graduate of Emmanuel, sequestered 1643: *ODNB*, under Holbeach, Martin (his kinsman).

119 'Papists and others who had borne arms against Parliament' were to depart from London and Westminster or within 20 miles by 25 May 1648 or be 'imprisoned and proceeded against as Traytors': *Acts and Ordinances*, I, p. 1140.

prevent all writing by spedy hastening hither. In the mean time I shall be glad to serve you. Your 3rd vol. of the bible I have by me.[120] Mr Thorndike & Mr Chamberlayn salute you, Mr Thurscross doth as his custom was: & so doth Dr W. only on Sunday he preacheth also in his chamber.[121] Mr Gayer is busy about Stoke buisiness & probably that will hinder his writing to you this day. My brother is well at his living.[122] The last I sent to you I wrote in Leicestershire. Since that time I have not heard from you. My mother is not yet perfectly recovered. Mr Gayer hath brought with him the Councils in 37 vollumes.[123] Mr Frost died of the small pox about 10 days since.[124] Mr Lant was with me to desire Mr Gayer send word to the aldermen for Mr Jefferyes of your acquaintance.[125] He is willing to leave his living in Northamptonshire for others. Dr Sclader is dead & the parish desired my Lord of Exceter to be their minister which he refused.[126] I was with my Lord at Sunning (7 mile from Bramsil) lately. He desired to be remembered to you. He doth not much complain of infirmityes. He will stay there all this winter. Then with my service to you I take my leave & remain

Your affectionate friend & servant
G.D.

J.G. at Stoke.[127]

---

120 Brian Walton's Polyglot Bible: L. **5**. Vols I to IV contained the Old Testament and the Apocrypha, V the New Testament and VI critical appendices: *ODNB*, under Walton; *ODCC*; Introduction, p. 27.

121 Herbert Thorndike (?1597–1672), biblical scholar and theologian. Hebrew lecturer at Trinity College, Cambridge, 1640. He contributed the Syriac section of Walton's Polyglot Bible: *ODNB*. The reference to Thurscross's custom is probably to his continued use of the Prayer Book services: above, pp. 5, 8. Dr W. = probably Dr Wild: L. **10**; *ODNB*.

122 West Rasen, Lincs.: L. **17**.

123 *Conciliorum omnium generalium et provincialium collectio regia*, Paris 1644, in 37 folio volumes: H. Quentin, *Jean-Dominique Mansi et les grandes collections conciliares*, Paris 1900, p. 28.

124 John Frost (1626–56). He obtained his B.A. from St John's College, Cambridge, in 1646 and B.D. 1656. Fellow of St John's in 1647. Died in London of smallpox, 2 November 1656. A volume of sermons was published in 1657: *ODNB*.

125 Thomas Lant: L. **3**. Jefferyes: unidentified.

126 Perhaps William Sclader or Sclater, rector of St Peter le Poer: Hennessy, appendix, p. 469 gives this date of death but *ODNB* and *Al. Cant.* give 1661. Davenport may have received false information.

127 J.G.: probably John Gayer.

19 **1 December 1656**
T. 52.215
G.D. to W.S. from London.

Lond. Dec. 1.

Sir, Yours was not brought to my hands till such time as the carryer was ready to part hence, so that I had not time then to answer it. < > [non libet, I ghess, & ampliandum est] runs much in my mind. I do not expect to see you before the spring. But to the hard questions. I have not turned over the voll. of the councells.[128] They lie at Mayerne House whither they were sent so soon as we rec{eived} them.[129] I think the print equals /that of\ the Byzantin Hist.[130] The price is 30 pistolls. I have heard that Sir H. Spelmans councils make one vol. by which you may ghess what makes them sell so largely.[131] I have received a note < > /to get in\ the 5th payment for the great Bible against Christmas next. It will contain all the N{ew} T{estament}. They /have\ been in the Epist{les} about a month and talk as if it would be finished by Candlemass. They left off printing the Apocalypsa soon after they began it. Royston saith that the Countess of Devonshire (who can do much with Dr Tailor) hath got the impression of Dio. Just. and will not suffer it to be made common.[132] Others say that Royston or the Dr. will not adventure it abroad.[133] For Dr Owen /I hear\ hath caused the unum necessarium (as I take it) or else another book to justify it; to be burnt at Oxford by the hangman.[134] Above half of Dr Cos. booke is

---

128 See L. **18**.

129 Presumably as referred to above in L. **5**.

130 Unidentified.

131 Henry Spelman (1563/4–1641), historian and antiquary. In 1639 he published his *Concilia* (part I of his plan to document all the church councils in Britain or in which British representatives had been present): *ODNB*. The Paris edition included Spelman's Vol. I as one volume: Quentin, *Mansi et les grandes collections conciliares*, p. 28.

132 Countess of Devonshire, Christian Cavendish (1595–1675), Royalist, whose house at Roehampton, Surrey, from about 1650 was a Royalist centre: *ODNB*.

133 Richard Royston (1601–1686), court stationer and bookseller, frequently charged with selling unlicensed books during the Interregnum: *ODNB*; Packer, *Transformation of Anglicanism*, p. 191n; Plomer, *Dictionary of Booksellers and Printers, 1641–67*, pp. 158–9.

134 John Owen (1616–83), theologian and Independent minister, made Vice Chancellor of Oxford University in September 1652. One of the Cromwellian committee for licensing biblical translations. The unum necessarium = one thing necessary: Luke 10.42: *ODNB*. But which book is referred to?

printed.[135] Last night I had a letter from him, in which he salutes you. Mr Gayer surely hath answered the question about hogeys.[136] But what know I not what is done at Westminster, or what is their temper. Mr Paman was to take the 2 statute books, and not I.[137] And for the secundum usum, it is the use and custom of the times; a conceived prayer at night. My Ld of Exceter is well. Sir Rob. Shirley died on Friday morning last in the tower of the small pox.[138] Mr Sandeland had lately given up your name to Sir George Savil as a fit chaplain for him: but I adventured to bid him withdraw it; and put Mr Chamberlain in the room, but I think, though he hath left the Marchioness, he will not hearken to it.[139] Dr Stokes was here lately and sends his service to you.[140] Mr Thrusscross desires to be remembered to you and so doth Dr Wild. They both preach and pray in their chambers and Mr {Mossom} at his house.[141]

20 **19 January 1657**
T. 52.190
G.D. to W.S. probably from London

Jan. 19. 1656.

Worthy Sir, I am now satisfyed about my engagement of meeting you. Mr John Gayer is now at Bramsil, whither he went on Saturday last: this day he goes from thence to Stoke, & on Wednesday, I suppose, returns home.

---

135 John Cosin, probably *A Scholastical History of the Canon of Holy Scripture*, London 1657, printed by R. Norton for Timothy Garthwaite.

136 Unidentified.

137 Henry Paman (1623–95), a physician, former pupil of Sancroft in Emmanuel and his life-long correspondent: *ODNB*.

138 He died on 28 November 1656: *ODNB*; L. **18**.

139 George Savil, Marquess of Halifax (1633–95), Royalist, living at this time in Carlisle House in Linclon's Inn Fields. The Marchioness would be his mother Lady Anne (d. 1662). He did not marry until 29 December 1656: *ODNB*. Mr Sandilands must be kinsman to the family of Lord Torpichen. Walter Sandilands (1629–96) became sixth Lord Torpichen in 1649: *ODNB*, under James Sandilands, seventh Lord Torpichen; J. Balfour, ed., *The Scots Peerage*, 9 vols, Edinburgh 1911, VIII, under Sandilands, Lord Torpichen, pp. 393–4; L. **21**.

140 David Stokes (1590/92–1669): *ODNB*.

141 If Mossom, probably Robert Mossom (1617–79) who, when sequestred in 1650, preached at St Peter's Paul's Wharf, using the Book of Common Prayer, and later kept a school: *ODNB*.

The writings were sealed by Mr Villiers this day sennight: so that I think the fish is now as good as done.[142] I wrote not anything of Stoke in my former letters: because Mr John Gayer was unwilling I should: & sayd he would do it himself, but through forgetfullness & buisiness he seldom wrote.

Mistress Russell told me last night, that they intend this summer to begin to set up their rest at Stoke: & not to come to London in winter. Mr Gayer hath not said so much to me: but he told me once, that our landlord desired that a Gentleman (who was willing to take the house for a longer term than Mr Gayer had in it) might see the house. Mr Godolphin lives with Mr Henley. Mr Thrus. Mr Gonning, Mr Coldham salute you.[143] Mr Chamberlain is gone into Leicestershire. A century of sequestered ministers about a fortnight since published a paper (but my diligence could never meet with it) in which they desired reliefe & purposed to send letters or men or both into severall counties to begg: some professed /publically\ that they were fayn to go to Hide Park to hak around, others that the reason was, because some of their brethren who were other men's Almoners, gave them nothing: the chiefs were Dr Swaddling & Dr Uthy.[144] After this some other men put out a paper to revoke this, & their reason say some because the first was scandalous, say others because they themselves were excluded. < >Amongst these latter were Parson Johnson & Mr Harley with one eye & such men.[145] These last nominate a </treas\>urer as well as the former & warn the century & all other sequestered ministers of what <u>order</u> soever, to come in & receive their appointment. I think both parties will dwindle away for of the 100 {p. 2} about a week since above 60 had renounced their remonstrance (for so I think they call it)

142 Robert Villiers sold the reversionary rights of Stoke Poges Manor in 1656 to John Gayer, who acquired the house at Stoke Poges in 1656/7 on the death of Sir John Villiers. John Gayer died in 1657 and the house was bequeathed to his elder brother, Robert: *VCH, Buckinghamshire*, III, pp. 303, 306–7.

143 Gonning: Peter Gunning (1614–84). He held Prayer Book services at the chapel of Exeter House in the Strand, with communion once a month: *ODNB*; LL. **27**, **30**, **32**, **35**. John Coldham: Fellow of Queens' College, Cambridge, from 1633 to 1644 when he was ejected: *Al. Cant.*

144 Dr Swaddling: Thomas Swadlin (1600–70), D.D., Oxford, 1646: *ODNB*. Dr Uthy: Emmanuel Utye D.D. 1628; vicar of Chigwell, Essex, 1615–43, 1660–1: *Al Cant.*

145 Henry Johnson, St John's College, Cambridge, B.A. 1653/4; rector of Washington, Co. Durham, 1662–83: *Al. Cant.* William Harley, admitted pensioner at Emmanuel College, Cambridge, 7 September 1631. Became clerk of Eastchurch, Kent: *Al. Cant.*

& since I hear that so little money was come into the treasurer's hands that they propose to return it to those who gave it. This is the best history of them that as yet I can meet withall. Pray hasten as fast as you may to London. I received yours & write this whilest Mr Gayer & the Lady sister are asleep in bed but they mean their service to you. I have received from my brother but one letter for 2 months last past. My mother I think will scarce overcome her last sickness: for her greatest journey for this 4 months hath been but into the yard. I suppose you may know that with Grotius there will be printed many other good books as all Druisus, /de dieu\ Fuller, Mister Masins, Munster, Vatablus, Isid. Clarius & Castellies notes & so many others that the price they say will be 6£.[146] They are now in Joshuah having done the Pentateuch, which was their hardest work * * being printed & they have another press about the N. test{ament}. Then a voll. of the great Bible will be printed about 3 weeks hence.

Your humble servant
G.D.

Tho. Fuller (my acquaintance) is about to write one county- graphy.

146 Hugo Grotius (1583–1645), published *Annotationes in Novum Testamentum* (1641–50), *Via ad Pacem Ecclesiasticam* and *Votum pro Pace Ecclesiastica* (1642). His principal religious work, *De Veritate Religionis Christianae*, was popular in England: *ODCC*. Johannes Drusius, or Joannes van den Driesche (1550–1616), Flemish Protestant orientalist and exegete, studied in Louvain and Cambridge and taught in Oxford in the 1570s: J. McConica, ed., *The History of the University of Oxford, III: The Collegiate University*, Oxford 1986, pp. 61, 316–17; L. **23**. Thomas Fuller, see L. **16**. Masin = Francis Mason: L. **15**. Sebastian Munster (1488–1552) produced the first German edition of the Hebrew Bible (Basle 1534–5) and also published Aramaic and Hebrew grammars and *Cosmographia Universalis* (Basle 1544), a German geographical description of the world. The Psalms of Coverdale's Great Bible of 1539 were based on his Bible of 1535 but revised by reference to Sebastien Munster's Latin version of 1534–5. This was used in churches with the 1549 Prayer Book and printed as part of the Prayer Book in 1662: *ODCC*. Franciscus Vatablus, *Annotationes in Psalmos etc.* and summaries, paraphrases and translations of works of Aristotle. Isid. Clarius was Isidore, Bishop of Seville (c. 560–636). His most important works were *Etymologiae* – an encyclopedia on medicine, agriculture, architecture and theological matters; *De Natura Rerum* and *Sententiae* – a manual of Christian doctrine and practice: *ODCC*. Edmund Castell (1606–86), B.A. Emmanuel College, 1625, B.D. 1635. In 1653 he became chief assistant to Brian Walton in the supervision of the printing of his Polyglot Bible, published 1658. Castell and Samuel Clarke produced a Heptaglot Lexicon, intended to assist with the Polyglot Bible. Three hundred copies of Volume I were destroyed by the Great Fire of London. The *Lexicon* was published in 1669: *ODNB*.

That is of the profit & weakness of such country: in it will be 1500 lives: some think as many lies & mistakes.[147]
{*Below the text are scribbled a few short illegible notes.*}
Address: For Mr Sandcroft.

21 **9 February 1657**
T. 52.193
G.D. to W.S. from London

London. Feb. 9. 1656.

Sir; Yours I have received; & am not a little sorry that they give me no better satisfaction about your journeying hither. I hope your mind will soon alter, & you be better resolved. I had no purpose of going into Leicestershire: & asked the question about your coming hither, onely in relation to that satisfaction I should find when it happeneth & I hope I shall not be defeated in what I proposed.

Mr Henley went from hence about a fortnight before Christmass & then met Mr Godolphin & his family at Bramsil, where they table with him. Your statute books are in Mr Pamans hands.[148] The questions I will propose to Mr F. when I next meet with him. Yesterday was a sennight I preached for him at Waltham-abbey.[149]

I have heard Mr Wk. reason very highly < > against the ordination by presb{yters} in so much that a gentleman asked him whether if all our bishops were dead, after the death of this generation of clergymen, </all\> should be all laymen?[150] He waved the question & would not answer to purpose. But I will endeavour to remember to aske him the question when I next see him. News I seldom hear: I ghess it will be no news to you to tell, that the major generalls power & stipends are taken away.[151] Yet I think, the books never yet said so much. Some say

147 Thomas Fuller: L. **16**. The reference is to *History of the Worthies of England*, published by his son John in 1662, which groups the Worthies by county: *ODNB*.

148 Henry Paman: L. **19**.

149 Thomas Fuller served at Waltham Abbey from 1648.

150 Mr Wk. = probably Philip Warwick (1640–83), son of Charles I's secretary of the same name. Admitted to the Inner Temple in 1656: *ODNB* under both persons.

151 The Major Generals had been responsible for local administration and the militia, and their costs had been met by Royalists for the latter. They were removed in the autumn of 1656: Durston, *Cromwell's Major Generals*, p. 5, and Conclusion.

decimation will fall with them.[152] It hath been said by some that none shall preach, but such as will pray for his highness: & indeed the act for the thanksgiving exhorts us therto.[153]

Yesterday Dr Gauden preached at St Gregorys & spake of the use of the cross in the primitive times in baptism, in highways, in signing their forheads often with it; & of the //keeping the passion day: which some expected no more than others did that he should say the grace of God be with you etc. the rest of this sabbath etc.[154] Mr Thrs. landlord hath warned him to depart his house next Ladyday, & so is like to effect that which no Parl. nor army yet have done.[155] Is it not strange that banished men should fall out by the way? Mr Gayer & his Lady & brother are your servants.

Your affectionate servant
G.D.//

highly < > against: 'when' erased.

22 **18 February 1657**

T. 52.191

G.D. to W.S. from London

Lond. 18 Febr. 1656.

Sir;

I had hoped to receive more satisfaction from your brother[156] than I have done from you, about your coming hither but he is such another

152 Decimation: tax levied on Royalist estates worth £100 p.a. to support the Major General system and the militias; began 21 September 1655. Only three payments were collected (December 1655, June and December 1656). Those Royalists who refused would have their estates sequestered. The tax failed because of the difficulty of assessing the Royalists accurately (many had sold their estates to trustees); many were slow to pay: Durston, *Cromwell's Major Generals*, pp. 118–20.

153 His highness: Oliver Cromwell. On 19 January 1656/7 a service of thanksgiving was ordered by the government to celebrate Cromwell's survival of a number of attempts on his life: Abbott, *Writings and Speeches*, IV, pp. 382, 386, 409.

154 John Gauden (1605–62), chaplain to Robert Rich, Earl of Warwick. Although he had Parliamentarian sympathies, he was also a staunch Royalist. He continued using the Book of Common Prayer and was critical of civil marriage. He preached the funeral sermon in the Temple Church for Ralph Brownrigg, Bishop of Exeter, on 17 December 1659: *ODNB*. John Evelyn mentions this sermon: *Diary*, III, pp. 187–8.

155 Thr. = Timothy Thurscross.

156 Sancroft's elder brother, Thomas, gave him shelter during the Interregnum at Fressingfield, the family home in Suffolk.

as yourself: ask him of the quando,[157] & he answers the ways are fowle; but he doth not secure the utrum.[158] I hope you will hasten seeing the spring is so forward yet I cannot dissemble with you (otherwise Secretum meum mihi est).[159] I was told in town that you was no more to like to stay here again than to sojourn in a remote place which you never saw. Your friends in town salute you, particularly Mr Thurs. Mr Coldham, Mr Thorndike, Mr Britton & Mr Sandelands.[160] I hear we have brought almost 40 Dutch vessels into the Thames; because the Hollanders hath taken 7 of our ships, some whereof are East India ships.[161] T'is confidently reported by some that the Spanish Plate-fleet is come home.[162] The last mentioned person saith that he hath good Polish intelligence that the Swedish horse are totally routed, 3000 taken & slayn.[163] The Prot{ector} he said feasts the house on Friday & hath provided 400 dishes of meat for them.[164] I know not yet whether Sundercomb be buryed (the chief justice searched the crown office for presidents in the like case) or whether he shall be quartered: nor I can tell what to think of the cause of his death.[165] Yesterday I heard a man

---

157 *Quando* = when.

158 *Utrum* = whether.

159 *Secretum meum mihi est* = My secret is mine.

160 Thorndike: L. **18**. Britton: John Breton, Master of Emmanuel College, Cambridge, after Sancroft 1665 (see below, p. 125). Sandelands: L.**19**.

161 The First Dutch War was concluded in 1654 but war with Spain resulted in English shipping being plagued by attacks from Flemish and Biscayan privateers. In the summer of 1656 the government sent ships to blockade Ostend and Dunkirk to prevent the privateers attacking the English merchant ships: Firth, *The Last Years of the Protectorate*, I, pp. 42–3.

162 The English fleet was used to harass the Spanish ships returning with precious metal from the West Indies: Firth, *The Last Years of the Protectorate*, I, pp. 47–58; Abbott, *Writings and Speeches*, IV, pp. 506–7. For the activities of the Spanish Plate Fleet in assisting the forces of Charles II in 1657: Venning, *Cromwellian Foreign Policy*, pp. 137, 140, 144.

163 Reference to the Baltic conflict between 1656 and 1658. Cromwell was concerned with safeguarding the interests of Protestantism and wished to avoid any move which might result in total commitment against the Dutch (Protestant) and hostile action by a Catholic Hapsburg coalition. However, Anglo-Swedish treaties were signed in 1654 and 1656 because of the importance of the Baltic for maintaining naval supplies: Venning, *Cromwellian Foreign Policy*, pp. 202–7; G. Clarke, *The Early Stuarts*, pp. 225–8.

164 Prot. = Protector (Oliver Cromwell). For the dinner: Abbott, *Writings and Speeches*, IV, pp. 409–10.

165 Miles Sindercombe was responsible for a plot to kill Cromwell which was exposed in January 1657. His aim was to remove Cromwell and return to government by the Rump Parliament. Abortive attempts were made at Hyde

say (& he saith he had it from his friend, who was Sund. bed fellow) that he was always a </mutinous\> fellow & that he once told him, that he would be hanged, to which he replyed /with an oath\ that it should be then for a crown or kingdom: he would oft bragg, what men he had killed in cold blood, & amongst the rest the Lord Francis Villiers.[166] T'is said by some that the French, /not Protestants\, have turned the K{ing's} souldiers out of Bullen & another town in Picardy & refuse to levy men for this Champaign.[167] My Lord of Exceter, I hear, is now as well as he useth < > to be: but was lately Apoplecticall.[168]

Pray let us hear from you & if it may be assure us whether & as you can, the when. Thus wishing your health & happiness, I commit you to Gods protection, & remain

Your affectionate friend and Servant. D.G.

</mutinous\>: over 'seditious' erased.

23 **2 March 1657**

T. 52.197

G.D. to W.S. from London

London March 2nd 1656.

Sir, I perceive my letters gave you not that </satis\>faction which you desired but I pray consider, that they are usually written in great hast to you: for I seldom have above an hours time after I have received them in which I can answer, in which if I have other avocations (for sometimes I have been fain to dispatch 8 letters on a Munday morning) it is no marvail: and sometimes onely whilest /Mr Beaumonts\ messenger stays upon me for my answer. For the utrum and the quando, you know what you wrote, and < > soon after I had received

---

Park, near Westminster Abbey and at Whitehall Palace. Found guilty of treason, he was sentenced to be hanged, drawn and quartered but escaped this fate perhaps by taking poison: *ODNB*; Abbott, *Writings and Speeches*, IV, pp. 291, 380–2 for scepticism about the details. Presidents = precedents.

166 Lord Francis Villiers, son of George Villiers, first Duke of Buckingham. With his elder brother, George, he was brought up with the children of Charles I. (George was later to become second Duke of Buckingham.) After their education at Cambridge (Trinity College) they joined the king at Oxford. Francis was killed 7 July 1648, near Kingston, Surrey, in a skirmish with the Parliamentarian forces: *ODNB*.

167 Bullen = Boulogne?

168 My Lord of Exceter: Brownrigg. Apoplecticall = showing the symptoms of a stroke: *OED*.

it, Mr Thrusscross told me (& not as a secret) that you would come no more to this place, for you would travail with a scholar, at your own charge, but not yet. I put both these together & thought they spelled a strong suspicion of </the loss of you\> & sometimes began to think with my selfe, that I had best communicate your letter to Mr G{ayer} but even carryed it in the negative till at length /he\ being in my study and professing some wonder that he was no better assured of our coming, & saying he would buy 100£ worth of books for publique use in his house at Stoke, & I knowing that I should be sufficiently blamed by him hereafter if you came not (of which I justly doubted) I showed him that passage in your letter & desired him to write effectually to < > you about it & I even thought I had done well. I thought the going beyond seas might be much noised about (it *{not}* being told me as a secret) & I not not[169] knowing the 2nd person (for Mr G*{ayer}* refused to tell me who that was, though if you would not think it like my suspicious selfe, I would ghess it a divine of Northfolk who went out of his chamber, as I came in) I asked Mr Holdsworth if he knew anything, which he said he did not, & then I desired him to keep it in private & I said I would, & this was the secretum meum, if I forget not my selfe:[170] but now I am glad to be freed of that suspicion for Robin saith after another quarter of a pound of coffee, you will come to London: not confirmed by act) that is, you say, not taken away.[171] That the Major Generalls power is broken & declared illegall, one of that house hath told me, & that no one dare gather up the decimation, for fear of the house.[172] I know not that the single person hath given his consent, but such he neither can nor will refuse & when the next sealing of acts cometh, this will pass. I know nothing said of the act concerning the clergy.[173] I have not seen Mr Fuller since your former letter which were your questions. This much for apology now for news.

{p. 2} This day /sennight\ Alderman Pack adventured to bring unto the house a Remonstrance in the name of the < > nobility, gentry &

169 Sic.

170 A divine of Northfolk: perhaps John Cosin.

171 Robin = Robert Gayer?

172 Major Generals' power; Decimation: L. **21**. The house: Parliament, essentially the Commons at this time.

173 The Act concerning the clergy may be the act of 28 August 1654 ejecting scandalous ministers: *Acts and Ordinances*, II, p. 968; or a confirmation in June 1657 of the Act of 1653 appointing commissioners to approve public preachers: ibid., II, 855–8, 922, 1025–6. The question was under discussion.

commons of England, in which (towards the settlement of the nation) they desired that his highness would accept of the name & office /or prerogative\ of a king & that there might be a house of blank (understand Peres or Lords) at no time less than 40 or more than 70, men that had never assisted the late k{ing} & to sweeten it to some, that taxes might not be raysed but by Parl{iament} which should be frequent, that all that are chosen for Parliament < > men hereafter, should sit therin, & not be denyed there places as of late & that an oath of abjuration should be ministered & they who refuse should be banished. This at first met with much opposition & some talked of </turning\> the mover out of the house, others of bringing him to the barr & sending him to the tower, as one that went about to alter fundamentalls.[174] Lambert & all the Major Generalls violently opposed it, insomuch that many said t'was because they hoped to be what the Prot{ector} now is, but at length thrice as many voted for Pack as against him & now they say there *{are}* 3 for 1.[175] Many are for it out of spleen to the souldiery. I know not what moves the Lawyers thereto. I have this relation from one of the house present at all the debates. He saith that he thinks it will take up 3 months' time. By this act all sales of the k{ings} lands must be confirmed; & the custom settled upon the heirs of this man & his successors, the next of which he is desired by it to name, that so their may be no interregnum or violence offered by the souldiery to the council when a new one shall be chosen. Some say that what he is desired to nominate, in amendment to bills, will be charged unto his heirs. It must be taken into many pieces, every of which is to be read thrice & amendments & at length all passed, or none. The Lord Richard, they say, is going into Scotland to be Generall there & Monk must be his lieftenant.[176]

174 Christopher Pack (c. 1599–1682). Merchant. Lord Mayor of London 1655. M.P. 1656. On 23 February 1657 he presented a new constitution providing for a second house and offering the crown to Cromwell: *ODNB*.

175 John Lambert (1619–84) was Major General for Cumberland, Durham, Northumberland, Westmorland and Yorkshire, but remained in London as a member of Cromwell's Council and was responsible for the details of operating the system of the Major Generals. Lambert is thought to have been the instigator of the decimation tax: Durston, *Cromwells's Major Generals*, pp. 97–9; *ODNB*.

176 Lord Richard Cromwell, son of the Protector. George Monk (1608–70). His support for the exiled Charles II was an important factor in his Restoration: *ODNB*.

Some say that some pieces were lately discharged against Ch. Stw. & James his brother as they were walking in a garden, whereby a page standing by was slayn: others say it is onely a report.[177] Mr Gayer is not in town. < > He lives with the Lord Capell about 20 miles from this place.[178] {p. 3} I know not what you mean by prayers for the church. I never saw the Book of the Psalms in {liturgy?} published by Q. Eliz. which are by Munster.[179] That Fuller Miss. will be printed you'le not wonder if you consider that < > Drusius Trigonisium will also.[180] I suppose /both\ at the end of the commentaryes. Mr Goldman[181] desires you would send him your scholium upon the 9th Iliad.[182] I hope to see you here ei'r long: but I wish you had confirmed it {in} your letter. Mr G{ayer} & his brother are your servants, to morrow they are for Stoke. Thus begging your parden for {my} former indiscretions, I remain

Your affectionate friend & servant
D.G.

I once saw the books of the Lord Verulam.[183] It is in folio as bigg *{as}* the naturall hist. But as I was reading the life in a bookseller *....* the customer called for it. I think there are in it many fragments formerly published, & some new treatises (which as the Dr saith were designed to be left by him in some library, but now published by him (who knew more of that Lord than any other) to prevent others)[184] and some letters. Mr Beaumont will give you a catalogue of them the next week.

To < > you: 'him' erased; the < > nobility: 'gent' erased; parliament < > men: 'should' erased; </turning\>: 'sending' erased; in town < > He: 'neither' erased.

---

177 Ch. Stw. = Charles Stewart (Charles II).

178 Arthur Capel (1632–83), of Little Hadham, Hertfordshire, succeeded his father as second Baron Capel when the latter was executed by Parliament in 1649: *ODNB*.

179 Munster: see above, L. **20**, for the Psalms in the Book of Common Prayer of 1574.

180 Drusius Trigonisium = Johannes Drusius: L. **20**.

181 Francis Goldman. He compiled an English–Latin and Latin–English dictionary: L. **8**.

182 scholium: an explanatory comment on a Greek or Latin author.

183 Verulam: Francis Bacon (1561–1626). The works referred to are probably *Historia naturalis et experimentalis ad condendam philosophiam, sive phoenomena universi* and *Historia vitae et mortis*: *ODNB*.

184 Dr: perhaps Cosin.

24 **5 June 1657**

H. 3783, f. 163

G.D. to W.S. from West Rasen, Lincs.

West Rayson Jun. 5.1657.

Sir; I came hither on Saturday last & found no brother. He went 4 days before with his mistress to the place from whence he fetcht her.[185] Nor is he yet returned, though expected ever since I came. In the mean while I have the daily company of the parish clerk, a grave weaver in a seemly-wrought night cap, who at first word entreated me to offisticate for his master; & by whom I much profit in learning the language of the countrey. I think my brother is fast seated in a living of good reverence; & amongst people of quiet & good conversation. For they tell me, that there is not a man in the parish (the Papists excepted for such is the Lord of the whole town, Sir Phil{ip} Constable, who lives in Yorkshire)[186] but is a good church-goinger, and hath good respect for their minister, & pay </their\> tithes as willingly as any papist in the parish. I hope to go for Leicestershire this day sennight, by Newark & Nottingham: for I fear my brother will not have leisure to go to York as he promised. I pray let me hear from you before you go to Tunbridge Wells: Rob{ert} Beaumont to whom my hearty respects will convey your letter I should be glad to hear of Mris Godolphins safe delivery. My humble service to Mr J. Gayer & his Lady, & Mr R. Gayer (to whom I </sent\> on Munday last by the post < > at home: & abroad to Mr Thrusscross, Mr Gunning, Dr Wild, Mr Thorndike & any of my friends whom you shall meet with.[187] Perhaps I may see Mr Chamberlan in my return: I hear he intends to be shortly in London. I long for some good news. God send you all health at the Wells & us a joyfull meeting at Stoke. Pray remember Dr Stokes' book.[188]

Your humble servant. G.D.

</sent\>: 'wrote' erased; post < > at home: 'from' erased.

---

185 Long Sutton was the family home of John Davenport's wife, Sarah Thompson.

186 Sir Philip Constable, Lord of the manor of West Rasen, with his household, failed to take the Protestation oath in March 1641, being recusants: *Protestation Returns 1641/2, Lincolnshire*, transcribed by W.F. Webster, Nottingham 1984, p. 93. West Rasen was a mass centre for Catholics: R.W. Ambler, *Churches, Chapels and the Parish Communities of Lincolnshire 1660–1900*, History of Lincolnshire 9, Lincoln 2000, pp. 79–81. The family seat of the Constables was at Everingham in the East Riding of Yorkshire: *Miscellanea*, ed. C. Talbot, Catholic Record Society 53 (1960), index under Everingham, for regular penalties for recusancy.

187 Gunning: L. **20**.

188 David Stokes: L. **19**. For his book: L. **25**.

25 **15 June 1657**

H. 3783, f. 164

G.D. to W.S. from Wigston Magna, Leics.

Wigston. June 15th 1657.

Sir; I have received yours & give you thanks for it. I returned on Friday last from my brother, who presents his service to you. I stayd a full week at his house, before he came. I believe you have heard before this time that e'er long he is like to be a marryed man. He would have persuaded me to have stayd 3 Sundays & preached for him, whilst he is asked in the church:[189] for when the poor register tells the neighbours that N & N are in a way of marriage, it is the unhandsome custom of the youth of the parish to turn < >towards one of the porches & with acclamations say, God give you joy. Now he is affrayd he shall blush. On the 1st or 2d of the next month I purpose, God willing, to go to him: & not to leave him till I have marryed him; & perhaps by that time you may have enough of Tunbridge & be for Stoke. I am not altogether satisfyed about Dr Stokes' book, which, you say, is like to rest in Mr Thorndike's hands till I come.[190] You may remember I told you, that I promised the Dr, that he should have it about midsummer: for about that time he said, he should have a scholar in his house who should transcribe some part of it. Pray unless the Dr know in whose hand it resteth, be pleased to let him know in a letter, which you may send before you go to the Wells, or else leave behind you for the next opportunity. That passage doth perplex me, that you will deliver Dr Erskin's papers to Mr John Gayer for me.[191] I am very glad for Mris Godolphins safe delivery: & wish them good prosperity with their son. My service, I pray, to Mr Henley & his Lady, who, as I suppose, are now with you. I would you had sent some news: for I have neither seen pamphlet nor heard any intelligence since I saw you. I believe few West-rayson men ever saw a diurnall.[192] My service to Mr Thorndike, Mr Gunning, Mr Thruscross & all my friends. Thus wishing to all of you a good journey to Tunbridge, happy success there, & all of us a joyfull meeting at Stoke. I commit you to God.

Your affectionate friend & servant,

G.D.

---

189 'asked in the church': the reading of the banns of marriage on three consecutive Sundays.

190 Stokes' Book: *Paraphratical Explication of the Prophecie of Habakkuk*, Oxford 1646.

191 William Erskin, D.D.Oxon. 1642. Died 1660: *Al. Ox.*

192 Diurnall: journal: see J.B. Williams, *A History of English Journalism to the Foundation of the Gazette*, London 1908, pp. 3–9.

26 **6 July 1657**
H. 3783, f. 165
G.D. to W.S. from Lincoln

Lincoln. July 6th 1657.

Sir;

I came to my brother on </Wednes\>day last: & accompanyed him hither this morning to put him into his wedding dress. I think he will be marryed about the middest of the next week: which will be assoon as you can receive this.[193] By that time you have done with the Wells, I hope, I shall have done with this, & all other buissiness in these parts, & be ready to meet you at Stoke. My brother presents his service to you. My service I pray to Mr Henley, & his Lady: & to Mr John Gayer & his Lady, & to Mr R.Gayer: not forgetting Mris Russell. I am almost dead with hot weather & *   * for want of company. Yet I meet now & then with * * honest people, who eat wholesome meat & green sauces, & *   *mustard with rost beefe. At Grantham, in my way hither, I fell in with the Lecturers of the place, some of them of the house of Iman.[194] & as they sat prophesying (it was over ale in my chamber, for bibbers that they were, they drank me 19d) one mightily scrupled to bowle on the Lecture Day, & because he was weak they would not urge him.[195] Afterwards by way of prophecy a young divine was censored for saying dish-clowt in the pulpit < > at the Lecture: but he presently wiped of their objection, when he told them, that if they had observed him, he said not simply dish-clouth but dish-clowt with reverence be it sayd. The Cathedrall of this city is the best that ever I saw, & kept as handsomly as any I know in England.[196]

---

193 John Davenport was married on 24 July at Long Sutton, Lincs. This would probably have been a civil wedding as church weddings were banned. Perhaps G.D. carried out a private church ceremony.

194 Iman. = Emmanuel College.

195 Grantham Lecturers = two preachers: Packer, *Transformation*, pp. 137, 176.

196 John Evelyn, on 19 August 1654, describes Lincoln Minster as comparable to York 'abounding with marble pillars' and 'a faire front' but records that 'the soudires had lately knocked off all or most of the brasses which were on the Gravestones': *Diary*, III, p. 131. The cathedral was one of the first to be 'purged'. The city was besieged by the forces of the Eastern Association under Manchester and Cromwell in May 1644: Lehmberg, *Cathedrals under Siege*, p. 31. G.D.'s appreciation is perhaps an indication of his churchmanship.

I wish you all much prosperity at the Wells: but fear I shall not be assured of it before I see you. In much hast I am

Your affectionate friend & servant
G.D.

//I have written to Mr Beaumont to call for Mr R.Gayers Lad's cloaths of a carryer who hath kept them a month in London.//

Address. For my very worthy friend Mr William Sandcroft. /Att Mr Downes his house att Bownes {shelfe}...Neare Tunbridge.\

Pulpit < > at the: 'there' erased.

27 **30 December 1657**

H. 3783, f. 178

G.D. to W.S. from Stoke

Stoke. Dec. 30. 1657.

Sir, I wrote to you about a fortnight since, & had sooner, but that Mr R. Gayer undertook to do that, which at that time he was not willing I should mention. I never heard from you since you made your 1st voyage towards Holland (& escaped my last not above an hour though I knew not so much then) & very rarely of you since that time. Ipse veni,[197] I would say, if it might stand with your affairs there, as well as it seems to concern you hear. I keep close here, & as well as I can oversee buisness: Mr Gayer hath been here but 2 days since the funerall.[198] Mr Gayers most pious & Christian end doth much comfort his friends. I absolved him, gave him the communion & buryed him.[199] My Lord of Exeter was ill </otherwise\> he should have preacht for him, & he did desire that he would do it. He gave 100£ to the poor clergy: & My Lord hath distributed it. Mr Gunning, Mr Thrisscruss & Dr Wild were disturbed on Christmas Day, & I hear imprisoned.[200] But I hear that good words were given them, & that they preacht as formerly on Sunday last. I do much mistrust my Lord of Exceter's health: for he is often ill, & is scorbutical, hydropicall, & some say asthmaticall & podaquicall.[201] Mr

---

197 Ipse veni = I myself came.

198 The funeral: John Gayer's funeral: L. **28**.

199 Absolved him: an indication of G.D.'s adherence to the Book of Common Prayer and earlier rites.

200 See L. **10**.

201 Scorbuticall: afflicted with syptoms of scurvy. Hydropicall: afflicted with dropsy. Podaquicall: suffering fluid in the feet: *OED*.

Widdrington hath been in great danger by his ague:[202] but Mr Beaumont tells me he is much amended at his retirement at Hisson.[203] Mr Lynford is dead.[204] My brother presents his service to you. He lately escaped a great hazzard of being drowned in the sea, through the mistake of the guid in a misty day.[205] Dr Worthington (who a while since marryed the governor of Windsors daughter) is Vice-Chancellor.[206] If I may not see you here, I hope I shall somtimes hear from you. You had heard oftner from me, but that I wanted sometimes leisur, & somtimes opportunity (not knowing which way to send to you,) & somtimes both: </and\> this letter is written by snatches, which will a little plead for its rudeness: for I want not employment out of my study. God in mercy comfort us after the death of Mr Gayer (of whom I have said the less, because I know his brother hath said the more) & indeed though he be dead, yet is he as though he were not dead: for he hath left a brother behind him that is like himselfe. I hear that Dr Cosin is minded to come into England, & I partly believe it: for the gentlewoman that told me so said, he intimated so much in a letter to her. B{isho}p King lives about two miles from this place: & to him I have recourse sometimes.[207] I have written to Dr Cosin this day, & acquainted him where you are. If in anything I can serve you, during your absence, I hope, I need not say, you may require it from me who am

Your affectionate friend & servant

G.D.

</otherwise\>: 'when' erased; </and\>: 'yea' erased.

---

202 Widdrington: either Thomas (c. 1600–64) or Ralph (1614–88). The latter carried out much correspondence with Sancroft: H. 3785, ff. 78, 79 (1656–61): *ODNB*.

203 Hisson: Histon?

204 Samuel Lynford, of Bedfordshire, who gained his B.A. from St John's College, Cambridge, in 1629/30, M.A. in 1633 and B.D. in 1643. He became a canon of Exeter in 1642 but was ejected. His will was dated 1657: *Al. Cant.*

205 Probably in the area of Long Sutton (near the Wash) where J. Davenport's wife's family lived.

206 Worthington: L. **9**. He married Mary Whichcote on 13 October 1657, daughter of Christopher Whichcote, niece of his former Emmanuel tutor Benjamin Whichcote. About three weeks later he became Vice Chancellor but did not hold office very long, finding it 'too burdensome': *ODNB* under Worthington and Benjamin Whichcote.

207 Henry King (1592–1669), Bishop of Chichester. In 1657 he may have been either at Langley or at Hitcham with his sister or his brother: *ODNB*.

28 **21 January 1658**
H. 3783, f. 181
G.D. to W.S. in Utrecht, from Stoke

Stoke. Jan. 21. 57.

Sir; Yours of Jan.1. I have received; as I hope you have mine of Dec. 31. In which what I wrote I have utterly forgotten: but write I am sure I did, & I think, about Mr Gayers; wherefore if I write anything again that was in that letter, or omitt anything, presuming it might be in that letter, I pray excuse it. You desire the particulars of his sickness, death, & buriall, & so doing-jubis renovare dolorem.[208] He went to London with his brother, the Wednesday sennight before his death, in his coach, in a very cold day through a sharpe wind. The next day he complained of a cold that he had taken, & so again the 2^{d} & 3^{d} day, but on that day he eat (for before he could not) & returned to Stoke because he would not affright his wife. So soon as he came home he took his bed, complaining of a cold & a pain in his neck; & the next day being Sunday he did sweat, & had some ease, yet got a pain in his head. In the night he bled at nose, & finding himselfe feaverish, he sent for me, who< > went immediately to London (when I arrived at day break) for Dr Scarborough whom I brought with me that day.[209] He caused him to be let blood & stayed with him till Wednesday. He called his disease an inequall or irregular feaver. On Thursday he had a fitt of it: he burned 3 houres or thereabouts, & then did sweat freely for 8 or 9 hours. In this fitt we were minded < > to send for another Dr to advise with Dr Scarburgh, but he telling of us we were affrighted more than needed, bad us try Wednesday night, & if we thought his case more dangerous on Thursday to send a messenger < > to him and he would bring another with him. We conceiving his case to be much better sent not, & the Dr at his return that night said he saw little danger, but thought it would prove a lingering sickness, as it commonly is (for I think it was the same disease that took away Mr Wilkinson, & that which the people call the new disease.[210]) On Friday he was, we

208 Vergil, *Aeneid*, II.3: You order me to renew the grief.

209 Dr Charles Scarborough (1615–94), B.A. Studied medicine and mathematics at Emmanuel College. Fellow of the College of Physicians 26 September 1650. Later physician to Charles II: *ODNB*.

210 Mr Wilkinson: unidentified. There were many epidemics of agues and influenzas during the period 1657–9: C. Creighton, *A History of Epidemics in Britain*, 2 vols, Cambridge 1891–4, II, *A.D. 1666–1893*, pp. 5, 21.

thought, in a very good way of recovery: & caused his wife (who never stirred from him till the last hour of his death) to eat her dinner upon the bed side, & sayd he could eat of that meat (venison pasty) heartily & drink claret wine, yet would abstayn for his healths sake. About 3 of the clock he fell into a looseness & had stools of good consistency, I think 5 or 6. Afterward 2 or 3 without consistence (then began the danger) soon after he fell into a burning fit very violent, & then did sweat all the night, without rest. On Saturday morning we sent for Dr Rydgley & Dr Glysson.[211] Dr Glysson came that night. Dr Rydgly was coming the next day < > when he was dead. Then Dr Scarburgh discovered that he had had always a very untoward pulse, & that not with standing all the benefits of nature < > (as bleeding, sweating, purgation) his fever never abated. His < > pulse rather moved than beat: & was such an one as physitians, if I mistake not, do name pulsus vermiculans:[212] but I did not hear them give it any name. This night the Dr told me of the danger, yet gave us good hope. {p. 2} Att midnight we were called up, & saw little hope of life, & then I gave him the communion & absolved him. I had done it sooner, as he desired, but somtime the Dr </h\>indered & sometimes his fitt. He had to the last good naturall strength; but his spirits fayled. Many heavenly expressions he had in his mouth: & died full of comfort, & out of love with this world. Saying, he renounced the world, & had overcome death & between 10 & 11 of the clock he fell asleep in {Christ}.[213] His will I wrote on Saturday, but first I desired them to send for Mr Abbot,[214] or in the mean while for the Scrivener at Windsor (Judg Jenkyns we forgott) but they would not.[215] If the child his wife now goeth with be a daughter then his brother is his heir, & she shall have 13000 to her portion. He gave the

211 Luke Rydgely, B.A. Christ's College, Cambridge, 1634/5 and M.D. 1646. He died in September 1697: *Al. Cant.* For his father, Thomas: *ODNB*. Dr Francis Glisson (1599–1677), Regius Professor of Physic, Cambridge, 1636–77 and prominent in London scientific circles: *ODNB*.

212 Pulsus vermiculans: 'to beat with peristaltic motion, i.e. with rhythmic wave-like contractions': *OED*.

213 Text has Xt.

214 Perhaps Robert Abbott of Cranebrook, Kent, who obtained his B.A. at Oxford in 1637 and M.A. at Emmanuel College in 1640: *Al. Ox.*; *Al. Cant.*

215 David Jenkins (1582–1663). A prominent Royalist judge tried and imprisoned several times for his attitude to Parliament and its power. In 1657 he was living under surveillance in Gray's Inn: *ODNB*; *Cosin Corr.* I, p. 232n.

clergy 100£, my Lord of Exeter 50£, you 20£, me 10£ & every of his servants 10£. He desired that my Lord would bury him: & he promised more readily to preach; but his infirmity hindered him. Therefor the funerall was deferred another week but he was still hindered. So that at length being honourably attended with about 50 coaches he was carryed from this house to Cree church, being met at Charing Cross with 200 torches: & then I read the office. He lay in state in the chappell here after the best manner. The great parler was also covered with black, & the hall hung with a breadth & the passages[216] & so was < > Cree-church.[217] His library he gave his brother. You would know how I dispose of my selfe: I answer at present I employ myselfe as a steward in looking after affairs here, from whence I have not stirrd since the funerall, nor can I imagine when I may, for my buisinesses are very many. Mr Gayer is at London for the most part; but will live here, I take it, if it prove his manor. Mr J.Gayers books were never opened: nor can I ghesse when they will. When they be I shall be able, I believe, to know most of yours, & will separate them: attamen ipse veni.[218] I have spoken to Mr Beaumont (who was here 2 days since in his way to Oxford & is expected again to night to take this to London) for the books you desire. I hope you will excuse me that I wrote not sooner to you (for Mr Davies promised to send the sad news within 2 days after: & Mr R.G. chose rather to do it, than that I should do it) & that I have written so rudely at this time, but I have not time to write a le{tte}r twice over.

Your affectionate friend & servant

G.D.

Address: For Mr Sandcroft. At Mr Honeywood's lodging in Utrecht.[219]

His < > pulse: 'feaver' erased.

216 Breadth = a piece of cloth of the full width: *OED*.

217 St Katherine, Creechurch, City of London, where his father was also buried: *ODNB* for his father, Sir John (1584–1649).

218 Attamen ipse veni = However, I myself have come.

219 Michael Honywood (1596–1681), formerly of Christ's College, rector of Kegworth, Leics., in 1639. He was sequestred in 1649. From 1643 he lived abroad, mainly in Utrecht, where Sancroft, his friend, stayed with him. An avid book collector: *ODNB*.

29 **8 March 1658**
H. 3783, f. 187
G.D. to W.S. in Holland, from Stoke

Stoke. March 8. 1657.

Sir; Yours of Jan. 15 I received long since. I hastened not then to answer it, because I believed before I received it, mine would come to your hands; in which, as I remembered, all you queries would be answered. Afterwards I purposed to write to you, but an ague hindered me, which took me this day moneth, & this is the first day that I dare adventure confidently abroard, though it left me the 2^{d} time (for I relapsed after I had missed 3 fits) above a week since. Last night I received your other of Febr.19. which came to London but 2 days before. I am beholden to you for your good acceptance of < > my letters, which you cannot but perceive are always either written in great hast, or by fits & starts. Yet, knowing your friendlyness, I am loath to write them over a second time. I know not what you mean when you say after Mr G. answer you may have occasion to use me:[220] but you may be assured I shall not refuse any friendly office. For the firre box,[221] if you please it may be sent elsewhere: but it is safe here: & it is very uncertayn when & where the library may be opened. I should be glad that you would come & make use of them here, or elsewhere with Mr G. as you say, it may please God you may. My Lord of Exceter, I think, is now at High-gate: he hath long talked of coming hither, in his way to Mr Rich.[222] I perceive you read in Gazets, therefore perhaps you may know our news better than I do, who have not been 5 miles from this place since my return from the funerall: & seldom see either news-book or news-monger. Yet this I am told, that all that sat in the other house shall have patents of honor sent them & peerages given them, & none but those, & such as are added to them shall be accounted peers that about the 7 of May we shall have another Parl{iament} chosen as formerly; that is all the ancient corporations have their privilage of sending Burggers as formerly. The K{ings} party by 2 proclamations are commanded to keep their dwellings, & not to stirr above 5 miles from thence till the 1 day of the term, that is Ap{ril}

220 Mr G.: probably Robert Gayer.

221 firre box: box of pine wood.

222 Thomas Rich, later Sir Thomas, at whose houses in Sonning, Berks., or at Wimbledon Brownrigg usually stayed. *ODNB* on Brownrigg. Rich: L. **10**; Introduction, p. 7.

28.[223] The great Bibles Apparatus, they say, will be finished by Easter.[224] I have received the Apocrypha etc. & now propositions are sent for a Lexicon of the severall languages. I mean to subscribe for 6. The price of each 50s but 6 may be had for 12£ 10s. 30s for each to be paid in hand the rest afterwards. Mr Beaumont hath been here this week {&} Mr Gayer 3 weeks, & this letter is now going for London with them. My brother remembers his service to you. Dr Burgess is supplanted at St Pauls by one Dr Annulo a civilian.[225] I shall be glad to hear from you, when you have a little time to cast away & what occurres here worth relation (you see at present how barren I am of any such things) I will communicate to you. I hope the Holland air is not offensive to you: for your good health is much desired by me who am

Your assured friend & servant.

G.D.

Of < > my letters: 'what' erased.

30 **12 May 1658**
H. 3783, f. 194
G.D. to W.S. from Stoke

Stoke. May 12 1658.

Sir; Yours of March 19th I received in good time: but I deferred an answer because I daily expected the packet through Mr Beamonts hand (but as yet he hears nothing of it) & also the delivery of Mris Gayer (who on Friday last was delivered of a very <u>handsom son</u> whom God make inheritour of his fathers virtues, & bless with a much longer life) & now I can deferr no longer. I demurr at one thing in your letter, viz. <u>the bond</u> to be dated from Lady {day} last (yours is dated Mar. 19) that is 1657. Your letter is playn for it & I only question it because it /will\ look above a year backward. Mr Gayer is not </able\> to resolve this doubt. Annulo the civilian is preacher at St Pauls. Dr Baker is dead.[226]

223 2 proclamations: Packer, *Transformation of Anglicanism*, p. 37 nn. 4 and 5.

224 Walton's Polyglot Bible: LL. **18**, **20**, **30**; *Cambridge History of the Bible*, II, Cambridge 1963, pp. 64, 93, 208, 214.

225 Cornelius Burges, vicar of Watford 1618–45; chaplain to Charles I. He was appointed lecturer at St Paul's in December 1643. Although he sided with Parliament, he spoke out strongly against the king's trial, at great risk to himself. He seems to have lost the salary after 12 February 1656: *ODNB*. Dr Annulo: unidentified, but evidently a civil lawyer.

226 Samuel Baker, chaplain to Bishop Juxon of London, probably assisted in the production of Walton's Polyglot Bible: *ODNB*, with no certain date of death.

Mr Balcanqual dangerously sick.[227] I have not yet subscribed for the Lexicons. R.Beaumont dissuades me from it at present. My brother is your servant: so is my neighbour, Mr Adams:[228] I saw him about a fortnight since, & then he had been sick of an ague for 6 weeks space. I hear that 500 dye per week in London. The bills acknowledge but one a week of the plague.[229] The distemper predominant there & here in the countrey some < > call the new cold, others the new disease. Mr Gayer saith the annuity cannot be assured by land: for no man hath power to bind the land. I suppose we shall leave this place ere long: but to whom I know not, I suppose to the trustees in the marriage articles: & whither we shall go, I am also to seek. Mr Riccard, Mr Gayer & Mris Abdy answered for the child & my Lord christened it.[230] My Lord came hither 2 days since, & intends to remove from hence to day to Sunning. He is now in pretty good condition of health: but lives medice.[231] He desires to be remembered to you: & so doth Mr Gayer, who came with my Lord & will speedily be for London agayn. Mr Molle of Kings, I hear, is very dangerously sick there, if not dead.[232] The H[igh] Court of Justice, I hear, sat yesterday: but what was done I hear not.[233] Some think that Dr Hewet shall be first questioned: Mr Gunning, Dr Wild & Mr Thrisscross were silenced a fortnight since:

---

227 Perhaps Samuel Balanqual, M.A. Edinburgh, 1611. Incorporated Oxford, 1618 and Cambridge, 1618. Fellow of Pembroke College, Cambridge, 1619. Proctor 1637. Ejected 1650: *Al. Oxon.* and *Al. Cant.*

228 William, son of Thomas Adams, alderman and ex-Lord Mayor of London. He was admitted fellow commoner at Emmanuel College, Cambridge, 1651. He entered the Middle Temple in 1654 and succeeded his father as baronet, 1667. They belonged to St Catherine Cree parish: *Al. Cant.*; GEC, *Baronetage*, III, pp. 37–8.

229 Bills of Mortality were compiled by the parish clerks of London and some provincial towns weekly at the height of the plague outbreak. Since the 'searchers' reporting the plague deaths to the clerks were medically untrained, the statistics were unreliable: J. Litten, *The English Way of Death*, London 1991, pp. 143, 154–5.

230 Andrew Riccard (or Rickard – see L. **16**), lived in the parish of St Olave, Hart Street, London and was Royalist. M.P. for London in 1654: *ODNB*; L. **7**. Mistress Abdy was Catherine, daughter of Sir John Gayer of London, and aunt to the child: GEC, *Baronetage*, III, p. 34.

231 Medice = on medicine.

232 Henry Molle or Mole, born Leicester c. 1597. He was ejected from his Cambridge Fellowship and died on 10 May 1658: *Al. Cant.*

233 The trial of Hewitt and others: Evelyn, *Diary*, III, pp. 214, 216.

there is a report (but I believe it is no more) that they are permitted to preach agayn.[234] The Apparatus to the great bible is finished. What books are lately printed come not within my view. Onely the Life of K[ing] Ch[arles] by Sanderson, the E{arl} of Hollands secretary (the same who made the Sanderson Doctoure at Cambridge) I lately saw, which some censure as partially written on the K{ing's} partys side.[235] The E{arl} of Warwick died about a moneth since: & Mr Calamy commended him at the funerall.[236] Dr Stokes is well. It is a moneth since I heard from Dr Cosin: he was well then. I pray at your leisure & convenience let me hear from you: & excuse my not writing, of which I have now given you the true account. Mr Tovey is about to remove to a better living, Botsworth near Belvoir Castle, /being\ presented to it by the E{arl} of Rutland.[237] Mr Honeywood knows the man, perhaps the place also.[238] Mr Thorndike was well on Munday last & Mr Tovey also.

Your affectionate friend & servant,
G.D.

31 **8 July 1658**
Add. 4292, f. 212
G.D. to W.S. at Utrecht

My Lord Mr Brownrigg Bp of Exeter lay at London all the winter. He hath voided many stones & hath been very fearful of a dropsy and the scurvy but now is pretty well, & within two or three days he will leave in his journey to London, whither he goeth to marry the Lord

234 Evelyn, *Diary*, III, pp. 165–7, 203–4, 204–5; for Gunning: L. **20**.

235 Sir William Sanderson (1586–1676), a Royalist historian. *A Compleat history of the life and raigne of King Charles from his cradle to his grave*, London 1658, provoked a pamphlet war. He was secretary to Henry Rich, Earl of Holland, when the latter was Chancellor of Cambridge University in 1628: *ODNB*.

236 Earl of Warwick: Robert Rich (1587–1658) second earl, died 19 April 1658. He had studied at Emmanuel College, and the Inner Temple: *ODNB*. Edmund Calamy the elder (1600–66), clergyman and ejected minister, whose grandson was the biographer and historian, had a long personal connection with Rich: *ODNB*, under Edmund Calamy.

237 Nathaniel Tovey, after ejection rector of Ayleston (1654–6), adjacent parish to Davenport's home village of Wigston Magna: Nichols, *Leicestershire*, IV/1, pp. 28–30. Botsworth = Bottesford, near Belvoir Castle, Leics., the seat of the Earl of Rutland: L. **31**.

238 Michael Honywood: L. **28**.

R {son in the c{ounty} of Rutland} to one of the Marquis of Dorchester's daughters.[239]

I cannot tell whether Dr Cosin is about to writ anything about Trent Articles.[240] I was told and I cannot tell whether he himself said it to me that he had written the History of Transubstantiation that was the received determination of the Church touching the body of Christ in the Sacrament by centuries or the History of the Canon of Scriptures.[241] In his last letter he desired me to acquaint him with my Lord's opinion touching his referring of the Canon etc. & the opinions of other learned men both so he might either be encouraged in publishing more of that nature or else resolved to write no more. And I told him from my Lord that he highly approved it & desired me in his name to move him to justify the Doctrine of our Church against the Trent Doctrine of Transubstantiation if he had any such history by him as being a better subject than the other or of more concernment but I have had no answer from him.

Old Mr Jackson is dead and died Mr Dr {?W} in the Tower.[242] Therefore ever false that the same died after release. Likewise while he ascended he made a pause and said 'God said unto Moses 'Get thee up unto the mountain and die in the mountain whither thou goest up'[243] As I am informed two others suffered to whose charge were laid that they desired to fire the city and a third had his righteousness {tested}[244] They were quartered.[245]

---

239 Lady Anne Pierrepoint, daughter of Henry, Marquis of Dorchester, married John Manners, son of the eighth Earl of Rutland in 1658. He became the first Duke of Rutland. The marriage was a total failure: *ODNB*, under Manners, John, first Duke of Rutland.

240 The Trent Articles = Decrees of the Council of Trent (1545–63), including on Scripture and Tradition and Transubstantiation (the Catholic definition of the real presence of Christ in the eucharist): N.P. Tanner, ed., *Decrees of the Ecumenical Councils*, 2 vols, Washington (DC) 1990, II, pp. 663–5, 695, 697–8.

241 The works of Cosin are *Historia Transubstantiationis Papalis* (written in exile in 1656 and published posthumously in Latin in 1675) and *A History of the Canon of Holy Scripture, or the certain and indubiate books thereof, as they are received in the Church of England* (written in exile in Paris in 1657): *ODNB*.

242 Old Mr Jackson: unidentified. The entire sentence is almost illegible.

243 Deut. 32.49, 50. The reference is probably to the execution of John Hewitt, who had been beheaded for treason on 8 June: *ODNB*.

244 Righteousness tested: i.e. by torture.

245 Quartered: the body divided into four sections. The punishment for treason.

32 **1 October 1658**

H. 3783, f. 220

G.D. to W.S. in Holland, from London

Bowstreet. Octob. 1. 1658.

Good sir; Yours of July the 16th met me at London when I had quitted Stoke. I then answered it in a bitt of paper, & promised more paper in my next, but since that time, I have not sent to you. This day 3 weeks I wrote a letter to you & brought in my pocket with me /from Albyns\ to London,[246] but through many of my triffling occasions (for I had not seen London of 6 weeks before that day, & then returned again that evening) I forgott to send it: & perhaps it was not amiss: for it was (as all other from me) of no concernment: besides I heard that the letters were stopt at the Post-house. Mr Th{omas} Sandcroft hath received your bond.[247] I have been but little at London of late: having been living with Mr Gayer at Mr Abdyes house of Albyns, where I think no one is more wellcome than Mr Gayer, & so he is most assured. On Saturday last I attended my Lord of Exceter thither, on Wednesday he went to Ansty & intends soddainly to be at Bury & there to winter.[248] He is in pretty < > in good health, as you may conclude by his preaching there in that church on Sunday. He desires to be heartily remembered to you; & so doth Mr Lant who went with us, and Mr Harris who enjoys a small living about 2 miles from that place.[249] I believe you have heard of the death of Mr Tovey & his wife {*who....*} were buryed in one grave about a moneth since & perhaps of Mr Estwicke, (formerly his colleague at Christ's College, & who enjoyed the living of Botsworth 2 or 3 moneths) & his wive's death also, who dyed (as the former paire) within a day of one another.[250] I visited Mr Tovey severall times in his sickness:[251] but had left that countrey before

246 Albyns, the Essex home of Sir Robert Abdy, son of an important alderman, married to Catherine Gayer: GEC, *Baronetage*, III, p. 34; L. **30**.

247 Th[omas] Sancroft, William Sancroft's elder brother.

248 soddainly = immediately, without delay: *OED*.

249 Perhaps Malachi Harris, B.A. Emmanuel College, Cambridge, 1627. Vicar of Navestock, Essex, 1656–60: *Al. Cant.*

250 Nicholas Estwick, rector of Bottesford in 1656: Nichols, *Leicestershire*, II/1, p. 97. *Al. Cant.* gives a Nicholas Estwicke, of Christ's College, rector of Barnwell, Northants, 1617, and of Warkton, 1617–58, buried at the latter 9 September 1658, who is probably the same man.

251 Tovey: L. **30**. B.D. Christ's College in 1627. He was buried with his wife at Ayleston, 9 September 1658: Nichols, *Leicestershire*, IV/2, pp. 28–30.

his death. In the beginning of his sickness he sealed the marriage articles betwixt his daughter & one Mr Vincent an atturney of 160£ lands per annum.[252] I the rather tell you this because, I know, he had a good friend with you. I know not who you mean by that other champion of our church with you (heere you say) unless it be the B[isho]p of Derry.[253] But little passeth through my fingers. I was this morning with /Mr\Thorndike: he cannot dispatch his business before another moneth pass at the soonest. Mr Gayer will not stay so long, if he can get away sooner. Mr Thorndike mistook, if he said I should come with Mr G. Perhaps himself & I may be there in the spring for a short time. For of such a thing we spoke together to day. Mr Gayer wrote to you this day sen'night: & that letter will satisfy you in all things you desire, as I am told. But least it should miscarry he saith he will write again tonight if he have time. Mr Holdsworth desires to be remembered to you & sings as followeth

Olli dura quies oculos & ferreus urget
Somnus, in aeternam clauduntur lumina noctem.[254]

Dr Heylin hath a book in the press of observations upon Sanderson Hist. & Mr Fullers Church Hist.[255] Mr Samways is gone to his great living in the North near Rippon which the Earl of Elgin gave him.[256] Mr Thriss. & Dr Wild preach in their old places. Mr Gunning is not yet removed /from\ Hatton House to Exceter Chappell.[257] I say there is no likelyhood of seeing you here. We are told that you mightily admire butter, & Dutch toasted cheese. Wishing you happiness, I take my leave & rest

Your humble servant,
G.D.

---

252 Elizabeth Tovey married George Vincent of Shepey, gent.: Nichols, *Leicestershire*, IV/1, pp. 28, 30.

253 John Bramhall (1594–1663), became Bishop of Derry in 1634. From 1650 to 1660 he spent his exile in The Hague, Antwerp, Brussels, Ghent, Utrecht and Flushing: *ODNB*.

254 Olli dura ...: Vergil, *Aeneid* X, lines 745–6. 'Ungentle rest and iron sleep fell heavy on the glazing eyes, and their lids closed into eternal night.'

255 Peter Heylin (1599–1662). Polemical writer. He attacked William Sanderson's *History of the Life and Reign of King Charles* in his work *Examen historicum, London 1659*. He accused Fuller of pro-Puritan bias in the latter's *The Church History of Britain till 1648*, published in 1655: *ODNB*.

256 Peter Samwaies: (L. **10**) became rector of Wath, presented by the Earl of Elgin in 1658: *ODNB*; LL. **57**, **136**.

257 Hatton House in Holborn. Gunning had been tutor to Lord Hatton's family. He began to officiate in Exeter chapel in 1656: *ODNB*; L. **35**.

33 **15 October 1658**
H. 3783, f. 222
G.D. to W.S. from London

Bowstreet Oct. 15.-58.

Sir; Yours of Oct. 8 I received this morning after Mr Beaumont (who came to see /me\ before he takes his journey to Oxford) had showed me yours of Oct.1. The man was in a little rage at the Bedlam women who laughed at him when he enquired for fine Cotswold lambs-wooll yarn; but hopes he shall speed better about the unperfumed musk-coloured cordalrint prick-seamed treblepointed etc. gloves, by which you may ghess we were well & merry.[258] As for the toasted cheese let Capt. Pinkney answer the allegation.[259] Your single walk I can but ghess at: but conclude your pashe mashe is like our Pell-Mell Walk. The letter I wrote before, I think, was as bad as this: however Vulcan had it.[260] We came to town on Thursday last: Mr Gayer from Pirford, & {*I*} from Stoke, at which places all our friends are in health. Mr Farringdon died at his house at Old Windsor last Saturday.[261] Mr Cutts also is dead.[262] I cannot tell what Mr Gayer wrote to you but he told me it would be satisfactory & wheras you say you are not yet satisfyed, perhaps you mean you shall not till you see him, for if you had told me what further satisfaction you desired, I would have given you it if I was able. He purposeth to leave us within /few\ days. <I have sent your letter to him at Lime Street: but I believe I shall not see him till evening, & my letter must be at the Post-house before that time; therefore you must excuse me if I send nothing from him.> Mr Thorndike mistook me if he informed you any thing of /Mr G.\ present thoughts for Italy.[263] He told me you had thoughts for that place: but he said he liked France better. Yesterday the Independ{ent} Ministers Dr Goodwin (the spokesman) Dr Owen, Mr Nye, Mr Griffith

258 Bedlam women: a reference to the inmates of the hospital of St Mary of Bethlehem, originally a priory but converted to an asylum in 1547; Cordalrint: cord edged?: *OED* for both.

259 Capt. Pinkney: unidentified.

260 Vulcan had it: i.e. it was burnt.

261 Anthony Farrindon (Farndon) (1598–1658), Church of England clergyman, Lecturer in Divinity, St George's Chapel, Windsor, and later clandestinely preaching in London, supported by charity. He died 9 October, buried in St Mary Magdalen, Milk Street: *ODNB*.

262 Henry Cutts, of Suffolk, Attorney. Died 31 August 1657: *Al. Cant.*

263 Mr G. = Robert Gayer.

& many more were with the new Prot{ector} to condole & to congratulate & to propose something in behalfe of their congregations & for accomodation with the Presbytery:[264] one who stood by told me they were courteously received & dismysed & their great moderation commended. The Old Pr{otector} is not yet in his full state at Somerset House:[265] nor no talk yet /of the time\ of the funerall, which for pomp, tis said, shall exceed K{ing} James's.[266] Your friends in town I heare, be well: but I have not seen any since my return last to town. I desire I may heare from you at your leisure, & in anything I can serve you, I know, you are assured, I will. I am so great a stranger heare, that I know not either what books are now printing or lately printed. Hereafter I shall at my {bare} leisure better know & inform you, for I mean to abide in town this winter, but when the spring comes (if God lengthen my life so long) I shall desire to quitt this place, though not the nation: yet to see Mr Gayer & you at Utrecht & to have Mr Thorndike in company thither, will tempt me, if I mistake not, from all my friends here. But I would not have you take it for a vile complement because I see little probability of your being there at that time. My brother is wed & desires on all occasions to have his service presented to you, & so doth my mother also who at present is < > in so good health that I cannot but give God thanks, and write to let my friends know though shee be a stranger to them.

Your affectionate servant,
G.D.

<I have sent … from him> is scored over in the text.

---

264 On the death of Cromwell representatives of about a hundred Independent churches met at the Savoy to try to produce a declaration of faith to achieve unity. The leaders included those Independent ministers given here: Thomas Goodwin (1600–80), Master of Magdalen College, Oxford, 1649–60 and Fellow of Eton College 1658; John Owen (1616–83), Dean of Christ Church 1651–60, Vice Chancellor of Oxford 1652–7; Philip Nye (1595–1672), rector of St Michael's, Cornhill, and St Bartholomew, Exchange. The meeting, for which George Griffith (1618–1699/1702) was scribe, produced a *Declaration of the Faith and Order of English Congregational Churches*: *ODNB* under the respective names; Hutton, *Restoration*, p. 25.

265 In his full state: presumably lying in state. Oliver Cromwell's effigy, richly dressed, was shown on 18 October 1658 at Somerset House: Abbott, *Writings and Speeches*, IV, p. 874.

266 John Evelyn refers to Cromwell's funeral under Nov. 22 1658: *Diary*, III, p. 224. Cromwell died 3 September 1658. The public funeral was held 23 November in Henry VII Chapel, Westminster Abbey: Abbott, *Writings and Speeches*, IV, pp. 874–5. K{ing} James's: James I.

34 **28 November 1658**

H. 3783, f. 224

G.D. to W.S. in Holland, from Great Wigston, Leics.

Wigston. Nov. 28. 1658.

Dear Sir; Yours of Nov. 12. came to me 2 days since & you may be assured was very wellcome, for in it I had the first newes of Mr Gayers welcome to Utrecht, or any part of Holland. I pray present my humble service to him. I sent 2 letters after him before I left London: the latter would acquaint you with my journey hither. My Mother continues so very weak (though she hath missed 3 fitts of her quartan ague)[267] that we have very small hopes of her life. Mr Th. book is divided into 3 pts.[268] The title of the first I remember not, the 2^{d} is of the Covenant of Grace, the 3^{d} is of the laws of the Church. The substance is briefly cowched (as I have been told) in a sheet or two of paper formerly printed. Mr Th. Holds. is gone into Yorkshire having left B[isho]psgate Street saith Mr Beaumont.[269] I received with yours one letter from him: but he acquaints me not with his purposes. Mr Beaumont & he used me so friendly as to open yours to me. I staid very little in town after I had your first intimation of Mr Parkers book:[270] & of those I then enquired of I could learn nothing, not so much as the title or subject of the book. Mr Thorndike told me of a book in the press of conversing with spirits written by Jo. Dee the Mathem{atician's} own hand, published by Dr Casaubon out of Sir R. Cotton (who bought his < > papers & books) his library.[271] The Dr proposeth it to the Reader to judge whether they

267 Quartan ague = fever recurring every four days: *OED*.

268 Herbert Thorndike: L. **18**. His principal work was *An Epilogue to the Tragedy of the Church of England*, 1659. This consisted of three parts, the first being *The Principles of Christian Truth*.

269 Thomas Holdsworth was born at Middleham, Yorks.: L.**3**.

270 Perhaps Henry Parker (1604–52), political writer. He produced many political pamphlets and was the focal figure in the pamphlet wars from 1642 as The Observator. His last publication was *The Chief Affairs of Ireland Truly Communicated*, 1651. Perhaps Alexander Parker (1628–89), a Quaker controversialist, who produced several tracts in 1658: *ODNB* for both.

271 Meric Casaubon (1599–1671), born in Geneva, a classical scholar and church historian. He lived at Cotton House, Westminster, during the 1650s, where he had access to Sir Robert Cotton's Library. He published John Dee, *A true and faithful relation of what passed for many years between Dr Jn. Dee ... and some spirits*, in 1659. Dee (1527–1609), a mathematician and astrologer, had believed that he could talk to benevolent spirits through a medium. The book gives detailed accounts of the sessions. The 'spirits' persuaded him to share wives with the medium: *ODNB*, under Casaubon and Dee.

were good or bad spirits: but, I ghess, they may readily be considered evil, because Dee was by them, as I was told, seduced to carnality. My brother presents his service to Mr Gayer & your selfe. My mother thinks it vayn to say so much, (for he hopes she shall not live (& I have cause to fear it) till I receive another letter from you) but give /both of\ you the well wishes & blessing of a dying woman. My next, I fear, will acquaint you with her death. If it be Gods will so to deal with her I shall not be long from London. Gods will be done. To his protection I commit you both & remain

Your servant G.D.

His < > papers: 'library' erased.

35 **11 February 1659**

H. 3783, f. 225

G.D. to W.S. in Holland from London

London Feb. 11. 1658.

Sir; Yours of Jan. 21. I received 10 days since. By it I perceive that you no more affect my wandring on English ground, than I do yours in Holland (& secretly in my heart, for myne own sake, I often wish you & Mr Gayer at < > home agayn) because you desire to find me in certo ubi:[272] & I myself do now begin to wish myselfe well settled somwhere. For since Mr Thorndike (of whose travail I once had some confidence) hath told me, that by what he heares from Utrecht he is not like to put over into Holland this spring, I begin to lay aside those thoughts I had of it also, in his company: especially since I perceive, that this winter (in which I thought you would have layn still, Mr Gayer if not you (for I cannot perceive by his letter to Mr Abdy this week from Rotterdam, or his to me from Amsterdam the week before that you was then with him) journey up & down. For when I proposed to my selfe so much happiness, as to see you in the spring, I thought I should see you, but part of the countrey also with you. And now, I think, the taking of a lodging in the < > city will not be most convenient for me. For, besides that I am somwhat oppressed with too much acquaintance here (though I love to see my friends & to preach for them sometimes) & too much business (for a man may have so much imposed upon him) for friends which live in the country, which steal away my time; I find the expence of this place too great for me: especially since my horse

272 In certo ubi = in a certain place.

exhausts my purse as well as my selfe (for since my mother is dead, I know not so well where to dispose of him, & if I should sell him, what should I do for another, when I have occasions) & is burdensom to me always, since I came to this place, except when I lend him to my friends.[273] And, as rolling stones gather no moss, so should I live sometimes here & other whiles ramble abroad in the countrey, & be no where tied, I should gather neither learning, nor wealth (which I expect not any where) nor (perhaps) health: but, on the contrary, spend upon the little stock I have of all. Some places have been proffered to me already, but most of them either too farr distant from mine own countrey, or where my horse will not be kept, as I suppose.[274] Amongst others, Mr Henley, when he was in town last week, sollicited me to come to him at Bramsil (for he hath parted with his Scotch Dr long since) & that I would consider of the matter before I came to his house or should meet him at Stoke at Mistress Gayer's wedding (for we had so little consideration as to think that happily we might be invited there).[275] I have thought of it, but will resolve nothing till I hear from you & Mr Gayer & perhaps then too I may resolve not to abide there. For I expect such conditions as may please me. By conditions, I mean not so much what I shall receive, as what I shall do, & how we shall joyn in prayer together. For I must needs say, that since the bulls of the people do < > make the Ark of God thus to totter,[276] I am not satisfyed how a priest that professes zeal to that ark, should forsake the service thereof, in such a needfull time of this,[277] wherein the number of his brethren & companions, is but small. If I may be {p. 2} satisfyed in all these (& in one thing more wherewith I have acquainted Mr Gayer) a good house, air, library, convenient distance from London, & mine own countrey & above all these liberty at my own discretion for myne own affairs will tempt me. Besides I account it very considerable, that if Mr Gayer should at any time require any service from me in his absence (& since I am so glad to serve him in anything I may, I will not despair of such employment) or that I should come to him agayn

---

273 Elizabeth Davenport, née Hales, does not appear to be recorded in the burial register of Wigston Magna, Leics. For her illness: LL. **20**, **33**.

274 Mine own countrey: Leicestershire.

275 Scotch Dr: unidentified.

276 the bulls of the people ... : I Chron. 13.9: 'when they came to the threshing-floor of Chidon, Uzzah put out his hand to hold the ark, for the oxen stumbled' (AV). The reference is to the Church of England.

277 Of this: sic.

when God gives him a safe return, if I live to see it, perhaps I may not so readily expect that freedom in another place, of which Mr Henley did assure me in this. Mr Thurscross & Mr Oley present their service to you.[278] Dr Gell hath a book in the press of annotations (as I take it) on the Pentateuch: the /last\ translation whereof he supposes may be improved.[279] I remember I heard of friend of his who had been his pupill say, that he had a design to translate the whole bible and make notes. You remember how ready he was, on all occasions, to mend the translation. /But here is no translation.\ Sir__Knatchbull hath notes in Latin upon some part of the Bible, I think the Epistles.[280] Ham. L'Estrange hath published a book of Liturgies, & a vindication of </ours\>:[281] I have not seen it. Florios Italian Dictionary is reprinted, with additions out of Crusca & an English & Italian Dictionary &c by Torriano.[282] I am now going to Exeter Chappell, where are prayers & Mr Gunning preaches (according to his custom every Friday afternoon).[283] Before my return I believe Mr Beaumont may return from Oxford (whither he went 8 days since on my horse) & then perhaps you may hear from him.

Your humble servant G.D.

do < > make: 'thus' erased.

36 **11 March 1659**

H. 3783, f. 226

G.D. to W.S. from London

Little Britayn Mar. 11. 1658.

Sir, The greatest news I can tell you, is that My Lord of Exceter is coming to the Temple.[284] The report hath been long of it. And yesterday

278 Probably Barnabas Oley (1602–86), Fellow of Clare College 1623, ejected in 1644. Vicar of Great Gransden, Hunts., 1633–86. Royalist and Laudian: *ODNB*.

279 Robert Gell (1595–1665), Church of England clergyman. Chaplain to Sheldon and rector of St Mary Aldermary, London, 1641–65. Published *Essay towards the Amendment of the last English Translation of the Bible* in 1659: *ODNB*.

280 Sir Norton Knatchbull (1602–85), politician and biblical scholar. He published *Animadversiones in libros Novi Testamenti* in 1659: *ODNB*.

281 Hamon L'Estrange, *The alliance of divine offices*, 1659.

282 Giovanni Florio, *Vocabulario Italiano e Inglesi, a Dictionary Italian and English*, London 1659, with additions by Giovanni Torriano.

283 The Chapel of Exeter House in the Strand where many gathered to worship according to the rites of the Church of England: L. **20**.

284 Bishop Brownrigg was invited to live in the Temple in 1658 and to become chaplain: *ODNB*.

Dr Beaumond did assure me of it.[285] For the day before, he received a letter from him, & another was inclosed in it [open] to the Benchers of the Middle & Inner Temple, wherein he promiseth to be with them before the next term. And they are furnishing lodgings for him. He may, if he please (but I believe he will not) be M{aste}r of the Temple. Dr Littleton being dead & Mr Johnson continuing, as he may, reader or preacher there.[286] All they expect from him is, to continue amongst them & to pray in the morning when he is able & pleaseth, but I know not whether all in term time or throughout the year. Mr Holdsworth is in Yorkshire still: I have not heard from him since he went thither. < > Mr Hardy this day tells me, that he now intends to write to him (he desired me to enquire how he might send his letter, for Ch. Hammond, to whom he used to send his letter, he fears is this day dead) & desire him to come to live with the E{arl} of Warwick, who for his health means to travail into France.[287] He is a man much reformed in his life, as it is said: & wholy devoted to the Church of England. I know not what this Parl{iament} will do about the C{ommon} Prayer: but it is thought they will enact more strictly against it than ever before. The great question that is, in the house (for no more than one /house\ we dare say we have at present)[288] is whether they shall transact with the other house or not. It < > is believed it will go in the affirmative. However (but what signifyes it?) a proviso /it shall have already\ is made [reserving to the ancient nobility /their\ right of Peerage, or such like words]. Besides they are now considering whether members returned & at present sitting < >for Ireland & Scotland shall continue in the house. If they, why may not the same power that called them, call as many as it liketh, if they do not, why should laws made here

285 Perhaps Joseph Beaumont who was chaplain to Bishop Wren in 1650 and married his ward, Miss Brownrigg.

286 Dr Littleton: possibly James, died 1645, Bencher of the Inner Temple: *Al. Ox.* Mr Johnson is perhaps Thomas, of Northampton. He may have been admitted to Gray's Inn in 1652 and became a Barrister-at-Law: *Al. Cant.*

287 Probably Nathaniel Hardy (1619–70), Church of England clergyman, well known in London for his sermons, despite his Royalism. Friend of the Gayers and preacher of a funeral sermon for Hewit after his execution. In June 1659 he preached at the Earl of Warwick's funeral, having ministered to him in his illness: *ODNB*. Ch. Hammond: unidentified. Earl of Warwick: Robert Rich: died after having been earl for only one year: GEC, *Complete Peerage*, XII/2, pp. 412–13.

288 The House of Lords had been abolished on 24 March 1649: *Acts and Ordinances*, II, p. 24.

(where they have no representatives) oblige these nations? This is the news at present, so farr as such a fellow as I can understand it. Mr Be/a\umont desires his service may be presented to you. Sir Lislebone Long a speaker pro tempore: the old speaker Chute having satt till his leggs are weary.[289] No Dutch post is yet come. I once thought to have gone for Stoke tomorrow: but I am now resolved to stay till that day sen'night.

Your humble servant,

G.D.

< > Mr Hardy: 'but' erased.

37 **9 June 1662**

T. 48.8

G.D. to W.S. From Bishop Auckland

Aukland. June 9. 1662.

Sir: yours of the 3rd I received before this. I hope you have received two from me: the one from Darlington this day sennight: & the other from Durham on Thursday last. Your course was yesterday supplied by Dr Dalton as one in the house that heard him tells.[290] My Lord continues in his mind concerning the frontispiece in the Monastic{on} for his books for the Goldsmiths work. As to Priests matters he saith sit pro non dicto, he knows neither the man nor the work.[291] If it be dedicated to him, when he has he can best judg of it. I am sorry that I can give you no manner of account concerning Houghton.[292] Mr Stapylton is not like to return these 10 days & I am so tyed up that I cannot stir from hence; so that I am not able to say anything thereof.[293] As for the Prebends of Westminster, I desire no more than a statutable salary, which I fear they

---

289 Chaloner Chute (1595–1659), lawyer, Speaker of the House of Commons, chosen in January 1659 but was only able to act until 9 March because of illness. Chute died 14 April 1659. Sir Lislebone Long (1613–59) was chosen to succeed him, but died 16 March: *ODNB* for both.

290 Thomas Dalton, rector of Barwick in Elmet, Yorks., 1661–72; canon of the fifth stall in Durham 1660–72. He died 22 November 1672: *Al. Cant.*; Mussett, p. 45. He had evidently supplied for the sermons and religious duties owed by Sancroft according to the Cathedral Statutes: *Durham Cathedral Statutes*, p. 109. By 26 July 1662 Sancroft had a royal dispensation from his residence: DCM, DCD/B/AA/4, ff. 59–60.

291 Priest : unidentified. Sit pro non dicto = let it be as if not said.

292 Davenport soon began to act as accountant for Sancroft for his living.

293 Miles Stapleton was Cosin's auditor, commissioner and man of affairs: *Cosin. Corr.* II, passim; *Stapylton Corr.*, p. 135.

will not give.[294] My service to everyone of them that you shall see. I like the place, & employment I have, very well as yet. You can ghess at the latter better than any one I know. The countrey or season or both are very cold for this time of the year. But here is a certayn sort of fewel much like to our Cambridg coal, which when it burns they call it /ingle\, & that warms us well.[295] If you see Bp. Wild pray present my humblest service to him.[296] I could not /see him to\ take my leave of him when I came away. I am glad my courses have been supplyed hitherto so well: & I hope they will be well supplyed till Mr Scrivener begins & then too.[297] If you chance to drop into the Church let me know: your opinion of the reader & preacher & auditory, for I like the parish huge well. If you happen to see my house //for Mr Scrivener's sake, pray ask for a tippet of Mary which I forgot to bring: & send it at leisure if you know how. Dr Potter hath possession of Gresham Hospitall:[298] but I know not who hath// the other vacant preferments. My Lord is hugely busy in building both here & at Durham. To most of your questions I gave answer in myne from Durham. The statutes I have now received from Mr Neil.[299] Your gown I have lockt up after 3 day *....* finding my mourning gown more convenient as being much lighter. Sir Rob. Gayer I suppose in the countrey: I would gladly hear * * his former design hath taken life again; inform me as you know. My service I desire may be presented to Sir R. Abdy & any of that family, or of my acquaintance you know.[300] Commending you to God's protection I remain

Your affectionate servant

G.D.

Endorsed: For Dr William Sandcroft at Mr Browne house in Maiden Lane in Covent Garden. London.

---

294 Davenport's position at Westminster Abbey cannot be identified but he seems to have acted as chaplain and appears to have preached on behalf of some of the prebendaries. See also LL. **41**, **43**, **52**.

295 Ingle = fire: *OED*.

296 George Wild had become Bishop of Derry in 1661; above, L. **10**.

297 Scrivener was perhaps acting as G.D.'s curate at St Peter's, West Cheap. He may be Thomas Scrivener, a Royalist, of Sibton, Suffolk, and Pembroke College, Cambridge. He died 1682: *Al. Cant.*; also L. **46**.

298 Thomas Potter became Master of Greatham Hospital, Durham, 19 May 1662: *VCH, Durham*, II, p. 122.

299 Mr Neil, under-sheriff in County Durham: see also LL. **59**, **70**, **118**, **121**, **136**; *Cosin Corr.* II, p. 28.

300 Sir Robert Abdy married Catherine, daughter of Sir John Gayer of London: above, L. **31**.

38 **16 June 1662**

T. 48.12

G.D. to W.S. from Co. Durham

</Aukland\> June.16. 1662.

Sir; yours of the 10th I received the 13th instant: & with it the letter for Peter House, which I gave to my Lord, who saith that he expects it should have been revised by you.[301] The Acts you mention are received.[302] Amongst the books you < > sent from Peterhouse, we have one vol. of Plut. Lives & two of his moralls, by mistake: so that my Lord saith it will be well that he have the other 3 imperfect ones from thence to complete these.[303] So also here is the 1st vol. of Ciaconius Vita Pontificum but not the 2d.[304] My Lord desires at all times to know particularly what progress you make in the Common Prayer.[305]

Mr Stapylton is just now returned: he only hath time to present his service to you, & say that Mr Cook the Curat & Philpot the factotum promised to look well after your business & to let your Parsonage to I know not whom, reserving grass < > for* * your selfe, whom then they expected in a short time.[306] I am resolved that shortly I will go over: though my Lord talketh daily of ordering his books & /of my\ preaching on Sunday sennight at an ordination, which put me out of order a little.[307] Mr Stapylton saith, if he can get leisure he will go with

---

301 'My Lord' from this point refers to John Cosin. Brownrigg died on 7 December 1659 and by the date of this letter Davenport had become chaplain to Cosin, replacing William Sancroft, who had become a prebendary of Durham and chaplain to the king: Introduction, p. 10.

302 Acts: a number of *Acta* survive in Cosin's Library but the volume mentioned here has not been identified.

303 Plutarch (c. 45–125), *Lives*, written in Greek and published in English first in 1579; and *Moralia* or *Moral Writings*, in fourteen books.

304 Alphonsus Ciaconius, *Vitae et res gestae pontificum … nec non s.r.e cardinalium*, Rome 1601.

305 Sancroft represented Cosin at the meetings of the Savoy Conference and the so-called 'Durham Book' contains many of Sancroft's annotations to the text of the Book of Common Prayer: G.J. Cuming, ed., *The Durham Book*, Westport (Conn.) 1961, repr. 1979, pp. xxi–xxii.

306 Cosin had presented Sancroft to the rectory of Houghton-le-Spring, a living in his patronage, in 1661. Mr Cook: curate at Houghton. John Philpott had been made parish clerk at Houghton on 15 August 1660: DCRO, EP/Ho 168, f. 171v; R.W. Ramsey, 'Records of Houghton-le-Spring', *English Historical Review* 20, no. 80 (1905), pp. 673–392, esp. 685–6.

307 Ordering his books = setting up his library.

mee. We are all well: & about 3 weeks hence are to go in to Northumberland to visit the diocese; & at our return I ghess the Assizes will be at hand.[308] I like this countrey well, yet must tell you, saving that I have been once at Durham, I never went out of this Lordship. The tippet I mentioned in my last I have now found.[309] I am like to do well, here, if I may ghess at my health by a good stomack & most profound sleep. I never waked in the night since I saw London. Pray present my service to Sir Robert Gayer, when you either see him or write to him: & let me know somthing of Sunning business, if there is any progress in it.[310] My service I desire may be presented to all my friends you see, as to Mr Thriscross & to whom not.[311]

Your affectionate servant

G.D.

</Aukland\>: 'Durham' erased; you< > sent: 'mention' erased.

39 **21 June 1662**

H. 3784, f. 58

G.D. to W.S. from Durham

Deanery at Durham. Jun. 21. 11 at night.

Sir, I came hither this afternoon with my Lord, who lies about half a mile off: but I know no better /place\ than this. From hence I went to Houghton < > Le Spring. Your curate & Jo. Philpot are your very servants. I meant to lie there but liked not my lodging (though my supper) at my inne & so returned: which I had not meant (for I had 2 sermons in my pocket) but that my Lord told me I must be with him before he goes to church in the morning: & I thought it but reasonable. Your living I like wondrous well: the church stands in the midst, & the extremityes are about 3 miles distant every way. Jo. Philpot hath acquainted you that all is let, & he hath bonds for the payment of rent.[312] The chancell is in good repare but wants beautifying: & about 2s-6s in glass, which I had him to lay forth, I mean the glass-work. The dean sowed about 8 acres, which is not considerable.[313] He saith the Dean

308 Episcopal visitation: *Cosin Corr.* II, p. xvi.

309 Tippet = cape: *OED*.

310 Sunning business: Sir Thomas Rich had bought the manor of Sonning, Berkshire, in 1654.

311 Sic.

312 'all is let': may refer to the tithes or the glebe land or both.

313 John Barwick, Dean of Durham up to 30 September 1661, had been rector of Houghton until 7 December 1661: *ODNB*; Mussett, p. 6.

layd not forth 100£, but almost so much in repairs of out-houses: but he never heard that he received Mr Batterslye's 100£.[314] The outhouses as barns, stables, cowhouses, kiln,[315] granaryes, dovehouse &c. I like wondrous well, being of stone, & well slated, & a strong wall about the house. But the house I like not, & assure myselfe you will not. It shows very well at 2 miles distant but very ill is it contrived. All the stairs are of stone & winding; the windows small, the walls of it thick, the doors low, & the floors from room to room not even, but by steps. The chappell is prefaced onely by < > a floor which must be taken down. Your tenths are paid by Philpot: & as I remember the curats salary.[316] If you can not down at the appointed time, let me {p. 2} advise you to give something to the poor which are many in the parish by reson of the cole-pits. The hall I believe may be repaired for 100£: & the house for as much, but not floored even, I mean particular rooms, which formerly were covered with rushes which you will not like. The people they tell me are excellent good as to conformity. About 3 keep on their hats at church: but one of the best men never comes thither.[317] In fine (for I scribble in monstrous hast), change not for a B[isho]prik worse than Sarum.[318] For I do not think that the saying of Secretary < > Cecil deserves to put amongst his Apothegms: I could have spoke as wisely my selfe. For Carlisle B{isho}prick (all things considered) is not halfe < > so sufficient. The Deans respects to you.[319] My Lord would have you every week to send him the news-book & news you hear: & when you cannot do it, you must bid Tim. Garthwait to do it.[320] No more at present but I desire your prayers, & tell you, what I trust you are assured of, that I am

Your faithfull servant

G.D.

---

314 Nicholas Battersbye had been rector of Houghton in 1659: *Durham Parish Books*, p. 304.

315 Kiln = maltkiln.

316 Tenths were a recurring annual payment to the Crown collected via the bishops: C.D. Chandaman, *The English Public Revenue, 1660–1688*, Oxford 1975, pp. 115–17.

317 The best man may be Robert Hutton: Introduction, p. 15. Keeping the hat on refers to the behaviour of the Quakers: *ODCC*.

318 Sarum = Salisbury.

319 John Sudbury was installed as Dean of Durham on 15 February 1662: Mussett, p. 6.

320 Timothy Garthwait, publisher first in Little Britain and then at the King's Head, St Paul's Churchyard. He printed Visitation Articles for Cosin in 1662: H.R. Plomer, *A Dictionary of the Booksellers and Printers who were at work in England,*

We supped very well for 2s 6d: I mean the curat & I & the clerk & schoolmaster: John Philpot would have had you to have paid all: but I would not, & was very glad it was so, when I saw the shoulder of mutton & pie, & such like reckond I thought for nothing; for we drank 3 pints of claret, besides Ale. By this you may guess its a plentyfull countrey. It was noised the parson was come: & John prophecyed a great congregation in the morning. But let them look to that. I wish you here each day. My service I pray to all: especially to Sir R.Gayer when you either see him or write to him.

Address: For Dr William Sandcroft at Mr Clerks house in Maiden Lane in Covent Garden London. 3d

By < > a floor: 'wall' erased.

40 **5 July 1662**
H. 3784, f. 60
G.D. to W.S. from Bishop Auckland

Aukland < > 1662 July 5.

Sir; I wrote to you two days /since\ something largely: yesterday I received yours which I now set to answer. And to begin with the latter end, which is the hardest, methinks it looks {like} my Lord's visitation articles, full of short questions.[321] To the 1st, he doth use me kindly: for the next I have almost nothing to do, but to follow my secular studyes: stay, though, I had like to have forgotten the Catalogue,[322] /again\ No one comes to wait – He carryes himselfe as a stranger, & I think is like always so to be as for any nearer relation. I hear nothing of Mr Greenvile.[323] My Lady Burton is at Mr Garrard: Mris Ann at the Spaw.[324] I cannot tell who shall have either the Archd{eaconry} or

Scotland and Ireland from 1641 to 1667, Bibliographical Society, London 1907, p. 80. Newsbooks, begun in 1641, improved with the development of regular postal services between London and the provinces: J.B. Williams, *Journalism*, pp. 8–10; J. Raymond, ed., *News, Newspapers and Society in Early Modern Britain*, London and Portland (Or.) 1999, pp. 52–3. See also L. **46**.

321 For the Visitation articles see below, n. 328.

322 G.D.'s duties included the preparation of Cosin's Library Catalogue: Introduction, p. 25.

323 Denis Grenville or Granville (1638–1703): Introduction, p. 14.

324 For Lady Burton and Anne Cosin: Introduction, pp. 13–14. The Spa may be Harrogate.

living or Prebend, nor can I ghess. The Dean hath had possession of the hospitall, the other giving place to him 3 weeks since /(& goes thither on Munday).\[325] That for questions. Tim. Garthwait (I guess for no name was in the paper) sent the news-book. I told you (or chode rather in my last[326]) that my Lord ordered the goldsmith to do as you in yours, he saith (for I saw it not) advised: that is that the goldsmith be left to his discretion to make a figure out of others, you know which.[327] On Munday we are for the Visitation at Newcastle, & so forward to Morpeth & Alnwick:[328] the next week we visit at Durham: and then my Lord asks whether any Prebend doth not repair his house; & whether they do not detayn his dividend that doth not:[329] so my Lord told me & then I told him again, then you must answer for Dr Sandcroft, knowing well enough that he cannot do it, being in his Majesteyes service: & he replyed, right: you'le say, Good. We are all well, God be thanked. And this countrey, I hope, will agree with my constitution as well as any. The weather is uncertayn, but generally cold. I find little use of an unlined cassock. My service to all my friends, as if named.

Your humble servant,
G.D.

//This day I had a letter from the school-M{aste}r of the free school at

---

325 John Sudbury was installed as Dean 15 February 1662: Mussett, p. 6. It is not clear whether Greatham or Sherburn Hospital is intended here, but Gabriel Clarke, canon of the first prebend, Archdeacon of Durham and former master of Greatham Hospital (from 1624), died 10 May, which probably explains the previous references: Mussett, p. 13. The other may be Thomas Potter: L. **37**.

326 Chode = past tense of chide, sometimes used at this time: *OED*.

327 Reference to the engraving of the title page for the Prayer Book. See also L. 43.

328 Visitation articles for canons: *Miscellanea*, SS 37 (1861), 252–60; for the diocese at large: Cosin, *Works*, IV, pp. 505–26; relevant questions and answers from the canons, Granville, *Remains of Denis Granville*, pp. 253, 262, 264; see also *Cosin Corr.* II, pp. xvi and xvii.

329 The dividend was any surplus of the corporate revenue of the cathedral, divided between the dean (2/14ths) and the prebendaries (1/14th each): *Durham Cathedral Statutes*, p. 117; Audit Bks, DCM/L/AA passim. In 1663 (figures for 1661–2 not available) the dividend was a little over £100 each: Audit Statement, DCD/L/LP21. It may have been less in 1662 because of the cost of repairs, though they had signed many leases and therefore received a large sum in fines paid at each signing. Sancroft received the ninth stall in March 1662: Mussett, p. 71. For enquiries made of him in 1668: Cosin, *Works*, IV, pp. 380–81.

Houghton:[330] something belonging to him is detayned, & he cannot sue till you & Mr Heath have nominated another Joynt Governour with Mr Tho. De la Vall, in place of one lately dead.//[331]

41 **15 July 1662**
T. 48.19
G.D. to W.S. from Auckland

Aukland 15 July 1662.

Sir; I have received two from you one of July the 5th at Newcastle the other of the 8th at Durham at our return on Friday last. As yet we hear nothing of the Statutes. Ministers come daily for < > certificates that they have renounced Anti-Christ the Covenant, & give the Secretary as I think what they please.[332] The testimonyall is in English & the words of < > renunciation are therin expressed. I drew /it\ as I remember, out of the words of the Act a little before the /form of superscription.\ You will be here time enough I recken, to do what is required of you, /I never studyed the Act since I left London\. In our return on Friday I saw Mr Wrench, who tells me that the letter is not yet opened & that Mr Dean (who is not very well) told him that he received it < > enclosed in one from my Lord of London, in which he

330 For Kepier Grammar School: Introduction, p. 18. From 1639 to 1682 George Cant was the Master: *VCH, Durham*, I, pp. 393–6; R.W. Ramsey, 'Kepier Grammar School, Houghton le Spring and its Library', *Archaeologia. Aeliana*, 3rd ser., 3 (1907), pp. 306–33, esp. 308–9. The appointment of governors lay with the heirs of Heath and the rector of Houghton: Surtees, *Durham*, III, p. 158. The letter is Cosin Letter Book 3. 79, of 3 July 1662, George Cant to Davenport. Cant explained, in desperation, to Davenport that his income depended on tithes of Bishopwearmouth and Ryhope, which had been lost to him during the 'time of distraction'. Any claim for redress had to go in the name of the governors and one of these (Mr Lambton) was dead and not replaced. Cant's concurrent letter to Cosin, in Latin, is Letter Book 3. 80.

331 Thomas De La Vall: third son of Sir Ralph Delaval of Seaton Delaval, Northumberland, who lived in Hetton. A JP, under the Protectorate he had been the most important member of the parish: *ODNB*, under Delaval Family; Ramsey, 'Records of Houghton', p. 681.

332 The Act of Uniformity received the royal assent on 19 May, intended to come into full force on 24 August but evidently was already being enforced in Durham. Clergy had to assent and read publicly the Book of Common Prayer; subscribe before their bishop that taking up arms against the king was unlawful; renounce the obligation to the Solemn League and Covenant: I.M. Green, *The Re-establishment of the Church of England, 1660–1663*, Oxford 1978, pp. 144–5; for the fee, pp. 147–8.

tells him, that it was without your knowledg.[333] I read to my Lord what you write of the Goldsmiths works: he answers here are more delays. I also read to him what you say of Mr Watson & he answered that Dr S. might do well to set some quick man upon Watson to take him to task by writing.[334] < > Next week about Thursday a man of the town will be at London < > with two horses for Sir Rob. Abdy which he desired me to buy. He talks of coming back by sea: if you have any goods or anything to send perhaps it may well be sent < > in the same vessel. I purpose to send him to you. Pray send </Dr M\> 5 letters by him.[335] My Lord saith he hath a catalogue of the books to come from Cambridg of your writing. Pray do not forget to let us know what you have from Sunning. Your friends here present their services to you. I pray present my service to Mr Stapylton & to all my friends. I like the countrey daily better & better, I never had a cold since I came hither.

//By the Act I was to testify my assent to the new book & to read it.//[336] I do not intend to go to London on purpose to do it.[337] I will rather abide the pleasure of my Lord of London as to the declaration of an impediment. And let my masters of Westminster say what they will.[338]//

{p. 2} On Thursday we go to Durham, < > the Visitation being the day following for the Diocese & on Saturday for the church. Mr Wrench (who presents his service to you) is to preach on Friday & I think Dr Dalton at the Assizes, which are this day fortnight: & till they be ended, I believe we shall be for the most part at Durham, & after I hope you will be here. My Lord suspended Mr Knightbridge at Newcastle because he refused to read prayers: & the living is

---

333 Richard Wrench, prebendary of the sixth stall, Durham: Introduction, p. 25.

334 Perhaps Thomas Watson (d. 1686) who was educated at Emmanuel College and was Presbyterian in outlook. He preached at St Stephen's, Walbrook, from 1646 and was imprisoned in 1652 for participating in a plot to recall Charles II but was re-instated at St Stephen's. He was ejected for nonconformity at the Restoration but continued to hold conventicles: *ODNB*. Gilbert Sheldon was consecrated Bishop of London 28 October 1660: *ODNB*.

335 Perhaps Charles Mason (1616/17–1677/8), Church of England clergyman, formerly of King's College, Cambridge, now rector of St Mary Woolchurch, London: *ODNB*.

336 G.D.'s assent to the Act of Uniformity and the Book of Common Prayer.

337 As rector of West Cheap, G.D. needed to give his assent there.

338 For G.D.'s position in Westminster, Introduction, p. 10.

sequestered.[339] Mr Hammond desired he might leave without suspension.[340] I can tell you nothing more considerable in our journey. My Lord hath his health very well & riseth some hours before me: but I think it is more than he knows. No more at present but that I am

Your most affectionate servant,

G.D.

Address: For Dr William Sandcroft at Mr Clerks house in Maiden Lane Covent Garden, London. 3

for < > certificates: 'their' erased; it < > enclosed: 'in one' erased; London < > with two: 'to bring up' erased; sent < > in the: 'by him' erased; </Dr M\>: 'these' erased; Durham < > the visitation: 'being' erased.

42 **22 July 1662**

H. 3784, f. 64

G.D. to W.S. from Durham

Durham Castle July 22. 1662.

Sir; Hither we came on Thursday last, & here we are like to stay till the Assizes be ended, that is, almost another fortnight. I wrote to you by the messenger that I sent with the horses to Sir Rob{ert} Abdy: But, I suppose, this may be with you as soon as it. To My Lord you must send Bp. Andrews' Life in 4 or 5 sheets written by Isaakson:[341] about 10 years since: & Abel Redivivus prefaced by Tho{mas} Fuller, /sometimes the former is bound up in this latter\ & Sir < > _____ Harrington's supplement to Godwyns Bishops.[342] I trust that now very shortly you will begin your journey. I care not how soon. Since I came

339 John Knightbridge, Fellow of Peterhouse, lecturer at St Nicholas's, Newcastle, 1657–60. He eventually conformed and was rector of Holy Trinity, Dorchester, 1663–70: *ODNB*; R. Howell, *Newcastle upon Tyne and the Puritan Revolution: a Study of the Civil War in the North of England*, Oxford 1967, pp. 243, 269; see LL. **49**, **65**.

340 Samuel Hammond (d. 1665), D.D., a Congregationalist appointed to St Nicholas's, Newcastle, in November 1652: *ODNB*; Howell, *Newcastle and the Puritan Revolution*, pp. 236–8, 266n; *Cosin Corr.* II, p. xviii.n.

341 Henry Isaacson, *An exact narration of the life and death of Lancelot Andrewes …*, London 1650/51.

342 *Abel Redivivus: or The dead yet speaking. The lives and deaths of the Moderne Divines written by severall able & learned men … And now digested into one volume, for the benefit & satisfaction of all those that desire to be acquainted with the Paths of Piety & Virtue*. The introduction was provided by Th. Fuller and included *The life of Bishop Andrewes, by the judicious & industrius, my worthy friend Master Isaackson*

hither I have viewed that Prebends house better, & find that a great part of ruins adjoyning, that I was told before belonged to the next house is yours.[343] So that the charge will encrease. I doubt you must expend 200£ before you begin to furnish. There is never a floor in the house, but two over the cellars, & one upper chamber, & they must be new laid. The Grand Chapter is begun here: I wish you a large dividend that may better enable you to build.[344] All the Prebends are here but your selfe, Dr Brevint, & Dr Carlton that is expected.[345] My service to all my friends and my true love to Mr Beaumont. Are you resolved never to mention him? I have sent for nothing by the messenger but another tippet at my house.[346] I long to hear < > some Sunning news: But shall never rest satisfyed till I see the wedding loves, or at least hear of the wedding. My service to Sir Robert Gayer, when you write. And if you chance to go to Stoke, pray remember to take a pair of French scissars that Sir Robert Gayer gave me & I left behind mee when I was there last, but now want: or if you write //send for them & pack them up in your trunks. My service to Mr Stapylton: but when you are ready do not stay for him. For he may have a mind to stay till the churching be past.

Your affectionate servant, G.D.

I hope I am mistaken in my former account: for since I wrote my letter the Dean told me that they are to allow you wood & he thinks lathes

... It was published in 1651: *ODNB*, under Isaacson (1581–1654) and Fuller. Sir John Harrington (1560–1612) continued the *Catalogue of the Bishops of England* published by Francis Godwin D.D. (1566–1633). Harrington's continuation was entitled *A Brief View of the State of the Church of England as it stood in Queen Elizabeth's & King James's reign to the year 1608* (published 1653): *ODNB*.

343 Sancroft's prebendal house was at the south-west corner of the College, Durham: Introduction, p. 20. According to the estimates produced in March 1661 (DCM, DCD/LP22/211) this house was one of the worst damaged, needing nearly £450 worth of repairs. Wood from the Dean and Chapter estates was routinely allowed to prebendaries for repairs to their houses and their corps lands: DCM, DCD/B/AA, passim.

344 DCM, DCD/B/AA/4, f. 59r/v, for the Grand Chapter, begun 20 July. Sancroft's letter from the king was presented and he was granted his full emoluments as if he had kept residence.

345 Daniel Brevint (1616–95), prebendary of the tenth stall 1661–95: Mussett, p. 80; *ODNB*. Guy Carlton, prebendary of the twelfth stall 1660–85, Dean of Carlisle 1660–72: Mussett, p. 94; *ODNB*.

346 G.D.'s house in London, location unknown.

too for your building. They have voted 400£ for aryiers & paid your Hamall letter in your behalfe.//[347]

Address as L. **40**.

43 **29 July 1662**
H. 3784, f. 66
G.D. to W.S. from Durham

Durham Castle, Jul. 29. 1662.

Sir, Yours I received. My Lord thinks that at present the number of 160 service books is sufficient: as for security you mention, he saith, as the books are taken off his hands they shall be paid for, & the money sent to Crook, or to whom it shall be appointed: & this is as much security as the King hath for the benevolence.[348] As for the bible & service book, you seem to believe they should be bound up together < > for as much as you say to be bound up with the Bible:[349] the Common Prayer Book is to be the largest you can get, & bound alone, & the bible also alone. Upon </both\> sides of </the Common Prayer\> is to be the figure in Dio. Datis bible & on both sides of the other that of Monasticon:[350] unless you prefer another & /on\ the top of both must be made /a rizing\ round like the top of a door, as you will see by the figure in the next page.[351] You must make as much hast

347 Hamall letter: Halmote court documents, e.g. a lease or patent. There are no Treasurer's accounts for this period. On 20 November the Dean and Chapter also allowed Sancroft the lead taken from his house: DCM, DCD/B/AA/4, f. 76v.

348 Crook: booksellers and printers in London and Dublin, 1648–69. Most probably G.D. refers to John or one of his brothers – Andrew or Edmond: *STC*, III, Index 1, Printers and Publishers; *ODNB*, under Andrew Crooke. The benevolence may refer to the 'Free and voluntary gift' to the king in July1661: E. Parkinson, *The Establishment of the Hearth Tax, 1662–66*, List and Index Society, Special Series, 43 (2008), p. 10.

349 Sic. The reference is probably to the matching books of Common Prayer and Bible bound in gold-tooled red morocco, given to King Charles II and placed in the royal pew of the Chapel Royal. Subsequently they were given to Nathaniel, Lord Crewe, as Clerk of the Closet, who donated them to Cosin's Library in Durham when Crewe became Bishop of Durham, in 1674, in succession to Cosin: DUL, SB++0020 (Bible) and SB++0021 (Prayer Book).

350 Monasticon: the architectural frame of the title page is similar to that in Dugdale's *Monasticon Anglicanum*, London 1655.

351 G.D. provided a rough sketch to illustrate his instructions.

as you can in this affair. Perhaps you may think that the goldsmith sent some patterns, but none came hither. I thank you for speaking to my Lord of London:[352] & if you see any of the Prebends of Westm{inster}, especially Dr Busby present my service to him & desire as much favour for me there.[353] The letter from my Lord of Cant{erbury} being not yet received, < > nothing at present is written to Crook, nor have we time if we would.[354] I am heartily glad of the news about Sir Rob{ert} Gayer:[355] my service to all the persons you mention when you see them. I cannot think this letter will find them with you. I hope you'll bring the gloves with you. I long extremely for your coming into these parts. That buisness is done effectually in the Chapter.[356] The Dean is very well. We hear the Dean of West{minster} is very sick.[357] The Assizes here begin this day.

Your most humble servant G.D

//Betwixt the pillars of the Bible figure /is to be\ this inscription in as large capitalls as it will bear: verbum Domini manet in aeternum[358] & on the Common prayer: The eyes of the Lord are upon the R{ighteous} & his ears are open to their prayers[359] – but in Latine. My Lord saith he ordered inscriptions// {p. 2} also for the other side of these books, but he hath forgotten them, & if you have also, you must find as apt ones as you can in their stead. To be set on the other side of these books. And let me hear no more of them saith my Lord. In wonderful hast, farewell. These instructions I read to my Lord. I hope you cannot mistake them.

---

352 Gilbert Sheldon, Bishop of London 1660–63: above, note 334.

353 Richard Busby (1606–95), prebendary of Westminster 1660–95 and Headmaster of Westminster School from 1638: *ODNB*; also L. **48**.

354 William Juxon (1582–1663), Archbishop of Canterbury 20 September 1660 to 4 June 1663: *ODNB*. He was by now very old and out of touch and the church was being run by Sheldon.

355 Perhaps Robert Gayer's knighthood: Introduction, p. 9.

356 Sancroft was inducted to Houghton-le-Spring rectory on 20 August 1662 and read the assent to the Act of Uniformity etc. on 14 September: Ramsey, 'Records of Houghton', p. 685.

357 The Dean of Westminster 1660–62 was John Earle (1598×1601–1665). His health was generally poor: *ODNB*.

358 Is. 40.8 = The word of the Lord remains to eternity.

359 Ps. 34.15.

44 **4 October 1662**

T. 48.55

G.D. to W.S. from Bishop Auckland

Aukland. Oct. 4. 1662.

Sir

I have acquainted my Lord with the contents of your letter.[360] He answers that if it will be for your content and advantage, he will consent (though he is heartily < > sorry that you are to leave these parts so much at least) that you exchange for Cottenham. Withall he bids me tell you; that once an overture was made to him of exchanging Branspeth & Elwick for the same rectory, and that he went to the place, but by no means liked the people, & for the value, he reckoned it not to be above 280£, and upon these considerations he left off thought of that matter.[361] I may say /also\ that your successor is not like to be as < > acceptable to my Lord (let others say for the people) as the present incumbent: but that is in your hat. He said also, that the Rectory of Kilkhampton formerly Bp Monks, & now Mr Grenvil's, he conceives is better than Cottenham, for Mr Grenvil saith it is worth 300£, & sometimes 400£ and if Dr Manby would take that, instead of Houghton in exchange, & you accept of Cottenham it would please him so much the better.[362] It is but nominating this matter to him /the Doctor\ for perhaps he may like that countrey /and living\ as well as this. /If you hold it convenient you may also\ //speak to Mr Grenvil now with you.// However I wish that you may not be deceived in the value of </Cottenham.\> On Wednesday if not on Thursday we are for Durham. The letter you desire my Lord hath signed; I wrote as you desired. I had rather a great deal have Mr

---

360 Sancroft became Master of Emmanuel on 31 August: Bendall, *History of Emmanuel College*, pp. 269–70. The salary was very small so he needed to augment it.

361 Cosin had been rector of Elwick from 1624 and Brancepeth from 1626. He had also held the tenth stall in Durham cathedral 1624–60: *ODNB*.

362 Nicholas Monk (c. 1610–61), Bishop of Hereford 1660–61. He held Kilkhampton from 1653, the patron being his cousin Sir John Granville, later first Earl of Bath, whose family held the living: *ODNB*; see LL. **45**, **46**. John Granville was Denis Granville's elder brother. Denis held Kilkhampton in 1662 and Sancroft wanted to exchange Houghton for Cottenham, Cambs., held by John Manby (1635–44, 1660–71). Cosin proposed that Manby should exchange with Granville: *ODNB* under Granville; R. Granville, *The Life of the Honourable and Very Reverend Dennis Granville, DD*, Exeter 1902, pp. 14–16. For Manby: *Al Cant*. The scheme failed.

Grenvil at Houghton, than Dr Manby, if it might bee. God direct us all to what is our last /rest &\ aim. I hear that my Lord of Winton inclines to have Dr Smalwood at Newcastle: but I have as yet no further account from Mr Duncon.[363] Tooker I have sent:[364] the other I cannot find & for the catalogue we have not yet done with it; though I admire it not.

Your most humble servant

G.D.

My Lord will be at Brancepeth in the morning.

Address: For Dr Sandcroft Prebendary of Durham.

As < > acceptable: 'great' erased; value of </Cottenham\>: 'the living' erased.

45 14 November 1662

H. 3784, f. 82

G.D. to W.S. from Bishop Auckland

Bp. Aukland Nov. 14. 1662.

Sir; I could not well return you an answer to your letter before this time. I told you </before\> that my Lord liked well of the proposition in your letter; & now I tell you the same from Mr Grenvil, who will be in London about the middle of December, where probably he will find you. And then if he can give you /such\ satisfaction as to Eton as will please you (that is that you may be assured of the next fellowship that is voyded, which is presumed will be before much time passeth) & also resign Kilkhampton to you, or whom you appoint: he will expect Houghton. On Thursday or Wednesday my Lord will at Durham, & with him you may expect

Your affectionate brother and servant

G.D.

</before\>: 'will' erased.

---

363 George Morley, Bishop of Winchester (Winton) 1662–84: *ODNB*. He had great influence over the Settlement of religion and was a close friend of Sheldon. Dr Alan Smalwood was vicar of Marske, Yorks., 1638–62 and Norton, Durham, 1661–3: *Al. Cant.* Duncon may be Edmund, Fellow of Trinity Hall, Cambridge, 1628–31, rector of Friern Barnet, Middlesex, 1663–73. He died 4 October 1673: *Al. Cant.*

364 Wm. Tooker (or Tucker) (1553/4–1621), a staunch monarchist, whose publications included *Charisma sive Donum Sanationis* (equating English kingship with that in the Bible and supporting the tradition that the king could cure scrofula), *Of the Fabrique of the Church and Churchmen's Livings*: *ODNB*.

46 **11 December 1662**

T. 144.96

G.D. to W.S. from Bishop Auckland

Aukland Dec. 11.1662.

Sir; Yours I received but an hour ago. First let me tell you my Lord is now, God be thanked, pretty well & much better than he was when I wrote last to you (for I have sent 2 to you by the way of Mr Garthwich & yet you tell me not where your lodging is.)[365] Yea so well is he that, I think, were it not for the weather he might go abroad, & so I pray tell all his friends. The dizzyness in his head he complayns not off: & into the gallery he goes without a staff. I was glad to see your letter because (though I regard not dreams) 2 nights since I dreamed a formall story, too long to be told, of your being drowned, going into Suffolk. I am very sorry, that my Lord of London despiseth Kilkh.[366] Pray God there be not reason for what he doth. I know nothing of R.W. being in news-book: nor can I tell who put that & the long story before in it.[367] Sure he was none of my admirers because he did not say that I christened the Qua{ker} Children & perhaps the same that told the long story of the ordination, & never said I made an excellent sermon. But have you seen what a letter of mine is printed in the Scotch Gazet, all the worthys that I have in print? Whereof some is nonsense:[368] but I wrote better. I have written to you twice in Mr Gardiners behalfe;[369] & in my last sent one to Dr Herbert, whom my Lord would have to be Vicar of Newcastle & Prebendary of Duresm.[370] My Lord of Winton wrote to him, with the Dean to find a /fitt\ person.[371] The Dean I think hath named Mr Bollen of Elwick & my

---

365 Garthwich, perhaps Garthwaite: L. **39**.

366 Kilk. = Kilkhampton.

367 R.W. = Richard Wrench?

368 See *Cosin Corr.* II, appendix, p. 342, for the cost of G.D.'s gazettes and postage from February 1666 to May 1666: 14s 9d.

369 James Gardiner (1636/7–1705), Emmanuel College from 1649, at this time prebendary of Lincoln: *ODNB*.

370 William Herbert (d. 1681), B.A. Trinity College, Cambridge, 1632; D.D. 1661; vicar of Trumpington, Cambs., 1641–2; rector of Great Whelnetham, Suffolk, 1646–80. Proctor of Suffolk clergy with regard to the production of the 1662 Prayer Book: *Al. Cant.* He did not become a prebendary of Durham: *Cosin Corr.* II, p. 21n.

371 Above, L.**44**.

Lord Dr Herbert.[372] I perceive Mr Duncon prevails not, because that after Mr Duncon's solicitation my Lord of Winton sends this letter to my Lord of Duresm, in which he saith {p. 2} the same he said to you.[373] However if my Lord of Winton say of Duresm he might not kill men for a Prebend: nor yet falsify his word to gratify those that /have\ abundance & frustrate the just expectations of those that have nothing: & so I durst with submission say to my Lord of Winton. Mr Grenvyl is expected to morrow from Durham: & within 2 or 3 days, if I mistake not, he is for London. I wish you would do what you can /to\ effect his busyness: if it cannot be effected, boggle not to say in downright terms where it sticks. That is as I suppose, why my Lord of < > London will not dispose of Kilkh. I shall be ready to serve you in any thing that I can here, & elsewhere I cannot do it. I ghesse you are for Imman. C. before your moneth be ended. Soon after I hope to be in London. In the mean time, I hope, Mr Scrivener will keep his charge, as I lately desired him by letter.[374] Commending you to God's protection (& Mr Gardiner to you, if he write to you) I rest in huge hast

Your humble servant G.D.

How doth Sir R.G? Write where you lodge: & if you go again to my house be acquainted with Mr Godman, & you will not repent it, if I have any judgment in a man.[375]

Lord of < > London: 'Win' erased.

47 **2 January 1663**

H. 3784, f. 90

G.D. to W.S. from Bp. Auckland

Bp. Aukland Jan. 2d 1662.

Dear Sir;

I had yours from Imman{uel} College with speed; & the same day I answered it, & directed my letter to be left at Royston. Since I have not heard from you: but I suppose you at London, & therefore I send

372 Daniel Bollen, rector of Elwick 1660, exchanged Elwick with Granville for Kilkhampton in 1664: Granville, *Life of the Honourable and Very Reverend Denis Granville*, p. 16; *Al. Ox.*

373 For Duncon, L. **44.**

374 Scrivener: L. **37**.

375 William Godman, B.A. King's College, Cambridge, 1646, B.D. 1659. Vicar of Ringwood, Hants: *Al. Cant.*; also L. **55**.

this to Mr Garthwait because I know not your lodgi{ngs.} God be praised my Lord is much mend{ed} I think coffee hath done him much good: but Dr Frasier & Dr Prujean advise him rather to drink tea.[376] He walks strongly in his chamber, & sometimes in the gallery without a staffe: but he keeps himselfe so warm in his cloathes, that I cannot ghess when it will be warm enough for him to stirr abroad. You will now have opportunity to enquire of the Printers what becomes of the Common Prayer Book, which you said they would bind & send to him. We have kept a jolly Christmas; dining some days, I think, 200 people. Pray send us some of your Court news: & let me know what chaplains you can provide me for the next term at Westminster. The term begins upon a Friday & ends on a Wednesday; yet I have but 5 sermons to preach //for my money: for the prebendarys look to Jan. 30. What doth my brother with his 100£.[377] I hear his purchase is at an end. The chapell here goes on. I have contracted with the glasiers to glaze the chapell & hall with blew & white glass for 9d ob. the foot: which I believe will amount to near 200£ which makes men say (I fear invidiously) the Bishop builds too much.[378]

Your humble servant,

G.D.//

48 **5 January 1663**

H. 3784, f. 92

G.D. to W.S. from Bp. Auckland.

Bp. Aukland Jan. 5.1662.

Sir;

I take this occasion (Mr Wm. Blackistons going for London) to tell you we are pretty well:[379] my Lord mending I hope much every where save in his legs, which continue swollen. I find by a letter from Mr

---

376 Alexander Frazer (Frasier) (c. 1610–81), Physician in Ordinary to Charles II. Born in Scotland. Fellow of the Royal College of Physicians 1641, Fellow of the Royal Society 1663. He was a relative of Bishop Cosin: *Cosin Corr.* II, pp. 216, 223, 299. Frances Prujean or Pridgeon (1597–1666). Fellow of the Royal College of Physicians 1626; President 1650–55. Knighted 1 April 1661. First Physician to Charles II: *ODNB*.

377 J.D.'s £100 was probably from a court case: see LL. **53**, **101**.

378 9d ob. = 9 ½d (ob. = obolus or obulus, the Latin term for 'halfpenny': *OED*). For the cost of Auckland Chapel furnishings see *Cosin Corr.* II, pp. 377–8.

379 William Blackiston, nephew of Sir Thomas B. of Blakiston, a Durham JP: *Cosin Corr.* II, p. 4.

Grenvil to my Lord that you are at London, whither I directed a letter to you 3 days since by Mr Garthwaits shop. My Lord had not < > health enough to go abroad on St Thomas Day:[380] so that your curate is but deacon yet: & I fear my Lord must keep his chamber till the spring. I pray remember me to all my friends at Court: but above all my service to our dean of Westminster, in whose time, I hope, the towers at the west end of the church will be finished.[381] I am thinking about the term sermons: and would fayn have 3 good Bs for the place.[382] When you see Dr Busby present my humble service to him, & if it be at supper give it to Mr Thorndike, & Mr Thriscross & all there.[383]

Your humble servant
G.D.

Address: For Dr William Sandcroft Chaplain in ordinary to his Majesty
Leave this with Mr Garthwait
At the Kings Head in St Pauls Churchyard.

49 **15 January 1663**
H. 3784, f. 96
From G.D. to W.S. from Bp. Auckland

Bp. Aukland. Jan. 15. 1662.

Dear Sir; Yours of the 10th came to me yesterday. I have been in a long mistake about the place of your present abode. Last week I sent another letter to you directed to Tim. Garthwait. Your letter came to day when Mr Dean & Dr Nayler were here.[384] I read to Dr Nayler that part of Dr Daltons being at Cambridg (you have heard that the Dr is likely to marry Dr Nailers daughter) but he was abashed at the report made of my Lord's health & surely if he conceived my Lord in so ill case, as he related, he was not to be excused that he passed by without visiting him. Pray, if you see the Dr: tell him the relation he gave,

380 St Thomas's Day: 21 December.

381 The Dean of Westminster 1662–83 was John Dolben: *ODNB*. The design for the towers of Westminster Abbey was by Sir Christopher Wren. They were completed by Nicholas Hawksmoor in 1745.

382 3 good Bs = 3 good briefs.

383 Dr Busby: L. **43**. Thorndike: L. **18**.

384 Joseph Naylor, rector of Sedgefield 1634–67 and holder of the second stall in Durham cathedral 1636–67. His daughter, Dulcibella, married Thomas Dalton, holder of the fifth stall, as her first husband: Hutchinson, *Durham*, II, pp. 176–7; Mussett, pp. 21, 45.

cannot be well taken. As for the books you have catalogued, keep them by you: & for those that are not catalogued, get some one to catalogue them & send the catalogue to my Lord. Pay the bill to the men /according to your discretion:\ but my Lord wonders that the mans pains should be worth 2£; & that 1£ should be given to the boat. But before all this I should have told you, that my Lord is daily better & better; & the swelling in his feet & leggs almost gone. I pray send word when your course is in Lent (for of late I have had no news-book from Tim. Garthwait:) if towards the end thereof I hope we may be in London then, I mean before you leave the city: but least you should look upon this /as a\ complement, I mean to see you & speak with you there, rather than to hear you preach. I am very sorry that Mr White is not sent hither for Newcastle.[385] Since I wrote first of him, I hear neither of him nor of any else for Newcastle: only Dr Nailer told it for a report (surely it is false) that my Lord of Winton had given orders to Mr K{nigh}tbridge, & so some conceived he was again fair for New- Castle.[386] But God forbid. I should be glad to send you 5£ or 10£ if I have it for /an\ organ in your chapell.[387] {p. 2} I am still of the perswasion that as many would give out of love to the college /as it is\ for such a purpose; so some would contribute out of spite to the college as it was. My Lord thanks you for your care & good wishes: & bids me take care of repaying you what you lay forth, which I shall do. I am glad you have gotten so many good fellows into the college: I know none of them but Mr Brown.[388] And if Mr Atwood & Mr Foster be gone (to Cadbury & Stand-ground I ghesse) I hardly know a person of the Society besides Mr Leigh & Mr Brown.[389] Mr Chapman's letter

---

385 Possibly Thomas White (1628–98), rector of Newark at this time and supported by Sheldon: *ODNB*.

386 'given orders': i.e. the Bishop of Winchester had ordained Knightbridge: appointed rector of Holy Trinity, Dorchester, on 30 June 1663 and had been ordained deacon and priest only on 20 March 1663: *ODNB*; CCED, person ID 51122; LL. **41**, **65**.

387 The new chapel of Emmanuel College: Bendall, *History of Emmanuel Collegel*, pp. 273–4.

388 Matthew Brown, Fellow of Emmanuel College 1662: *Al. Cant.*

389 John Atwood, rector of North Cadbury, Somerset, 1663–89: *Al. Cant.* William Foster, Fellow of Emmanuel College 1655; vicar of Stanground, Hunts., 1662–70: *Al Cant*. Thomas Leigh, rector of All Hallows, Lombard Street, London, 1658–62, when ejected. He did subscibe to the new chapel at Emmanuel: *ODNB.*

I still have:[390] for though I have written to Mr Blackiston, yet I have never seen him /since;\ & I would not trust it by a messenger.[391] As for Mr Gard. I never heard from him or of him since mine in December to you:[392] nor can I tell what to say. Res suas agat.[393] Mr Welsted surely deceived you, when he said my brother was with him: it could be but an agent; for certainly neither of my brethren have been at London this year.[394] You put the fairest interpretation that can be on building too much: one that complained to me therof was satisfyed when I said stone & lead would be kept easily in repair, & that the Bishop did not build his houses as other men did. As for Franklyn Patent, I waited on the Chapter & argued the case.[395] I thought I could have convinced any Chapter in England that it ought to have passed (as formerly ever but once) for 2 lives. Everyone of the Prebendaryes, I thought, seemed to yeild to me, especially when I proffered to reserve in the Patent a power of putting 200 deer, & also of the Bishop & his successors taking the top & bank to themselves; this moved not Mr Dean, who was willing the Patentee should have top & bank, but yet my Lord granted it not. I am not satisfyed that the Kings letter to Chapters against letting leases (not patents) for lives is anything to this purpose. As it is Mr Davison hath his own life: & what hath the chapter done?[396] My

390 Perhaps Thomas Chapman, at Emmanuel in 1665: *Al. Cant.* William Chapman was manciple and porter at Emmanuel: Bendall, *History of Emmanuel College*, pp. 137, 141.

391 William Blakiston?: L. **48**.

392 Mr Gard. = James Gardiner: L. **46**.

393 Res suas agat = He does his own things.

394 Welsted: a stationer or a goldsmith in London: Bendall, *History of Emmanuel College*, p. 589.

395 Frankland Patent was the grant of the Keepership of Frankland Park, which was part of the bishop's demesne. It was granted to Cosin's future son-in law, Samuel Davison, on 18 December 1662, but it appears here that the Chapter, who needed to countersign it, objected to its grant for two lives. The Chapter wanted restrictions on the patent if it was for lives, which Cosin did not accept. Since this was a patent and not a lease, royal objections to the number of lives did not apply. In the end the patent passed (24 April 1671) on Samuel's death to his son John, a minor, but not without further objection from the Chapter: Surtees, *Durham*, IV, p. 147; *Cosin Corr.* II, pp. 274, 277, 278, 279, 282, 285–6; Cosin's Letter Book 3. 55–62.

396 All Dean and Chapter leases were for twenty-one years, although the bishop still granted for lives. Cosin was against lease for lives, but this was not a lease. The objection may have been to the apparent nepotism: Anne Orde, 'Ecclesiastical Estate Management in County Durham in the Eighteenth Century', *Northern History* 45 (2008), pp. 159–71, esp. 160–62.

Lord bought in a man's patent that had no restriction, & now instead therof one {p. 3} is granted with the two restrictions above named. And so I told Mr Dean & the Chapter, when they told me how ready they were to serve my Lord. Dr Basire went Post to London on Munday about the tenants business.[397] You are, I think, to find an house, by order from the deputy Lieue-tenants. All your Brethren,[398] & my friends at Durham are well. The marryed pair, & Mris Grevil present their service to you.[399] Of the books that came from Cambridg the 2d volume of Plutarch's Lives is wanting; & the first volume of Vi{ce Comes} de Ritibus: when you pay Danks let him look {for} them, < > & bring them to you, who are desired to put them into the box with the rest that you keep by you till further order.[400] Our Vice Comes is titled Observat ecclesiast. Vol. 4tum.[401]

My Lord keeps his chamber still: & is carefull of his diet. Thus having given you trouble sufficient for once I commend you to God's protection & rest

Your most affectionate servant

G.D.

Address: For Dr William Sandcroft, Mr of Immanuel College, In Cambridge. Leave this with the Post master of Royston. Pd. 3d.

50 **24 February 1663**

H. 3784, f. 98

G.D. to W.S. from Bp. Auckland

Bp. Aukland. St Matthias. 24 Feb 62.

Sir; Your last I answered: your money due from my Lord & my selfe (unless you otherwise order) shall be paid you at London when we meet, which I hope will be before Apr. 1.[402]

My Lord now ventures into the dining room & chambers about the house, & hath been out of the house & in the chappel & new buildings, & caught no cold: and now his mind is set on London but I begin to be

397 Isaac Basire (1608–1676), holder of the seventh stall: Introduction, pp. 12, 24; Mussett, p. 59; *ODNB*.

398 All your Brethren: Sancroft's fellow prebendaries.

399 Marryed pair: Dr Dalton and Dr Naylor's daughter.

400 Thomas Danks: bookseller in Cambridge: Wing, IV, p. 280.

401 Joseph Vicecomes, *Observationum ecclesiasticarum … volumen quartum*, which dealt with the Mass. Earlier volumes treated the liturgy and ceremony and were published 1615–26: DUL, Cosin's Library Catalogue, D.432.

402 Your money due …: a subscription for Sancroft's building projects?

affraid of that place; for I find here as much work (ecclesticall[403] & secular) as one man can do; & there I expect the same, besides my Church work at Chepe & Westminster.[404] And how then shall I be able to visit the Knights my friends neer London as I have promised?[405] Or Cambridge as I designed? We have missed Mr White at Newcastle I know not how: & have a vicar there < > which for largeness B{isho}p Brownrigg was but boy unto. His name is Nayler; farther I cannot say of him; but beleeve very well.[406] I have been at Duresm but once since you went; & know not whether I shall go there any more before I go for London.

Your most affectionate servant, G.D.

51 **9 March 1663**
T. 155.47
G.D. to W.S. from Bishop Auckland

Bishop Aukland. Mar. 9.1662.

Sir; Yours of the 5th I received last night & after I had read & mused, to my Lord I went boldly & told him what you had designed at Imman. College which he liked /wondrous\ well < > & bad me to bid you to look well upon Christ College Chappel, & to take heed of making windows as low those in Peter-house Chappel.[407] After this I told him you had ordered me to present 13 – 06 – 8 toward the glazing of the Chappel here (I said somthing of what I knew of your want of money) he replyed, alas if he gives his money to another chappel he needed not to give any here, but however I /said I\ would give the money you designed: & so it is kindly accepted of him. The bill you sent is 08. 09. 06. 4£ I owed to you that I had of Mr Wrench & now some shillings are due to me from you. This tis to leave matters to my discretion.

For Immanuel Chappel (God speed it) I desire you to subscribe as much for me as I have paid for you towards this Chappel, twenty marks, which is as much as at present I have. If I have it hereafter I may do more. I write by this post to my brother about this matter. Twenty nobles I give to glaze the west window of this Chappel.[408] I had forgott

403 Sic.
404 Introduction, p. 10.
405 Sir Robert Gayer and Sir Robert Abdy.
406 Thomas Nayler, of Clyffe, Yorks., became vicar of St Nicholas's, Newcastle-upon-Tyne, in 1663 and was buried in his church 15 April 1679: *Al. Ox.*
407 For Emmanuel chapel: Bendall, *History of Emmanuel College*, pp. 273–5.
408 Noble: a gold coin worth 6s 8d (approx. 33p), half a mark. The mark was 13s 4d (approx. 66p): *OED*.

before to say, that they who glaze windows here are to have their arms put up in a window if they please. Perhaps you'le say, that yours were lost long since. But I would advise you to get arms assigned to you at the Heralds Office, which you may easily effect & severall presidents herof in the Kings Chaplains /are named\ in Sylvanus Morgan's late Book of Heraldry.[409] But to the Chappel again. {p. 2}[410] I need not to put you in mind of drawing a letter in the name of yourselfe < > & fellows & scholars to be sent to such persons as have been of your College. I know none of this countrey that hath be{en} of the College, Mr Dean excepted, & I have little hope of perswading any else. Some of the above said letters without superscription you should leave in friends hands who may superscribe & deliver them as they see occasion. And many will do that for a letters sake that will not be perswaded by a friend. Let Mr Waterhouse of Zion College (who was once a fellow commoner at Imman.) be ingaged in this business. When I come to London, I will bring him & you together for this end only.[411] He is a man of great acquaintance. Perhaps Mr Thriscrosse may do good service. I write this because I would have you to carry a great sort of letters with you to London. Be sure to send one to Mr Wright by a trusty messenger least it should miscarry.[412] Remember that Archdeacon Fulwood was of Immannuel.[413] I name him now because I may forget him herafter. There is another man in Zion College, a rich batchelor, I have forgotten his name, but he was a Master of Arts of our house. You will get money /enough\ I'le warrant you. I must say I never heard my Lord say that any benevolence towards the Chappel /here\was expected /from you\. I moved the matter of mine own head. My Lord grows better; but is troubled with obstructions which makes him short-breathed. I hope we shall perswade him to stay till April: so that I may see you at London though I do not hear your sermon at Court. I say nothing now of a gilded one. I wish Brother Laney was installed {p. 3}

---

409 Probably Sylvanus Morgan, *The Sphere of Gentry*, London 1661: *ODNB*.

410 The right-hand side is tightly bound and ends of words therefore are concealed.

411 Edward Waterhouse, heraldic writer, Fellow Commoner at Emmanuel College in 1635. By 1660 he was living at Sion College, an ecclesiastical institution including a clergy guild founded in 1624: *ODNB*.

412 Possibly Ezekiel Wright (d. 1668), former tutor of Sancroft and his regular correspondent: Bendall, *History of Emmanuel College*, pp. 168, 223, 251–3, 265–7, 271; D'Oyley, *Life of William Sancroft*, I, pp. 125–31.

413 Francis Fulwood, admitted pensioner at Emmanuel College 1644; Archdeacon of Totnes 1660–93, prebendary of Exeter 1662–93. Died 27 August 1693: *Al. Cant*.

in his Lords Prebend, I should be glad, as Edm. Duncan told me, to carry an half penny loafe to his house for house-warming.[414] It will be time enough to provide my brothers money against the next term: I cannot tell that he shall need it then. Thus commending you to God's protection, I wish we may have a joyful meeting and rest

Your most affectionate servant,
Geo. Davenport.

Address: For Dr William Sancroft. Mr of Immanuel College in Cambridge. Leave this with the Postmaster at Royston. Paid 3d.

/wondrous\ well < >: 'enough' erased; yourself < > & of: '& not of' erased.

52 **28 March 1663**
H. 3784, f. 50
G.D. to W.S. from Bp. Auckland

Bp. Aukland Mar. 28 1662. {*sic; recte 1663*}

Sir;

I go to morrow to preach for Mr Grenvil at Durham, & carry this with me for the Post. Mr Davies went yesterday to London, & left this office with me. Mr Gardiner is at London, & tells me < > that my Lord of Lond{on} hopes to do something for </him\> at your coming to London: which I heartily wish. I hope we shall begin our journey on Thursday sen'night. I have been very buisy for 2 or 3 days past. For /almost\ a week since a man came & upon oath informed against diverse persons in this county that they had a design to rise in arms to destroy this Parliament, & had taken an oath of secresy & the informant sayd he also took it.[415] Most of the persons are apprehended, & are Anabaptists, & do resolutely deny it.[416] But my Lord hath sent them to the gaol, & some days since acquainted the Lords of the Council with the information. O how I have turned over St Augustine De Civitate Dei & dispatcht Commission officers with musqueteers to severall places,

414 Benjamin Laney (1591–1675) held the eighth stall at Westminster 1641–63 while he was Bishop of Peterborough 1660–63. He became Bishop of Lincoln in March 1663. His brother may be Thomas Laney, who held a prebend in Lincoln from 1664: *ODNB*; *Al. Cant.*; Le Neve, *Fasti, IX: Lincoln*, pp. 3, 35. Edmund Duncan: Trinity Hall, Cambridge, 1624; Fellow 1628–31. His livings were Wood Dalling and Swannington, Norfolk, 1630–63, and Friern Barnet, Middlesex, 1663–73. He died 4 October 1673, aged 72: *Al. Cant.*

415 Refers to the 'Derwentdale Plot': Introduction, p. 12.

416 Anabaptists: a term used of many groups who denied the validity of infant baptism.

& Posts with Post hast for his Majestyes speciall service 7 /clock\ at night, & examined suspected persons & drawn warrants, recognisances, mittimuss & a great many such like matters.[417] {p. 2} Sometimes I am chaplain & reason with these men. And sometimes I supply the place of our Atturney Generall & accuse them out of intercepted letters either written by them or written to them. This makes some call me the Tormenter of the Anabaptists, as Dick Neil is of the Quakers.[418] I hope the danger is past & so we may be merry. I can say nothing of a gilded one this time. How doth Mr Dean of St Pauls?[419] Who shall have the Prebend at Westminster? Where do you lie? How long will you stay? What court-news? To all these you may make answer, if you will, on Thursday night when your work is over. I pray present my service to my Westminster friends. Mr Dean of Durham went towards London on Thursday last.[420] I shall find no Prebendarys but Dr Nayler & Mr Wrench at home.[421] Your Curat was made Priest, the last ordination.[422] When I had written this much I received yours, which put an end to some of my queryes. What else you mention in your letter I shall observe. And so I rest (< > tis time you'l say)

Your affectionate servant
Geo. Davenport.

53 **5 May 1663**
T. 47.12
G.D. to W.S. from London

May 5 1663.

Sir
I wrote to you but have no answer. As yet nothing have I done in that business. Dr Clutterbugg will not subscribe yet.[423] The other parsons

417 Mittimuss: the first word of a writ directed to a keeper of a prison by a JP, for the safe keeping of the person named in the warrant: *OED*.

418 Richard Neil, under sherrif of County Durham: LL. **37**, **60**, **72**, **123**, **138**; *Cosin Corr.* II, pp. 28.

419 John Barwick, nominated 30 September 1661: Mussett, p. 6.

420 John Sudbury, 1662–84: Mussett, p. 6.

421 Joseph Naylor: L. **49**.

422 The curate of Houghton had been made a priest probably at St Thomas (21 December).

423 Perhaps Thomas, son of Samuel Clutterbuck, rector of Dinton, Bucks. He was a pensioner at Emmanuel in 1639 but he received his B.A. from Oxford in 1643 and M.A. in 1646. He received his D.D. at Cambridge in 1669: *Al. Cant.* The letters were about subscriptions for Emmanuel Chapel: L. **51**.

Dr Waterhouse knows, but would have letters to them.[424] A letter will do more than the most effectuall words. Dr Carleton is dangerously ill at home at Wolsingham.[425] My Lord misseth you in town; & so do I for if he miscarry you may have a better prebend and shall if I want not my will. But preaching /be sure\ I told my Lord you would be here a fortnight this term. He wisheth you to come assoon as you can, so do I. And if you have any papers about Consecration of churches besides Peterhouse Chappell form, bring them with, hee desires you. I hope shortly to see you. In hast at Mr Welsted's shop.

Your humble servant

G.D.

54 **27 June 1663**

T. 47.26

G.D. to W.S. from London

London. June 27 1663.

Sir;

Yours I received yesterday. News I have little but the Portugalls great victory is confirmed.[426] The consecration is well approved by my Lord of London & it is committed to my Lords of Sarum, Lincoln, Litchfield & Carlisle as I remember. I called at Mr Welsteds as I came & he told me that your 100£ is received by him 2 or 3 days since. Your bond I will cancell, & wish my brother to call for the money. My brother this day got the victory of his adversary at the Chancery barr & will stay about a week longer in town. He presents his service to you. Mr Crouch I met an hour or two since: he desired me to tell you that Dr Holdsworths books had need to be removed shortly for they have need of their room.[427] < > I told him I had a roll for the Chapell, he

424 Edward Waterhouse: L. **51**.

425 Guy Carleton: L. **42**.

426 The Battle of Ameixial, 8 June 1663, which defeated the Spaniards and effectively established Portuguese independence. An English force under Thomas Hood took part: D. Malland, *Europe in the Seventeenth Century*, London 1968, p. 223; H.V. Livermore, *A New History of Portugal*, Cambridge 1966, pp. 188, 191.

427 Nathaniel Crouch, bookseller in London: Plomer, *Dictionary of the Booksellers and Printers … 1668–1725*, pp. 88–9. Sancroft was trying to get the books of Dr Holdsworth for Emmanuel Library: Bendall, *History of Emmanuel College*, pp. 270–2; D'Oyley, *Life of William Sancroft*, I, pp. 130–31.

desired to see it, & promiseth something & puts me in good hope touching Dr Wichcott, that he will be a benefactor.[428] I have been & sent very often to Sir Tho. Rich's lodging, but never saw him till yesterday at Sir Robt. Gayers lodging, where he spake very warmly & affectionately on our side & declared his opinion to me as fully as I wished: only he said they would refer the matter to be determined by the Coll[ege] & university.[429] I said rather let /the executors & College\ debate it & do their exertions determine, which he liked better. No more at present but that my Lord is well & I am

Your affectionate servant,
Geo. Davenport

Sir Robt. Gayer remembers him to you: & would know when you are for the north & when you mean to be in town. Surely an executor of an exec{u}t{ion} hath nothing to do *...* a trust.

I write from Sir Robt. Abdey house, who tells me as much as he will *..* to you & to the Vice Chancellor, to the end you may compare the matter amicably if you can, but withall to tell you that both of your opinions is for Imman{uel} College.

< > I told: 'he' erased.

55 **9 January 1664**
R. 100, f. 159
G.D. to W.S. from Durham

Durham Castle. Jan. 9. 1663.

Sir; (for I dare not say Mr Dean, least the news should want the circumstance of truth, but I assure you, it is talked all over this town (& I am to hear of it at Houghton to morow, because Mr Wrench hath a driveling cold & cannot keep his word with your curate, & is perswaded such a journey will be good for my dry cold) that on newyears his Majesty gave you the Deanery of York for a newyears gift.[430] My Lord hath had two letters from York, which say it not as

428 Roll for the Chapel = subscription list. Benjamin Whichcote (1609–1683), B.A. Emmanuel College, 1630; D.D. in 1649. He held a fellowship at Emmanuel College 1633–43 and became Provost of King's College, Cambridge, 1645–60, when he was replaced. He was a benefactor of Emmanuel: Bendall, *History of Emmanuel College*, pp. 123, 246–7, 259–63; *ODNB*.

429 The discussions were about Holdsworth's books.

430 Sancroft had been nominated Dean of York 8 January 1664: *ODNB*.

hearsay, but confidently: & this night Dr Burwell is come from thence, & saith he believes the same.[431] I would be sure.

I wrote to the Dean of Lincoln 10 days since, & told him that /Deanery\ would be a good place for us to meet at.[432] I wish we may. So much for that: when I return from Houghton I will give you as perfect an account as I can of what John thinks.[433] Yesterday Capt. Lilborn met me in the street, & told he & his neighbours desired to take their tithes at Ufferton (for he was told, he said, each township should be let by it selfe) I told him, I knew not how that report came: but if it would /let\ for more that way, & that as good security might be had; I thought it would not be refused.[434] But I said, every township then must be let: for I would {not} consent to let < > some, & hazzard others. My Lord is well: {p. 2} and rejoyceth much at the news, & saith he hopes to have more of your company in the north than formerly. We give Imman{uel} College for lost. In your ear, if that college should want a master, & seek for one in the town, I am perswaded a fitter than Mr Godman could not be found.[435] For he is a man of very good learning, but of singular honesty. But I am not wise enough to advise in this point. I shall not need any of your money as I expected in my letter which I sent to you by the post yesterday. No more at present from

Your humble servant,
G.D.

Address: For Dr William Sancroft. Chaplain in Ordinary to his Majesty. Leave this with Mr George Meddon at the Crown in Duck Lane, London.[436] 3

---

431 Thomas Burwell (c. 1603–73), LL.D., Spiritual Chancellor of the diocese of Durham before the Civil War and supporter of Cosin then. After the Restoration he was again Chancellor and also Chancellor of York: *Cosin Corr.* II, p. 197; *HPC*, I, pp. 752–3.

432 Michael Honeywood, Dean of Lincoln 1660–81: L. **28**.

433 John Philpot, parish clerk of Houghton since 15 August 1660: *Durham Parish Books*, p. 34.

434 Thomas Lilburne of Offerton: Introduction, p. 16; L. **82**, **113**; *Durham Parish Books*, p. 309.

435 For Sancroft's replacement: Bendall, *History of Emmanuel College*, p. 292.

436 G. Meddon: stationer in Little Britain, near St Paul's, London, called citizen and stationer in 1668: *A Transcript of the Registers of the Worshipful Company of Stationers, 1640–1708, AD*, II: *1655–75*, London 1913, p. 387.

56 **11 January 1664**
T. 150.49
G.D. to W.S. from Durham Castle

Durham Castle Jan. 11. 1663.[437]

Sir; Yesterday I preached at Houghton & there Duke Allison acquain{ted} the parishioners with the news of their Parson.[438] After dinner John Philpot & I fell to work. But I perceive he hath < > mistaken you: for he presented me with a particular of glebe, tithes, prescriptions, surplus fees &c which at length I understood was the value of this present year, & such an one as he had formerly delivered to you, amounting in all to 405. 15 02. I told him I expected one for the years to come, at what rate such township might be < > let & what the glebe let at /in\ parcells. He answered that could not be made. The glebe would hold the rate, he said; & perhaps increase a little, & but a little. For the tith, though each township were desirous of their own (& some had been so foolish so < > as to say, that if any stranger took it they would not pay) and had been oft with him about it, yet they would offer nothing unless he would bargain with him, which he said he could not do < >: But he tells me he knows he can raise it to 420£ with surplus fees (or to 415£ without them) & keep all the barns & stables & houses to yourselfe, which you /may\ let, as you see occasion. I wished him to raise it to what he could, & to tell them I thought you would let it apart to each township; & that I would write to you to know your mind. I said, I thought you would let it thus because he assured me that Mr Smith said to him he would not give more than 400£: besides he is not thought an over-excellent tenant, & Jo. Brignall, he saith, told him he would not take it for hims{elf} but be surety for another, who will not come up to the rate.[439] Again I took time to write to you, because, he saith, May-day is the best time to let the tith; (for then the year shows what is like to be. And if the corn appear good they will give the more: I answered & if bad then the less. He answered no for, then they would say it would be dear: but this

437 The original was probably 1663, now illegible.

438 Marmaduke Allison of West Rainton: *Durham Parish Books*, p. 323. The news was Sancroft's promotion.

439 Mr Smith: probably William of West Herrington: Surtees, *Durham*, II, pp. 183 and 187 for pedigree. John Brignall supplied Houghton church with building materials: *Durham Parish Books*, pp. 333–4; DCRO, EP/Ho 168, f. 187v.

will not hold both ways). Besides I knew not but you might have occasion to come into the north yourselfe before that time: & no man is so well served as he that is his own man. For the Glebe he saith this is a good time to let it: but it will be plowed that that is to plow: & so if men take it, they plow for themselves, if otherwise, they must be paid for it. He can also make such a bargain, as that you may take part /of the glebe\ into your hand if you should come to stay there. So that now you must tell us, whether we shall let it for 415 besides houses & surplus fees, by townships & parcells: none to have any particular townships unless all be let. He saith, he meant to have been with me to day, if I had not been there yesterday. For news from York, I suppose that you hear it almost assoon as we. Yesterday we had letters that <18> had been convicted by the Jury of life of death.[440] For other news there Mr Chancellor, who came home /from thence\ on Saturday /& hopes to meet you at York ere long\, tells me that {p. 2} he went into the chapter house on Thursday last to finish the Arch-Bishop's {Visita}tion; where requiring them to shew how they fulfilled his graces injunction * * /& nothing to S.P. prejudice pendente lite or visitation\ of paying St Peter his 900£, they shewed he had 300£ /in his chest\ & the other 600£ was or should be expended on the organ & church /& to this purpose shewed a new act of the chapter.\[441] He answered they offered a great indignity to his Grace /by making such a prejudiciall act\ & so decreed all the Residentiarys (for Dr Soresby & the others were in this business) be excommunicate.[442] But upon their earnest request (Mr Chancellor telling Dr N. of sharking < > over & over)[443] he respited the matter untill Febr. 8. & till that time the visitation is not like to be ended; at which time unless they comply, he

---

440 Life of death: sic. Perhaps reference to judgement on participants in the plot mentioned in L. **52**.

441 pendente lite = while the litigation lasts, referring to the quarrels about York Minster (St Peter) and its fabric fund. St Peter's portion was a share of the common fund and from fines for certain leases. In 1662/3 Archbishop Frewen ordered these funds to be safeguarded and asked for new statutes to be drafted: G.E. Aylmer and R. Cant, *A History of York Minster*, Oxford 1977, pp. 231–2, 239–40; J. Raine, ed., *The Statutes of the Cathedral Church of York*, Leeds 1900, pp. 45–6, 94–5.

442 Robert Soresby, B.A., Emmanuel College, 1628/9, Precenter of York 1660–83: *Al. Cant.*; Le Neve, *Fasti, IV: York Diocese*, London 1975, p. 10.

443 Dr N. = John Neile, Archdeacon of Cleveland and residentiary from 1638: Aylmer and Cant, *York Minster*, pp. 235–7, for some of his remarks about the situation. Canon of the third stall of Durham since 1635: Mussett, p. 26. Sharking = swindling: *OED*.

purposeth to excommunicate them. The Quire < > are there /in\ rebellion against the visitor & refused to execute the prayers on Thursday night last.[444] But enough of that.

Now if you are to be D{ean} there /(the place is valued in the king's Book at 600 marks)\ : I would advise you before you are installed & take an oath, to move his majesty that the old statutes might be reviewed, & a new body made. For (besides that those statutes which they now have, seem some of them to be absurd, others voyd or never well grounded, & yet all difective.) he that is Dean seems to be prejudiced by them . For Mr Chancellour tells me 1. the Dean is /no\ Residentiary unless he be canon. [At this time no canons place is voyd, but one that hath a mean one will resign if the AB will give him the next that falls be it better or worse, his name I think is Tolly][445] And then he /is capable to bee\ but of necessity is not /Residentiary\, which seems wondrous absurd. 2. His power is little or none: for he can convict only < > cum judicio capitali.[446] And what is such a dean above a cypher? 3. By some /of\ these statutes, if such the Dean is every day in the year to feed 40 poor people (that is 20 < > more than the Arch Bp. of Toledo /is bound to\ feed, saith my Lord of York).[447] These statutes are < > Antiquas consuetudines, called corruptelas by H{enry} 8 & statuta per Henricum Decanum & others made by the Dean & Chapter (who gave these power to make statutes?) & lastly new statutes made by Hen.8 which concern little besides Residence:[448] a miserable farrago & Hotch-potch.[449] It seems by the Chancellor that St Peter is a residentiary & pays no more to the repair of the church than every residentiary doth: & the rest is to lie up in his treasury (as the 200£ doth here) & not taken forth but by consent both of Dean & chapter, & that I suppose, in some urgent causes. I have told you my tale & tales-master. Now if it concerns you, So; if not, So. For the news of your being

---

444 The choir at York.

445 A.B. = Archbishop. Timothy Tully was prebendary of Givendale 1660–1700: Le Neve, *Fasti*, IV: *York Diocese*, p. 38.

446 Cum judicio capitali = with the judgement of the Chapter. The Dean had the greatest revenues but little power against the Chapter: Cant and Aylmer, *York Minster*, pp. 62–5, 216–17.

447 Archbishop of York: Accepted Frewen 1660–64. For his duty to feed people: Raine, *Statutes of the Cathedral Church of York*, p. 3.

448 Raine, *Statutes of the Cathedral Church of York*, pp. 1–42, 43–52; Aylmer and Cant, *York Minster*, pp. 197–8, 228–32.

449 Antiquas consuetudines ... corruptelas = ancient customs ... called corrupt.

Dean of York is neither confirmed from London nor contradicted from York. We long till we are assured what is the truth therof.

Your humble servant,

G.D.

Address: For Dr William Sandcroft. Chaplain in Ordinary to his Majesty. Leave this with Mr George Meddon at the sign of the Crown in Duck lane. London. 3

Might be < >: 'taken' erased; could not do< >: 'so' erased; quire < > are: 'also' erased; statutes are < > 'partly' erased.

57 **19 January 1664**

R. 100, f. 161

G.D. to W.S. from Durham

Durham Castle. Jan. 19th 1663.

Sir; Yours of the 14th in answer to 3 of mine I received on Sunday after evening prayer (the days are not yet so long that the post from the south can come before that from the north goes from us). And first I am so glad of your news that you write of Sir Robert Gayer &c. As for Mr Holdsworth business the Chancellor saith that he must come in person to be absolved (for though the sentence should be unjustly layd on yet it binds, till an absolution be procured, & will not be made a nullity) & then upon his alleging an exemption from Archb{ishop's} Jurisdiction he shall be absolved: if he shew it presently the Chancellor will desist, otherwise he may have time set him to do it, which if he do, then Mr Holdsworth hath right on his side, if he do not, then he must submit to the visitation or be excommunicated again.[450] Which seems as much as Mr Holdsworth desires; who the Chancellor saith mistakes in saying he will appear by a Procter with a protestation: for he must do it personally. The Chancellor gro{u}nds his jurisdiction upon the s{t}atute of 31.Hen.8.c.13. in fine.[451] I hope this will do: /I write to him this post.\ I am glad to see you so confident on Mr Holdsworth side. For Houghton business I expect another letter from

450 Thomas, probably nephew of Richard Holdworth, Master of Emmanuel College 1637–43, was Dean of Middleham, North Riding, 1660–80. The church claimed exemption from the Archdeacon of Richmond and its deans were largely independent of the archbishops of York: *VCH, County of York*, III, p. 366.

451 Act for dissolution of the abbeys, 1539, in fine (= at the end): *Statutes of the Realm*, III, London 1817, p. 738: churches hitherto belonging to religious houses were now subject to visitation.

you, which perhaps may come this day. We cannot find any one man desirous to be your tenant. For none ever came {to} us. And Jo. saith Mr Smith will not give above 400£: & besides he likes him not: & he is as confident that the parish will give 420.[452] Now by John's note /for this present year the tith is 202.13.06 and\ the glebe & prescriptions & surplus fees are 203.1.8. without any barn /or houses\ & these can be raised but little.[453] Why should not these (all but surplus fees) be let alone /if we can get a single tenant? (or to severall if we cannot?\ And the other tithes which are 10 in number /(for Pittington Ford at 0.2s. 6d. I reckon not)\ be set severally, especially if they will give good security & advance 20£ in the rent more than a single person will give: 12 to 22£. or more?

{p. 2} We must trust John * *{in} many things, whether we will or not. For who else can tell us the valuation & we cannot let it to one man, unless we can find that man. I will do /as\ much for you, as I can for myselfe, & take Mr Morland's advise, & as punctually as I can observe your directions in this affair.[454]

You say you shall not stir from London (hence) till Mar. 9. Soon after I think we shall be there /(but afterwards I perceive you intend for Cambridge in Febr.)\ And by reports you may have another Archb{isho}p of York by that time: for by letters on Sunday he was reported to be in very ill case: for which I am very sorry.[455] I wish you good success about Dr Holdsworths library. When you can foresee, let us know, who is like to {be} your successor at Im{ma}n{uel} College.[456] I suppose the fellows choose. Trouble yourselfe no further about your course in this church which happens on Quinquagesima Sunday Febr. 21.[457] For money I shall need none. I send this letter directed as the former; for I know not where you lodge. With yours I received a letter from my Lady Gerard, who is very glad for what hath

452 Jo. = John Philpott, parish clerk of Houghton-le-Spring: L. **55**. Mr Smith: Houghton tenant, frequently in debt: L. **67** and others.

453 Surplus fees = surplice fees, paid for marriages and burials to the incumbent of a parish. Prescriptions = money owing from the past.

454 Mr Morland, probably John, of Durham city, JP: Surtees, *Durham*, III, p. 276 for pedigree; *North Country Diaries*, SS 124, p. 120.

455 Accepted Frewen died 28 March 1664.

456 Sancroft's successor at Emmanuel College was John Breton. Sancroft resigned 26 April 1665, Breton was probably his choice: Bendall, *History of Emmanuel College*, p. 272.

457 Your course: the beginning of Sancroft's residence and sermons as prebendary of Durham.

befallen you at York.[458] I am glad now that you changed not your living for Cottenham: and if any should suggest a change for any in Yorkshire, I cannot imagine what they should nominate unless it be Bedall, of which Dr Samways told me he makes but 300£, besides a private patron pretends title.[459] But for Houghton again; I would not, were I as you, despise that which any calls the conveniency of the neighbours: for as they will hold themselves obliged by having /the tith\; so they will clamore, as if they were disobliged by missing it. Mr Church dyed on Thursday last.[460] I hear that the plague is at Hull, & that severall houses there are shut up; & that the Lord Major of York hath forbidden the citizens intercourse with that town. God bless our seaports: for it is thought the plague was brought from Amsterdam.[461] Mr Wrench {p. 3} desires to be remembered to you: I was yes{terday} at your house where the carpenter was drawing up timber to lay for dormars over the uppermost windows. Dr Wood's peice is to be made conformable to yours.[462] When I was at Houghton they told me, they thought the roofe of the chamber at the </west\> end of the hall would fall this winter. And that it rained into many places of the house though they had been mended. Think you that Mr Dean of St Paul's will be able to preach his course in Lent?[463] I pray present my service to the friends you mention in your letter.

Your humble servant.,
G.D.

Address: For Dr William Sancroft chaplain in ordinary to his Majesty. Leave this with Mr Meddon at the sign of the Crown in Duck Lane. London. 3.

</west\>: 'east' erased.

---

458 My Lady Gerard, Cosin's daughter: Introduction, p. 13.

459 Peter Samwaies, rector of Bedale 1660–93: L. **10**. The Crown exercised the patronage but Richard Peirse, lord of half the manor, claimed and eventually recovered it: *VCH, York: North Riding*, I, pp. 294, 300: H.B. M'Call, *The Early History of Bedale in the North Riding of Yorkshire*, London 1907, p. 109. The *Valor Ecclesiasticus* valued the living at £89 9s 8d, ibid., p. 107, but by this time it was worth £600.

460 William Church of Durham city, under-sheriff of Durham, buried at St Mary's South Bailey 14 January 1663/4: *North Country Diaries*, SS 124, p. 162.

461 Plague: Introduction, pp. 21–22.

462 Thomas Wood, prebendary of the eleventh stall at Durham 1660–92. Dean of Lichfield 1663. Mussett, p. 87.

463 John Barwick, Dean of St Paul's 1661. He died on 22 October 1664: L. **39**.

58 **15 February 1664**
R. 100, f. 163
G.D. to W.S. from Durham

Durham Castle. Febr. 15.1663.

Sir; Haec est finalis concordia.[464] Your last to me was Jan.30. and in prosecution of what you wrote, & what I before intimated to you, Mr Wrench, Mr Morland & his man & I went this day to Houghton, where the bonds were sealed, & I have them tyed up in red tape & indorsed, & to morrow morning I deliver them to Mr Treasurer.[465] The Newbottle men came /not\, its thought our message did not reach them, & we forgott to send for them till it was too late, that is after dinner: but they were the first men that agreed with us, & will certainly seal: I know 2 of the 4. Jo Brignall one of the 3 for Pencher had earnest business that hindered him, but he promised to seal, & the other 2 sealed. One other man for Waterfalls was absent, but will seal as his partner did. So these bonds & articles we left with John, for to see them sealed, & to return them to us. The Glebe men gave bond, & had a lease partl: the tithmen made articles with us; (one part we keep, the other they have, severall articles for each township but all of one form & gave us bonds. Mr Shadforth I have not yet seen; but John saith he will take Mr Huttons tithes.[466] Mr Dobson entreats you again to go to Coll. Hollis, who will be in town in the end of this month, & stay there all the next.[467] Mr Morland hath been twice over with us: for the articles & bonds the townsmen paid. But I thought good to give his clerk 5s. For his reward I referr him to you; though I told him I would pay him if he pleased. In the articles we covenant that __ shall have the tithes (prescriptions excepted) of such a township for 3 years from Michaelmas last & to gather the tithes after Michaelmas if they be not then inned, if you live parson so long. And they covenant to pay us so much money yearly

---

464 'This is the final agreement' from the beginning of a legal document or 'fine' recording a conveyance: D.M. Walker, *Oxford Companion to Law*, Oxford 1980, p. 471 under fine.

465 Richard Wrench: Introduction, p. 25. Morland: L. **57**.

466 Probably Thomas Shadforth of Eppleton, gentleman, of Houghton parish, one of the leading parishioners and a former supporter of Parliament: Surtees, *Durham*, I/2, pp. 219, 221; *Durham Parish Books*, 312, 323, 324, 326–7. Robert Hutton was his son-in law, Surtees, *Durham*, I/2, pp. 147–8, pedigree 149.

467 James Dobson, sexton of Houghton, succeeding his father in 1662: DCRO, EP/Ho 168, f. 174. Coll. Hollis: possibly Gervase Holles (1607–75), MP for Great Grimsby 1661–75, former colonel in the French army: *HPC*, II, pp. 565–6.

by equall portions at Michaelmass & * *{Lady} (Our Lady{Day} next is for the last years profit) & one halfe years rent after the expiration of the lease. The lease ends at Michaelmass< > therefore the rent must be reserved for Lady after. We set down Lady & Michaelmas but promised not to call for the money till Mayday & Martinmas which are the paydays in this countrey.[468] To perform these articles severall persons give bond for each town ship. The condition of the bond for the Glebe is whereas you have let _______ such ___ ___ glebe for 3 years from Mayday next, < > under such a rent at Michaelmas & Lady, if they pay the same during the term. I hope we have done all things to your satisfaction. And now I have done with that secular business I will study for Sunday, & see what I can say of blind Bartimeus.[469] Of Mr Dobson /for coneygarth\ we would take no bond: but let him be tenant at will.[470] I told you in my last that we abated 8s of what with rigour we might have gotten from 16 men for Waterfalls: & now we abated 2s in Rickland garth, & now I account all besides house at 418.19.10. You see the account that I make of it, by the inclosed. And if I be deceived in any particular John hath deceived me. I write in hast (& indeed too great a hast for this affair) & besides can scarce hold open mine eyes, & in the morning I am to go abroad with My Lord betimes. I heard Mr Wrench speak as if he was to return you 100£, but could not do it under 50s. We are all well: but we hear My Lord of York is likely to die, for which I am sorry. No more at present,

From your humble servant,

G.D.

59 **24 March 1664?**

T. 47.103

G.D. to W.S. from London

London March. 24. 1663.

Sir,

I went to Stoke on Saturday last & returned on Tuesday night late, so that both your letters found me yesterday. By the way 1.</your letters\> are well directed (but if you will you may say to me at my

468 Which are the pay days …: i.e the first instalment was due at Lady Day (25 March) and paid at May Day (1 May) and the second was due at Michaelmas (29 September) and paid at Martinmas (11 November).

469 Mark 10.46–52.

470 Coneygarth: rabbit warren: *OED*.

Lord's lodging in the middle of Pell Mell /we will be a little sooner)\ 2. There is never a word of my Lords Grace whom other letters report to keep his bed, & to have a hiccough, & to take cordiales that may preserve him till Our Lady be past.[471] Sir Robt. Gayer is well & his Lady: & she expects to lie down about Easter, at which time I have promised to bee there, because their minister is sick: & perhaps I may go again on Saturday next.[472] I was yesterday with Sir Tho. Clarges about the tith of Stoke.[473] All he would yield to was, to part with it at 18 years purchase, on condition it should be given to the vicar of Stoke, & he still keep the patronage, which he saith he will by no means part with. I know no particular business that my Lord had with you. But he was sorry that he missed you; & you may ghess how I was. My Lord was in the Schools at Cambridg; & when they shewed him the old modell for the schools & wished they could tell how to carry it on; he told them men would subscribe to pay so much for 7 years as they did before, & that he would willingly give 100£ for 7 years.[474] They thanked him but had little hopes of getting others in. This was for the schools & not for a commencement house only. Mr Vice-Chancellors mind ran upon building K{in}gs College & the M{aste}r of Trinity was for building a theatre near their bridg. Here I stept in (you know my bolt must be shott) {p. 2} & told them, I thought it would be the best way to build K{in}gs College, & to leave the Theatre & school alone: for if they could effect that, K{in}gs College should afford us a theatre & Commencement house and /as\ much room for schooling /as was needed\. This was very well liked by the Drs.[475] But, I think, the wisest sort of men thought all would be built assoon as any & so we dissolved. I was glad that the university excepted against my Lord. I should have been loath to have trusted any Cambridg Bp. And therefore I marvail that you did not * <|>* {choose}[476] Oxford Bps. which were like to be more indifferent sons. They would never have referred it to Imman[uel] College men. However I am glad the

471 Lord's Grace: Archbishop of York.

472 To lie down = to have her child.

473 Sir Thomas Clarges, brother-in-law to General Monk, active in London. His country seat was at Stoke Poges: *ODNB*.

474 Cosin would be in the Old Schools. The discussion was about the new buildings needed: V. Morgan, *A History of the University of Cambridge, II: 1546–1750*, Cambridge 2004, p. 54. Anthony Sparrow (1612–85) was the Vice Chancellor and John Pearson (1616–86) the Master of Trinity: *ODNB* for both.

475 Drs: doctors.

476 Concealed in the binding.

business is ended. Sir Tho. Rich's eldest son dyed at Stoke about 3 {weeks} since of the small pox, as is supposed.[477] Dr Franch preached for you.[478] Do you intend to come to Cambridg at Easter? I will labor what I can in Mr Holdsworth's business but I have not yet seen the Chancellor. I was yesterday {at} London when I received your letter & went forthwith for Lin{colns} inne to find the first fruit office, but before I came thither I heard it was removed but I could </not find\> till last night that it was settled in Dr Massons house at Puddle Wharf and thither I am now going.[479] Where I have given in * <|>* that is mine own. Mr Beaumont & G. Meddon, Mr Farringdon advised to compound untill after tomorrow because of the subsidyes.[480] Besides dignitys of above 40£ value must have the security first approved by the chancellor of the exchequer & for that we must stay for his hand. So this day sennight is appointed for the day. The value is as you set down & not 400£ as I imagined. I have not yet seen Mr Beaumont since that < > letter but I was there & told his man. He was packing up Dr Holdsworth's books.[481] I met Mr Jo. Buck this morning.[482] He bids tell you that he is {p. 3} sending down the books to Cambridge. I am glad the chappell will * * on. I will begg of men for it as I can. My Lord is very well & I am glad you are pleased about Haughton, or in anything that can be done by

Yr. humble servant,

G.D.

The Dean of Lincoln (as his letter to me saith) will be here about the end of this month.[483] All your friends are well. I find a note here in my

477 Sir Thomas Rich's eldest son, Thomas. His memorial is in Sonning church: *VCH, Berkshire*, III, p. 222.

478 Perhaps Mark Franck (1612–64), Master of Pembroke College: *ODNB*.

479 First Fruit office: First Fruits were a tax levied during an incumbent's first year, annexed to the Crown by Henry VIII in 1534, payable in variable instalments. The First Fruit office was a department of the Exchequer: G. Best, *Temporal Pillars: Queen Anne's Bounty, the Ecclesiastical Commissioners and the Church of England*, Cambridge 1964, pp. 22–3; Chandaman, *English Public Revenue*, pp. 115–17. Dr Mason was probably Charles Mason, from whom several letters to William Sancroft survive in the Harleian (BL) and Tanner (Bodleian Library) collections: *ODNB*.

480 G. Meddon: L. **55**. Anthony Farringdon, a barrister of the Inner Temple, *Al. Ox.*

481 Dr Holdsworth's books: L. **54**.

482 John Buck: 1625–68, printer and bookbinder in Cambridge, with his brother Thomas: *STC*, III, p. 31.

483 Michael Honeywood: L. **30**.

study of a book Alex Irwins dialogue * * iam Regnis.[484] I < >know not that I had such a book, is it /good\ for ought?

Address: The Reverend Dr Sandcroft, Dean of York. pd 3d.

</your letters\>: 'they' erased; </not find\>: 'tell' erased.

60 **9 April 1664**
H. 3784, f. 162
G.D. to W.S. from London

London Apr. 9. 1664.

Mr Dean;

I received yours of the 6th yesterday. As for the days of payment they might not be set as you would nor as I would, nor as Mr Farrington would as he said, but as Mr Chancellor pleased, who for the Kings sake deals hardly < > in that particular, as it seems to me. I urged all I could in vain. For what you write concerning Litchfield clergy I am a stranger to it: but I know Mr Machon went in wet weather to subscribe as not daring to trust him for his subscription & reading of prayers.[485] I imagine it concern not you who have done I suppose what is requisite or will do it within the time. It is good to be sure. You give a sad account of your deanery:[486] & indeed since you had it, that is since I enquired about it, I never thought it better. Make much of Durham. I adventured last night to speak to Dr Frank about the mastership of Immanuel College if it must be quitted.[487] I spake freely of Dr Utram & spake well of Mr Holdsworth.[488] I thought the /Dr\ was of my mind. I urged not much: because I knew not for whom you /are\ resolved for another. Therefore I was cautious, as it became me. I hear Dr Britten named:[489] & Dr Holbech I am told desires

484 Alexander Irvine, *A dialogue between A. & B., Two Plain Country Gentlemen, Concerning the Times*: Wing, 1050, printed in 1694.

485 Thomas Machon, prebendary of Lichfield 1631–71: Le Neve, *Fasti, X: Coventry and Lichfield*, p. 72. His brother John was Master of Sherburn hospital, Durham, in 1661: Hutchinson, *Durham*, II, pp. 596–7. The reference is to the acceptance of the Book of Common Prayer etc.

486 Deanery of York.

487 Dr Frank: L. **59**.

488 William Utram, Fellow of Christ's College, Cambridge, 1648–57; D.D. 1660: *Al. Cant.*

489 Dr John Breton was elected Master 22 May 1665: L. **56**; Bendall, *History of Emmanuel College*, p. 273.

/it\:[490] but he never said so much to me. My Lord is well & desires to me[491] remembered to you. Mr Stapylton & Mr Neil are your servants. I am now taking horse for Stoke where I stay till Tuesday. Your debt to me may be paid in that countrey: I am not in hast for it. I like not the potion in your belly, but hope it was only for prevention. In hast

Your humble servant
G.D.

The dean of Lincoln is well in town.

Address: For the Rd. Dr William Sancroft. Dean of York. York. 3

61 **21 July 1664**
S. 813, f. 77v
G.D. to Sir Andrew Henley Kt. & Bar. at Bramshill from Auckland Castle {Copy}

July 21st 1664. Aukland Castle

Sir
I must intreate you to put a seale to this inclosed & send it by someone to Dr William Burstall.[492] I would not have given you the trouble of it, but that I know not how otherwise to send it to him. I humblie desire of you, that if there may bee a friendly composure of all quarrells between you that it may bee made accordingly. You know the man & his conversation better than I doe. But this I know as well as you, that if the priest & people strive; the priest may sometyme or another incumber them with many unnecessary troubles, especially if hee bee not given to peace. There is noe sweetness in what people call revenging of quarrells but there is in peace. And there may bee peace where there is noe extraordinary kindness & freindshipp: & such is good where better cannot bee had.

---

490 Thomas Holbeach, B.A. Emmanuel College, 1626; D.D. 1660; Master 1675–80; prebendary of St Paul's 1660–80: *Al. Cant.*; L. **18**.

491 Sic.

492 Dr William Burstall, rector of Eversley, near Bramshill, seat of the Henley family. He received his D.D., King's College, Cambridge, 1662: *Al. Cant.* There was a serious and long-standing disagreement between him and Sir Andrew Henley, which was still continuing in 1667. Sir Andrew was trying to get rid of him but did not succeed apparently: Introduction, p. 24; *HPC*, II, under Henley, Andrew; *CSP, Dom. 1667–8*, p. 125; ibid., *1668–9*, p. 212.

I know it may easily bee answered that I know not the quarrell: but I should reply, lett it bee what it will, it may bee composed. And I have commonly observed that in controversies that last longe both parties are to bee blamed before they end. I say not this out of any mistrust I have of you, (I thinke you & I know one another better than hee,) but because I am very desirous you should have a life as free of disturbance as of want. Most controversies are in one of the parties' power to compromise: & the things which wee comonly contend for are not worth the ado wee make about them which I leave further to your consideration. Soone after M{i}ch{ae}l{ma}s I thinke wee shall bee in London; but in the meanetyme I should bee glad to heare of the health of your selfe & family. Wee are quiete here; but have a troup of horse in arms & on Wednesday next all the horse both militia & volunteers shew themselves.[493] Wee expect above 500 of the last sort according to theire subscription. I pray, faile not to present my humble service to my Lady: & excuse my not comeing to Bramshill according to promise.[494] I thinke I breake my word with noebody but her. But wee that are at other men's disposall cannot doe as wee would or as you who doe as you list. The Deane of Yorke was here on Munday in his way to Durham. Hee presents his service to you & to my Lady & is as sory as I am that your quiet is disturbed. When I come to London I intend to bring you some bridles: we have the best in England, they say, here at Barnard Castle. I have nothing more to present you with but the service of

Your most obliged servant,
Geo. Davenport.

Address: For Sir Andrew Henley Knight and Baronet at Bramshill. These.
Endorsed: paid per me, Fr. Tompson.

493 The Militia Acts of 1661–3 put the raising and training of local armed forces into the hands of the lord lieutenant and his deputies, who also raised the money locally to pay and equip each soldier. Richer local people provided the horse and the poorer the foot. Parishes might be charged and pay for one man. Volunteers could be added, recruited in the same way, but either serving at their own expense or paying another : J.R. Western, *The English Militia in the Eighteenth Century: the Story of a Political Issue 1660–1802*, London 1965, pp. 16–20, 25–6.

494 My Lady = Lady Henley.

62 **21 July 1664**
S. 813, ff. 78v–79v
G.D. to Revd. Willam Burstall, rector of Eversley from Aukland Castle {Copy}

Aukland Castle July 21 1664.

Sir, Yours of July 1st I received, as also that mentioned in it to bee formerly sent to mee. But that former letter as you rightly coniectured I showed to Sir Andrew Henley, when I was att London, that soe hee might answere to certaine particulars contayned in it which concerned him. It was soe long & my story att that visit so short, that I could not have tyme to reade it: and therefore left it in his hands & whether hee returned it to mee I cannot say: if hee did it is at my house in London. As for answer to that former letter I give none for these reasons. First you desired a full answere to all that longe letter: now such answer I had not leasure to make; for I could not write it in a dayes tyme. 2d I knew I had both given that by word and in writing alsoe & you sayd you /had\ my letter) /an\ answer to some things which you demand of mee afresh. 3 I thought you question my discretion more than was necessary, for charity would have directed you to have thought mee as regular in my proceedings as yourselfe especially when I had affirmed it unto you, & your neighbours could testify of my proceedings. 4. You tould mee not how I should send a letter to you & I know no other way than by Sir Robert Henley & Sir Andrew Henley. And though it bee not very fitt that I use theire helpe in conveying this to you, yet I am fayne to doe it. As for the question you proposed to my Lord by mee, hee took them not well, saying, Non vacat tam exiguis rebus adesse: & hee sayd indeed they became noe man that studied the peace of the Church.[495] I remember a minister of this diocese came above 40 miles to complaine to them that one in his church was married that could not say her catechism and that was the onely inormitie that hee had to complaine of in his parish, & that hee came for that onely end: he was well chidden for his paynes, especially, when I justified to his fall he came to profer mee 100£ for a presentation to a living then in my disposall. What a strange thing is it that you should send to a Bishop for advice, what you should doe with a woman that had received the communion from you & had not beene churched. I knew that she had thankes given att hand after a convenient tyme & the other infirmitie kept her from church for

495 Non vacat = there is no time to deal with such small things.

3 or 4 monthes after her lying in. And if women are in noe case to give thankes at home: then some women (beeing never able to come to church though they live many yeares) are never to be churched; & if they may bee churched att home (as they say) then this woman might: for shee was well recovered from her lying in, but yet had other infirmities that kept her in her chamber.[496] And you could not but know that shee kept her chamber : but it was enough if you might have known it upon enquirie. However how came it to pass that you did not rather question her about this matter before you gave the communion to her? As for the private christening as you call it in noe consecrated chappell, I can assure you & 40 of your neighbours (for evening prayer was done at the parish church before we began) that publick baptisme was & that after you had given mee leave & that in a consecrated chappell; for your predecessor Mr Blithman tould mee he was present when Archbishop Abbott consecrated it.[497] As for what you say of speaking so scandalously of your Diocesan in his letter I cannot remember it, but if there was any such matter, I have soe great an honor for my Lord of Winton, that though I never spoke to him in my life, I would not conceale it:[498] But as I sayd I remember it not; & have not the letter by which I might enforme myselfe. I have spoken to the Deane of Yorke (which was one cause why I sent this noe sooner) but there is noe likelyhood of his beeing in the south, as he sayth & therefore cannot doe what you desire. And as for myselfe I am needy on all occasions to doe what lyes in my power to make a Christian pacificacion beetweene any that are att difference; I have now written /to Sir\ Andrew Henley about this affaire but you must give mee leave to tell you that your friends who never heard of Sir Andrew Henley that I know of) have heard reports of you which makes them call your discretion in question. I was tould of severall personall reflections you made in your sermons, & such so meane, that if such preaching was allowed, yet the people would despise the preacher: examples thereof were of French cookes, not comeing to church, yet making visits to nurse children (you know men must goe to church at a sett houre but make visits any hower of the weeke) of hastninge to a landlord's dinner though they dyed by the

496 The churching of women, in the Book of Common Prayer, was a ceremony of purification carried out for a woman soon after the birth of a child. It involved an offering given by the woman and often took place at the Eucharist: *ODCC*.

497 Robert Blithman, predecessor of Birstall as rector of Eversley from 1634: *Al. Ox.* George Abbott (1563–1633), Archbishop of Canterbury 1611–33: *ODNB*.

498 George Morley, Bishop of Winchester 1662–84: L. **44**.

way, of fricassies & I know not what. I am noe orator, yet I think I never could perswade myselfe to name fricassee in a pulpit. I remember when I was a youth I heard a grave divine name a pudding in a pulpit, & it lookd like a gest in the church, & the people could not easilie cease laughing when they had once begunn. As for personall reflections; Axes, Hammers & saws of contention were not to bee heard in building the materiall temple nor are to bee suffered in those that are to build up the living temple.[499] I am sure that such preaching is not like his, who did not strive nor cry, nor cause his voyce to bee heard in the streets; & being the prince of peace hath called us to peace & made us embassadors thereof.[500] I pray mistake me not, & looke upon this as brotherly advise; and not busie intermeddling in other men's affayres: for I assure you in the word of the preist, it is not att the least soe intended by mee. For I would bee rekoned amongst those that are peaceable in the land, & a lover of those that follow after the things that make for peace with good advice. For piety will make a good Christian, and learning a good scholar: But a good Churchman a man cannot bee unlesse hee hath discretion as well as both the other. I shall never forgett what my Lord of Canterbury sayd to mee when hee gave me Institution (viz:) you have a Rule to go by, observe it, bee stout, but bee sure you bee discreat withall.[501] If the salt bee without saver (peace) it is good for nothing but is to bee cast out.[502] You know what quarrells you have had at Sherbarn, what in London, & if you have the same att Eversley, will not your friends bee doubtfull of your disposition? For God's sake consider of these things & doe like a man that studies if it bee possible, & as much as lyeth in him to bee att peace with all men.[503] If I have erred herein I assure you, it is not maliciously. I have taken the boldnesse I confesse, to give counsell to one better than my selfe: but my meaning is good. I am

Sir
Your most affectionate Brother & fellow servant
George Davenport

Address: To the Reverend my worthy friend, Dr Willm Byrstall Rector of Eversley

---

499 Axes, hammers and saws … : restrictions on the builders of Solomon's temple in Jerusalem, I Kings 6.7.

500 Isaiah 53.7.

501 Gilbert Sheldon was archbishop at Davenport's institution (archbishop 1663–77).

502 Matt. 5.13.

503 Rom. 12.18.

63 **8 November 1664**
T. 145.103
G.D. to W.S. from Pall Mall, London

Pall Mall. Nov. 8. 1664.

Mr Dean, we have been here ever since St Simon & St Jude's Day.[504] And we have been made beleeve by many so soon as we came, that you would follow us at the heels. But now I can meet with no one that can ghess when you are to be here. I beleeve I know nothing < > concerning your new Dean{e}ry that will be worthy the relating to you.[505] The houses near Ratcliff (so many in number that they pay 200£ per annum for chimney money)[506] are held by one life, & </I think\> that person, /however,\ the person for whose use they are held is a prisoner in the King's Bench & so poor as not in capacity to render so he must either be bought out, or else you must higg for it & so make a hog or a dog.[507] If you outlive the life, it is like to be better worth than 10,000£, saith the Dean of Canterbury.[508] The living of Tharfild, I hear, is like to fall to the /Dean of\ Canterbury's son's share, who is chaplain to the Duke of York.[509] The Chapter are a body without the Dean, they say. The Deanery I hear is valued at about 200£ in the Kings Book, /though they pay a yearly rent to the King.\ But these things I suppose you know better than I. Many make suit for places, as one of the last Deans servants that waited on him till his death, & is a verger, my Lord's undercook Rich < >Little would be something in the church, & my countreyman Paybody wellknown to all the chapter would be a bellringer, & your hattmaker I hear hath

---

504 St Simon & St Jude's Day: 28 October.

505 New deanery: St Paul's. Sancroft had become dean in October 1664.

506 Chimney money = Hearth Tax. Levied on each hearth in every house at 2s a year from 1662 to 1689: Parkinson, *Establishment of the Hearth Tax*, p. 17. Ratcliffe manor was in the parish of Stepney.

507 higg = dispute about terms, from higgle?: *OED*.

508 Dean of Canterbury: Dr Thomas Turner (1592–1672). A friend of John Barwick, ex-Dean of Durham. His son Francis was chaplain to the Duchess of York. He became rector of Therfield, Hertfordshire, on 30 December 1664: *ODNB*. Francis's brother William was Archdeacon of Durham: *ODNB*.

509 Tharfild: Therfield, Hertfordshire, a rectory received by John Barwick in 1662. Barwick died 22 October 1664: see previous note.

a mind to speak with me.[510] God send you well up, & then you may, I perceive, have choice enough. No more but that I am

Yr. Humble servant

G.D.

Address: For the Reverend My worthy friend, Dr William Sancroft, Dean of York. York pd 3d.

Rich < >Little: 'John' erased.

64 29 November 1664

Cosin Letter Book 1B, letter 117

G.D. to Isaac Basire[511]

Pall Mall. Nov. 29 1664.

Sir, Yours of the Oct. 29 with the postscript of Nov. 18 I received. As for what concerns Mr Prowse[512] my Lord knoweth /not\ what to answer/yes my Lo{rd} might sequester for the K{ing}s tenth or for want of incumbency or present upon the lapse\ nor how to remedy him. If he came in well (as he hath protested to me he did, though he confessed that he gave </160£\> by way of gratuity, which I understand not) the law will give him remedy, my L{or}d cannot. For how should he give him possession, when another takes it violently from him? The law must do it. For what you write of that (concerning the excommunicated persons) if you have not already determined anything, my L{or}d thinks you had best pass it by. One you say desired absolution, and so it may be the better passed over. The church is not yet so surely established as to do everything that in former times, I think, it might more safely do. All the friends you mention are well.

---

510 Thomas Paybody: book-dealer in London. Perhaps he was from Wigston or Leicestershire: Plomer, *Dictionary of Booksellers and Printers, 1641–67*, p. 146; LL. **79**, **86**.

511 Basire: Introduction, pp. 12, 24; L. **49**.

512 Edward Prowse, rector of Bolam in Northumberland, had replaced John Thompson who had been ejected in 1662 but lived on in the parish as a centre of dissent. In 1663 Prowse was accused of scandal and negligence by Basire, perhaps for failing to deal with Thompson: R. Bibby, *A Survey of a Northumbrian Castle, Village and Church*, Newcastle 1973, p. 222; J. Crawford-Hodgson, 'A Survey of the Churches in the Archdeaconry of Northumberland, temp. Charles II', *Archaeologia Aeliana*, 2nd ser., 17 (1895), pp. 244–62, esp. 246–7.

Mr Thorndike is at Cambridge. The Dean of St Pauls is expected tomorrow, as men say; but I have it only by report.[513] The Commons have voted /at a committee\ the 2500000£ to be raised by a regulated subsidiary way, and are now to consider how it may be best done. What it will mean, I know not: but I ghesse it must not be called a monthly tax, because they formerly declared ag{ain}st having more such, nor a subsidy, because it cannot be raised but by a great many, which cannot be paid in a few years.[514] My service to M{istres}s Basire and to all my friends in the college. Your sons I saw very well. I am

Your humble servant

Geo. Davenport

Address: For the Reverend my worthy Friend Dr. Isaac Basire, prebendary of Durham. Durham. Pd 3d.

</160£\> : over 180 erased.

65 **9 April 1665**

H. 3784, f. 263

G.D. to W.S.

April 9 1665.

Mr Dean;

The occasion of the inclosed is this: My Lord hath been informed that my Lord < > of London hath admitted one Mr Shafto to the cure of Dedham in Essex, as formerly Mr Knight-bridge to the vicarage of Dorcester in Dorset.[515] Since when he was Bishop of Sallisbury (both which were crept into Newcastle) without letters dimissory. The former of these cast himselfe out at St Bartholomews, < > refusing to take orders though B.D. The other was not suffered to continue, the place being a curacy & so not to be held without the Bishop's license.

513 The Dean of St Paul's was Sancroft, from 11 November 1664.

514 In December 1661 the Commons had prohibited the use of Assessments (monthly payments), but they were very lucrative. For the various types of subsidies and Assessments: Parkinson, *Establishment of the Hearth Tax*, pp. 10–11. For the debate about this levy and the use of the phrase 'a regulated subsidiary way': Chandaman, *English Public Revenue*, pp. 145–6.

515 Humphrey Henchman (1592–75), Bishop of Salisbury 1660–63; London 1663–75, a friend and supporter of Sancroft: *ODNB*. Leonard Shafto was vicar of Dedham, Essex, 1665–71, and of All Saints, Newcastle, 1671–6: *Al. Cant.* Knightbridge: LL. **41**, **49**.

My Lord thinks my Lord of /Londons\ chaplains were too facil in these men's affairs. No more at present from

Your humble servant
G.D.

I write by command & not of choice: & had I had opportunity to /have\ seen you again I had not written. The business of the clergymen I think should be used tenderly.

Address: For the Rd. Dr William Sancroft, Dean of St Pauls, London. {With other scribbling including part of the Hebrew alphabet.}

66 **21 April 1665**
R. 100, f. 164
G.D. to W.S. from Bp. Auckland

Aukland Castle. Apr. 21. 1665.

Mr Dean; on Thursday last we came safe to this place. Yesterday we went to Durham, & returned this morning. At Durham I find that in the Chancery sitting last Mr Turner in your & my name did something I know {not} whether he exhibited a bill, or how to call it. The end of it (the former part being recitall of the order for Dr Marshall) is as followeth.[516] It was therefore prayed that a subpoena in the nature of a scire facias[517] returnable upon the _____ day of _______ next might issue out of this court to be directed to the said Wm. Smith son & heir of the said Hen. Smith & Robt. Ayton, son & heir of the sd. Robt. Ayton deceased, & unto the said Eliz. Smith to show cause why the s{ai}d severall sums of < > 30£ per annum & 8£ per annum together with the respective arrerages therof incurred & become du{e} aforesaid should not be paid unto the s{ai}d Dr Sancroft & Mr Davenport respectively & also to show cause why a commission should not be awarded out of this court to certain Commissioners for the setting forth of a certain quantity of the lands in the s{ai}d decree mentioned for the securing of the s{ai}d 8£ per annum to the s{ai}d Mr Davenport & his successors Rulers of the s{ai}d Rectory, & why the s{ai}d 30£ per

516 Mr Turner: a lawyer: LL. **72**, **81**, **89** etc. Hamlet Marshall, rector of Houghton 1633–45: Hutchinson, *Durham*, II, p. 541; Surtees, *Durham*, I, p. 157.

517 Sub poena: a writ directing a person to come before the court subject to penalty for non-compliance. Scire facias: a writ requiring a person to show cause why someone should not have 'advantage of the record': Walker, *Oxford Companion to Law*, Oxford 1980, pp. 1107, 1195.

annum should not be also secured according to the intent & true meaning of the s{ai}d decretall order which Mr Chancellor thinks fitt, & doth hereby order the same accordingly.[518]

So soon as I had gotten a copy of this (the fees of councill & attendance on him & copy of order came to 51s.04d) I went to Mr Mickleton & he went with me to bespeak 3 severall writts to be left at the houses of the partyes, & his man is to execute them.[519] Mr Mickleton is to come towards you on Munday. And to him I gave all the papers in your trunk concerning Houghton. I desired him to come to you: because I beleeve you may be desirous to speak with him. These papers may be useful to you at present. But when you have done with them pray send them to me. But if in any you deprehend any falshood blott it now that it may not lead me into any mistake. I also desire what other papers may be useful to me, & not so to you. I perceive it is long since Mr Wrench & you exchanged letters. He tells me Shacklock neglects his work, yours I should say. And I beleeve it, because the smith told me that he about 9£ of work in barrs for </windows,\> & hooks for doors, which he could not set up, & consequently could not demand money for them, because the floors & doors were not made. The Glazier he said was in the same case about his glass. I long to hear that an end is putt to our business in the Arches.[520] In which you laboured much, but suffered more. I am about to buy timber & resolve to cast down all the walls of the Hall & the staircase at one end & the little vaulted room at the other end, & to build from /beside\ the end of the /little\ parlor to the end of the kitchen, one end wherof shall be stair case /to the dining room,\ buttery, & passage to the </little parlor\> & all the rest hall which will be about 40 foot long. The change will be as much as roofing the hall as it stands, but the convenience more. /(The entrance shall be at a corner looking westward).\ For now I shall have passages into all the house (which I had not before for it led well only into the kitchen); & also prevent cross beams in the hall (which it must have had by reason

518 Margin has: March 28. Sancroft and Davenport versus Smith etc. William Smith of West Herrington: L. **56**. Robert Ayton, senior, of West Herrington died 1642, pedigree: Surtees, *Durham*, I, p. 186. Elizabeth Smith, widow of Henry Smith, daughter of Robert Ayton senior.

519 Christopher Mickleton, attorney employed by Cosin: *Cosin Corr.* II, p. 3n.

520 Court of Arches was the provincial and appeal court of Canterbury through which G.D. must obtain dilapidations and arrears of tithes: Walker, *The Oxford Companion to Law*, p. 75.

of the weakness of the walls) that would have made it look like a barn. I intend to go to Houghton to morrow; and to warn the tenants to bring your rent on May the 3^{d}, when Mr Wrench & Mr Morland (if it snow {p. 2} not) are to meet them. The same day I am to provide dinner for the Halmott Courtyer & to let the tith & glebe if I can.[521] Now I am like to have some money in my purse. I have no patience untill I lay it & more out. I am told part of the garden wall & /part of\ the roof of Mr Dobsons chamber are fallen.[522] Mr Ch. Gerard is dead.[523] The Dean went to London the same day that we came home: he went to meet us at Darlington, & we came by Piercebridge. Dr Brevint is /to\ go into France on especiall business for the King, as it is said, but by some perhaps not beleeved, & his residence is to be excused.[524] At the visitation we shall find about a rump of the Chapter, some three or so. Mr Wrench saith Mr Dobson hath brought him no money. This day the chimney gatherer demanded of me 5s. < > so much being unpaid at Michaelmass last.[525] I will look after it on Sunday. Mr Stapylton presents his services to you. My service to Dr Barwick, & Mris. Barwick & to Mr Nicholls.[526]

Your humble servant,
G.D.

My Lady Burton presents her service to you: and desires to help Ra.Douthwait to a good place if you can; and so do I also.[527]

</windows\>: 'doors' erased; </little parlor\>: 'lower hall' erased; me 5s. < > so much: 'as being pa' erased.

521 Members of the Halmott or manorial court: DUL, Archives, DHC 1/ 1/83, f. 818 for this court.

522 James Dobson was sexton of Houghton from 1662: *Durham Parish Books*, p. 328.

523 Charles Gerard was buried on 15 April: *Stapylton Corr.*, p. 144n; Introduction, pp. 13–14.

524 Daniel Brevint, prebendary of the tenth stall at Durham 1661–95: *ODNB*. On 7 April 1665 an order from the king gave him a passport and told the Dean and Chapter that he was to suffer no prejudice since he was about to go to France: DCM, DCD/B/AA/3, f. 25v.

525 Hearth Tax collection, which was done locally from 1664 by a receiver or his deputy, 'the chimney man': Parkinson, *Establishment of the Hearth Tax*, pp. 24, 41; L. **67**.

526 Peter Barwick (1619–64), brother of John and a Dr of Medicine. John (L. **39**, **58**) was already dead: *ODNB*. Mr Nicholls: probably John Nicholls, *Cosin Corr.* I, p. 186; II, p. 203; *Stapylton Corr.*, p. 180.

527 Ralph Douthwait: *Cosin Corr.* II, pp. 12, 311, 336; *Stapylton Corr.*, p. 211.

67 **6 May 1665**
R. 100, f. 165
G.D. to W.S. from Bp. Auckland

Aukland Castle. May 6 1665.

Mr Dean; I wrote to you about a fortnight since: but perhaps my letter came not to your hand. I have been at Houghton both the Sundays since I came down. On Wednesday last I went thither again: & there I met Mr Wrench who received above 10£ of your rents; & all the rest I beleeve he will receive in Whitsunweek, when there is a fair at which they /tenants\ mean to sell cattell & raise money.[528] After this we celebrated the Halmot Court with a dinner, & in the strength of the rost meat subscribed 31£ towards the building of an organ.[529] Jo. Brignall subscribed 5£ (as Mr Shadforth did & I ten) and said you told him you would give 10£. However though you have left the parish (for I said that was coincidentally it should be done; while you was Parson) yet I pray give us as much as you can. Mr Lambton was not there, nor many gentlemen of the parish.[530] After this we celebrated a vestry, & agreed for new flagging of the church all over, with new free stone flaggs: & I agreed for doing the Chancell after the same manner, if I liked the work at church, which will be begun next week. I agreed with the rough wallers for the house, & /with\ the free mason for the windows & for making all the house towards the court with broached ashlar work, /as the new building at Durham Castle is\,[531] the work to begin on Munday next, that is the ashler to be wrought, & in six weeks time I hope to lay the foundation & to finish all by Michaelmass. But I long to hear that we have ended all in the Arches.[532] For till then I dare not pluck down the hall walls. I hope My Lord will give me leave to throw down the building at the west end of the hall, that so I may have a large window at the west end of the hall. I look to get 10 load of timber the next week into the yard: and am agreing for slates.

528 Wrench was now Treasurer of the Dean and Chapter: DCM, DCD/B/AA/4, f. 91.

529 *Durham Parish Books*, p. 332 for the organ and other work about the church.

530 Sancroft had resigned Houghton on becoming Dean of St Paul's but kept his prebend. Thomas Lambton of Biddick in Houghton parish: Surtees, *Durham*, I, p. 201 for Biddick. The Parish Council in Houghton comprised the Gentlemen and the 24: *Durham Parish Books*, SS 84, p. 323.

531 R. Brickstock, *Durham Castle: Fortress, Palace, College*, Durham 2007, pp. 42–5.

532 Arches: L. **66**.

To morrow morning I purpose to go over again. For last Sunday I had about 40 people out of Newbottle at Catechism (& hope for almost as many to morow from the Herringtons, they being warned to it as the others were) & about 200 people at church in the afternoon.[533] When all is done in the court then I shall take money of Mr Wrench. Mr Cant, /from whom comes the inclosed,\ would < > fain have your 20s: charge.[534] I showed him the condition of your subscription, which is not otherwise fulfilled {p. 2} than by the subscription of 3 others to give 30s. Mr Smith (who subscribed 3£ to the organ) is served with the writt, according to Sir Fr. Goodericks order to show cause why he doth not pay you your arrears & give me security for the future, according to the /old\ decretall order.[535] The like is or will be done with his mother, & with Mr Ayton.[536] Mris Shuttleworth remembers her service to you on Munday she leaves this countrey, & goes to live in Lancashire.[537] I desire the order of the court (if it be done) may be delivered to Mr Mickleton at Clyffords inne, if it be too large for a packet by the post.[538] My service to Dr Barwick, his wife, & brother.[539] My Lord is in good health, being bettered by his journey: he would fain hear whether you have spoken with My Lord Chancellor about his affair.[540]

Your humble servant,
G.D.

Address: For the Reverend Dr William Sancroft Dean of St Pauls at his house near St Gregory's Church in St Pauls churchyard. London. 3.

would < > fain: 'have' erased.

---

533 Catechism: questionnaire in the Book of Common Prayer used to educate in the Christian Faith.

534 George Cant, Master of Kepier School, Houghton, 1639–1682: L. **40**.

535 Sir Francis Goodrick (1621–73), younger son of Sir Henry, of Ribston, Yorks. Temporal Chancellor Durham Diocese from 1664: *HPC*, II, pp. 409–10; *Stapylton Corr.*, p. 175n; *Cosin Corr.* II, p. 147n. For the writ: L. **66**.

536 Robert Ayton, of West Herrington: Surtees, *Durham*, I/2, p. 186.

537 Mrs Shuttleworth: LL. **74**, **100**.

538 Mickleton: L. **64**.

539 Dr Barwick was Peter: L. **66**.

540 Lord Chancellor: Sir Edward Hyde, first Earl of Clarendon: *ODNB*. Cosin's affair may be the lead mines of Stanhope: L. **93**.

68 **9 May 1665**
T. 45.6
G.D. to W.S.

Yours of Apr. 30 I answered the last post, but was not at leisure to give so full an answer as now as I am. You was myred in the account as you say: I seem to <wade through>. If any myre stick; you know, mistake is no true payment < > & you are in as good condition as you was. I am quite tyred: therefore I am for a merryer subject, read what follows at leisure.

A Gentleman is with me who coming from a place within 3 miles of Carlisle with the relation following. One Gillemont a Scotch witch long since prophecyed, that when Rainbow was Bp & Stanicks major of Carlisle, when Skarrows well there went dry, when all the subofficers were Tom's & the castle was on fire, & a wench went to milk a cow upon Stanicks banks /where cows go not,\ then should the wench say, where is fair Carlisle now, for it should sink.[541] You know who is Bp. (untill he look upon Lincoln). Tho. Stanicks is major, all his officers are named Tom. Scarows well is dry, the castle was on fire in the Sessions week, a cow hath /a\ broken legg upon Stanicks bank (some advise not to milk her, but in vayn, the wiser are for removing her upon a sledge:). This possesseth the people with such a fear, that a great part are fled, for fear of the cityes sinking. And the grave people fleeing /&\ meeting with flouters, say they are like to Lots sons in law, that would not beleeve the destruction of Sodom.[542] One old woman that could get no lodging lay in the field, whither she removed her bed. Another tells me that Mr Dean is gone thither to see if he can quiet the mad people.[543]

More mirth yet. This morning my Lord sent for me, & put all forth the room; & I began to think of all my offences. At length he told me that though Dr Sancroft said he might know better than himself who was to succeed at Elie,[544] yet he knew not, but beleeved the man would be Dr Sancroft. And the rather he thought so, because one had

541 Edward Rainbow (1608–84), Bishop of Carlisle 1664–84: *ODNB*. Thomas Stanwick was mayor of Carlisle in 1666–7. There is no printed list of mayors; I owe this information, from a manuscript list in Carlisle Library, to Mr Ian Caruana.

542 Gen. 19.14.

543 Probably Guy Carleton, prebendary of the twelfth stall at Durham, as well as Dean of Carlisle: Mussett, p. 94.

544 The Bishop of Ely was Matthew Wren, who died 24 April 1667: *ODNB*.

been which *{came}* to begg your Prebend. The truth is a visitor of this countrey, hearing from a {neighbour} that came lately from Cambridge of such a matter, rode (as never man rode) he rode /14 miles\ upon the outside of a grey mare booted & spurred (but no hith on his neck)[545] with the strongest wind in his face that ever he felt (which he was resolved to say </that\> he should /not\be thought to have drink in his face) /which was somdeal saucy\ lest he should have come too late to my Lord: but when many (for he was loath to believe anyone) answered in such cases the King bestowes the preferment, he returned home a slower pace. Still my Lord believing the report of the man from Cambridge (though he said the Bp. was not then dead but very sick), would have perswaded me to write to you (the greatest part of this was written before) to desire you to use your interest for me here: which when I peremptorily refused, he bad me then to write to you in Dr Herbert's faver, forasmuch as my Lord St Albans told him, he would move the King, that if you was promoted, Dr Herbert might be your successor.[546] I tell you this piece of merryment not to please my selfe, but in obedience to him who would not be gainsaid.

Mr Dean, I am your humble servant,
G.D.

May 9. 1665.
My humble service to Sir Robt Gayer & his Lady & to Sir Tho. Rich. I pray let me hear that they are well, if you can. I go betimes in the morning to measure my work at Houghton: the masons having finished.

Address: For the Reverend Dr William Sancroft, Dean of St Paul's at Mr Benbows house in Maiden Lane in Covent Garden, London.[547] 3

<wade through>: 'wade through it' erased; to say </that\>: 'lest' erased.

545 Hith = twisted rope: *OED*.

546 For William Herbert: L. **46**. Henry Jermyn (Germain), Earl of St Alban's (1605–84), courtier and government official, at this time an opponent of Clarendon and close to Henrietta Maria: *ODNB*; L. **14**.

547 Benbow: unidentified.

69 **21 May 1665**
R. 100, f. 167
G.D. to W.S. from Durham

Durham Castle. May 21. 1665.

Mr Dean; at my return this evening from Houghton I found yours, which doth a little perplex me about a man you mention. But I think you are more affraid than hurt. As for Herrington tithes /10£ 10s.\ I paid them at London to you (as you remember in the margin) & have your acquittance; and as for Pensher tithes Mr Dobson paid them to Mr Wrench when he was last there: & then Mr Wrench received Mr Huttons tith rent due at May, & the arrear for E. Houden.[548] So that all that may go; & will be with your good liking: and all that part of your letter had been spared, if Mr Wrench had been as good at writing as he is at reading. To morrow morning we go to Newcastle to visit: but before I go I mean to speak with Mr Wrench. But I think he hath received little more money for you. But I have no reason to doubt of the payment of any. I do not remember that ever I heard of the 18.06.06 that you left in Mr D. hand.[549] I brought you with me to London, an answer to the particular summs that he was to receive: but that /answer\ you said was defective. If I can I will be there the next Sunday & do as you desire & take your letter of Atturney. I have /been\ at Houghton for 5 Sundays past, that is every Sunday since I came down, & had 45 persons this afternoon at Catechism, & 38 < > the Sunday before, & about 40 another day, & hope for as many next Sunday. I divide the parish into 7 parts for Catechizing. I have about 200 at church in the afternoon & 98 were at communion last Sunday & about 6 or 700 at Easter. My Easter book I gave to the binding of boys to apprenticeships, & so about 4£ was gotten: but I doubt you got little: & as for surplice fees I let the < > curat have them, because /I\ thought he would get them better for /himselfe\ than for me.[550] My Lord dined with me at Houghton last Munday, & with him Sir Gilb. Gerard, & severall gentlemen.[551] He will make me (I am as willing as

548 Robert Hutton, gentleman, whose house in Houghton-le-Spring was taxed for fifteen hearths: Green et al., *Durham Hearth Tax*, p. 55; Introduction, p. 15.

549 D = Dobson.

550 Easter Book: the Easter offering to the incumbent. His curate in July 1664 was Lancelot Dobson: Ramsey, 'Records of Houghton-le-Spring,' p. 686.

551 Sir Gilbert Gerard, married to Mary, eldest daughter of Cosin: Introduction, p. 13.

he) to cast to the ground the building at the west end of the hall, that so I may have a west window in the hall that I shall build, the wall wherof will < > stand about 4 foot within that building. I long to see the sentence of the judg. I am about to burn lime. To morrow carpenters square timber for carriage to Houghton, & the free mason goes to make windows, chimneys, and doors. I have free stone brought already into the yard. But I know not what to do for money, to finish all I would do. You say nothing of the organ. By which I ghess you received not my letter that I wrote to you the day after Mr Wrench was at Houghton for your rents. If I can buy the old organ in this church at an indifferent rate, I hope to hear it in Houghton church within 3 months. Mr Dean is sent to about it: I pray when you see him speak to him in our behalfe. I have not done yet. You must know that on Friday last I preached the visitation sermon at St Oswalds church.[552] And this morning {p. 2} My Lord told me he had a mind to have the sermon printed, & bad me bring it to him. I said little, & perhaps his mind may alter. The text was, But thou, O man of God, flee these things,[553] which from v.3 & v.4 I said were schism, teacheth otherwise &c, pride, he is proud, ignorance, knowing nothing, contention, doting &c about strife &c & covetousness; I added the man of God must girtt himself like a man, & so idleness is to be fled. My Lord said the instructions on these heads were wholsom, & that if the sermon was printed it should not be sold but he would give < > copyes to the ministers of his Diocese, & hoped they might do good amongst many. Now if I could beleeve that, I should think my selfe bound in conscience not to oppose My Lords desire, which otherwise I see no reason why I should gratify. I tell you this, that so if this must be done, I must adjure you by all kindness you have for me, to look over this sermon with as severe an eye as you can, before it go to the press, & with as favourable an one as may be afterwards, if you chance to see it. For I mean not to give it to any friends: nor see I any cause why I should set my name unto it. I stand not /or but little\ upon right printing & the aptest words; but fear ne sit aliquid per {im}prudentiam aut per minus studium dictum.[554] I'le say no more now; & perhaps I may not herafter. But let me know your opinion. I have told you what weighs more with me, than my Lord's importunity should. I would willingly secure both my

552 St Oswald's, Durham; for his preaching there in 1662: *Durham Parish Books*, p. 199.

553 I Tim. 6.11.

554 'lest anything be said through imprudence or too little study'.

modesty & credit: & yet not refuse to /do\ Gods service, though by incompetent arguments, if I could do it.[555]

Address: For the Reverend Dr William Sancroft. Dean of St Pauls at his house in Angel Court in St Paul's churchyard. London. 3

70 **19 June 1665**
T. 144.152
G.D. to W.S. from Durham

Jun. 19. 1665. Durham Castle.

Mr Dean,

Vous avez enough of the release. I came hither this day & return within an hour or two. Mr Wrench has paid the 100£ & 5£ for the organ. If Dr Berwick have paid the first fruits that is well, if not I desire you to see it done.[556] All the remainder of the money /due from him\ I desire may be to Mr Royston at the Angel in Py Lane: for I have money of his in my hand.[557] Shaechlock saith he hath done much work for you (above that which Mr Wrench discharged) about laying of floors & making of doors.[558] He said he would bring me note: but it comes not & I cannot stay for it. Mr Wrench pays none: because he was in your debt before: & he knows not what other bargain he made with you. He lets him go on, because he would have < > him to be out of your debt. Shacklock talks as if you was 15 or 16£ in his debt. Shall the glasier and smith set up their work? Mr Wrench, /is with me & salutes you,\ desires to know whether you have received the bill of exchange for 200£ charged upon Chaplain & which he sent inclosed in a letter about a fortnight since. In great hast,

Your humble servant

G.D.

Address: For the Reverend Dr William Sancroft, Dean of St Pauls at his House in Angel Court in St Paul's Church Yard. London. 3

Discharge of dilapidations at Houghton.

have < > him: 'you' erased.

555 There is no greeting.
556 Dr Berwick = Barwick.
557 Richard Royston (1601–86): L. **19**.
558 Shaechlock = Shacklock.

71 **1 July 1665**
H. 3785, f. 1
G.D. to W.S. from Aukland Castle

Aukland Castle Jul. 1. 1665.

Sir; yesterday I received yours of Jun. 27. I have this day written to Mr Wrench, & acquainted him with all the particulars needful in your letter. But, as I remember, when Shacklock talked with him {and} me about his bargains with you, Mr Wrench was at a stand, & said you had the Articles & that he had no copy of them. I beleve he was deceived (but could not stay to see the truth) & that they were either in his study or your trunk: however we may see the Articles in Shacklocks hand. I will do what I can & assoon as I can, in this affair. But I have no hope of seeing Durham before the Sessions which will be the 10th of this month. I have many men at /day\ work at Houghton & yet cannot go to see what they do. I am very sorry to hear the sad relation you make about the Pestilence. Wee are in great fear, it </will\> be brought from /London to\ Newcastle.[559] I perceive you have left Immanuel but I know not to whom: but I guess to Dr Brittayn.[560] I am glad to hear that Dr Barwick will pay the 38£-10s-04d remaining to Mr Royston.[561] I have written as much to Mr Royston: And am ready at any time to seal the release, which I will send to him. I suppose he is still in the same house with you. I have not yet written to Mr Mundie, because he said he would send me a bill which he hath not yet done: but I intend to do it by the next Post.[562] Thursday last my Lord consecrated his chapell, & named it after the saint of the day, St Peter . The Dean & Prebendarys & many clergymen; but abundance {p. 2} of Gentlemen & gentlewomen were present, & had a great fea*{st}* made to them. My meanness (as Rabbi Wheelock said) preached on, he is worthy for whom he should do this, for he loveth our nation & he hath built us a synagogue; then Jesus went with

559 The Plague which raged through 1665 was mentioned by Sancroft in his letter to G.D. dated 20 September 1665: T. 467.52; H. Barnes, 'On Quarter Sessions Orders Relating to the Plague in County Durham in 1665', *Archaeologia Aeliana* 15 (1892), pp. 18–22.

560 Dr Brittayn: John Breton, Master of Emmanuel College: L. **60**.

561 Royston was paid for gazettes and postage: *Cosin Corr.* II, p. 342; L. **70**.

562 Perhaps Francis Munday, son of John of Markeaton, Derbyshire, educated at Westminster School and St John's College, Cambridge: *Al. Cant.*; L. **81**.

them.[563] In the end of the sermon, I moved all the clergy & laity to be </persuaded\> by the sight of the < > beauty of this chapell, to repair & beautify their own churches & chancells, & pressed it so fair on them, that at length I onerated the Bishops conscience, & his Chancellor & Archdeacons, with care of seeing it done: saying Bishops, Chancellors & Archdeacons took too much upon them & did they knew not what when they spared either laity or clergy in this case.[564] This was well enough taken: & at dinner Coll. Villiers, the Governor of Tinmouth moved my Lord to have this sermon printed for the use of the Diocese, saying, he would give a copy of it to his brother in law, the E{arl} of Northumberland who had many ordinary churches in Northumberland.[565] More words were said; but I am not willing to have anything done in it, & hope I shall wear </out\> the humer in them, as I did in the other sermon at the Visitation, though both were now spoken of. Let the worst come that can; if either or both do go to press, I am resolved neither of them shall be sold, but all of them given away in the Diocese. And then if the former make any minister better in his place; & the latter cause any church to be repaired, I shall get some credit in the work, though none in the sermons. I trust I shall be solicited no more: but if it must be done, I must find some way of sending these papers to you for a review. For I have none here I can advise with but Mr Wrench. But enough of that. Pardon this boldness in

Your humble servant
Geo. Davenport.

I pray let me know when you go for Tunbridge. & how you may be sent unto there. My last told you that I am indebted 5£ to you for the like sum I received of Mr Dobson for you. If you will, take that of < >Dr Barwick, & let Mr Royston have the rest 33£ 10s 04d.

</will\>: 'should' erased.

563 Luke 7.4, 5. Abraham Wheelock (1593–1653), noted for his modesty, was a teacher of Hebrew, Professor of Arabic, a librarian and Anglo-Saxon scholar of Cambridge: *ODNB*.

564 Chapel: at Bishop Auckland.

565 Algernon Percy, tenth Earl of Northumberland (1602–68), had married as his second wife Lady Elizabeth Howard, daughter of the second Earl of Suffolk. The third earl, Elizabeth's brother James, married Barbara Villiers, daughter of Sir Edward Villiers: *ODNB* under Algernon Percy and James Howard.

72 **14 August 1665**

T. 45.22

G.D. to W.S. from Aukland Castle

Aukland Castle. Aug. 14. 1665.

Mr Dean; Yours of July 26 came to my hand about an hour since. I am very sorry to hear of the sickness of your contrey man: & therefore long for another letter from you. Mr Wrench told me he had received money from Mris Wildbore (I take it) & so was inabled to let me have 50£ upon your account.[566] I have herin sent you a bill for 50£ from my brother: & least it should miscarry I have written a letter of advice to Mr Welsted who knows your hand. I came this day from Houghton: but there I had so much business of mine own that I forgott all yours. My hope is in Mr Cant that he may help me, for as yet I * *spoke with him about the 21£. If the arrear bill would *....*good I can copy it out, & return you the original. Bridget (as the neighbors say) will pay, being rich enough: but I advised Mr Wrench to send to her: & if she delayed payment to sue the bond.[567] All the assize time, Shacklock was < > in Westmoreland (as I remember) but some little matter was done upon the staircase. Mr Wrench told me that upon Jo. Rowills counting, there appeared but about 200 boards used by Shacklock.[568] When the assizes held the College gates were locked up for fear of infection[569] (as they were before & since) & I had much business, & Mr Wrench being to preach the Sunday we hardly saw one another. So that you owe us but a little thanks. That sermon puts me in mind of you. But dormi

566 Frances Wildbore, tenant of corn tithes at Heighington, which belonged to the ninth stall of the cathedral. Gilbert Wildbore, her husband, had been vicar of Heighington, ejected 1651, restored in 1660, died in 1661: Surtees, *Durham*, III, pp. 307, 315.

567 Bridget: perhaps Bridget Ayre, mentioned in Cosin's Survey of 1662 as a tenant of Ryhope: DUL, Sharpe MS 167, ff. 130, 131.

568 John Rowell, mason, of St Margaret's parish, Durham, involved in building and paving Sancroft's prebendal house in Durham: *North Country Diaries*, SS 124, p. 141.

569 A quarantine was placed on ships from London and Great Yarmouth by Co. Durham justices but plague was still brought from the south. Jeremy Reed seems to have imported it from Kent (dying 5 July 1665) and there were thirty other cases in Sunderland in the following months. Further outbreaks occurred in Gateshead and in Newcastle later in the year: J.F.G. Shrewsbury, *A History of Bubonic Plague in the British Isles*, Cambridge 1971, pp. 114–16; Surtees, *Durham*, I, p. 534; Barnes, 'On Quarter Sessions Orders Relating to the Plague'.

securè.[570] Dr Dalton coming home the week before his course not to preach, was not provided for it: & none would exchange. He begged hard of me & I preached for him, on condition he should preach your course, which he hath undertaken, & that is on Sunday sennight.[571] Do you not forget our Chancery business?[572] Mr Smith upon conference at the Assize told me he saw he was in a wrong box, & would submit to me, for Mr Turner for his fee had told him I should be too hard for him.[573] For you alleged that he could prove that Jo. Philpot for one year had let him his tith /with glebe\ for 22£ 10s & so will yield to pay no more, for that year. For he saith that was all and as if you had chosen to take it in < > kind, as by the decree you might. I said you had not entrusted Jo. so to do. He said he thought {you} would not swear, that John was not trusted by you to let all glebe & tith. {p. 2} I confess I wish you had all your money from him though that 5£ 10s was abated. I pray write your mind, for the Chancery sitting is on Sept. 12 but do not say do as you will for me. I think Mr Ayton owes little. But he comes not at me.[574] Mr Smith I am told is much in debt, & was cost in 150£ at the assizes. I believe he cannot pay you at present, nor can I tell what bondsman he will get, if you should accord: but who hath power to take a bond? Mr Baker is the attorney for I could not get the matter with his willingness out of his hand: & I think it is not the worse he executing the Chancery Registery Office.[575] I have paid for writts & fees 50s. & to Mr Turner 20s, (perhaps you gave him a fee also) & his man had 20s for drawing the motion & given him by Mr Neil in my absence, which I have paid /him\ so that here /is\ some change for you. Besides I paid 19. 04 ½ for the building the Session /House\ (besides my gift of 03.06.08) which was laid on two years since & now paid by all the countrey aswell clergy as laity, after the rate of 5£ per pound. I {* *think} that will fall to your share to pay, being it was laid on at the Assizes * * years ago though little was paid until the last year, when the agreement was made with Langdale for 490£,[576] the house is almost quite finished. We hear little talk of the sermon printing now.

570 Sleep safe!

571 Thomas Dalton had said he would come into residence on 15 August: DCM, DCD/B/AA/4, f. 104.

572 Chancery business: see L. **73**.

573 Mr Turner: L. **66**.

574 Robert Ayton of West Herrington: L. **66**.

575 Possibly George Baker of Crook Hall: *Cosin Corr.* II, p. 210n; Surtees, *Durham*, II, p. 358, III, p. 166; *North Country Diaries*, SS 118, p. 59.

576 Langdale: unidentified.

Keep my brothers bond. About the latter end of the week my building I hope will be 17 foot high. The lead I have, & carpenters work daily at the roof. I have spent the dilapidation money (though not all in building) & owe Mr Wrench 60£ & this 50£ I doubt will not serve my turn.[577] But Martinmass I trust, will pay my debts.[578] The sickness hath been a fortnight at St Hild's (commonly called Sheelds) which is a town belonging to the D{ean} & Chapter betwixt Gateside & the sea mouth.[579] Two houses are suspected in Gateside. Sunderland buryed two of the sickness the other day: but God be praised it spreads not. At my instance with my Lord, the Judge, the Bench & Grand Jury, I got an assessment of 5s per pound to be laid in all the countrey (which will amount to 250£) the money to be laid up for occasion if the infection spread. In which I think I did no ill service. God send us a good meeting after all your wanderings. Let us pray for one another. It grieves /me\ to read the last bill of mortality. God hear our prayers & give us grace to amend our lives. The Duke of York & Dutchess have been 10 days at York. Some think they may come into this countrey: but alas none desire his company these dangerous times, though all wish him prosperity. I hope Sir Robt. Gayer & all friends are well; because you mention them not. I am

Yr. Affectionate servant
G.D.

If you send the bill to Mr Welsted write on the backside of it: that so he may know it comes from you, & not from any that might intercept it. I have told Mr Welsted that you will endorse the 50£ upon the back of his bond.

Address: For the Reverend Dr William Sancroft Dean of St Paul's London.
To be left with Mr Stephen Bing at his house in Knight-Riders Street. or with Mr John Tilleson at the Dean of Canterbury's house in St Pauls Back house at Pauls Chain.[580] London. 3.

Was < > in Westmoreland: 'at D' erased; take it in < > kind: 'hand' erased.

---

577 Dilapidation money, received from W.S., the previous incumbent.

578 Martinmass: 11 November.

579 St Hild's = South Shields. Gateside = Gateshead.

580 Stephen Bing, minor canon of St Paul's. A letter from Sancroft to him is in T. 145.106, dated 20 September 1665.

73 **19 August 1665**
T. 45.24
G.D. to W.S. from Auckland Castle

Aukland Castle. Aug. 19. 1665.

Mr Dean; By the last post I sent you a long tedious letter, concerning all particulars that I thought was needful for me to write of. In it was inclosed a bill for 50£ charged upon Mr Welsted. If that letter came not to your hands (for I perceive it must /pass\ through many before it come to yours) I pray write to Mr Welsted or his Agent, not to pay any money but by your order. I am not a little troubled in my thoughts (& so shall be untill I hear from you again) because of what you write concerning your countreymans sickness. The sickness, God be praised, in these parts, is not worse than it was a fortnight since. We think the D{uke} of York may come into this countrey but have no other ground but our own conjecture. The fanaticks are this day serviced because of a plott spoken of: & so much the D. adviseth.[581] I pray remember in your next to send your directions about the Chancery business: for the time Sept. 12 draws on.[582]

Your humble servant
G.D.

Addressed as L. **70**.

74 **7 December 1665**
H. 3785, f. 55
G.D. to W.S. from Durham

Durham Castle Dec. 7 1665.

Mr Dean; although you write not to us: yet, I beleeve, you may be willing to hear from us. Therefore in the first place, God be praised, we are all well. And I do not < > hear that any place either in the county or Diocese is infected with the pestilence. (We have gotten you no more money. But Newbottle tith is expected this week. And Bridgets fortnight (which Capt. Newton desired for her) will be out

581 Perhaps the aftermath of the Derwentdale Plot: L. **52**. Serviced: serving of a writ to those who had been involved: *OED*. D = Dean of Durham?

582 Chancery business: L. **72**. The case seems to have concerned debts owed (perhaps by Mr Smith) for the letting of tithes and glebe land in Houghton parish.

this week /& he tells me the next week the money shall be paid.\[583] Whether any prebendall money comes in I know not: the Audit is ended, & the Prebendarys are going.[584] Dr Smith is gone, having left his service for you.[585] The same Mris Shuttleworth sends by letter. Mr Smith told me on Sunday last, he would be with me this week. If he be, he doth a little deceive me: but if he brings money he deceives me more. I doubt we must have more law: but then you have the shorter cutt. I am perswaded an Attachment may serve your turn. But I doubt I must do my successors business throughly. I have gotten almost all my moneys due this Martinmass; (his & Mr Aytons excepted) but debts still pinches me. I'le build leasurably in the spring: & finish the inside of what I have done as I see occasion. In my last, I think, I told you, that Smith was paid about 14£ & skints for boards & nails /etc.\ about 18£ & Shacklock must have about 33£ when all is done. /Jo. Rowell had 5£ for flagging the kitchen.\ I know not how much Mr Wrench hath paid /Shacklock\: but I think Shacklock hath little to do but laying the boards, which are ready plained, but not nailed down. Langstaff tells me he fears the hall chimney will smoak. Green hath had no more money: about halfe the glass is up.[586] Some lime is brought in for plaistering in the spring but we want wood for lathes: for which I call in vain. {p. 2} Mr Wrench begins residence to morrow. Mr Wood is to succeed at Heighington & with Mris Wildbore would be tenant of your corn tith there.[587] I told him Mr Wrench onely had to do in it & perhaps might have set it already.[588] But indeed I think he might be no ill tenant; for the minister, if anybody, will get the tith of those who will pay, & those who do, will rail sufficiently upon those who refuse. If you have heard of Sir Robert Gayer of late: I pray let me

583 Perhaps Bridget Ayre, mentioned in records of Bishop Cosin's Survey of 1662 as a tenant at Ryhope: DUL, Sharpe MS 167, ff. 130, 131. Captain Newton may be mentioned in *Cosin Corr.* II, pp. 311, 333, 343.

584 The financial year of Durham cathedral ran from Michaelmas to Michaelmas. The audit was in November, after which the dividend was distributed. There are no audit books for this period.

585 Thomas Smith held the fourth stall in Durham cathedral 1661–8: Musset, pp. 14, 36; *ODNB*.

586 Green: a glazier: LL. **76–78**, **82–83**; *North Country Diaries*, SS 124, p. 148 records the death of 'old Nicholas Green a glasier' on 30 December 1699.

587 John Wood, successor to Wrench: Surtees, *Durham*, III, p. 307. Mistress Wildbore: L. **72**.

588 A reference to Wrench supervising the preparation and sowing of his part of the open field.

know. For I hear nothing, though I wrote to him. I suppose < > you do not think of removing to London before the spring at the soonest: & that you will have your house cleansed again and again. I should be glad to hear that the bill of 50£ upon /Mr\ Welsted was paid to you. Mr Wrench speaks as though he meant to write to you: but neither you, nor I, nor he can tell whether he will or not. I am

Your humble servant,
G.D.

We say my Lady Burton is with child. And Mris Gerard hath had another son since her husbands death.[589] My Lady Gerard is at Windsor; where she hath another son also. Thus, < > God be praised, my Lords family increaseth. Mris Grenvyl is well, but childless.

I do not < > hear: second 'not' erased; I suppose < > you do: 'to do' erased.

75 **12 December 1665**
H. 3785, f. 61
G.D. to W.S. from Durham

Durham Dec. 12. 1665.

Sir; I wrote to you by the Friday post & now do it again, because yesterday Mr Ayton paid Mr Wrench 06£ and I was fain to promise him to write you to know whether you would abate him anything of the remainder. I told him there was no reason you should: & he may easily ghess at your answer. I write this at Kepier where I am come to baptize a daughter of Sir Nich. Cole.[590] In my way I met Capt. Newton, & he told me he had this morning paid Mr Wrench the 30£ & taken up the bond.[591] I was not present, & so said nothing of what else you may expect from Bridget: nor was I willing /to name it\ before the bond was discharged: but now I intend to speak of it. This all the occasion of this present from

Your humble servant,
G.D.

589 For Cosin's family see Introduction, pp. 13–14.
590 Sir Nicholas Cole, of Brancepeth castle. Created a baronet in 1640. His sons were Ralph (second baronet) and Thomas, who died at Brancepeth 13 October 1694: *Cosin Corr.* II, pp. xxxvii, 210n; *North Country Diaries*, SS 124, p. 179, for his death July 1701.
591 Capt. Newton: L. **76**.

76 **9 January 1666**

H. 3785, f. 71

G.D. to W.S. from Durham

Durham Castle Jan. 9. 1665.

Mr Dean; Since July 26 I have but one letter from you dated Oct.6. Mine, I trust, have come safe to your hands. In my last I acquainted you, that Bridgett had paid the 30£ to Mr Wrench, & in a former that Mr Ayton had paid to him 6 I remember. Since that time I know of {no} money paid from our parish, saving that last week Bridget paid, (that is abated out money due for oats) Mr Dobson 04.01.03. due to you for May-Day rent 1664. & also 40s for surplus fees & Easter book. But this money he hath not yet paid to Mr Wrench. I </deducted\> nothing </out of\> his salary at Christmas towards that debt. The other money due </from Newbottle & Herringtons &\> for last years rent, is not paid, though often promised, though I assure my selfe in very good hands. Some that had their tithes have not yet paid those who were your tenants.[592] Your house stands still at present: but lime is bringing in for playstering. But I find it very troublesom to get lathes. Green plays the knave, & I have threatened to sue him upon his bond. So soon as the season will serve, all things shall be hastened. Mr Wrench talks daily of writing to you. But I think doth not. He makes me beleeve he hath a great deal of money for you. But what I must {p. 2} not know, least I should be acquainted with dividends & chapter secrets. He is now at Bolden. Capt. Newton and Mr Dobson assure me that Bridget hath paid more /money\ than ever she received of Johns, that is more than the inventory did amount to.[593] If so, you see, in what case you are as to other accounts with Jo. Ph{ilpot}. Cocken is now sold to Mr Ra{lph} Carre of Newcastle;[594] but whether we shall get arrears of tith is doubtfull. He that sold it is still in the gaole.
I long to hear from you, or of {you} & so do many here.

Your humble servant,

G.D.

---

592 A reference to the subletting of the tithes.

593 John's: Bridget's deceased husband presumably.

594 On 14 May 1662 and 18 December 1665 the whole Cocken estate, except its coal mines, was first mortgaged and then sold to Ralph Carr of Newcastle. 'He that sold it' (Francis Carr, esq.) was of a different branch of the family: A.W. Purdue, *Merchants and Gentry in North East England, 1650–1830. The Carrs and the Ellisons*, Sunderland 1999, pp. 13, 27; Surtees, *Durham*, I, 208–9, for pedigree; pp. 206–7. For the transactions; *North Country Diaries*, SS 124, p. 179n, and below, L. **82**.

Address: For the Reverend Dr William Sancroft, Dean of St Paul's London. To be left with Mr Steven Bing at his house in Knight-Riders Street or with Mr Almond at the Dean of Canterburyes house in Pauls Backhouse, London.[595] 3

</deducted\> nothing </out of\>: 'abated,' 'in' erased.

77 **23 January 1666**
H. 3785, f. 82
G.D. to W.S. from Durham

Durham Castle. Jan. 23. 1665.

Sir; the business of this is to convey the inclosed, which tells of money sent for the poor of London, though the plague is again at Gateside, & this county hath been taxed about 250£ for that place & others that have been infected. Last night dyed Anth{ony} Pearson, after a lingering sickness of five moneths.[596] He declared his constancy as to our church to me very largly before his wife: & desired me to send for his children, & that they might be confirmed in the religion in which I had baptised them. Mr Stapylton is like to be Auditor.[597] My Lord remembers him kindly to you: & would be glad to hear from you. I can say nothing of your businesses since my last on Friday: only the glasier hath promised to be with me this day. I am going with my Lord to dine at Dr Basire's residence.[598] In hast, I rest

Your humble servant,
G.D.

Address: For the Reverend Dr William Sancroft, Dean of St Pauls London.
To be left with Dr Berwick at his house in Angel Court near St Gregoryes church in St Pauls Churchyard. London. 1s

595 George Almond, formerly of Emmanuel College, B.A. in 1638: *Al. Cant.*
596 Anthony Pearson, under-sheriff of Durham: *Cosin Corr.* II, p. 316n for his previous radical history in the Derwentdale Plot. He had been a Quaker.
597 Stapylton was auditor for Cosin, *Stapylton Corr.*, p. 135n.
598 Isaac Basire (1608–76): Introduction, p. 24.

78 **27 January 1666**
T. 45.58
G.D. to W.S.

Jan. 27. 1665.

Sir, Mine and my wife's true love to you remembered. This is to let you understand that I received youre university letter the last night. But why should you be amused at my marrying a Lady. A man may affect a Lady as well as a woman of worse quality, & love where there is money as well as where there is none. Now for the gloves you mention, I fear this countrey will not afford such as I would have for you. I know the measure of your hand, but then again I know not whether ribbons or fringe would best become them, that is I know not the fashion. I should fancy wrought gloves best; but I remember we used to call those Presbyterian gloves. But the true reason of the name was because other ministers could not go to the price of them. Mr Wrench knows not how to advise herin. Besides he gave me none at his wedding: & therefore /by the way\ I need not give him any now. Do you think that Mr Dean of Lincoln would accept of a pair, & send me my bill that lies with him?[599] I pray do not acquaint him with the news, least you spoil a composition. Mr Thriscross hath heard the news at York, & sends joy hither but perhaps his talk may not be heard at Lincoln. My brother knows not of it, I dare say: & therefore will not reveal it: but your discretion may be trusted in all things by

Your humble servant
G.D.

I had thought to have ended here: but one thing I would speak off, if you would not take it amiss. You know my house will not be habitable this summer. But I hope yours will by the end of the spring. And if you come not down this summer I hope my wife < > & family may have your leave to abide therin / for as yet I want an house & a fire to put her head in.\ Wee bring you good security to do harm. Fires would be comfortable to the house.

But {p. 2} another postscript must follow. For reading the premisses I perceive I have not told you the womans name, which thing is enough

599 Michael Honeywood (1596–1681), Dean of Lincoln 1660–81: Le Neve, *Fasti, IX: Lincoln*, p. 7; L. **30**. Gifts of gloves were made to those attending weddings or funerals.

with some to say matrimony makes men mad. But I had rather acknowledg my error than write this over again.

Know ye therefore, in all earnestness, that I am neither marryd nor about to marry: but verily think I am as /good as\ marryed that is, better than married. How these reports are raised about me I cannot imagine. Almost every week I am likened (as they call it here) to one body or other, widows old & young, maidens rich & poor, fair & foul.[600] And yet for all this here is never a Gentleman in this countrey will sell me an horse at day of marriage. I was once about to buy the D{ea}n of Litchfields coach & three horses to be paid for at that day, but he flew off.[601] Indeed honest brother Ralph sold me both his horses on such an account.[602] But reporting for one, the next day, I (like a conscientious fool as I was called) let him have it again (though I told him plainly I gave him an horse out of my purse) & the other I keep, & he is our trooper. What luck had I had, if my Lady Henley & other Ladyes of my acquaintance had sent my wife presents of napery for smocks & gaugets or such fine matters?[603] Keep this matter to yourselfe & let them beleeve the former news, & if you can perswade them to send the wife any presents, you shall go halves. It might easily be efforded, if they did but know that it is the custom of this countrey. I could promise, if they would do it, to laugh at them all the days of my life.

After all this lost labor I am glad to hear that my Lord of Canterbury is so well recovered (God preserve his life) & that the sickness is abated to you the last week.[604] I wrote to you by the post on Tuesday & in it sent one from my Lord who is very well: but voyded a stone that night, & kept his chamber two days after it. If you go to London I must desire you to speak with Mr Mundy about my matter. I never had an account from him.[605] I left 1£ with Mr Dyer & 5£ Mr Mundy had of Mr Martin.[606] I must gratify Mr Mundy for his pains: but I would first learn how accounts stand. I have had 28£ in Mr Royston hand for a moneth past to be paid for my 2^{d} payment of first fruits: but the office

---

600 'Likened' is noted as a Durham usage in the sixteenth century: *OED*.

601 Thomas Wood, canon of the eleventh stall, Dean of Lichfield 1663: Mussett, p. 87.

602 Perhap Cosin's brother-in-law, Ralph Blakiston (1608–77), rector of Ryton (1660–77): *Cosin Corr.* II, p.27n.

603 gaugets: gorget-collar or other adornment for the throat: *OED*.

604 Gilbert Sheldon, Archbishop of Canterbury 1663–77.

605 Mr Mundy: L. **71**.

606 Mr Martin: probably a stationer at 3 Nuns in Cheapside: L. **79**. Dyer may be a proctor in the Arches: L. **81**.

was not </open\> untill of late, if it be now.[607] How do you charge about your first fruits of York? I have chidden Mr Green this morning & put him into some fear. He hath promised mee on Munday morning with another man to begin again your work & never to leave off untill it be finished.

Address: For the Reverend Dr. William Sancroft, Dean of St Pauls To be left with Dr Berwick in Angel Court over against St Gregorys church. London. 3

</open\>: 'held' erased.

79 **7 February 1666**
H. 3785, f. 121
G.D. to W.S. from Durham

Durham Castle Shrove Tuesday 1665.

Mr Dean: My soreness is over (for I preached for you on Sunday last) & so will yours of the court also, by that time this comes to your hands. As yet no return can be gotten for the 200£ though I make daily enquiry, unless I would pay 4d per pound, or allow 3 moneths time for payment, which is the worse proposition of the twain. I will enquire further; & no delay shall be in mee. I have taken the bonds for Houghton Parish due at Mayday last into my hands, & on Sunday next will be rough with your creditors. I told you in my last how Newbottle /tith\ was paid; that is all but 08.10.04. which I must pay out of Mr Dobson's salary /at Ladyday\. I can get no wood for laths of the Chapter: who will not cutt down until the bark run, which will be about St George's day:[608] though I offer to pay Mr Duncon the price of the bark.[609] But further consideration of it is promised. Green hath brought in some more glass & promiseth daily progress. If we had glass & lathes all the rest might soon be done. For floors are laid, partitions made & almost all the doors.

I am
Your humble servant
G.Davenport.

607 Royston: L. **19**. First Fruits: L. **59**.

608 The felling of timber on Dean and Chapter land needed Chapter approval. St George's Day was 23 April.

609 Edmund Duncon, keeper of Bearpark: *North Country Diaries*, SS 124, p. 126.

I know not what to do about your Herrington business. Richmond with the Gaolers leave is not to be found here: but at Heighington. So that no answer at present can be given about him.

About 5 weeks since I sent a bill to Mr Martin of 41.12.07. charged by my brother on Mr Welsted. And though I have sent 3 letters to Mr Martin, as yet I have no answer, which doth amuse me. I pray do me so much favour as to send a servant to him at the 3 Nuns in Chepeside, & know whether he hath the bill: for I fear it may by lost, or come into an ill hand: & then I hope he will stopp payment at Mr Welsteds, if it be not too late. Pardon this trouble: for I have no friend at London (Mr Paybody & all his family being dead of the plague) to do this for me.[610] What becomes of R.Beaumont & George Meddon?[611]

Address: For the Reverend Dr William Sancroft, Dean of St Pauls at his house in Angel Court, St Pauls Churchyard, London. 3

80 **8 February 1666**
H. 3785, f. 94
G.D. to W.S. from Durham

Durham Castle Feb. 8 1665.

Mr Dean;

Yours of the 2d I received the last night, when my Lord & Mr Wrench received your others. For that of mine of Jan. 18 not yet come to you, you should enquire after it of Mr Bing or Mr Almond, for to them it was directed:[612] yours of the 20th Jan. first bidding me to direct mine to Dr Berwick. In it among other things (for it was very large) I told you, that I needed not money here at present. Because Lady Day next would pay my debts, & put something in my purse for other building. Besides I know not how to return my brothers money again, if I should make use of it. Therefore there is no thought of returning your money the way that you then, & now again propose. I have indeed taken 30£ of your money of Mr Wrench; but I will repay it to him at any time upon a days warning: for I have good credit. Yet if you please to make any use of what money Mr Welsted hath of my brother, you may freely command it, & deliver in his bond. I told you long since, now the plague increased, that he desired you in kindness to take it into your hand: but then you was gone into the countrey. You

610 Paybody: died 15 October 1665: L. **63**.
611 George Meddon: L. **55**.
612 Stephen Bing: L. **72**. George Almond: L. **76**.

may do it now, if you please (when the same occasion is not) & pay it again to my brother when you think good and I am sure he will be well pleased. In the last letter I told you, that Mr Ayten had the day before at Herrington paid me all he owed to you, & that Mris Smith had also paid me 5£ for you: both which sums I had then paid to Mr Wrench for you. I said also Richmond's surety was fled & that now he proffers, if he may have his liberty, to give a good surety, one Garth, to pay 4£ per annum for 5 years & Mr Morland & Mr Crosby who know the man advise to take it.[613] I wrote to you to know the resolution: & now desire it again. I said also in that, or another letter, that the 04–01–03 due from Bridget for the May Day Glebe 64 was stopped by Mr Dobson who owed her money for oats, & also 2£ more /stopt\ for surpliss fees. The Chapter owes him money, & if they would pay it, Mr Wrench is to receive so much out of it for you. It was before this {I} think, that I said Bridget had paid more for John Philpot, than she received: so that now the 30£ is paid, I know not how you /can\ expect any thing more from her, who hath not assets in her hand. In this letter I also asked whether Dr Berwick & you, would be at charge of setting up his brother & your arms in painted glass in my new hall. If you would, I would set up also my Lord's & mine own. All the rest I have forgotten. The marriage I perceive is off: at least is < > put off until April, which is as great a riddle as the former unto mee: My Lord may be glad to hear the report of his own death. {p. 2} I cannot but think, had Mr Dean of Westminster & you (poor < > man I pity you) when you spake concerning the marriage, said, there is an honest fellow lost.[614] Mr Wrench tells me he can return 200£ to you: and I have spoken to Mr Steward to find out a speedy return if he can, & he is looking for one for himselfe.[615] My Lord is very well. I am sorry it goes so ill with you about York Deanery: but I pray, how speeds Dr Berwick about Houghton? For I am more afraid of those bonds, than those that were entered for the Deanery at York. For they may levy the first fruits upon the place.[616] I am glad that the pestilence hath made so considerable an abatement: God in mercy put a period to it. We long

613 Richmond: tenant imprisoned for debt: L. **79**. Mr Crosby may be Nicholas, attorney at law, of St Nicholas parish, Durham, who died February 1694: *North Country Diaries*, SS 124, p. 136.

614 John Dolben, Dean of Westminster 1662–83: *ODNB*. The marriage is probably Davenport's.

615 Steward: a reference to Cosin's steward?

616 First Fruits: L. **59**. John Barwick held Houghton from 1645 to 1660/1.

for the letters this evening, which will tell us what the bill of mortality amounts unto. Commending you to Gods protection. I rest

Your humble servant

G.D.

My service to Dr Berwick & his wife. I am in hope of hearing of a return for your money to morrow by one Mr Sanderson a justice of Bernard Castle.[617]

is < > put off: 'not to' erased.

81 **20 February 1666**

H. 3785, f. 112

G.D. to W.S. from Durham

Durham Castle Febr. 20 1665.

Mr Dean;

Yours I received yesterday at Houghton. At which time I got your Newbottle tenants to me: it so happened that Mr Dobson was in debt to some of them 08.06.08 & so they paid the rest, & I promised to pay that & to get them their bond from Mr Wrench who went on Saturday to Bolden, & from thence yesterday to Newcastle. I thought this was the best way, & not to delay any longer. So that assoon as the quarter /is\ ended I will both abate < > Mr Dobson & pay you. For the 06£-01s-03d (for /Bridget's\ rent </at Mayday\> & 04.01.03 & surplice fees 02£) it is still in his hand. And Dr Dalton tells me they will pay but halfe a years augmentation to him; that is from the time of his incumbency & not from the last incumbent's death.[618] Besides the Dean tells me, he shall not hold the living unless he resides upon it. When I reckened with Mr Dobson at < > Michaelmass, I abated 2£ for you, as I had done 5£ before at Midsummer. But after all this I know not what he owes upon the old account: I sent the copy to you, & have none myselfe. The 5£ was accounted /to you\ with the 45£ that < > I had of Mr Wrench, & the 50£ you now receive of Mr Welsted (as your last saith, though that of Jan. 13. saith you had then received it the

617 Sanderson: unidentified.

618 By a letter of 7 August 1660 Charles II instructed bishops and deans and chapters to augment poor vicarages up to a value of £70 per annum, using fines from new leases if necessary for the purpose: *CSP, Dom. 1660–61*, p. 183; Chapter Acts, 3 November 1660, DCM, DCD B/AA/4. Thomas Dalton was rector of Berwick in Elmet, Yorks., and of Dallam in Ely diocese: Hutchinson, *Durham*, II, p. 188.

week before; the mistake is not materiall) is in lieu thereof. The other 2£ remains in my hand: & I would fain know what I owe you as to fee or fees given < > at Doctors Commons for us all,[619] in our case, or to Mr Turner or otherwise: for you owe me above 4£ about our Chancery suit: & 19s 04 1/2d for an old < > assessment in 63 to the Assize House; & the 5 ½ part of a fortnight's pay to our trooper since I wrote last.[620] I again desire that when Mr Mundy comes to London you would cause him to get the procters bill for me, (Mr Dier is his name) & see it discharged.[621] I left 1£ in </Mr Dier's\> hand, or 2£ but I think but 1£, & 5£ < > Mr Mundy hath had of Mr Martin. I think I had best give Mr Mundy 1£ besides the payment of the Proctors bill, out of which I suppose he hath some advantage {p. 2} or if you think good, give him more on my account. I know not that I have anything more to do in the Arches in this case.[622] I have a copy of the sentence. And if an exemplification be needfull, that will concern you & Dr Berwick for whose indemnity it is, & not me. And surely I think you may do well to look for that. Yesterday I spake with Mr Wm. Smith who saith he is providing for the discharge of the debt to you. He said nothing of what he owes me. There is some hope of getting the 10£ due to you from Cocken for I have affrighted the tenants, & the new purchaser resolves to make good that a prescription is there, & will rather pay for 4 years past, than loose it, especially seeing he can pay himselfe with purchase money still in his hand. I think if he paid me for one year I durst not refuse it (& that was Mr Turner's advice to me:) but if bustling will do the matter, I will get all the 4 years. You are about to pay the York firstfruits: another man would let the Deanery be sequestered for them. And I am perswaded they < > would never sue me, so long as York is between them & me. It was an unfortunate Deanery to you. But your Advocates advice is better than mine. As yet we cannot fix upon a return for 200£ for you. We will do it as soon as we can. I will now enquire & look after

619 Doctor's Commons, the London organisation for practitioners of Civil Law set up in the 1490s.

620 Presumably Militia Money, levied by the Militia Act of 1662: Chandaman, *English Public Revenue*, p. 327.

621 A notary public called Alexander Dyer acted in the Court of Arches at this time: *Cases in the Court of Arches, 1660–1913*, ed. J. Houston, British Record Society 85 (1972), nos 2945, 2947.

622 Two cases were brought by Davenport in an attempt to obtain tithe payments from his period as rector of West Cheap: Davenport v. Hinde 1663 (*Court of Arches*, no. 2569), Davenport v. Towell 1663 (*Court of Arches*, no. 2571).

Richmonds business: but I wonder that he should never look after me, since he made the proposition.

Your humble servant,

Geo. Davenport.

Abate < > Mr Dobson: 'him' erased; in </Mr Diers\> hand: 'his' erased; 5£ < > Mr Mundy: 'he hath' erased; they < > would: 'will' erased.

82 **16 March 1666**

H. 3785, f. 141

G.D. to W.S. from Durham

Durham Castle Mar. 16. 1665.

Mr Dean; a letter of yours of the 3d hath layn 10 dayes upon my hand, (which is not usuall) & therefore I write, though to your small satisfaction. I come now from your house (where I was with Mr Wrench, who is your servant) where we find Shacklocks work done, as we suppose: & to morrow we are like to pay & discharge him. The plaisterer is putting on the borrowed laithes, which we must repay, when we have wood given us for lathes. And the next week he begins to plaister. We have agreed for 2s 6d to have the house cleansed in order to his work. But oh the glazier, Green, I beleeve, hath wrought out the 5£: but is like to do no more. For we will not trust him with money, & he hath none to buy glass. And one whispers to me, that this last week his goods were extended. I offred the same rate to another to finish his work: & he (though he dwells in the town) will not do it unless he may be paid for painting the windows above the 6d per foot. I sent an Awkland glazier to view it: & he never came to me again. What shall we do? We say, if we cannot get it done according to the rate agreed to by Green; we must give more. Others comfort us, & say it is best to glaze after plaistering. Richmond it is said will come to town tomorrow. I met yesterday at Houghton your Herrington tith-man & he saith, the next week he will pay his bond of 10£ 10s. I wish the curat hath no money in it. Mr Smith I see not. Your chancery work must on. The week before Easter is the sitting: & if you give no directions, I must be advised by your counsail. The tax for the Assize House was laid on by the Jury & Judg when you preached the assize sermon: & most of it paid whilest you were /Rector\ at Houghton. And you must not fare the better for /Mr Dobson's\ delay in payment /of it for you\: so that the 19s is clearly yours. Every one in the countrey hath paid it. I pray, remember Mr Mundy. {p. 2} On Munday next the end of /my\ dining room & parler & as far as to the corner /eastward\ goes down in order to better building. The next week the chancell will be flagged: & in a fortnight after, all the walls plaistered & all the walls round it wainscoted; most of the work being already wrought.

You know that with our /Houghton\ School an almshouse for 3 poor people was founded. These were to have a penny a day apiece. But forsamuch as we want maintenance for many /& most\ years we have /had\ no almspeople, but mortmain enough.[623] Now for less than 10£[624] this almshouse might be endowed, the allowance for all 3 being /yearly\ about 4£ 10s. If Sir R.G. hath not disposed of the money he spoke of, </perhaps\> by your perswasion, he might part with so much. For considering we have mortmain & governors & statutes, no almshouse can be cheaper founded. There is an house too, by the churchyard, as I remember. But mention this, or let it alone, as you shall think best. I confess, I prefer the place where I am before all others and this was my mind when I was in Chepeside. Think a little seriously of it, if it be a feisable matter: if otherwise, let it be as if not said. My Lord is well.

I had like to have forgotten the Cocken < > matter. Mr Carre in the Jail saith he will pay nothing for tithes.[625] The tenants are affraid. And to encourage the fear, I have ordered Mr Dobson to take their names. But in earnest, if I go to law, I see not how I can recover any more than myne own 03.06.8.[626] I hope fear will work with them, or if that will not, that then Mr Carre, who hath bought, will pay all arrears, that so he may make good the prescription. I will handle the matter as wisely as I can: & to tell you true, take somthing rather than nothing, & nothing we are like to have, unless either the purchaser or tenants pay us. For though Cocken be sold, Mr Carr is likely still to be a prisoner. With my service to all friends, I rest

Your humble servant

G.D.

---

623 For Kepier School: Ramsey, 'Kepier Grammar School', passim; *VCH, Durham*, I, pp. 393–6; Surtees, *Durham*, I, p. 162. The house was probably that bought by Gilpin. Mortmain: lands or tenements granted to be held inalienably by an ecclesiastical or other corporation were free from taxation but the king had to be paid for the privilege: *OED*.

624 Second 0 possibly deleted.

625 Francis Carre of Cocken, gentleman, younger brother of Ralph Carr (who had died): R.E. Carr, *The History of the Family of Carr of Dunston Hill, County Durham*, 3 vols, London 1893–9, I, p. 125 for pedigree; *Records of the Committee for Compounding*, SS 111, p. 147. A relative had bought him out, presumably because of his debts: L. **76**.

626 What was owed to G.D., rather than W.S.

Another matter (the worst of all) had likely to have been omitted. We are as farr from getting a return < > for the 200£ as we were a month since. The money is ready at an hours warning. But we can get no one to return it. I daily lay out: & we will take the first opportunity. I wish a speedy one.

</perhaps\>: 'but' erased; return < >: second 'return' erased.

83 **24 March 1666**
H. 3785, f. 149
G.D. to W.S. from Durham

Durham Castle Mar. 24. 1665.

Mr Dean; I have now agreed with an Aukland glazier for glazing the remainder of your house, and this morning he hath taken measure of the windows & will forthwith go about them. But after they are wrought, they must lie in cement for a month. Green, I think, hath set up asmuch work as will come to 5£. He hath had no money of Mr Wrench. His goods & instruments are seised on by an execution /by one of whom he bought his glass.\ No glazier I could meet with, (but this man I now employ) would glaze it for the rate agreed to by Green. The hall, parler, dining room, & 2 chamber </eastward\> are glazed all but the casements: & most of them plaistered. This afternoon a man comes with straw to stopp the windows < > towards the garden < >: & then the plaistering works will on apace. It is not possible, in my judgments that the stable can be endured under the parler. I remember Dr Daltons hall smells basely in summer time when the hay is heated, & that is over the stable & flagged with stone. Therefore, I think your vaulted room must be preserved /for stable & hayroom:\ which I would do thus (& Shacklock applauds me for my invention). I would pave it over with < > pebbles (as a bridge is) & leave on each side a channell for descent of water, & then at the further end have the stairs down to the garden. This is a small cost: & the wood that is above it will pay the charge twice over, as I reckon. But then on the end adioyning on your hall, I would make a tofall, which will be a small charge: for /I\ do not see where both men & maids /(servants)\ can conveniently lodge as the house now is.[627] Mr Wrench saith the same thing with me: & do you consider & resolve. When this /old\ house goes down, I would be a chapman for the boards that lay under the

627 Tofall = a lean-to building: *OED*.

lead, if they be found good enough to lay under lead again, & that you have no use of them & at present I < > foresee none.[628] For having said this of your house, I have but a sad story to tell of mine own. On Munday last I began to pull down the end of the parler southward & the wall adjoyning eastward. When I had laid the top a little open, I found the chimney of the parler, & the room next the dining room in wretched state & took them down. This made a way under the roof that covers the last named room /the < > stoned hall betwixt the parlers\: & there I found the slates hung upon rotten lathes without pins; insomuch that I took all that down from the dining room eastward. Then forasmuch as the dining room /wall\ < > westward was to go down, (because in decay & for building of two chimneys,) I uncovered it, & then seeing but little left, I ordered the taking down the length of that whole building also from south to north, the kitchen chimney, & the bredth of the old larder (which larder stands untill next year) excepted. And most of this is already done. So that now there stands nothing of the old house, but the chapell & parler /adjoyning\ with the room over it: & the old larder east of the kitchen. I intend to make the kitchen one yard shorter, that so the timber may rest on the walls north & south, which formerly it did not do & to cutt /shorter\ < > the other building that runs east from the parler to the garden by 6 yards, & so to make one low chamber next the parler, & another above it /to the dining room.\ The kitchen, parler, dining room, to be as they were before; & all this I hope to have covered with lead < > by Michaelmass, if I so long live. Lead is about 12£ per fodder:[629] & if the warre continue it will be cheaper: and I have timber enough.[630] But boards are scarce. If I should /build\ a part of the house this year, & another next, it would not < > bee< > so firm, as now it is like to bee: which puts me upon {p. 2} this resolution: of which, I hope I shall never repent. And if I do not repent: I think the successor will have no cause to do so. Within a week I trust to lay the foundation. I have this day sent a citation against 7 Cocken tenants /for last year's tithes.\[631] They are to appear on Friday next. I hope this will < > affright them & make them pay what they owe you. If it doth not work this, I loose my design: for I am told they would gladly pay me. The men can

628 Chapman = a man whose business is buying and selling: *OED*.
629 A fodder or fother was a measure (19½ hundredweight) of lead or coal etc.: *OED*.
630 The Dutch War: Introduction, pp. 22–23.
631 citation = a summons to appear in a law court: *OED*.

secure themselves out of their rent. I will use all the witt I have in this affair. Richmond was with me this morning. And now he saith, his security is one Rich{ard} White of Redworth.[632] We must send to enquire of him. And he, he tells me, had rather pay the < > money in two years; & so would have us to take two eight pound yearly. I offer to take 2 9£. In this I will consider with Mr Wrench, & enquire of the ability of the man. The return of your money is in as bad case as formerly. Neither Mr Wrench, nor I, can yet find out a way; but the money is ready. I wrote to you on Friday last was </a\> week. I desired you to use your interest with Sir Robert Gayer for getting money for </Houghton\> hospitall /lost for want of maintenance.\ I remember he told me the money was at your disposall. This he said when I last saw him. If the nature of the guift would bear it, & this might be done at your prosecution, there would /bee\ 100£ (or what you please) for you at London & I might take it here of Mr Wrench. I am not without hope that you can, & will say <u>fiat</u> to it.[633] Remember you was once parson there. The work is good: & seriously I know not how the money can be better disposed off. But this I mean if it /(or all of it)\ be not already condemned for impropriations.

If the Cocken tenants come to me, I shall be unwilling to compound unless </all the 4 years\> be paid.[634] If they come into the court, Mr Wrench is to tell them, that the like sute he is to have /with\ them for you. This course, we hope, will operate upon them. If not, I am to try the purchaser, whom I have already told, that he will find no prescription, & therefore he had best < > to pay for 4 years past, < > if he means to maintain a prescription, for which he pretends a chancery decree, but saith he hath it not, nor any of the old writings as yet.[635] My Lord is not altogether so well as he useth to be. And I am sure he is not fit for a London journey, so that I hope he will easily be excused this parliament. I am sure the cause is reall, & no pretence: & that such a journey would be with perill of his life though I see no danger at all, if he stay at home. In your ear be it spoken, it is a kind of rupture or some such matter, but secrecy, I pray, to all people /whomsoever.\ I have no desire to see you at London this year: (& to speak truly I am affraid of coming there where the infection hath so

632 Redworth near Heighington. Two Whites were freeholders there in 1685 as were two Richmonds: Surtees, *Durham*, III, pp. 307–8.

633 Fiat = let it be done.

634 Compound: to settle a debt by partial payment or by a lump sum. *OED*.

635 Prescription: an ancient custom regarded as authoritative. *OED*.

raged) & I have but small hope of seeing you here. God Almighty assuage the contagion; that we may have a thankgiving after so many fasts.[636] The Dean preached the first fast day; & this day he hath sent me word that, in course, the next falls to your lott, which I will provide for. Are you at law yet with the D{ea}n of York?[637] And have you paid your first fruits as you said you must do ? There is too much trouble for you for once. God almighty keep you.

Your humble servant

G.D.

Mar. 25 I am now going to my cure, & I hope to find your East & Middle Herrington tith ready

Towards the garden < >: 'with straw' erased; I < > foresee: 'can' erased; /wall\ < > westward: 'eastward' erased; it would not < > bee< >: 'have' 'n' erased; pay the < > money: 'two years' erased.

84 **30 March 1666**

H. 3785, f. 155

G.D. to W.S. from Durham

Durham Castle. Mar. 30. 66.

Sir;

Yesterday I was at West Herrington /with commissioners\ who set out land for the securityes of 8£ per annum for Glebe. There I gott 09£ 10s for the tithes of E{ast} & Middle Herrington due at Mayday /last to you\: there is yet an arrear of 1£ for which I keep the bond. This morning most of the Cocken tenants appeared /in consistory\ & said their /old\ Landlord bad them to pay my year's tith: I said I would compound for all the 4 years.[638] At length they agreed to pay all charges forth with: & amongst themselves to raise 13.06.08 for the payment of

636 National fasts ordained by Parliament, intended to show penitence and obtain divine mercy in time of trouble or rejoicing. They had been numerous since 1660, and especially 1665, when there had been three (5April, 4 July in the provinces, 2 August in the provinces): *British State Prayers, Fasts and Thanksgivings and Days of Prayer, 1540s–1950s*, ed. P.A. Williamson, S.J.C. Taylor, N. Mears and A. Raffe, Church of England Record Society (forthcoming), reference nos 1655-E1, E2, E3. Information supplied by Dr N. Mears, one of the investigators of the AHRC project on British State Prayers, Fasts and Thanksgivings.

637 Robert Hitch, Dean 1664–77, successor to Sancroft: Le Neve, *Fasti, IV: York Diocese*, p. 6. At issue were dilapidation payments for the Deanery of York.

638 Consistory: i.e. the tenants appeared in the bishop's ecclesiastical court.

you & mee. The difficulty is some have been tenants but 2 or 3 or 1 year: & they are to pay you but proportionably, /they must speedily & are to pay at Whitsuntide.\ What order will you give about Mr Smith? The Chancery sitting is Apr{il} 9 and you are more concerned a great deal than I am. </Mr Smith's\> mother is at London.

I go this afternoon with Mr Wrench to view the corps by the town: /part\ which the tenant is paring & burning without leave, as I am told.[639] I am sorry to tell you, that the D{ean} & Chapter have refused to confirm 2 or 3 concurrent leases to my Lord though the K{ing} hath required them to do it by letter, which my Lord Chanc{ellor} procured & My Lord Cant{erbury} consented to, & helped forward: and they themselves had said that if either of the K{ing} or Lords mentioned would signify their pleasure to this effect it should be done.[640] I think nothing but an act of Parl{iament} can hold them: and truly the matter is not worth all the stirre hath been already. For it will be but a triffle though they be confirmed from year to year as the letter requireth. I heard this day from Sir Andrew Henley, with whom Sir Robert Gayer & his Lady were the day before the date. In much hast that I may not miss the post.

Your humble servant,
G.D.

</Mr Smith's\>: 'his' erased.

85 **31 March 1666**
H. 3785, f. 157
G.D. to W.S. from Durham

Durham Castle. Mar. 31 1666.

Mr Dean: I wrote to you by the Post yesterday: and in the afternoon Mr Wrench & I & a skillfull husbandman went to Relly, where we found your tenant Pleasington paring 5 acres & not more (though I

639 Pare and burn: the custom of cutting the turf to a depth of two or three inches and burning it to provide ash for manure: *OED*. Corps: the lands assigned to each prebendal stall were known as 'corps' and the tithes as its 'by-corps'. Sancroft held the ninth stall (1662–74), which carried with it the corps of Amners (or Almoner's) Barns, Relly and the tithe of Heighington and Thickley: *Durham Cathedral Statutes*, p. 121 and appendix p. 249; Introduction, p. 20.

640 Lord Chancellor of the diocese of Durham, Francis Goodricke, MP for Aldborough, who in 1666 chaired the committee allowing Cosin to lease his lead mines to Humphrey Wharton for three lives: *HPC*, II, p. 410; L. **67**. My Lord of Canterbury: Gilbert Sheldon.

was told 12). This man in his articles hath liberty to pare & burn so much, & so hath the other < > Kirkley. But in Kirkley's articles the place is to be assigned by you, & no such thing in Pleasingtons. No new articles have been /made\ since Michaelmass; & the tenants say, you told them, you would not put them off, & Mr Wrench examining the papers left with him by you, finds he hath not power to let. < > At adventure, we appointed the tenants to be at church on Wednesday & after sermon to seal bonds for the former rent, & we must engage they shall have the land untill Michaelmass.

This afternoon I got my Lord to go from church to your house, & showed him the design with which I acquainted you in my last but one; he consents it shall be done as I proposed. But by all means, he would have you to make a porch to the hall door towards the College; for he saith a portall will not be sufficient to keep out wind & the charge will not be much. (Dr Nayler hath neither porch nor portall).

Another thing I have to say, which I forgott yesterday (though it was principall matter I intended): my Lord wants money /at present\ & borrows about 600£ that he may furnish the K{ing} with 1000£ (its lent upon the tax)[641] I have agreed with Mr Steward to pay him 200£ here, on condition he, /my Lord,\ shall pay you so much at London by July 1st /or sooner:\ & this bargain is to hold, unless you contradict it by the Post that comes from /London\ on Thursday next, & will be here on Palm-Sunday. By that Post, I pray, let us know your intention, as to Mr Smith & your house. This is the surest way, (& the spediest too) that I can find for return of your money.

{p. 2} Your plaistering goes on. And the casements are sent this afternoon to the glazier to be coloured, & fitted with glass. I hope by midsummer you /will\ have an habitable house. Mr Grenvyl is gott to London; & there his complaint is against my Lord, out of whom, as he saith, he hopes to squeeze some money.[642] My Lord answers with good reason, when he deserves a portion he will give one. However he hath provided for his daughter, if her father die. Keep this to yourselfe. But if you meet him, I pray, chide him & send him home. But that, I doubt, is more than you can do. I think you have 40 fodder of coals due to you from Renton pitt, for it was a going colliery for two

---

641 'Loans' on the security of tax yielded 6%: Hutton, *The Restoration*, pp. 234, 241.

642 Denis Grenville or Granville, at this time prebendary of the first stall and Archdeacon of Durham, married to Anne Cosin: Introduction, p. 14; *ODNB*; Granville, *The Remains of Denis Granville, Dean of Durham*, ed. G. Ornsby, SS 47 (1865), pp. 2–10.

of your three years: & you had but once 40 fodder of coals. I will enquire, & demand them, if they can be gotten.[643] I am glad to hear that there is so considerable decrease in the plague the last week.[644] Within a month we are for Aukland: and about that time my Lady Gerrard is expected. This County is about < > to advance a whole yeare together before hand for his majestys service.[645] Particular persons lend the money (as my Lord 1000£ & the Dean 500£) & receive it again of the countrey: they pay it quarterly. I am for Houghton in the morning; & therefore it is time to bid you a good night. Doth Shadwell stick still?[646]

Your humble servant,
G.D.

power to let. < >: 'it' erased; is about < > 'a whole' erased.

86 **13 April 1666**
H. 3785, f. 163
G.D. to W.S. from Durham

Good Friday 1666 Durham.

Mr Dean; Yours of the 5th instant I have, & return this briefe answer (for the bells are ready to toll, & I am to preach being desired to it the last night) The Chancellor is gone away to day; & yesterday he decreed an attachment against Mr Smith & Mris Smith, unless we be paid before Penticost: & also that the tithes shall be hereafter secured by land, as the glebe is. The glass for your house is made. Mr Wrench & I will take care for pulling down, & then for making up, at your house. I have notes for about 10£ of Cocken tithes to be paid at Penticost. Your tenants have given bonds for Relly; & they are in Mr Wrench's hand. The D{ean} & Chapter, upon further consideration of his Majestyes

643 Rainton coal tithes: LL. **95** and **109**. For Rainton, Surtees, *Durham*, I, pp. 210–11.

644 This is true only for London but was premature elsewhere: Shrewbury, *History of Bubonic Plague*, pp. 484–5.

645 Reference to the loan to the king.

646 Sancroft and Thomas Neale endowed St Paul's, Shadwell, as a new parish, carved out of Stepney. Shadwell was part of the estate of the Dean of St Paul's, recovered after the Restoration. Neale was already involved as a builder, for instance of its chapel from 1656. The bill for creating a new parish was submitted to Parliament by Neale and Sancroft together, though the parish was not set up until 1671: M. Power, 'Shadwell: the Development of a London Suburban Community in the Seventeenth Century', *The London Journal* 4/1 (1978), pp. 28–46, esp. 42; D'Oyley, *Life of William Sancroft*, I, pp. 148–9.

letters have sealed the leases & all is well. I am sorry I was too late about Sir R.Gayer's money. If ever herafter you know how to help us, I pray remember us. Your 200£ is ordered to your steward. My Lord pays it here to the K{ing's} Receiver Generall: & must return about Penticost, a larger summ to London, & in it yours must be included. I will look after the repayment. What you say of Shadwell I cannot understand. But I wish you be not cheated. Your words are so doubtfull that I fear. My Lord is not very well; & hath kept his chamber for almost 10 days. Onely yesterday he came to dinner. In great hast,

Your humble servant,

G.D.

My new house is /in\ building up. I pray let your servant enquire < > what becomes of Mr Paybodys goods,[647] for as I remember, he had my brothers new Lexicon in his hand, if nothing else. This at leisure.

87 **21 April 1666**

H. 3785, f. 165

G.D. to W.S. from Durham

Durham Castle Apr. 21. 1666.

Mr Dean; I wrote to you on Friday sennight past; & have little to add to what I then wrote in hast. This day I gave instructions to Mr Jackson for drawing up the act to be passed for pulling down the old house adioyning on your new one.[648] Mr Smith said both you & I should be paid at Pentecost. I[f] he should /intend to\ be as good as his word, & then demand what power either Mr Wrench or I had to receive his money & discharge him, we could not answer him. Therefore I think you had best to make a letter of Atturney either to him or me, & to do the same for Cocken tithes. I hear nothing more of Richmond.[649] Yesterday I had a letter from my brother, who desires you to keep the bond at present. If the danger encrease he will take further order, I beleeve, to get away his money. He saith also he wisheth you could help him to another living; for his lawsuits have almost tired him out of this, though he still gets the better.[650] I have sent him word, that most of the

647 Paybody: L. **63**.

648 Gabriel Jackson was a Durham proctor in 1688: *North Country Diaries*, SS 124, p. 121.

649 Richmond: L. **83**.

650 Brother's lawsuits: L. **54**, **103**.

livings in the disposall of you & the Chapter of St Paul's are in London (where he cares not to be) & the rest are commonly small, & that the Prebendarys, which are many, expect to be first served. But if on occasion you should know how to help him, I said, I beleeved, you would. Your 200£ is paid to the steward: & I think Mr Steward delivered Mr Wrench a bond for it this day. My Lord is not yet well: but was yesterday on the place-green to set out ground for an almshouse for the building of which he hath contracted with workmen.[651] Had he been well, he tells me he meant to have preached at Houghton tomorrow: //(I wonder where he meant to have dined) but since he cannot, I hope I shall. My new building is raised about 2 yds. high & yesterday I contracted for 6 fodder of lead for 60£. I paid the last year 83£ for the like quantity. Mr Wrench (who of all the Preb{endarys} is the sole Residentiary) presents his service to you. Your humble servant, G.D.//

88 **4 May 1666**
T. 45.75
G.D. to W.S. from Durham

May 4. 1666. Durham.

Mr Dean; Yours of the 28 of April /& the letter of Atturney\ I have. First I am glad my fear is over as to Shadwell. Next, I wonder whether you should < > resolve to bestow livings onely upon those that have none already. Mean you to plant churches with novices? I am apt to think, you mean, such as have /livings\ that they mean to keep; & that is not the case of him I mentioned. But enough of that. Your act is passed before my Lord for taking down the old building to the arch: & the carpenters are about the work. And truly I mean to take you at your word about preemption of what will not be used there. The old boards prove rotten, & the new not very fitt: but /of\ such as they are, if they be not used about the house, Mr Wrench means to have < > some & I to have others. 50 or 60 I think are the number /of what are usefull.\ I took another carpenter thither today, who values all the timber at 20£. We will make as much of it as we can. I intend to buy some to make a new screen /& folding doors & finishings\ betwixt the church & chancell at Houghton, & to make pillasters for a staircase,

651 The modern Palace Green between Durham cathedral and castle where the almshouses still stand. For the almshouses: *VCH, Durham*, III, p. 142.

which should be of old seasoned wood. And for this purpose the studds of this house are very good. The beams & wall plates & sparres which will not be used again may serve my purpose also /seing I make a leaded roofe as that of yours was:\ for </which\> if I have them, you shall be honestly paid. And perhaps better than by the College, who as Mr Wrench saith, said that if the materialls would serve for any building about the College, they would allow something for them. But I believe some, perhaps, the greatest part, will not like of paying money out of the treasury for timber, as long as Beare Park will afford it for nothing.[652] However, if they will have any, I will raise the price as much as I can, by bidding. They do not so pretend that this timber belongs to them: & when the price is laid out in other materialls for building, I am sure they cannot complain if it be sold. I did not intend that you should trouble yourself so much /about\ Paybodye.[653] I think he had nothing in his hand but the 1 vol. of /the Oriental lexicon for\ my brother < >.[654] And this makes me inquisitive about </the edition of the 2nd vol.\> I think I left Dr Castells note for the 6 2^{d} vollumes (when printed) with you, tyed in a green sattin ribband. The Dr told me he hoped to have them finished by Xtmas last: but I fear the plague obstructed that work. You left not sufficient authority with Mr Wrench for the purpose for which I desired the letter of Atturney. As for preaching here you need not to come untill Aug. 26. For last Sunday I preached for Mr Wrench, on condition he should preach for you the 27th instant, when we are like to be {in} Aukland. I was yesterday at Houghton. Most of my new building is up to the floor: & the building where the drick stood < > at the bottom of the kitchen is cast down & its foundation is to be laid to morrow: nothing now remains but the kitchen chimney, chappel & room adjoyning of the old house.[655] I trust to have it all covered with lead by Michaelmass Day. I pray if you hear any good news of likelyhood of peace, send it with speed;[656] that so I may buy what lead I want, whiles it is at 10£ the fodder. But if the warre continue 6 months, I beleeve 8£ will be a good price here. {p. 2} If I can possibly, I will perswade my Lord that no toofall may be built to your house (& the

652 Bearpark was the chief source of timber for the Dean and Chapter: L. **91**.

653 Paybody: L. **63**.

654 Edmund Castell, *Lexicon*: LL. **20**, **101**.

655 Drick = decayed part of timber: *OED*.

656 For the Anglo-Dutch campaigns at this time: Hutton, *The Restoration*, pp. 241–2.

act is drawen simply for the taking down without any mention of building) for it will cost money, & not be handsome either within or without, & as you think of little use. The old walls above the arch shall suddenly down & paving stones shall be provided.

Richmonds bondsman hath appointed to morrow sennight for his coming. I like not his delay. But the Jailor saith he came one day when I was at Houghton. In the mean time I tell the Jaylor it is at his perill if Richmond go abroad. I can add no more than what I have formerly said in other letters: for I have gotten no more money. Mr Wrench has Mr Arden & Mr Stapyltons bond for your 200£.[657] My Lord is not yet got abroad, but now & then walks into the air & was once abroad in his coatch. I pray let me hear how Sir Robt. Gayer & his relations do in your next. I never heard from him since I saw him. My service to him & to all my friends.

Yr humble servant
G.D.

Address: For the Reverend Dr William Sancroft Dean of St Pauls at his house in St Pauls Churchyard, London. 3

to have < > some: 'for' erased; to make < > a new: 'the' erased; for my brother < >: 'Lexicon' erased; stood < > at the bottom: 'on the back' erased

89 **11 May 1666**
H. 3785, f. 181
G.D. to W.S. from Durham

Durham Castle May 11. 1666.

Mr Dean;

I have this /day\ written to my brother desiring him to send order to Mr Welsted to pay you 41£ upon his account for my use. This if he do, I shall desire you to pay my 3d payment of the first fruits due June 1 and to send me the bond cancelled, and the other 13£ to pay to Mr Royston (& about two or three shillings more which I will repay you) & to take of him a generall discharge & to send it me. I am this bold, because I have none else to trouble at London in this affair: and I make the greater hast < > lest the sickness should drive you out of

657 Edward Arden was steward to Cosin and then to Crewe, to whom he was perhaps related. Died 17 August 1695. He may also be the person referred to as 'Mr Steward': *Cosin Corr.* II, p. 332; *North Country Diaries*, SS 124, p. 139; Surtees, *Durham*, I, appendix, pp. clxiii–xv; LL. **85**, **87**.

the city. This morning I paid to Mr Wrench the fourty shillings that Mr Dobson paid to me for you at Michaelmass, & I received a bill of him as followeth:

An assessment for the assize house made 1663 & pd. by every one of the countrey (but neglected by Mr Dobson)	00.19.04 ½
5th part of 36s being a fortnight pay to the trooper 1665	00.07.00
Chancery Sute	
Halfe 50s paid to Mr Barkas 1665[658]	01.05.00
Halfe 40s to Mr Turner & his man then	01.00.00
Halfe 20s to him < > Septem. 12.65.	00.10.00
Halfe 03.06.06 to Mr Mickleton Nov.6.	01.13.03
Halfe 20s to Mr Turner Apr. 9. 1666	00.10.00
Halfe 38s. 6d. to Mr Barkas then	00.19.03.
Half 20s. to Mr Mickleton	00.10.00
Halfe 8s to Clerks for writing & serving subpoenas	00.04.00.
Halfe 4s for serving subpoenas & making affidavit	02.02.00
	07.19.16 ½

What concerned my selfe alone (as /did\ the commission) I paid. I paid also to Mr Wrench 30£ which I borrowed /of him\ upon my note Febr.1. Of your money as /then I\ < > reckoned: but he never placing the loan to your account, received it as his own money. But I am indebted to you for the tith of Newbottle {p. 2} 21.05.00 & for E. & Middle Herrington 09.10.00. which I have received, & 1£ is still in arrear. Two other bonds (besides Philpots or now Bridgets of 2£.04.06) that is Tho. Rutters, on which is due 03.01.08. & Jam. Wild 02.05.02, I have, & am promised < > the money speedily, & then I will pay that & what I owe you to Mr Wrench.

We went to your house </this morning\> & every one is for a tofall but myselfe. The timber will pay for it: but that money I think may be spared. The walls /round about\ will be down, I think, low enough to morrow night. Advise what we shall do in it. Mr Wrench goes to Bolden tomorrow. Dr Basire went to Eggscliff this day & next week calls upon Dr Neil for London:[659] & < > no Prebendary will be in the College. My

658 George Barkas, attorney at law, clerk to every mayor of Durham during his career, notary public, died 31 March 1690: *North Country Diaries*, SS 124, p. 124: *Cosin Corr.* II, p. 239. Note his gift of a book to Davenport, no. 50 in G.D.'s catalogue, Appendix I below.

659 Dr John Neil (1635–75), canon of the third stall in Durham cathedral 1645–75, Dean of Ripon: Mussett, p. 26.

house goes on apace; God send it well up. My Lord was abroad in the Coatch yesterday: & is pretty well. My service to all my friends.

Your humble servant,

G.D.

hast < > lest: 'because' erased; to him < > sep: 'in' erased; </this morning\>: 'again' erased.

90 **14 May 1666**

H. 3785, f. 187

G.D. to W.S. from Durham

Durham May 14. 1666.

Mr Dean; on Saturday last Richmond came to me & told me that now no one will be bound with </him.\>[660] But he paid me 40s in part of his bond (a little is better than none) which I paid presently to Mr Wrench. To him also I paid the 21£ 05s 00d. for Newbottle tithes < > due a year since & 03£ 01s 08d which I received on Sunday from Mr Dobson for Tho. Rutter being the relikes of his bond for Houghton tith. Jam.Wild arrear & Joh. Philpots is still unpaid. The last I mistrust. Herrington bond I have, but onely 1£ is arreared: the other 09£ 10s I have. I think besides these little will be had, but what comes from Mr Smith, Mr Carre & Mr Dobson. I could abate no more of his stipend for you this quarter, because he owed one of my tenants more than is due to him & he desired abatement /in rent\ from me.

Now we are like to have a tofall again. For Shacklock & Rowell say, a building was always intended there, & upon that presumption they left the old wall /of the hall\ standing, < > in which the hall chimney & dining room chimney are carryed up, & that the wall is not most secure without it, </and that\> it will /be\ as good a buttress against it. The best is, I think it will not cost much. You are like to be in the end of this month 7 Prebendarys besides the Dean at London. I beleeve you will meet & order some business. I pray propose to them the giving me 2 trees out of Beaupark towards the building of my house (I think I have deserved them in sermons but must not say so for many wherof I had no thanks nor pay.) Sir Nich. Cole hath given me 4 & my Lord hath given me 2.[661] If I could get them, I intend them for wainscoat for my dining room. Mr Wrench tells me they will not be

660 … no one will be bound with him: i.e. no one will be his surety. See also L. **88**.

661 Sir Nicolas Cole: L. **75**.

denyed by the Chapter. My Lord is now going to the place green to lay the foundation of his hospitall for 8 almsfolk, for which work he is to {p. 2} pay above 300£. From thence he goes to church, where no prebendary will be found. In hast, for he calls me.

Your humble servant,
G.D.

</him\>: 'me' erased; standing < >: 'to the hall' erased.

91 **19 May 1666**
T. 45.80
G.D. to W.S. from Durham Castle

Durham Castle May 19. 66.

Mr Dean; I wrote to you by the Tuesday post & have little to add now. Mr Wrench is gone to Bolden < > this day, & from thence he came on < > Thursday, having left his wife making cheesecakes.[662] On Munday Shacklock & Jo. Rowell go /to him\ about reparations, & there is great likelyhood his fingers will be in morter speedily. Dr Grey is come to preach to morrow & I beleeve may stay untill Mr Wrench returns on Friday.[663] In absence of the Prebendarys my Lord went to church daily, & on Tuesday next purposeth to remove to Aukland. This evening I have had paviers to view the vault, who will pave it for about 20s (I mean for workmanship) & perhaps 30s more will pay for sand & stones. The tofall is up almost to the eves: & the cost will be little besides slates. The plaisterers are again at work. And if Mr Wrench will but call apace upon the workmen three weeks time might finish almost all your work. The flaggs upon the vault, I purpose to translate into your cellars & passage. And on Munday I mean to speak to Jo. Rowell for a door-sted for the vault. I have /now\ gotten 3 trees of my Lord for my house & chancell. I pray use all lawful ways to perswade the D{ean} & Chapter to give me 2 out of Beau Park. Mr Wrench & Dr Grey are willing: & I hope none at London will gainsay. My Lord hath urged the two above named in my behalfe. Mr Rich. Berwick tells me that his brother Dr told me if I could get the Cocken tithes due for a year to his brother, the poor of the parish should have

662 Richard Wrench had married Ann Baddelay, 16 August 1664: *Durham Cathedral Registers*, p. 37.

663 Robert Grey, son of Sir Ralph Grey of Chillingham, Northumberland, prebendary of the eighth stall 1660–1704. B.A. Cambridge, 1627/8, and D.D. 1660: Mussett, p. 66; *Al. Cant.*

the money.[664] I remember it not: but he told me he meant when he got what </arrears were\> due to give somewhat to them. I pray present my service & ask. But I have little hope to get any thing, but by law, & then I must have a letter of atturney {p. 2} to enable me to sue for the poor, & perhaps some composition may be had. But if they must be sued for the Drs use, the letter of atturney had better be made to Mr Nicholas or to a Proctor.[665] Dr Basire went from < > Eggesclyff towards York on Thursday & meant to stay at York untill Munday; & then to set foreward with Dr Neil for London. The painter hath been at work all this week in my chancell; & I hope will finish his work the next week. On Munday my masons begin to work again upon the house, and if I can but borrow money, I hope to give /a good\ account of my work at Michaelmas, if God lend me life: but wo to my * * {heirs} if I see not that day, unless God /send\ a mercyfull successor.[666] I am very desirous to be the author of a good parsonage house there. I wish we might have your company here this summer but I have little hopes thereof. My service to Mr Dean & all the Prebendarys you see. If my brother send a note for 41£ charged upon Mr Welsted, I pray, pay /28 for\ my first fruits & pay 13£ to Mr Royston. I am not sure that I mentioned this in my last letter, as I designed. I go to Houghton in the morning to take leave, having a chapell to look after at Aukland on Sundays.

Yr humble servant

G.D.

Address. For the Reverend Dr William Sancroft Dean of St Pauls at his house in St Pauls churchyard, London. 3.

Bolden < >: 'from' erased; < > Thursday: 'Wed' erased; </arrears were\>: 'was' erased; from < > Eggesclyff: 'Stanhope' erased.

92 **25 May 1666**

H. 3785, f. 205

G.D. to W.S. from Bp. Aukland

Aukland Castle. May 25.

Mr Dean; this day I received yours of the 22. And by good chance, I found the act you desire, here amongst my papers, which I transcribed

---

664 Mr Richard Berwick, brother of Dr John Barwick. The latter had been rector of Houghton 1645: Surtees, *Durham*, I, p. 157.

665 Nicholas: unidentified.

666 For Davenport's further views on this, see L. **134**.

forthwith, & send inclosed. I marvail at the neglect: but is not your Proctor to blame? I had a letter this day from Mr Mundy, who saith I need /not\ to trouble my selfe with an exemplification forasmuch as I have an authentick copy of the Record. I mean to write to him to deliver to you my libell, & the tax of dilapidations (for I know not to what use they should be in my Proctor's hand) & I think it were not amiss that the certificates I gave to Dr Barwick about the great kitchen & barn were also in my hands, though I could, if need required, procure others. My Lord is pretty well; but he did ill brook the Coatch in his remove hither. He is at chapell daily morning & evening. I think I may truly say but in your ear Mr G{renvyl} causeth as much trouble to him as all infirmityes.[667] For my Lord is tyred with letters there are so many from him & others, & all say he will give his daughter no portion. He hath put forth 1000£ < > for her use in trustees names some years since, & the profit goes on < > for her and in his will, hath given her as good a part as any of her sisters, at least as two of them. And this is thought to be nothing. What reason hath he to give a portion to one who can make no settlement upon her? & when he said once to me she should have one in Cornwall, he also said, it was to be for her life onely after his, & then I said it was not worth 3 years purchase. Besides it is almost 400 miles from this place, & was to be upon a person's lands who he confessed did not pay an annuity to him as he should.[668] Alas what then could a poor wife expect after his death? I wish heartily you could devise some way to make him sensible of his error, & to send him home. It grieves /me\ to hear that he speaks of squeezing money out of my Lord & of jerks in letters to him from his friends, & of his breaking my Lord's sleep.[669] Unruly words at best. Besides his wife is famed for a madwoman in letters which he sees before my Lord receive them. And if I was examined upon my oath, I think, I should say, she hath the most discretion of the twain. It is not a time to speak to my Lord about the 50£ which he hath set down in his will for Imman[uel] Chapell. He is desirous to buy 100£ per annum for scholarships in Peter house & Caius College: & to endow his new hospitall with 60£ or 70£ per annum. Some other good works he hath in design. But at present he is bare of money, having borrowed above 500£.

I thank you for your care about my first fruits & Mr Royston. I did not expect my brother Jo[hn] should write so soon to you. He is none

667 Denis Granville: Introduction, p. 14.

668 Kilkhampton, in north-east Cornwall: Introduction, p. 14.

669 jerks = fooling: *OED*.

of the Hastings. You ask so many questions about him that I cannot tell what to answer, save that, I am confident he is not for a London living, & I beleeve, not for one neer it. I have now bought 10 fodder of lead for 100£. But you may better ghess at the price than mee. For the price will be regulated by the warr or peace.[670] And if the warr continue this summer, I beleeve 8£ a fodder will be a good price. Bridget is able enough: but it is said she hath not assetts in her hands. I long to hear from Sir Rob. Gayer. To morrow morning I intend for Houghton, & /in my return in the afternoon\ to call at Durham upon Mr Wrench, as he desired, about the carrying on of your work. And then, if I have time, I may adde a post script. And so goodnight.

Your humble servant

.....

{p. 2} from Mr Wrenches House. May 26.
Sir; I have been at Houghton, & am thus farr in my return. There I received Bridgets answer that she would not pay, by reason she had not assetts. But then I also learned, that John died the same moneth that he entered upon his lease, & that Bridget let the land to about 03£ 10s advantage, & received the money.[671] So I desired one to tell her, that if she paid not before this day sennight she should be sued at law. I have paid this day to Mr Wrench 09£ 10s for E. & Middle Herrington tiths.The other 20s the tenant owes, but I have the bond. Jam. Wild owes somewhat. And more is not owing (besides what is above specifyed) of all that Mr Wrench & I let for you. The carpenters are putting on the roofe of the toofall to which end one of your dormants is saved.[672] Lathes are brought in for almost all your wood.

1000£ < >: 'in h' erased.

93 **1 June 1666**
H. 3785, f. 219
G.D. to W.S. from Bp. Aukland

Aukland Castle. Jun. 1. 1666.

Mr Dean; Yours of the 22th I answered as to the greatest part of it. Since I have received another in which was Roystons receipt for which I thank you. And this day I received yours of the 29 of May.

670 Reference to the progress of the Dutch War. See Introduction, pp. 22–23.
671 John Ayres?
672 Dormants = dormer windows.

For Mr Forsters business, I have read his letter to my Lord, who remembers nothing of him.[673] But when I had read what you said & /had\ told him of the Samaritan & Coptick copyes, & also of the Mss. Hebrew bible in Jesus Coll{ege} without points, cited in the mentioned sermon at St Mary's,[674] he bad me tell you: that he knows not whether he shall make 3 or 4 or 5 scholarships at Caius College; and that these he designed for lads born at Norwich & < > bred at that school, yet for your & Mr Foster's sake he means to dispense with his intention & to make his son of the number, so soon as they are established. But if he have so many children as he mentions, he had not need to commend his relict to a speciall friend for a wife. For Mr Thrisscross; my Lord saith he speaks too late. The last week my Lord wrote to my Lord of Man & the money will be speedily sent to him.[675] For our J{ohn}, < > his living was worth about 170£ per annum. But I beleeve is not that value at present. I do not beleeve that any exchange can be made, though the patroness be his wives sister.[676] And so farr as I can ghess a living of 120 might serve the turn. But I am sure, he will forgive us, if neither you nor I can procure such an one for him. I assure myselfe I could have done it heretofore in this countrey. And so much for the clergy. I was yesterday at Houghton, & called at Durham. Shacklock saith he will finish his part of the toofall tomorrow: and slates lie ready at the door to cover it. The house is almost quite lathed; & lime & hair tempered for the greatest part of it. I have no chapmen yet for your /7\ dormants: for which

---

673 Samuel Forster, rector of Kelling, Norfolk. He was at Caius College, Cambridge, in 1634, Fellow 1644–50. His son, John, was admitted to Caius 31 January 1664/5 and obtained his B.A. 1668/9: *Al. Cant.* G.D. speaks here of Cosin's intention to grant a scholarship to John, though not born in Norwich as the bishop originally specified.

674 The Samaritan Pentateuch which differs from the Massoretic (Jewish) Hebrew Old Testament text and was the only part of the Old Testament accepted by the Samaritan community. Brian Walton included it in his Polyglot Bible, published in 1657: *ODNB*. The New Testament of the Egyptian Church was translated into four dialects of Ancient Egypt: Sahedic, Bohairic, Fayumic and Akhmimic Coptic. The 'points' or symbols indicating the correct pronunciation of the Hebrew Old Testament text when the language was no longer spoken were introduced by the Massoretes or Jewish Grammarians: *ODCC*.

675 Isaac Barrow (1612/13–1680), Bishop of Sodor and Man 1663–76, former Fellow of Peterhouse, was raising subscriptions to improve the education of clergy in the Isle of Man: *ODNB*.

676 J.D.'s wife's sister = ? Ann Thompson, married to John Morden, vicar of Long Sutton 1646–62: *Al. Cant*.

the last year I durst have given 10£ for I found it a great difficulty to {p. 2} get timber of the same length the last summer. And had not Sir Nich{olas} Cole & my Lord helped me, my hall could not have been built < > that year, or if it had, it must not have been so wide. I have chapmen for them that would cut them shorter: but then the price will be as short. So that we will stay the selling for a time. No prebendary can be found at Durham. But Mr Wrench is expected tomorrow, being to preach the next day for Mr Dean. You spoke in your letter of writing to my Lord: and a little before he said, he wondered that you never wrote to him. The Gazet mentions a fast.[677] I wish we receive books in time. We had none the last fast for the navy. So that < > we cannot hope to make use of < > old ones. I pray let us hear before that time /what are\ the psalms & lessons, for fear of the worst. I hopd Mr Dean & the Chapter with him will take care for the Cathedrall. Richmond is not like to put you off, as you suppose. For within a few days, I mean to call him to his hole, & to chide the jailer for his liberty & then perhaps something more may be gotten. But, I fear, you will never have all that he owes you. I owe my brother 130£ but I am not in case to pay debts so that I shall buy no lead for him (I could say I give Mr Wrench as much). Besides, I am told that lead is worth 12 the fodder: though I have bought for 10£. And Mr Wharton hath promised me I shall pay no more for all I use, though it should rise to 20£: & I should use 20 fodder.[678] And more than all this, he will trust me, and as the King's maj{esty} bilmaker said, take myne own bond without either scripp or scroll. I hear nothing from Sir Robt. Gayer but live in hope. My Lady Gerard is on the way towards us: & I think will be here on Tuesday next. I pray remember to write to my Lord. With thanks to you for your care in my affairs, I commend you to Gods protection & rest

Your humble servant
G.D.

We make your staircase to the orchard in the end of the /late\ building

677 The *London Gazette* was two pages 'half a sheet in folio'. Since it had to be licensed its contents had authority: Williams, *History of English Journalism*, pp. 3, 8, 10. The fast would be that ordered on 28 May for 14 June in the provinces, for a blessing on the forces: L. **83**; Williamson et al., *British State Prayers*, code no. 1666-E1. The last fast for the navy may be June 1665: code no. 1665-E2.

678 Humphrey Wharton (or Whayton): *Cosin Corr.* II, p. 237 and Index; *Journals of the House of Lords*, XII, *1666–75*, p. 82, 18 January 1666, a committee concerning lead mines in the Palatinate has a note 'Wharton's lead mines bill'; see also L. **67**.

towards the east corner & Shacklock means an house of office under the highest part of it: the door to be towards the orchard.[679] We presume the ground to be yours (there being a doorsted in the wall) though it lie open to Dr Wood's yard. And Jo. Rowell saith you intended the said house there.

& < > bred: 'bread' erased; J{ohn}, < > his: 'the other' erased; so that < > we cannot: 'it is' erased; of < > old ones: 'our' erased.

94 **19 June 1666**
H. 3785, f. 227
G.D. to W.S. from Aukland

Aukland. Jun. 19. 1666.

Mr Dean; my last answered you that lead will not be had here at 10£ the fodder. I was yesterday at Durham & Houghton. I think it will be the end of the next week, before all your house be plaistered. The tofall is almost slated. Mr Stapylton is gone to Durham to pay the 200£ for you to one that must give a bill upon a merchant at London. This is to be done to morrow; & by the next post, I beleeve, it will be sent to you. Dr Brevint told me yesterday that he will build his Prebendal house this year; & I must give my advice.[680] I did: but for all that, he holds to wooden windows. But he saith it shall be covered with lead: which I was glad to hear; because I had been told, he meant to slate it. The work is not much. Over the hall he means to make a dining room & so the wall must be 6 foot higher, & the roof made flatt, so that halfe the lead will serve. The rest of the house remains as it did; onely a dead wall of the same height for uniformity must be made to it. My rough masons are like to finish there work in a months time. My services to all friends. Col. Tempest I hear is come home out of Lancashire:[681] so that now we are like to know soon what Mr Smith means to do.

Your humble servant, G.D.

---

679 house of office = domestic quarters such as a pantry or privy: *OED*.

680 Daniel Brevint: L. **66**.

681 Col. John Tempest of Old Durham who married Elizabeth daughter of John Heath of Kepier, October 1642. He lived usually at the Ile near Sedgefield: *Cosin Corr.* II, p. xxviii and pp. 155–6. For his gift of books to Davenport see Appendix I, nos 37, 38, 54.

95 **22 June 1666**
H. 3785, f. 232
G.D. to W.S. from Aukland

Aukland Castle Jun. 22. 1666.

Mr Dean;

You have a bill of 200£ drawn for you charged upon Mr Chaplin in Thames – Street, whom you know, which is to be paid to Sir Wm. Turner of whom you are to receive it.[682] This the steward I ghess (for he is not now within) sends this post to Sir Wm. Turner.

Cocken tenants say they will pay soon: but at present want money. For /Mr\ Smith I said in my last < > Coll. Tempest shall be spoken unto so soon as I can go to Durham. He & Jo. Morland are trustees for his estate, which is vested in them. The coals are denyed me (contrary to Haswells promise as I understood him) at Rainton.[683] When Mr Dean comes down I think he must be intreated to threaten him with the bond upon the < > covenants in the lease.[684] If you think good, you may speak of it. Mr Davis lies dangerously ill of a calenture /at Easington\:[685] & as they send us word under a grievous distraction, & bound in his bed. God help him: but we have little hope of his life. I say nothing of the trees now: but I hoped to hear good news before this & I hope still. Within a month the masons will call for the roof of my house, & for money too: and that is the onely circumstance at present needed by

Your humble servant
G.D.

I pray deliver or send the inclosure at leisure.

Address: For the Reverend Dr William Sanroft Dean of St Pauls at his house in St Pauls Church yard, London. 6d

last < > Coll: 'I h' erased; the < > covenant: 'articles' erased.

682 Mr Chaplin: unidentified. Sir Wm. Turner acted as Cosin's banker in London. He was Lord Mayor of London three times and was knighted in 1662. *Cosin Corr.* II, p. 100n; *Stapylton Corr.*, p. 208.

683 G.D. had hoped to receive coal from Rainton: L. **85**.

684 Probably Dean Sudbury.

685 calenture = burning fever: *OED*. Mr Davis: unidentified.

96 **16 July 1666**
H. 3785, f. 234
G.D. to W.S. from Durham

Jul. 16. 1666. Durham.

Mr Dean; I was yesterday at Houghton, & am now in my return towards Aukland. This Durham monk is gone again to Bolden; & cryes your Bolden servant sir. So that I could have no talk with him.[686] The plaisterer is still at work, & like to be so for a fortnight. The door to the stable is putting in, the stone stairs are laying: & the paviers begin not untill Munday next. The entry by your sellars is flagged with the old flaggs, & so is the larder. You may wonder that you here nothing of Mr Smith. If he had not been in Westmoreland I beleeve you had heard of him sooner: and when he returns I know not. I have gotten about 20 load of your coals, & the rest are promised. Mr Dobson saith he owes you but about 5£ or less. (besides the 6£ &c of Bridget which he saith Mr Wrench shall receive of the Chapter at St James tide)[687] & I have not the account or copy of it which I sent to you /but\ I think he saith right.

On Thursday I carry two of your Dormants, & the rigging tree to Houghton, & perhaps some less pieces for the chancell skreen. Shacklock shall value them. I am going to see Dr Basire, who is just now come. On Friday </a\> Dutch privateer new, having betwixt 20 & 30 brass guns was taken upon our coast & is brought into S'Hilds.[688] No more in this hast, but that I am

Your humble servant,
G.D.

97 **3 August 1666**
H. 3785, f. 240
G.D. to W.S. from Bp. Aukland

Aukland Castle Aug. 3. 1666.

Mr Dean; I think the last letter I had from you was about the /Chapter\ wood. I had hoped before this time that we should have heard you had received the 200£ of Chaplin, that so we might take the bond out of Mr Wrenchs hand. The late victory I trust also may

686 Durham monk: Davenport's nick-name for Richard Wrench.
687 St James' tide: Feast of St James – 25 July.
688 S Hilds: South Shields.

draw a letter from /you\: the Post this day, I trust will bring us some particulars.[689] The glazier told me, that this day he would go to Durham with your glass: whither he sent the casements coloured the last week. A door is made into the cellar or stable and it is paved above. But one reason why your work went no faster was because the monk carryed your workmen to Bolden. And now I will lay more blame upon him. The last night Mr Wood & Mris Wildbores man came to me with a letter from Mr Wrench desiring to let your Heighington tithes, which I reckened he had let long since (for I was no way entrusted therin): & the men told a great part of the corn was shorn. At first they alleged many reasons why they should have it for 35£. I told them I would have as much for you this year, as you had before: otherwise I would this day come with a friend to view, & then as I would abate, if I saw cause, so I would also rise if I saw occasion. They feared this friend, & wondered who it should be (& well they might for I knew not whom to take with me) & therefore agreed to pay as formerly, least the < > friend should prove the better chapman. But when wee {p. 2} came to bonds, & I asked for the old one, that so conditions on all side might be seen, Mris Wildbores man said, he was 3 days since with Mr Wrench to pay him the whole last years rent, but the bond was in his curats hand & so Thursday next was appointed to carry the rent to Durham; & then he must give by our agreement his Mris bond for 30£ & Mr Wood must give his bond for 10£. So much for Heighington. For Cocken: the tenants have paid to Mr Dobson /by my appointment\ about 7£ & I beleeve will make it 10£ before they have done. But this is all /at\ present for the 3 years, & my 2 years (I hear nothing of Dr Berwick's gift, Mr Mickleton being yet at London) But I will look out again either after the tenants or after the purchaser, & you shall fare as I do. For Mr Smith, what can I do? He is in Westmoreland or Lancashire, where our attachment is not worth a chipp. His friends say he will be at home ere long: & then have at him. But I fear it. Others say he is about a way to pay all debts: which I should beleeve, if I had not been told it so often. More can I not say, or do not at present. But for his mother, I fear, upon the last decree, it would appear shee < > hath p{ai}d more to you /by about five marks,\ than is due, but less to me by 9£. But I fear her payment of me more than yours.[690] At the Assizes you shall know more about

689 The defeat of the Dutch at sea on 25 July: Hutton, *The Restoration*, p. 244.

690 Five marks: a mark was worth 13s 4d (66p approximately).

your house. I beleeve you will find building chargable aswell as I have done. I shall owe above 400£ at Michaelmass /(when I have to leave building, having done all without & somewhat within)\ but the years profit if I receive it, I trust will pay it all when it comes in: & my comfort is it will be shortly due. If I thought you was a moneyd man I could almost perswade myselfe to ask whether you would lend me 100£ from Martinmass untill May day, when rents will be due to me or my executer. And if you could not, I could find in my heart to ask the favour of Sir Robert Gayer. For borrow of someone I must; or else my house must stand; which I {p. 3} would by no means, though I was sure never to live in it. It will be the greatest work I shall do whilst I live: and is like to justle out some lesser pious works designed by me. My Lord is out of all patience when they talk of my building (for he saith none but fools build without money, & indeed I now begin to be of his mind) & Sir Nich{olas} Cole to mend matter tells him oft, for building he is outgone by none but his own chaplain.[691] But enough of my foolery. Onely, I'll add, I have told many that are new building in this countrey, that they must meet me at the eating of a goose when all is done. For Bridget, I must advise with Mr Mickleton before I sue her. For the rest of your arrears, I carry the note you returned in my pocket: But, in earnest, I know not how to get a penny more than what I have now written about, and there is but hope in all these. I would very fain you had a clear account (I mean clear payment) at Houghton. But I know not how to effect it. For some will never pay, as widow < > Lambton. The 18.05.00 /for tithes\ at May day 1664 (besides the 02.15.00 paid for Penshar) is as great a riddle to me as ever; I know not of whom to ask any part of it.

I should be glad to hear that My Lady Gayer did not miscarry: & if she did that she & her relations are well. I should also be glad that my Lady Henley is the mother of another son or daughter.

Your humble servant,

G.D.

My Lord hath had an ill fitt of the stone the last night.

691 i.e. by George Davenport.

98 **4 August 1666**
T. 45.87
G.D. to W.S. from Aukland

Aukland Castle. Aug. 4. 1666.

Mr Dean; Yesterday after I had sent a letter to you, I received yours about Peloni Almoni.[692] You must not appear and must I. I dare not own any letter from you & should I say, let him write to me, perhaps I could not avoyd the owning of it. I dare deliver any letter: but if a letter be written to me, such an one I mean as I cannot avoyd an answer /to it\, I may, perhaps, be blamed for correspondence. About 6 months since I received a letter by the post as I was in my Lords chamber: in the cover was nothing written, but it contained another /from persons we knew not\ to my Lord, which was construed to be a libell against a Peer of the Realm. The Peer grew angry: & I justifyed myselfe. Why may not the party send a letter the same way? Indeed I would not be engaged to return an answer but I will promise to deliver what comes to my hand. You say he trails a pike: another saith he is aboard the Golden Pellican: a 3^{d} saith he is Mr Grenvyls bedfellow but a 4th saith he is a constant massing priest.[693] All these have been said confidently< > though to deal ingenuously, you (nay any < > of our acquaintance) are as often named in my hearing here, as that party. I can say no more: but leave you to use your discretion. My Lord was at chapell this evening. In hast

Yr humble servant
G.D.

Confidently< > though: 'said' erased; any < > of: 'man' erased.

99 **25 August 1666**
H. 3785, f. 250
G.D. to W.S. from Durham

Aug. 25. 1666. Durham Castle.

Mr Dean; My Lord is this day gone to Aukland, & left me here. Where first my business was to state the account with Mr Smith & his mother:

---

692 Peloni Almoni: Hebrew for 'unknown': Ruth 4.1–2. It seems that Sancroft has had an anonymous letter.

693 Grenville's bedfellow was Anne Cosin; the 'massing priest' perhaps Christopher Davenport (c. 1595–1680), G.D.'s Roman Catholic relative: Introduction, p. 2.

but the latter appeard not. Coll. Tempest & Mr Morland came for the former, & agree that Mr Smith owes us 77£ (& 2£ 10s more, say I, unless he paid you 20£ as they allege from him, whereas I acknowledge but 17£ 10s from you) wherof 22£ is mine (And indeed there was no difficulty about my account).[694] The woman owes you as I ghess (for I have not the payer from the Register who states the account) about 5£. This done, I now stay to preach your course to morrow.

The monk is at Bolden again. The house is not yet finished < > by the plaisterer. The glass is up. 333 foot of new work, & 214 by Green : so that he owes you little or nothing. And now Mr Morecroft son to one of your Predecessors & a Pettycanon, would live in it.[695] And so would Mistress Robinson, (my Lord's late cook's wife who hath onely a maid) and I'll warrant you 20 more. The latter will be ready to leave any time at 6 weeks warning. Do as you think good: but doubtless the house will be the better for an orderly housekeeper; such I take the cooks wife to be. My Lord means to return to the Chancery sitting about a fortnight hence: & not to see Aukland any more this year. Sometimes he talks of going to the Parliament, but I think he is not able to abide the journey. At least I hope I shall not go with him. His nephew Rush a Deacon is here & may do the chaplains work if need be at London.[696] {p. 2} My Lord went to Houghton on Wednesday to see my building: & to my great content (for he threatened so that I was ready to quake by the way) < > liked all the work there & commends < > the Chancell above all the chancells in the countrey: but I excepted Branspeth; and so /I\ returned merrily, /not\ fearing </any\> censure from any of his clergy.

And now, me thinks, I hear you say, that I speak to you, in my letters, more of myne own building, than I do of yours; which is more proper for you to hear. All is true: yet I am not negligent in your affairs: but my absence will not suffer me to /be\ very diligent. And the unhappyness of my seldom meeting with the Monk (let him keep the name) who dotes so much upon Bolden (where he hath been at great

694 Coll. Tempest: L. **94**. Mr Morland: L. **57**.

695 Edward Morecroft, ejected from his living of Monk Hesleden in 1651, was restored in 1660, but later resigned in favour of his son, Edward: *Walker Revised*, p. 143. Edward, the son, was a minor canon, 1665–72, curate of St Margaret's, Durham, and vicar of Monk Hesleden, 1682–1700: Treasurer's Books, DCM, DCD/L/BB/31, ff. 7, 33; ibid. 33, ff. 4, 18.

696 Samuel Rush, nephew of Bishop Cosin, was educated at Emmanuel College. He was buried in Durham cathedral, 10 April 1667: *Al. Cant.*; *Durham Cathedral Registers*, p. 96.

cost upon the house & quire) will in some measure plead for me. There are but two things which I have had in myne eye to have seen effected for you /here\ (& I am not at the end of either of them as yet) the finishing of your house, & making a clear account for all arrears at Houghton. I hope to effect both: & promise at my return to this place, to leave no stone unturned. Coll. Tempest & Mr Morland tell me of < > speedy raising money, or of good security for Mr Smith. I hope the best: but in a doubtfull case know not what to trust unto. I fear Mr Smith must be constrained to sell his land. The small pox is rife in this town: I pray God, it be not the forerunner of an heavyer visitation. Commending you to Gods protection, I take leave, & rest

Your humble servant

G.D.

finished < > by: 'for' erased.

100 **13 October 1666**

H. 3785, f. 256

G.D. to W.S. from Aukland

Aukland Castle Octob. 13. 66.

Mr Dean; I had written to you long before this, had I known how to direct my letter: & I question whether this may meet with you.[697] Mr Scissons can give me no aim.[698] The loss at London I know not how to mention: cura leves locquuntur.[699] I am altogether in the dark concerning a great many particulars about the city. For I never had a letter < > from London (but by letters) since it was burnt, nor had I spoken with any person that was there then or since.

Mr Stapleton brings me word from Durham that the plaistering at your house there is finished: I can not foresee any considerable thing now to be done at it : nor will I do more without your order, rebus sic stantibus.[700] Mr Wrench will not dwell in it, nor will I admitt of any without your direction: and perhaps the Chapter too will have their say in it (but by all means let it be inhabited) which I rather think

697 Sancroft was homeless at this time as a result of the Great Fire of London.

698 Arthur Sisson, the son of Cuthbert, an attorney, was baptised at St Mary-le-Bow, Durham, educated at Durham School, Houghton-le-Spring School and St John's College, Cambridge, where he received his B.A. in 1664: *Al. Cant.*; LL. **101**, **102**, **107**, **110**, **123**.

699 cura leves locquuntur: with anxiety they speak lightly.

700 rebus sic stantibus: with things as they are.

because some of them have complained in Ch{apter} that I disposed of wood in your house, though Mr Dean saith I acquainted him & them with the taking of it down which they liked well.[701] Yet he saith it was ill done not to ask their leave /to dispose of materialls\: though I told them I had Mr Wrench for a President who did the same before me. Then he told me, he thinks the wood would not have < > been denyed you: but they found new timber to build the < > new house & therefore might expect the old one. I answered I thought it was not reasonable, since it was not pulled down at the first: & had they doubted at first, they should have said so, & then the house should have stood, or else been[702] {p. 2} at least have been pulled down, & the rubbish removed at their cost & the act procured by them &c. Besides the price of the materialls are expended in building the toofall, & other reparations. In fine, I think, you do not understand all your Br{ethren} so well as I do. I think I shall at length get 10£ (or almost so much) for you at Cocken: for I have received about 8£ of the ten promised. & Mr Carre that purchased it hath promised 06.13.04. I have </now\> got land at Herrington < > set out for tith as well as glebe: but no money but hopes still. Mris Shuttleworth is this day delivered of a son. Your letter I had out of Suffolk. As yet nothing is done about Mr Scissons matter.[703] Their revision of his father's place was given, & < > the redemption is nothing worth in my opinion. We sometimes say, you may perhaps come & stay at Durham: but we have no other reason but because you have no other house. I pray let me know where you live or lodge. I heard long since that your library & goods were safely conveighed to Fulham. Our fast books came hither late on Munday night.[704] We disposed them by severall messengers as fast we could, & sent to Bawick by the post where they came not soon enough, they are required to keep it on Wednesday next.[705] My Lord is not very well, this weather: it hath rained for 5 days together in good measure. I get nothing from Richmond nor Bridget: but I threaten both. I question whether Mr Wrench hath set your corps for this year:[706] I will write to him about it, least he put it off as he did last year. I have sent Mr Wood

---

701 There is no record of this.

702 Sic.

703 See next letter.

704 The fast books for prayers in response to the Fire, ordered for 10 October: Williamson et al., *British State Prayers*, code no. 1666-E3. This is an insight into how the fasts were organised in the localities: L. **83**.

705 Bawick: Berwick?

706 Corps: L. **84**.

& Mris Wildbores bonds to him. I heard to day from Maj. Aldworth now at Durham that my Lady Gayer is great with child,[707] & all her relations well. I sent to him because I can hear nothing from elsewhere. God have you in his protection & send us a good meeting.

Your humble servant,

G.D.

Address: For the Reverend Dr William Sancroft Dean of St Pauls London. To be left at Mr Geo. Meddon a stationer in Little Britayn unless the messengers at the Post Office know where to leave it. 3 London.

</now\>: 'not' erased; Herrington < > set: 'for tith' erased.

101 **29 October 1666**
T. 45.116
G.D. to W.S. from Bp. Auckland

Aukland Castle. Octob. 29 1666.

Mr Dean I have received your letter, & with it that sad relation of your own loss, with which I am not a little affected. We are this day removing to Durham & then I will acquaint Arther with your letter.[708] The money I have not yet received of my Lord: so farr as I have it, I will make up the account betwixt us, & take the best order to return you your money. I have already sent to my brother about it, & perhaps it may be done that way by Mr Welsted, if he be in ease, as I hope he is, though I hear nothing. I have again spoken to my Lord about Arther for a patent of his fathers place, but as yet have no answer.[709] My Lord remembers him kindly to you, & desires to know from you how Dr Holbech & his wife do, & whether Mr Melsin be alive.[710] I hear that my Lord of Rochester is dead:[711] I would gladly hear of his /good\ works. He lived long Bp of Rochester, & scarce any Bp died in that see since John Fisher; & I hope /Mr\ Dean of Westminster (who, I hear, shall succeed him) will not die Bp of Rochester.[712] As for the Dean of

707 Perhaps Mr Aldworth, an auditor: *Cosin Corr.* II, p. 210; *Stapylton Corr.*, p. 197; L. **109**.

708 Arther Sissons: L. **100**. Now homeless because of the Great Fire.

709 See previous note.

710 Mr Melsin: unidentified.

711 John Warner, Bishop of Rochester 1637–66. Died 21/22 October 1666. John Fisher, Bishop of Rochester 1504–35, executed 22 June 1535: *ODNB*, for both.

712 John Dolben (1625–86), Dean of Westminster 1662–83; Bishop of Rochester 1666–83: *ODNB*.

York, I should think you might do well to get the Kings pardon under the broad seal: & if that will not do get the < > /Deans\ too /under the seal.\[713] If nothing will serve him, but an Irish Bishoprick, let him have it. I speak all this, because I have been told that he hath a very good Deanery house: and such an one as well might content an ingenuous man & good house-keeper. I have been told that dilapidations may be pardoned by the K{ing} & Chancellor Burrell < > is my author.[714]

I begun this letter at Aukland: but must end it /at\ Durham, whither we are now come safe. I have shewed your letter to Arthur, who read it with an heavy heart, but takes it patiently, & much magnifyes your kindness to him, despairing of ever having a like master. If it lie in your way, help him to some good place. I need not have asked it: for I know you will do it /if you can.\ Mr Wrench is at Bolden again. Seldom a week passeth over his head, in which he doth not ride thither & back again. I am heartily glad for the good news you write of my Lady Gayer. My service, I pray, to Sir Tho. Rich & Sir R.Gayer & to both their Ladyes. I pray at all times that you write, let me hear of them: for I expect no letter from Sir Robt. Gayer when I write to him. I heard about a month since from Sir Andrew Henley. In your next I pray let me know where Sir R.G. lodgeth, and whether all things be well with Mr Welsted. {p. 2} I would fain hear that Sion College is safe. The bill of mortality tells us the church adjoyning to it St Alphege stands. I hope Dr Castell & his Lexicons are safe. I never heard of Mr Martin my good friend, in whose house I had some things.[715] Commending you to God's mercy (who is better than ten cityes)[716] I rest

Yr humble servant

G.D.

Address For the Reverend Dr William Sancroft Dean of St Pauls at Mr Benbows house in Maiden Lane in Covent Garden London 3

Burrell < > is: 'told' erased.

---

713 Robert Hitch: L. **83**.

714 Thomas Burrell: L. **55**.

715 Mr Martin: L. **3**.

716 better than ten cities: perhaps an expression of faith based on Psalm 48; or Luke 19.17.

102 **4 December 1666**
T. 45.125
G.D. to W.S. from Durham Castle

Durham Castle Dec 4 1666.

Sir; I have much to say but first I'le vent my displeasure. I wrote to you, desiring to hear on all occasions how Sir Robt. Gayers lady sped with her great belly, & now Mr Scissons tells me from a letter he had from your servant, that you went to Stoke to baptize the child on Friday was a sennight. Whether it was son or daughter I hear not, God bless it; but I have heard nothing from you of it < > though I have been bigg with expectation & now am as full of joy. So the anger is over. The next thing is the baptism of the Jew you commended hither. On St Andrew day Dr Basire christened him in the Cathedrall & Dr Brevint & Mr Grenvyl were the Godfathers & Mistress Basire the Godmother.[717] The office was in English as in the book & the questions for him propounded in Greek (after the English had been first read) & his answers were in Greek, which the Doctor interpreted. His name is Andrew. My Lord confirmed him immediately; & on Sunday he received the Communion. The other Jew baptized by Mr Durell & interpreter to this, is about to return to London.[718] He tells me this Jew is about to set up a coffee house here.

From Jews I come to money. Mr Wrench saith he will shortly make up your accounts. But now again I must not see them. The reason because there is /now this audit\ same dividend & I must not know that secret.[719] For money betwixt you & mee: my brother writes me word that he hath sent you a bill charged on Mr Welsted for 50£ & I pray you again to pay my first-fruits with what hast you can. Mr Kirby hath promised to pay and the rest of the 80£ due from Mr Smith this day (50£ 10s I have already & also 6£ from Mr Morland). I told you in </a\> former that 89 was due; but I concluded for 86 & as I then apprehended the case, would have taken 50£ for all, rather than have lost all, as I feared, we should have done. So that I reckon you must

717 St Andrew's Day: 30 November. *Durham Cathedral Registers*, p. 9 records the baptism of Elias Turvill that day. He took the name Andrew. A Greek by nation, born in Constantinople. Frances Basire was his godmother. Cosin confirmed him and he communicated on 2 December.

718 John Durell (1652–83), a friend of Sancroft, who became canon of the fourth stall in April 1668: *ODNB*.

719 DCM, DCD/B/AA/4, f. 125.

have 54£-6s-8 for that </56£\> & I must have 31£ 13s. 4d. /for 33£\ you abating 5 nobles, & I 4 nobles.[720] I told you that probably you lost 50s before in the Registers account.[721] Your /note\ allows but 17£ 10 /received\ from Mr Smith; he alleged /in Chancery that\ he had 20£. But he was not hend to produce, acquittances, & rather than the Register should not tax it in the time allotted,[722] I chose to let his account pass: because the case seemed desperate {p. 2} and Coll. Tempest & Mr Morland who appeared for him at the {taxation} said (and I beleived them) you would be glad of the residue. What remains due to you from me shall be paid < > to Mr Wrench or as you appoint. Mirs Smith still owes you 6£ & me somewhat more. From Cocken I have received 9£ & Mr Carr promiseth 20 nobles. On Sunday the Dean & Prebendarys & wives & many more dined here. And speaking of your fire-sermon (which none of us yet saw) one in the company said the text was Ezra.4.15 at which we were amazed a little.[723] I said the words were the reproach of the adversarys, which I beleeved you did wipe off. Dr Smith & Dr Neil went away yesterday, leaving their services with me for you.[724] I pray write back & tell us the news from Stoke at large, that I may rejoyce with them.

Your humble servant
G.D.

Address: For the Reverend Dr William Sancroft Dean of St Paul's at Mr Benbows house in Maiden lane in Covent Garden. London 3.

of it < > though: 'from you' erased; </a\>: 'my' erased; </56£\>: '54£' erased; paid < > to: 'as you appoint' erased.

---

720 Noble, originally a gold coin worth 6s 8d (approximately 33p), reissued as a ryal worth 10s, and later as an angel which was discontinued in the reign of Charles II: *OED*.

721 Register's = Registrar.

722 Hend = ready at hand: *OED*.

723 Sancroft preached before the king on 10 October 1666, on *Lex ignea, or the School of Righteousness*, with his text Isaiah 26.9. He asked his contemporaries to look to their own sins and not blame foreigners for the fire: text printed in D'Oyley, *Life of William Sancroft*, II, pp. 355–403; *ODNB*. Ezra 4.15 reads: 'That search may be made in the book of the records of thy fathers: so shalt thou find in the book of the records, and know that this city is a rebellious city, and hurtful unto kings and provinces, and that they have moved sedition within the same of old time: for which cause was this city destroyed' (AV). See also L. **105**.

724 Thomas Smith, canon of the fourth stall in Durham cathedral 1661–8: Mussett, p. 36. John Neil, vicar of Northallerton, canon of the third stall in Durham cathedral 1635–75: Mussett, p. 26.

103 **2 March 1667**
T. 45.153
G.D. to W.S. from Durham Castle

Durham Castle. March 2. 1666.

Mr Dean; Yesterday I received your letter, Mr Wrench being then with me: & I need not tell how wellcome it was to us. I question not but before this, you understand that my Lord of Durham is a living man: and further, I assure you, to my thinking, he is as like to live, as ever he was since I knew him. But what becomes of my Lord of Litchfield I am yet to seek.[725] But his Dean was certainly /marryed\ about Michaelmass last to Sir Jam{es} Clavering's sister, whom he bedded about New Years day.[726] The Prebendarys' wives have not yet seen their new sister. But gulls they raise of their brother, & say that he threatens to lie alone, because the wife putts her arms out of bed, & lets the cold into </it.\>[727] They say in the south, shee is very young: but here it is as confidently said, he hath been a suitor to her for almost 30 years. Perhaps you may report your putting me into a way of getting letters from you. I am < > exceeding glad of what you write concerning Sir Andrew Henley & Sir Rob. Gayer & his relations. I had a letter this week from my brother, who in great merryment tells me, that whilst the < > sisters wept over their dead brother in law one (an Atturney I take it) who marryed one of them & had < > more insight than the rest, made a presentation to my Lord of Lincoln who, without more ado, gave him institution, & he as suddenly had induction.[728] And now the man is not like to be removed, unless the right of presentation was in /the executor\ Mr Thompson of Trompington, as they say it is, all the sisters being not yet at age, & so the Parsonage to which the presentation is appendent being in < > his hand /according to his brother's will.\[729] The best is, our John careth not. And he is the

725 John Hacket (1592–1670), Bishop of Lichfield 1661–70, seriously at odds with his dean, Thomas Wood: *ODNB*.

726 Thomas Wood (1607–92), Dean of Lichfield since 1663. Canon of the eleventh stall in Durham cathedral. He was negligent and quarrelled with Hacket. His wife Grace was the daughter of Sir James Clavering of Axwell Park, Newcastle, whom he had baptised as an infant: *ODNB* under Thomas Wood.

727 Gulls = tricks, deception, fraud: *OED*.

728 Dead brother-in-law = John Morden, husband of Anne Thompson: *Al. Cant.*; L. **93**. Benjamin Lany (1591–67) was Bishop of Lincoln 1663–6: *ODNB*.

729 Mr James Thompson of Trumpington, brother of Anthony, rector of West Rasen (1624) and Sutton St Mary, Lincs. (1637–45): *Al. Cant.*

less carefull, because his adversary hath lately /paid him\ most of the money he recovered in Chancery & now offereth conditions of peace for the future.[730] I wish I had a copy of the account I sent to you < > almost two years since concerning the {p. 2} reckening betwixt Mr Dobson & you. The Chancery sitting here is Apr.2 and then you may hear what will {be} done as to Mistress Smiths arrears & what costs we shall have.

Your most humble servant,

G.D

Address as L. **102**.

</it\>: 'the bed' erased; in < > his hand: 'their' erased; you < > almost: 'about two year' erased.

104 **24 May 1667**

T. 45.192

G.D. to W.S. from Durham Castle

Durham Castle. May 24. 1667.

Mr Dean;

You was taxed here as a Dean to the Poll bill & so were the Deans of Lichfield & Carlisle, & they paid here.[731] It is not questioned, but you paid at London: but the Commissioners say they must either have a certificate that you did so, or else you </are to\> be returned according to the Act, into the Exchequer. They have promised me not to return your name, on condition that I promise to procure a certificate: which I pray send so soon as conveniently you can. Dr Neil is in the same case.

I have nothing more to say, having answered your letter of Apr.30 (which is your last) as fully as I can in three severall letters. On Thursday next we are for Aukland. Hereafter you may direct your letters to me at Aukland to be left at Darlington. I shall have them two hours sooner, & if need require may answer the same day. But mention no Rector of Houghton least they be carryed to Mr March by

730 John Davenport's court case: L. **54**.

731 The Poll Tax of 18 January 1667. People were assessed at their normal residence with a certificate of discharge for property elsewhere. Levied on those not receiving poor relief, in theory it amounted to 1% of the value of their estate: Chandaman, *English Public Revenue*, pp. 146–7, 173 180–81; Parkinson, *Establishment of the Hearth Tax*, pp. 9–10. Dean of Lichfield, Thomas Wood: L. **103**. Dean of Carlisle, Guy Carleton, canon of the twelfth stall in Durham cathedral 1660–85, Dean of Carlisle 1660–72: *ODNB*.

mistake.[732] My service I pray, to Mr Dean of Lincoln, if he {is} still in town: & to Sir Robert Gayer & his Lady & to Sir Tho. Rich. I hear a bill of indictment is found against Sir Andrew Henley as well as against the Ld. St John but I hear not at what price either of them is fined.[733]

Your humble servant
G.D.

//We went yesterday & the day before with the justices viewing the high way by Relly. And 60£ is demanded by workmen to turn the water course not to hurt you.[734] At the sessions we represent it: before the Deanery will undertake to do it.//

Address: For the Reverend Dr William Sancroft Dean of St Pauls at Mr Benbows house in Maiden-lane, Covent Garden, London 3

</are to\>: 'must' erased.

105 **17 June 1667**
T. 45.197
G.D. to W.S. from Bp. Auckland

Aukland Castle Jun. 17 1667.

Mr Dean: to your letter of Jun. 1. I have returned two answers, & the last was as large as confused. I hope they are come to your hands & /are\ in some measure satisfactory. For as for West Herrington, Mrs Smith pd. 3£ that you take no notice of & Jo. Philpot had 5s. more of Mr Aiton than you acknowledg, or else I greatly mistake myselfe.[735] For May day tith 64: 14£ 15s being a moyety of West Herrington (as John let tithes & glebe together) is plainly included in the 21£ arrear, as appears by John Philpots book.[736] To this add the 2.15. which Geo.

---

732 John March, rector of Haughton le Skerne: Hutchinson, *Durham*, III, p. 179; see also *Stapylton Corr.*, p. 225.

733 Ld. St John: Charles Paulet or Powlett (1630–99) of Basing: *ODNB*; *Cosin Corr.* II, p. xxix. The two had come to blows in Westminster Hall. Paulet was pardoned but a prosecution began against Henley in the King's Bench and he was not pardoned until 1668: *HPC*, II, p. 523, under Henley.

734 Under the new foundation the manor of Rilley was assigned to the ninth prebendal stall of the cathedral, which was held by Sancroft. Relly Woods near Langley are at the confluence of the rivers Browney and Deerness.

735 Mr Aiton: Robert Ayton: L. **67**.

736 John is Philpot. Moyety = moiety, half.

Watson p{ai}d for Penshar.[737] & you want only 3£ 10s & who owes that I cannot yet find, nor have I time so much as to go /to\ Houghton to enquire: & if I had I fear I should be little better. I told you before, our Trooper was waiting for the Dutch at Sunderland, & there (by letters this day from the Privy Councill) he is like to stay: but it grieves us that they have such havock upon the coast neer you.[738] God free us from all our iealousses. I pray you send me by this bearer (who liveth in this town) one of your fire sermons: for I have none.[739] The brother in Leicestershire that owes me the 50£ wrote to me the last week to have patience untill a little before Michaelmass & then he would pay it at London to you.[740] I condiscended to it, because, he said, otherwise it would extremely prejudice him in selling some goods now which give a very small rate. I presume that time may serve your turn. Have you begun your Deanery House? {p. 2} I mistrust your learned contrivers 1500£ will not pay for the building of such an house as /is\ fit for a Dean of St Pauls. For by that time I have finished mine (which will be a very good parsonage but a mean Deanery House) I think it will cost me little less. And yet workmanship is cheap here, & so are materialls: & if lead be excepted, I had the greatest part of all my materialls in the ruins of the old house: & such you want. If you make not the house /fully\ large enough, contrive conveniently for a supplement by some uxorated successor. Women generally mislike my house, because they can find no room in it fit for a nursery. I confess to them, I forgott it, & so I did: but it had been all one, if I had remembered it. Let them that have wives build for them.

I would fayn hear how Sir Robert Gayer & his Lady do. My service to them & to all friends.

Your humble servant,
G.D.

Address as L. **102**

737 George Watson had a lease in Ryhope in 1662: Cosin Survey, DUL, Sharpe MS 167, f. 130.

738 In June the Dutch had come as far as Chatham, destroyed several ships and then blockaded the Medway: Hutton, *The Restoration*, pp. 268–9. The trooper was presumably the soldier whom the parish paid for: L. **81**.

739 Fire sermon: L.**102**.

740 Steven, who farmed the estate in Leicestershire: Introduction, p. 1.

106 **22 June 1667**
T. 45.199
G.D. to W.S. from Bp. Auckland

Aukland Castle. Jun. 22.1667.

Mr Dean;

We have a report here that severall of the Bankmen at London have shutt up their shops, & deny all bills sent to them.[741] This occasioneth this letter to you, desiring you to do my brother so much favour (if you apprehend cause for it) to call for the remainder of the money out of Mr Welsteds hand & to keep it by you. It was lent, as I remember, at 4£ per cent. His book will shew. I have written to my brother about it this Post. He intended for London about Michaelmas, to do this himselfe. But if he have no further occasions there, I conceive, it would be but a frivolous errand, when I know you would do so much for him, as to clear the account. I can say no more at present to your letter, than what I said in my three last in answer to it. I was yesterday at Durham with my Lord, at the mustering of the volunteer horse.[742] I saw Mr Wrench who is in Residence. God send us better news than what we yet hear. Thus in hast, I subscribe my selfe,

Your humble servant,

G. Davenport.

Address: as L. **102**.

107 **8 August 1667**
T. 45.208
G.D. to W.S. from Durham

Durham Castle. Aug.8. 1667.

Mr Dean, the last week I wrote to you as I was going to Heighington, & now I will give you an account of that journey. Mris. Wildebore gave me this positive answer that unless she might have the tithes at 26£ she would foregoe them, & so I took her at her word & parted fair, & in my hast forgott to ask her for her rent, which she had said she would send for the whole year that week.

With Mr Wood I concluded this bargain that he should have halfe the tithes for 17£ 10s. And withall promised that in case he was a looser by

741 In July 1667 the parlous financial state of the government meant that bankers refused further credit and the government was reduced to borrowing even from the gentry: Chandaman, *English Public Revenue*, p. 213 n. 1.

742 Western, *English Militia in the Eighteenth Century*, pp. 25–6.

it, corn being at a low rate, it should be considered. < > Since I have agreed with an Aukland man (who sometimes dwelt in that town) for the other moyety at 17£ 10s absolutely. And moreover he tells me, that in case you will make him a lease, be it in writing or parole for 7 years after this, if you continue in that Preb{end}, he will give you 40£ per annum. This /year\ he would not because of the rate of corn. But your barn there must be repaired. Proceed we now to Relly: Pleasingtons rent you know for the last halfe year is paid in bills and moneye.[743] Kirkly left yesterday with me (Mr Wrench being absent) 09£ 15s 06d & 01£ 09s in bills: the rest of the halfe years rent he saith he will bring this next week, it being in a sure hand. But he urges with open mouth, as the others for abatement. And also for four years spoyl of his winter eatage, by reason a high way was fain to be made by the waterside.[744] /Mr Wrench and\ I promised him some abatement for it this {p. 2} year, and he saith Mr Wrench promised for the others. We have an order of the last sessions for turning the course of the river from your ground at the charge of the Countrey.[745] But oh how I was fain to tugg for it! The black justices </made\> little help. But I wonder you can have so little compassion on a man, as to tell him Sir Tho{mas} Rich is dangerously ill, & after twice requesting, neither by yourselfe nor Mr Scissons let me know how he doth. Some say Dr Nayler mends: but I much doubt it.[746] If it be Gods pleasure to take him, I could wish you had his prebend in exchange for your own: I am perswaded it is almost 100£ per annum better than yours, & your revenue is much diminished, & my Lord said, he would give you a better, when he gave you this. By no means refuse, if such a case should happen as to have it in your power.

Yr humble servant,
G.D.

Aug. 9. I am just now come < > recking hott out of your pulpit after the Assize sermon. I met in the Church Mris Wildbores man, who is gone to Mr Wrench to pay her rent. I met there also Mr Wood & his partner who come to give bond for this year's tith.

Address as L. **102**.

< > Since: 'but' erased.

---

743 The rent was to be paid for the land which constituted Sancroft's 'corps'.

744 Eatage = the grass grown after the hay is cut: Wright, *English Dialect Dictionary*, II, p. 232.

745 turning the course of the river: L. **104**.

746 Joseph Naylor, canon of the second stall since 1636, died 6 January 1667/8: Mussett, p. 21.

108 **1 September 1667**

T. 45.212

G.D. to W.S. from Houghton

Houghton Sept. 1 1667.

Well SAID, Tutor, in truth. Your /letter\ of Aug. 22 I received the last night. In which said letter, me thinks, you do so say, and unsay, with your yea-says & nay-says (is the Dean of Lincoln at London still?) that I do not well know what to say. But this I'le say & you cannot gainsay, that I received yours in the midst of my workmen Harvestmen (& I have 60£ but town tiths & as much glebe in my hand) joyners, smiths, masons, setters up & pullers down; & the messenger telling them that he < > heard the peace proclaimed at Durham, they all ran from their work beleeving I had the proclamation, so that I say they neglected their work, & they said they would to the kirk & ring for joy & so they had done, had not the churchwarden luckily < > borrowed one of the Bell-ropes for a cart-rope.[747] I say further, though you be for monkery (& as a monk slight rents & townships with a generous neglect) yet the premisses will say, that I look more like a secular, or a lay brother. And as such I ride & tith my selfe (I have a man Sir Reverence, Hind Nicholas, so is his name, Gods with me) & tear my stockings in //the stubble. I say also I am this morning going to Durham to preach for you: the monk promised & broke his word. If you go to Stoke with the Lady, do not name me at dinner, lest your meat be spoiled.[748] And now I have said all that I will say at this time (& you'ld say this letter is not worth 3d and reading) and more cannot be said in this page, when I have said that I am

Sir,

Your George.//

Address: To the Reverend Dr William Sancroft Dean of St Pauls Thomas at his lodgings at Mr Benbows house in Maiden Lane (Covent Garden) London 3

luckily < > borrowed: 'and' erased.

747 The Second Dutch War was concluded by the Treaty of Breda in July, proclaimed on 24 August 1667: Hutton, *The Restoration*, p. 274.

748 The Lady: Lady Gayer.

109 **1 November 1667**
T. 45.232–3
G.D. to W.S. from Houghton

Houghton. Nov.1. 1667.

Mr Dean; They are mightily beholding to you here that can /have\ a letter from you. I thought you would not have failed to have answered that letter which I wrote to you about 2 months since in which I told you 40£ per annum was proffered for Heighington tithes: for three years or as long as you continue Prebendary, by the parish tenants, & since by Mr Wood solely.[749] Which man (now I have named him) often hath desired me to solicite you to give something to their poor. I long to hear from you, that the 50£ is returned to you from my brother in Leicestershire.[750] If it be not, according to his promise, I would write to him again of that matter. I would gladly hear from you also how Sir Robert Gayer & all his relations do: (I think he is resolved that I shall hear no more from him) & the rather because Mr Auditor Aldworth about 3 weeks since told me he left Sir Thomas Rich in a dying condition: but the next day brought him a letter from his wife, which told him that he was mended.[751] God, of his mercy, give /him\ good health. A lick of news too now & then would do well in a countrey town (my Lord of Durham is the best intelligencer I have at London) where no news is, but that certainly we have peace, which the neighbours conclude because of the number of ships that pass by them. But of late they begin to mumble, that the Parliament is {p. 2} about to humme the late Lord Chancellors Gigge.[752] I beleive almost all the rents for the last year are paid by the tenants of your corpse. So soon as I can meet Mr Wrench, who, I take it, is now at Bolden, we will make up an account. You do ill, & not well, in letting your house stand idle. I passed by the door the other day, & the walls to the stepps of the hall door are rubbed down, & the standers by say it was with Dr Woods coatch. You had better hire a tenant than put no one into it: you may do well to tell Mr Dean so, who told me above a year since that

749 Wood: L.**74**.

750 Stephen Davenport: L. **105**.

751 Mr Auditor Aldworth: L. **100**; for Rich see next letter.

752 Edward Hyde, Lord Chancellor from 1658, Earl of Clarendon, was forced out of office in August 1667, threatened with impeachment in November, which caused a confrontation between Lords and Commons. On 30 November he went into exile: *ODNB*.Mussett, p. 21.

you had written to him to dispose of it. I verily believe that if it stand empty 3 years longer, it will then begin to think of falling down: for it is not a strong house northward, & was hardly even yet warmed. I keep a sorry house here, whither my old house-keeper is come to me, & fretts me everyday with rules for health. I hold, that if I was once out of debt, this would be a comfortable place. For I live amongst kind neighbours: though I am likely to go to law with some for increase of tithes. I think I told you, that Renton Pitts have yielded /some yearly\ 40 fodder of coals in right of my rectory in lieu of tith coles, according to depositions which I found recorded in Chancery, as I was seeking after another matter. My next care is to prove Eppleden without a prescription for corn: & to make West Rainton Park, now it bears no wood, but a great deal of corn, to pay tithes; & there no prescription is pretended. Pittington ford acknowledgeth corn in kind; but I am not content unless I have hay also. A good corn close straggled out of the {p. 3} parish in the rebellious times but I have wonned it back again. These things (if I effect them) will make good for succession. But I want much the papers & books of my predecessors & so good night from

Sir your humble servant
G.D.

110 **24 January 1668**
T. 45.261
G.D. to W.S. from Houghton

Houghton. Jan. 24. 1667. Mr Cosins 24£.

Mr Dean; this is the greatest soreness that ever I knew you to have; for it hath lasted almost 3 months. Your last of Nov. 7. told me of the death of Sir Thomas Rich & Sir Robert Gayer's daughter, & of the sickness of his Lady.[753] And both she & you may be dead for ought I have heard to the contrary, though I wrote to you about her condition the same day I received your letter, & since I think, twice /or thrice.\ I now remember it is your waiting month, but that is almost at an end: you may be also a Lent Preacher, for I know not who are. But if Dr Beaumont be now /in\ attendance with you, I desire you (for I have small acquaintance with him) to recommend a nephew of my name to his favour, whom my Lord hath designed to be one of his

753 Sir Thomas Rich died 15 October 1667, aged sixty-six: *VCH*, *Berkshire*, III, p. 222; GEC, *Baronetage*, III, p. 180.

scholars there, who shall be sent to him so soon as the scholarships are settled which I trust will be very shortly.[754] I would fain hear of Sir Robert Gayer & his Lady, but know not from whom it can be, unless from your selfe. And if I had any hopes you would tell me I would ask also after Sir And. Henley & what end he hath of his trouble, & Sir Robt. Abdy, & whether either of them be marryed or about to marry.[755] Your money burns in Mr Wrench's purse: & though I asked you about six weeks since whether you would have it returned, you /do not\ answer.< >I hear Dr Smith is likely to have Dr Naylers Prebend & Dr Durrell to have Dr Smiths.[756] Much joy may they have. Mr Lilborn of Sunderland hath promised 200£ towards the errecting & endowing an hospitall here for 6 poor folk at 2d a day,[757] as much more I think will do the work: now if you hear of any well disposed person that will do us good herein, they may come in as co-founders or lone-factors, at their own proper costs & charges. I would gladly know whether Sir Thomas Rich left money for the founding an hospitall at Gloucester.[758] {p. 2} You see how many questions I ask: & in earnest I fear, these are more than you will answer. But if you will give Directions to Mr Scisson, I doubt not but he will do so much for

Your humble servant

G.D.

Address as L. **102**.

754 Joseph Beaumont (1616–99), Master of Peterhouse from 1663, had married a daughter of Robert Brownrigg of Sproughton: *ODNB*. The nephew was George, second son of G.D.'s brother Stephen, who was admitted pensioner at Peterhouse, Cambridge, October 1668. He received his B.A. in 1672/3, and M.A. in 1676, and became rector of Steeple, Essex, in 1678. He died in November 1736: Leicester RO, Will, 5 February 1736/7; *Al. Cant.* He received £100 in G.D.'s will. His brother, John, was G.D.'s sole executor.

755 The indictment mentioned in L. **104**. Henley's wife had died on 30 July 1666: *HPC*, II, p. 523.

756 John Durel became canon of the fourth stall in Durham cathedral in April 1668, in succession to Thomas Smith who moved to the first stall, replacing Denis Grenville who obtained Naylor's prebend: Mussett, pp. 14, 21, 36–7.

757 George Lilburne: Hutchinson, *Durham*, II, p. 561; L. **55**.

758 Sir Thomas Rich was well known for his benevolence in Gloucester. For charities founded in accordance with his will: *VCH, Berkshire*, III, p. 224; L. **115**.

111 **20 February 1668**
T. 144.110
G.D. to W.S. from Houghton

Houghton. Febr. 20. 1667.

Mr Dean; This day I received yours: & considering you live sine cura, I am the more bold to trouble you with this scriblement.[759] He is a witty Dr, I'le warrant him, that bestowed the sine cura upon you. I wonder you could forbear his name: but I am perswaded he shows most of his witt in a pulpit. I thank you heartily for your relation concerning Sir Robt. Gayer & all his kinred. I am sorry for Mris. Godolphin's death & for the mistake in Sir Tho. Rich's will.[760] I live in a place where as little news cometh, as any melancholy man can wish. I heard from Mr Stapylton that you are to have 12£ 10s of Mr Cosin's money & so {we} shall when we can get it.[761] As likewise any part of your arrears in {this} place of which as yet I have not received one penny, nor can I say that I am like to get any thing in a short time. For the 12£ 10s you need not doubt. The Hospitall is in hand, & almost 20 men in work in winning & hewing of stone for it. But when I have < > the two trees from the Dean & Chapter towards it, I know not where to get any thing more besides the 200£ promised; to which I mean to add the like summ if I can procure no part of it from others: but that is a secret which I will impart to my executor. I hope it will be finished by midsummer: and then beg for Bow-Church at Durham, to which my Lord & I & some others have subscribed, & the subscription now lies before your brethren at Durham.[762] I beleeve your 4 long dormants must be employed in the quire therof. Take you that. We talk also of enlarging the school-masters house, at the charge of such as have been scholars here. I love such works at my heart: & hope I shall not onely talk of them but also see them effected. I pray you to remember the nephew when Dr Beaumont comes to town. And if you think to keep me at the staves end as you have done for the last 4 months, I am like enough to lay the said sine cura in your dish. Oh how Wrench will laugh when he hears it. I am Sir

Your humble servant, G.D.

have < > the two: 'not' erased.

759 sine cura: without cure of souls.

760 No source found.

761 Probably Bishop Cosin's estranged son, John, for whom G.D. and Stapylton administered an allowance: Introduction, p. 13.

762 Bow Church: St Mary le Bow, in the North Bailey, the parish church at the east end of Durham cathedral. It was in ruins: *VCH, Durham*, III, p. 137.

112 **3 April 1668**
T. 44.5
G.D. to W.S. from Durham Castle

Durham Castle. Apr. 3d. 1668.

Mr Dean; I came hither on Tuesday to the synod & the sessions & a cold hath kept me hitherto, & now the cold, I think, will keep me another day. In two letters of late gloves have been demanded in your name:[763] but I know of none due as yet & how they will at any time be due is more than I understand. For certainly my marriage is more in your head, than it is or ever was in mine. And so much for wedding. Was the nephew ever recommended to Dr Beaumont? Is not my Lady Gayer ready to lie down? & how doth shee & her husband & mother? We have no news here. But Mr Flowre puts us in fear of subsidyes.[764] I care not which way it be, if the necessityes of the King be supplied: though you know well that a subsidy will be in the poor parsons of Houghtons parishe. Our hospitall work goes on bravely and halfe being ready hewen. And what is better I have found a freestone quarry beside Howden Hill in my glebe for the work: which had I discovered 3 years since, I am perswaded, it would have saved me 40 or 50£. I got no more money for you. But Mr Wrench wonders he heard not from you for what he hath in his hand, which I beleeve (for I must not know the secreta capituli) will be neer 156£.[765] Mr Wood hath not yet given security & it is time enough to do it within 2 months.[766] But I would gladly perswade him to take in the former partner, whom I hold to be the better paymaster, as being both more able, & more sure, & one that can make /more\ profit of it, though he live at Aukland, for he was tenant at Heighington for many years. Mr Grenvyls collation /to the 2d Preb{end}\ is expected the next week: but he fears he shall not be installed untill the great chapter for want of a chapter.[767] He is possessed

763 Gloves: L. **78**.

764 William Flowre, vicar of Leek, Northallerton, 1667. He became domestic chaplain to Cosin and his amanuensis in his latter years: *Cosin Corr.* II, pp. xxx–xxxi. For the financial crisis: Chandaman, *English Public Revenue*, pp. 146–7.

765 secreta capituli = secrets of the Chapter. Presumably Sancroft's share of the dividend.

766 See L.**74**.

767 Great chapter = the full chapter. There were two Great (or Grand) Chapters a year, on 20 July and 20 November. All prebendaries were under an obligation to attend and those who did not could be fined part of their stipend. Chapter Acts, DCM, DCD/B/AA/4, for this period. Granville was installed 16 April 1668: Mussett, p. 21.

of Sedgefield: and as I am told, is bidden 600£ per annum by quarterly payments for it. I wish you would send me your picture for my house: it is but a modest request to a friend. I hear Dr Berwick was never taken & his brother here cannot help me to his arms.[768] But he lately brought me 3£ from his brother for the poor. My service I pray to the friends above mentioned. I am

Sir Your most faithfull servant,
G.D.

113 **26 September 1668**
T. 144.108
G.D. to W.S. from Durham

Durham Castle. Sept. 26. 1668.

Mr Dean, I have yours of the 22[d]. I beleeve the widow will be soon with you.[769] My nephew I think is now upon his journey for Peterhouse: when you have a fair opportunity of writing to Dr Beaumont or of speaking to him, I pray have him recommended: but do not write on purpose.[770] There cometh in mind charge to me by this lad.

For the hospitall I hope it will be finished in a month, the roof being almost set /up\ & the slates lying by it. I have gotten by begging of my Lord & D & Ch.[771] & others about 20£ of timber & of my neighbours some carriages towards this building, & nothing more. I expect Mr Lilborn who is to be at halfe charge & the other halfe I must either procure, or find myself, that was our bargain. The house is for 6 people, & hath 6 ground chambers built of good stone, & a front of Ashlar & will cost about 200£. I think it would have cost 40£ more had not I luckily found a freestone quarry in mine own ground, which might have saved me much money had {it} been discovered 3 {years} since.[772] This house is intended for 6 aged men – 3 of our parish & 3 of Weremouth (< >in which parish Mr Lilborne dwelleth) unless he will choose, as I desire, that one of them shall be named for Offerton in our Parish where he hath an estate. We mean to indowe it with about 20£

768 John Barwick (L. **39**), who had been Sancroft's predecessor at Houghton, died on 22 October 1664. Of his three brothers the relevant one may be Peter, who wrote his Life. Peter lived in London but leased the rectory of Brantingham: *ODNB* and DCM, DCD/B/AA/4, p. 132.

769 Perhaps Sir Thomas Rich's widow.

770 My nephew is probably George: L. **115**.

771 D & Ch: Dean and Chapter.

772 Mine own ground: G.D.'s glebe.

per annum which will cost about 300£ or more. This will pay every of the poor men 2d a day, and benefactors may afterward encrease it to more. We may make it a new foundation by a statute of Q. Eliz. or else have it upon our old charter {p. 2} which I the rather like, & then we have both governors & collector (& usher) & statutes.[773] You know it is the free school & hospitall of Kepyer at </Houghton.\> But then we must < > petition the King about mortmain & I told both the judges that I hoped neither the Lord Keiper nor Atturney Generall would not take any fees, /hope beene*..*opinion.\ We are allowed by our letters patent 50£ per annum & have already about 40£.[774] After all this you may give if you be so disposed, what sum you please to this good work. For though Mr Lilborn will have no benefactors as to his moyety, I declare I will have all I can get. And the rather, because I am indebted at this time neer 400£; though in < > truth, corn & hay & rent at Martinmass & Mayday, I think will pay < > all that summ: and my personall estate would pay my 150£ for lands for the hospitall, if it please God that I dye before that time. I have now acquainted you, as you desired with my case, I am so poor as you see: an executor could handily spend 10£ on my buryall & yet get as much by me. I have also told you the intent of the foundation, & God bless you < > for your pious design & remember you for good. I pray let me have the resolution, when you see good. I should be glad to hear that Sir Robt. Gayer & his family are in health. My service to them when you see any of them. I meant onely that my executors should not know as yet that I was in hand with an hospitall. Mr Wrench & Mr Stapylton dine in my chamber this day, & being both come, I must attend them: but first they present their service to you & so doth

Your humble servant

G.D.

Mr Stapylton would have me to tell you, that Mr John Blackiston hath this day promised him to receive & send the 60£ & that assoon as he hath it, he hath provided a return for it.[775]

---

773 Letters were granted by Elizabeth on 2 April 1574 to John Heath of Kepier (who had bought the dissolved Kepier Hospital) and to Bernard Gilpin, rector of Houghton-le-Spring, to establish a free grammar school and alms house in honour of the Blessed Trinity: Hutchinson, *Durham*, II, p. 554.

774 Lord Keeper: Sir Orlando Bridgeman (1609–74); the king's Attorney General was Sir Geoffrey Palmer (1598–1670): *ODNB* for both.

775 John Blackiston of Newcastle, a cousin of Bishop Cosin, *Stapylton Corr.*, pp. 200–1, 218n.

Address: For the Reverend Dr William Sandcroft. Dean of St Pauls at Mr Benbows house in Maiden Lane Covent Garden. London. 6d

< >in which: 'who' erased; </Houghton\>: 'Durham' erased.

114 **11 October 1668**
T. 44.39
G.D. to W.S. from Houghton

Houghton Oct. 11 1668.

Mr Dean;

Having this oportunity, the bearer being a parishioner at Hetton in the Hole, I send my service to you. I am told that the next week we are likely to have our annuity for Mr Cosin.[776] I wish it may so prove. I have sent Sir Robt. Gayer's Coat of Arms under the King of Arms hand, which is as good testimony as may be. I the rather do this because I was told the last week that the Heralds wreked some displeasure upon Sir Tho. Rich & other Gentlemen in the South of late.[777] The Coat was given me by Robt. Beaumont (where is he?) who found it in a bookbinders hand. I ghess it was delivered to have a stamp made by it for marking of books. I offered it to Sir Robt. Gayer in my lodgings at London; but he despised it; & perhaps did not well in so doing. I pray proffer it to him again, with my service to himselfe & Lady. In hast for the bells ring us in to evening prayer. I am

Yr. humble servant
G.D.

115 **25 November 1668**
T. 44.62
G.D. to W.S. from Houghton

Houghton Nov. 25. 1668.

Mr Dean;

I this day received your letter with no little joy. Gods blessing and poor mens, be upon the head of my Lady Rich for her kindness to the hospitall here. I doubt not, but she will reap benefitt from their prayers. And indeed to say the truth that I might have poor people's /prayers\ whilest I live, I chose rather to put forward this work with an empty purse, than to deferre it to such a time, when I might probably have

776 Above, L. **111**.
777 The Gayer coat of arms was a lion rampant sable, supporting a spear.

more money & little need of it. I used the same argument to Sir Tho. Rich, when he acquainted me with his charitable design for Gloucester: but was answered by him that he would certainly make provision for it;[778] but nothing should be done in it while he was alive, least evill-minded men should accuse him of ostentation, of which I know he was clear; & so I trust in God I am also. In his sickness, when I was at London last, he sent me with 20£ to the poor of St Olaves in Suthwerk, for which I took a receipt of the churchwardens for an unknown person: which when I showed to him he went & buried, least it should appear amongst his papers.[779] I meant to have kept the receipt, as well to testify mine own honesty, if the Parishioners should at any time /have said\ it had not been paid, as to cut off all occasion of deceipt in the churchwardens. I tell this the rather to you least you should be so served with my receipt when I send it to you. I go to Durham on Friday; every Saturday I attend there upon my Lord's affairs, on Sunday is your course & on Monday I am for Brassenton. I will give you an account by the next post what Mr Wrench can do as to the 91£. I wrote to you on Munday last desiring you to get a discharge from Mr Cosin for Mr Stapylton & me, for what we have hitherto paid him of his annuity.[780] With it I sent an old account between you & me. Of the nine pounds not here mentioned, I must say, I thought the 4£ to my kinswoman had not been received because she sent me word she would not have it, hoping I would take her son for /G.\ Meddon's 5£. I thank you that I came off so well: you told me famously what you meant to do as to him & I answered as I do now, that I should take it kindly. I wish the man be sound.

For Ra.Bl.[781] (prettyman!) I sold him /an\ horse the last assizes * * & he was to pay me for him the next morning: but he never did yet. But very kindly yesterday he sent me my horse again. I took him & thought there was no need to reward the messenger.

For my nephew you needed not to have employed any to my Lord about him.[782] He being the first scholar that is nominated by my Lord

778 See also L.**110**.

779 St Olave's, Southwark, was a London church in the dock area opposite the Tower, now demolished.

780 Above, L. **111**.

781 Ra.Bl.: Ralph Blackiston, brother-in-law to Bishop Cosin, son of Marmaduke of Newton Hall, Durham (1608–76). Rector of Ryton from 1660: *Cosin Corr.* II, p. 27n; Introduction, p. 13.

782 See L. **113**.

& I one of the trustees for paying the college. I desired onely {p. 2} that Dr Beaumont would take notice of him as of my nephew, and so to afford him a < > gracious nodd as he passeth by him. You tell me the first news of my legacy from Mr Weston.[783] I knew Dr Rogers very well: but I know not where he liveth in London. One Dr & his unknown abode brings in another. Dr Samuel Collins (I think there are 3 of that name but I mean him of yr. & my acquaintance who was Physitian to Sir Tho. Rich) about 16 months since left a lame horse with me to be sent to my Lords park,[784] where he went till about this time the last year & then nothing bettered, I sold him for 03£ 10s. 00d to be paid about Pentecost last & Coll. Wren passed his word for the money. The man never returned again & Coll. Wren desired me to have patience till Michaelmas, & now I have stayed longer: & therefore 3 days since I wrote to him for the money.[785] He shall do as much for his friend as I do for Meddon. I have told the Dr. so much; & the reason was because I know not where he dwelleth. I pray /if you can learn\ let me know against the time that I get his money. But there /are\ some triffling charges upon the horses head to the farrier. I heard the horse dyed soon after: & so much for the horse.

I pray present my humble service to my Lady Rich with my hearty thanks. God willing, at my return, I mean to trouble her with a letter. I wish I had her picture for the hospitall. I will write also to Sir Robt. Gayer, to whom & his Lady, I pray present my service.

I wish any other Church officers could tell me the dimensions of St Paul's pulpit cloth, which fashion I like very well. As I remember the middle payn was red damask, & the outward side purple & the cushion red on one side & purple on the other . I pray at your leisure let me know & say of yr. servants may learn most exactly of some officer of the church. And now thanking /you\ for all your favours, especially for this last. I commend you to God's protection & rest

Yr. obliged servant,

Geo. Davenport.

a < > gracious: 's' erased.

---

783 It appears that G.D. was left a legacy by the unidentified Dr Rogers. Weston may be Henry, who entered at Gray's Inn 23 December 1637, or Richard, entered 10 August 1642: *Stapylton Corr.*, p. 178n.

784 Dr Samuel Collins: *ODNB* for possible identification.

785 *Records of the Committee for Compounding*, SS 111, p. 47 for the Wren family. Col. Francis Wren was a sincere supporter of the Parliamentarian side but behaved with moderation towards the Royalists and lived to old age. He was buried in the church of St Andrew's, Auckland, 24 September 1684.

116 **17 June 1669**
T. 44.112
G.D. to W.S. from Bp. Auckland

Aukland Castle Jun. 17 1669.

Mr Dean;

I have received yours of May 27 & the other since. I thank you for your care in my affairs with Mr Birch & I wish he may now rest satisfied.[786] I am extreamly grieved for the ill news you send concerning Sir Robt. Gayer; to whom I pray God to repair this great loss.[787] My service to him & his Lady, & my Lady Rich. I should be glad to hear that my Lady is with child again. For Mr Wrench I last saw him May 29 when he preached. Otherwise I have not been at Durham since Ascension Day. I hear he is now in Residence.[788] For my 3 1st volumes of the Lexicon, I intend to send for them so soon as I have opportunity.[789] I pray deliver Dr Holbech to him with my service.[790] My Lord is very well: & about 10 days hence, I think, he will be for Durham to stay there: & then the books must be placed in the new Library.[791] In the meantime I have fine work about the Classicall Catalogue. The 5£ I will repay with thanks. I wonder I never hear anything from Dr Collins or Dr Rogers, or whether he have received the 3£ legacyes : if he have not I still owe him 3£ for his horse; & I wish you would pay that also. You see what a fellow I am. On </Tuesday\> last I buryed Mr Geo. Shadforth, the old man's eldest son.[792] I pray let me know whether Mr Thurscross be fellow of Eton, as I heard it reported, three weeks since.[793] With my service & thanks I take leave. & rest

Your affectionate servant
G.D.

</Tuesday\>: 'Wednesday' erased.

---

786 Mr Birch: unidentified.

787 Great loss unidentified, probably a miscarriage.

788 Certainly from 20 July: DCM, DCD/B/AA/4, f. 142.

789 Above, L. **20**.

790 Above, L. **17**.

791 The new library, founded by Bishop Cosin on Palace Green, Durham: A.I. Doyle, 'John Cosin (1595–1672) as a Library Maker', *The Book Collector* 40/3 (1991), pp. 335–57, for the building and stocking.

792 Mr George Shadforth, son of Thomas, of Eppleton, Durham. He died 15 June 1669: Surtees, *Durham*, I/2, p. 221, for pedigree: Introduction, pp. 16–17.

793 L. **3**.

117 **6 July 1669**
T. 44.119
G.D. to W.S. from Durham

Durham Castle Jul.6. 1669.

Mr Dean;

Mr Wall an Atturney of Aukland went for London about a fortnight since, & I desired him to call upon you for the 3 voll. of the Orientall Lexicons which and for me which[794] I pray your servant may deliver to him if he call for them.[795] I have little more to say; the monk bids me present his service to you; but he is willing to see the grand chapter over before he write to you.[796] His residence is over & Mr Durell hath begun. I was promised 3£ for you on Friday for Mris < > Smiths arrears of 6£ but I have it not yet, but stay in daily expectation of it. We have 4 poor people in our hospitall & we pay them out of our purses till we can provide land the other two rooms are not fitted, but will be, I trust, in another fortnight. My Lord is removed to this place, I think, for all this summer & is very well. My service to Sir Robt < > Gayer & his Lady & my Lady Rich when you see them. With my humble service to your selfe, I rest,

Your faithfull servant
G.D.

< > Smiths: 'Ayton' erased.

118 **25 July 1669**
T. 44.136
G.D. to W.S. from Durham

Durham Castle July 25 1669.

Mr Dean; Since I wrote my last I have received 3£ of Mr Ayton in full satisfaction of the 6£ which Mris Smith owed you for tithes at West-Herrington which I took because I know not how to recover in law, she being dead. Robt. Kirkley paid almost his halfe years rent this week: but he owed an arrear of 3£ for last year, which with your lease Mr Wrench & I promised to abate (by reason of the dearness of his farm as we conceive) when he shall have paid the next halfe years rent entirely:[797] that is not above 30 £ per annum for the year past, & as

794 Sic.
795 Mr Wall: L. **118**. For the *Lexicon*: L. **29**.
796 The chapter: DCM, DCD/B/AA/4, f. 142.
797 A Houghton tenant: L. **85**.

much for this. Mr Wall is returned home without my Lexicons: because he found you not at home when he came to enquire for them. John saith he will appoint one to take Mr Welsteds account the next Term. Dr Smith & Dr Brevint are not here this chapter.[798] The rest are well. My Lord hath placed his books in the new library which he built. But oh! What a life have I in shifting them hither & thither /& this life I reckon I must lead till Michaelmas.\ I have no more to trouble you with at present, but that you would present my service to Sir Robt. Gayer & his Lady, & my Lady Rich, & all my friends. And if you can let me know what he is about to build at Stoke. For a man of this countrey told me that he lately rode by his gate; & that many builders where[799] hard at work.

Yr. humble servant,
G.D.

119 **3 August 1669**
T. 44.142
G.D. to W.S. from Durham

Durham Castle. Aug. 3. 1669.

Mr Dean;

Yours of July 29. I received yesterday & am glad you are so well satisfied with what I did with Kirkley & Mris Smith's executor. But as for my preaching your courses here, why should you imagine that I would sell sermons to you?[800] As for others preaching your course, it was by way of exchange, sometimes for my convenience, at other times for theirs. Indeed for last Trinity Sunday, being the ordination at Aukland, I could not be spared, nor could I get any but honest Elias to supply that place, whom I promised to pay, or else to repay in kind at his pleasure.[801] I have not done either as yet: but if he will be paid for it, I will take money of Mr Wrench to do it. But the money you have laid forth for me I will repay. I'll write to John about the Lexicon.[802] But doubtless you are mightily mistaken when you think you paid me

798 DCM, DCD/B/AA/4, f. 142.

799 Sic.

800 Payment for preaching 'courses', for instance DCM, DCD/L/BB/36, f. 25 in 1673–4.

801 Elias Smith (c. 1605–76), minor canon 1628 until his death, precentor of Durham 1666–76, and librarian 1633 till his death: DCM, DCD/L/BB/27–39; typescript by B. Crosby in 5 The College, Durham, 2002, minor canons.

802 John: G.D.'s brother.

4£ for the Lexicon. I beleeve you paid me by Robt. Beaumont or some other 50£ about 11 years since, you being then at Utrecht & about 2 or 3 years after, when the new propositions were /made\ either the 5th or 6 part of the other 5£. The like Dr Holbech will tell you. In the like manner I subscribed for 6 great Bibles & paid a like share with my partners, by the same token I received my own copy as a Procurer for my pains. I am sure the supernumerary copy is all mine own /& that I paid for it.\ For the nine shillings you expended I must pay 6 for myselfe & John; the other 3s Dr Holbeach & you must pay.

It is very well that Dr Collins is paid for his house with the legacyes: but you need not trouble either yourselfe or him for an acquittance. God bless Sir Robt. Gayer & his Lady & daughter & send them a long life. I thank you for the news of the birth of his daughter. I think my Lord is about to send to Mr Scott for some books & if he doth, I will send for the Lexicons with them.[803] Our Assizes are on Thursday & Monk is as buisy as a fly in a glue pott in making briefes etc. for a suit about the boundary of his parish. He is so waspish, I can hardly get a good word from him: yet I think he will be here anon to have me review his Breviat.[804] He hath /not\ time, he saith, to make accounts. I will give you no further trouble at present but remain

Sir

Your affectionate & obliged servant

G.D.

120 **17 August 1669**

T. 44.148

G.D. to W.S. from Durham

Durham Castle. Aug. 17. 1669.

Ah, Mr Dean, that you should deal thus with mortall flesh! Could you think, I had so little ingenuity as /not\ to spend a few hours, for one to whom you must needs (let me at least) say, I owe so much both of my education, and < > preferment? For the time to come I had best to keep out of your debt (you'l say do if I can) & then I'le be as stout as you are. But I see at present your pleasure must be observed; & therefore I now return you my thanks, which I should have done two posts since had I been at this place: for I was at myne own house not very well.

803 Robert Scott, a London bookseller with an international trade: *Cosin Corr.* II, pp. 218, 274: Plomer, *Dictionary of Booksellers and Printers, 1668–1725*, p. 264.

804 Breviat = a short note or summary or a lawyer's brief: *OED*.

And now let me tell you a tale & my talesmasters. George the son of Dr Nayler & Mr French (that is now at Hetton) both your neighbours tell me, that you have gotten a fine of about 7000 for Shadwell, & that one Mr Neil that marryed Mris. Gold is your tenant at 100£ rent.[805] Much good may it do the heart of you. But doth it not want the circumstance of truth? I pray let me know.

The law case at present is over, & the jury are to tread the bounders against the next Assizes.[806] But I have gotten, I think, the tithes of Rainton low pit houses (worth about 2£ per annum) from the Dean & Chapter, by a reference to two lawyers at this Assizes. The case is they enjoyed the tith as being Rectors of Pittington & we maintained the poor < > because they said they dwelt in Houghton parish. And now the tith is to be paid to the parish church, which was not done before. You must know the place was divided < > about the beginning of the times & before was a moor & nothing tithable upon it & those tenants got the tithes those times, when thieves durst not sue at Law for other mens right.

It is just 6 of the clock & my Lord calls me to the Library. I wish I could say of it, as the woman did of the fish, the fish is done. This cataloguing is errand toyl. But I must to it, & so break off for this time. I'le now call on monk for the account. I am Sir

Your most faithfull servant,

G.D.

My service to Sir Robt. Gayer, his Lady, my Lady Rich, when you see them.

and < > preferment: 'my' erased; the poor < > because: 'as' erased; divided < > about: (?)'beforr' erased.

---

805 Above, L. **85**.

806 Tread the bounders = perambulating the boundary of the parish. The case concerned a quarrel about poor relief in Rainton Low Pit and High Pit houses between Pittington and Houghton parishes. Ralph Flair and his wife were charged as poor upon Houghton parish, whereas Houghton said they belonged to Pittington. The case was heard over several sessions, finally being decided in 1691, with a verdict for Pittington against Houghton. The Pittington case included a plea that the tithes from the lands in the township of Pittington, held by lease from the Dean and Chapter, had been taken by Davenport when rector of Houghton. In 1668 the parishioners of Houghton could not say how Davenport came by the tithes, but were sure that before his time the tithes went to Pittington. Pittington pleaded that fifty years previously the lands had been divided and given wholly to Pittington: DCRO, EP/Pi 53 is the brief for 1689, including the 1691 verdict.

121 **16 November 1669**
T. 44.167
G.D. to W.S. from Houghton

Houghton. Nov. 16. 1669.

Sir;
Yours of Oct. 27 I received in due time, & the good news of my Lady Gayers recovery did < > please me /not\ a little. I think we have as good weather here at this time, as you had lately in Suffolk. I have now sown all my winter-corn, 38 good acres upon Howden Hill, which yielded no rent, & I have about 20 more there for sowing in the spring. Where furze did grow, now ploughs do go. The oldest man in the parish never saw it so before. And besides all this I have lately paid about 200£ of my debts. Enough of that. I am glad to read what you write as to the acts for your house & Shadwell. I wish you good success in them both. It is /an\ even wager, < > that they will cost you a sermon before the H. of Commons. I wish Shadwell fine had been as good as was reported.[807] Wrench writes not to you. He is every day about it: & then he leaves off again, & is angry with his Bretheren, & saith to me, Write you; for why should I write unless I had money to send him. I think you must expect no more from this parish. Mr Smith & Mr Ayton owe us 10£ for Chancery charges but I nowe expect it. And so much for that too. And yet I cannot but muse a little why Shadwell money should all go in an house, where the scite costeth nothing. But it is no matter, make it handsome & good, whatsoever it cost: </for\> now I think on it, the leasing out of the remainder of the ground may do you some good. I told you, I think twice, our John will have the 2nd vol. of the Lexicon at 40s. And, as I remember, he said he wrote to you to that purpose.

I intend shortly, so soon as Mr French comes to you (he is going every day) to rid you of my 3 copies. When they come, I intend to sell two, if I can get customers. I pray what rate bear they ? Perhaps they will buy </two oxen,\> & they are cheap & I have but 9 of them: which Parson Gilpin had 18.[808] I wrote to you long since about the dimensions of St Paul's Pulpit cloath & desired you to enquire of any of your officers about it, for I liked the fashion of it. But I had no answer. I would gladly get an Altar Cloath of about 13 or 14£ price

807 Shadwell: L. **85**.
808 Bernard Gilpin (1516–84), G.D.'s famous predecessor at Houghton: Introduction, p. 18, and *ODNB*.

against Christmas. I think Damask will be best, & the colours purple & crimson. If you will advise me herein, I'le thank you. But the charge (mistake me not) shall not be mine, but good friends here. I doubt the fring must have more silk in it than gold: & that we shall have no front cloath at that price. I </now\> write to Mr Nayler shortly about it. Therefore if you please to lend me any advice, do it soon. And now, if you'le present my service to Sir Robt. Gayer & both the Ladyes, I'le thank you and trouble you no more at present.

Your humble servant.

G.D.

did < > please: 'not' erased; wager < > that: 'but' erased; </two oxen\>: 'a goat' erased; </now\>: 'mean to' erased.

122 **23 December 1669**

T. 44.186

G.D. to W.S. from Houghton

Houghton. Dec. 23. 1669.

Mr Dean;

Wrench, plain Wrench (I'le call him no better, for would he light though </it\> snowed?) was at the gate this afternoon: & I protest, quoth he, I forgott to write to /D.S.\ & you must.[809] And then when he got me farre enough from walls, he told me very softly, wish him to get a bill of 300£ assoon as he will & charge it upon me (Wrench I mean not myselfe) for saith he, I have already 270£ /for him\ & have some rents to receive. And so he vanished, as if he was affrayd that I should ask after secretum capituli.

I meant to write to you notwithstanding, if it was to no other end but to enclose one to Sir Robt. Gayer: for I know not what other way to send it: & here it is. I heard lately that the gowt vexeth him. I wrote to Mr Nayler about an altar cloath, & I hoped to have it finished before this: but I never heard from him since. I asked your judgment about it at the same /time\ & directed him to come to you but I heard not of either. And now I have no more to say, but that I wish you a good Christmas & rest

Yr. most humble servant.

Geo. Davenport.

---

809 D.S.: Dean Sancroft.

123 **15 January 1670**
T. 44.188
G.D. to W.S. from Durham

Durham Castle. Jan. 15. 1669.

Mr Dean;

Yours of the 11th I received here yesterday & have acquainted Mr Wrench with it. I could not expect to hear anything from Mr Walt. Etterick this day: /if the bill was sent by the last Post\ but assoon as I do, I will fit my business for the conveyance of the culpa, unless he will choose to have it here.[810] The man I have known for 7 years past & I & Mr Neil & Mr Stapylton /& others\ agree he may be trusted with a greater summ. But you must know I came hither on Epiphany night to make provision for my Lord Lawderdales entertainment on Saturday after: & he is not yet come nor can I ghess when he will come (having no letter from any about him of late) /nor when I may get away\.[811] About Christmas Dr Frazer (now with the /said Lord\ Commissioners) wrote to Mr Dean desiring him to tell us (whose names he knew not) that the Commissioner meant to lodge at this Castle Jan. 8.[812] As for the enquiry after me letter after letter, I beleive I can unriddle it (though I cannot tell whether the enquirer hath either son or daughter or kindred) for Jo. Jopling who dwells at that town, & was arraigned here once as being supposed to have been in a plott, hath reported in many places that I was Fleetwoods Chaplaine & Preacher to one of their Congregationall Churches:[813] so that I suppose the letters were to enquire after that, in which you could have resolved them better than any one in London, if they had but asked the question. Mr

810 Walter Etterick, Collector of customs dues at Sunderland and Registrar of the Bishop's Admiralty Court: Surtees, *Durham*, I, p. 238; *Stapylton Corr.*, p. 202n. Culpa = blame.

811 John Maitland, second Earl and first Duke of Lauderdale (1616–82). He ruled Scotland through most of the reign of Charles II as Secretary of State (from 1660) and Lord High Commissioner (from 1669): *ODNB*; DCM, DCD/L/BB 35, f. 2r/v (1671/2): 'ringing for the Duke of Lauderdale, 7 Oct.'

812 On 14 December 1669 Cosin instructed Stapylton or Davenport to write to Sir Alexander Phraser 'so that they might provide entertainment for him as he passed through Durham': *Cosin Corr.* II, pp. 215–16, 223, 224, 225, 228n.

813 Jo. Jopling: Derwentdale plotter (L. **52**). Fleetwoods Chaplaine may refer to Charles Fleetwood (1618–92), head of Cromwell's army. He was noted for the number of preaching officers in his army and his sectarian affiliations: *ODNB*. G.D. was perhaps confused with his radical Coventry relative, John: Introduction, p. 2.

French went to London Jan.3. & will shortly ease you of the Lexicons. Our John's it seems you know how to send. The price as I remember /you said\ of the 1st vol. was 2£. But you do ill & not well. (Quoth Almond of Immanuel) to tell me of sermons & therefore I pray say no more of it, but </set down\> the book & binding etc cost so much.[814] Mr Dean hath heard from my Lord of Cant. of his Course in Lent which I perceive by you will be the Annunciation day.[815] I am tyred with this attendance in expectation of the Commissioner: but so soon as I am at leisure I will not neglect your business. But for all that I will have 3 or 4 strong carles with pistolls sir reverence to go with me.[816] And so I rest

Yr. humble servant,
G.D.

I would gladly have the Altar Cloath against Easter. For in Lent I would not have it up. But I have severall times desired of you to let me know the dimensions of the pulpit cloath at St Pauls, & a description of it (or whether it was paned & how) Mr Scissons can enquire it from of[817] an officer. I remember I liked it well.

124 **26 February 1670**
T. 44.185
G.D. to W.S. from Durham

Durham Castle. Febr. 26. 1669.

Sir;

Mr Stapylton tells me from Mr Flower, that you are well & remember me.[818] I am glad it is so, & now the soreness is over, I wonder you do not look after the 300. I hear not yet of Mr Etterick's return home. I have received damask for an altar-cloath from Mr Nayler a week since: but no bill nor no letter. I think neither you nor he will even tell us the dimensions & fashion of St Pauls pulpit cloath & cushion. John intends the next term to send one Mr Ward to account with Mr Welsted.[819] I have written to him that you have a 1st volume of the Lexicon, which you say from him, must be paid for /by\ me & let it be so: but be not paid for it by sermons, I pray you. But I hear

814 George Almond: L. **80**.
815 25 March.
816 Carles = country men: *OED*.
817 Sic.
818 William Flower: L. **112**.
819 Ward: unidentified.

that Dr Fr. Turner is Residentiary of your church, & since that he is made M{aste}r of St John's in Cambridge & that in both these places he is Dr Stillingfleets Precentor quoth Hugh Broughton of Bp. Bancroft.[820] Much joy may my good friend have in both his places. I am heartily glad for old generous gentleman his father's sake, that he hath so good a neighbour, & also for Mistress Turners sake; to both which, if you would give my service, as also to the young Residentiary, I would thank you.[821] If I was sure the Dr was at St John's I would write to him in behalf of a poor sizar there, whom for what I perceive, by a letter thence I am like to maintain (because his mother is my kinswoman & hath 6 or 7 children besides) if he stay there, unless he can get some help. If the Dr would make him his sizar, it would be brave; & it would be very well if he could do any other good for him, if that cannot be done. And I pray you if he be at London do as much for me, as tell him, I desire him earnestly by all the friendship he hath for me, to look upon that poor lad, whose name is Dan & Mr Birlick's pupill.[822] But now what a stirre have I made if the Dr be not the Precentor at St John's, as said the aforementioned Hugh. You see how plainly I use you: & I pray do what you can for me in this behalfe. I know both Mr Dean & Mirs. Turner will second my request.

I took my leave of Mr Dean this afternoon.[823] I beleeve he will begin his journey on Munday or Tuesday. And so I take my leave of you for this time but on all occasions my service to Robt. Gayer & his Lady & to My Lady Rich.

Your most humble servant,

G.D.

---

820 Francis Turner (1638–1700), prebendary of Sneating in St Paul's 7 December 1669; Master of St John's, Cambridge, 11 April 1570: *ODNB*. Edward Stillingfleet (1635–99) was prebendary of St Paul's 1667–89 and Chaplain to the king 1668–89: *ODNB*. Hugh Broughton (1549–1612) was a pupil of Gilpin at Kepier School, prebendary of Durham 1578–80, and rector of Washington, Durham, 1580–83; he was deeply critical of Richard Bancroft, Archbishop of Canterbury 1604–1610, for the latter's views on biblical chronology: *ODNB*. Precentor may mean he sings on his side.

821 Thomas Turner (1592–1672), Dean of Canterbury from 1644 till his death. He was renowned for his generosity: *ODNB*.

822 John Dan married Ann Davenport, the daughter of Henry Davenport (George's uncle). The boy was thus George's cousin once removed. He was educated at Oakham School, Rutland, before entering St John's College in June 1668. He obtained his B.A. in 1672/3 and M.A. in 1677: *Al. Cant.* A sizar was charged reduced fees in exchange for performing menial tasks. Mr Birlick: unidentified.

823 Dean Sudbury.

125 **5 April 1670**
T. 44.195
G.D. to W.S. from Houghton

Houghton. < > Easter Tuesday 70.

Mr Dean;

Etterick will not have the money at Sunderland, but at Durham, to my good liking. I listed Stapylton & Carnaby & Foster & some other stout fellows for the translation to morrow & intimated so much to Mr Etterick, who returned answer that he would receive it at Durham shortly: & so I dispacht a messenger to Durham to bid the Carles come over on Wednesday morning sine culpa.[824] For you must know, I had invited them all to dinner and to ride out 2 or 3 miles with me. I might as well have saved the rost meat, as have bestowed it upon the inculpabilis.[825]

But now, you say not a word of your speaking to Dr Turner of St John's in my name in behalf of Dan there, whom I would desire to make him his sizar or /a\ servitor in the hall or chapell clerk /for I am told it will be voyd shortly\ or anything he is fitt to be. And truly I thought I should have heard from you long since of this matter.

We are about to build Bough Church by the Cathedrall: the expense whereof will amount to about 400£.[826] I am chief beggar; & I think I shall get the money. Now you must know, that your good Br{ethren} Wrench, Wood, Grey, Grenvyle & Smith have subscribed 05£ a piece, & Dr Basire 7£. Dr Carlton, Brevint & Dalton have promised /me\ to subscribe as well as their Brethren. Dr Neil is absent, & I must desire you to speak to Dr Durell & also to signify your own pleasure. For we intend I think to go forthwith about it. I have subscriptions already for about 150£ & I think it may easily be doubled, severall having already promised: & there is about 80£ in bank of old store. But our gentry come very hangedly (as we say in this countrey) to this work.[827]

We have an Altar Cloath hung up. It is brave, & to the admiration of a thousand who saw it on Sunday. Wrench went to Bolden on Saturday, & is to meet the foresaid supposed culpable people tomorrow at dinner: but he is affrayd of putting me to charge: though

824 sine culpa = without blame, but in this case without the money. Carnaby: possibly *Cosin Corr.* II, p. 255.

825 inculpabilis = blameless, but again a pun on without the money.

826 Bow Church: Introduction, p. 14.

827 Hangedly = languidly.

now I am but in 200£ debt: having overcome other 300£. This is well you'l say. But what walls am I to build this summer about the house!

For the rest, my service to Sir Robt. Gayer & all friends as if named. And so I rest, for it is almost to time to choose churchwardens & other officers.

Yr. most obliged servant,
G.D.

Houghton < >: 'Whitsun' erased.

126 **15 April 1670**
T. 144.111
G.D. to W.S. from Durham

Durham Castle. Apr. 15. 1670.

Mr Dean;

The culpa is here still & yet I am not culpable in your business. On Saturday last Mr Etterick sent me an order to pay 200£ to one Mr Sedwick a lawyer of this town whose sister he marryed.[828] I sent for Mr Sedgwick & offered him the money. He answered that indeed his brother Etterick owed him 200£, but he was to have three months warning before he received it: & forasmuch as he knew /not\ how to dispose of it, he would not receive it. With this answer I sent my man on Saturday last to Mr Etterick: who took the matter ill from his brother in law, & ordered me to bring the whole 300£ to him any time within 10 days. Now Tuesday last was the synod here & the same day I had a reference from the Chancery to hear & to Christen Dick Neil a daughter.[829] Wednesday /&\ Thursday were our Sessions: this day is the Visitation: and every Saturday I attend my Lords affairs here, on Monday Mr Stapylton & Mr Kirby (two of the priest carles) are to be employed: so that Tuesday is appointed for portation: of which I have given Mr Etterick notice by a letter this morning.[830] And so much for culpa at this time.

I have spoken with Mr Wood who hath, since I came to town, cleared the former year, & payed 10£ towards the last years rent & is to pay all the rest without abatement, before we let him the tithes for

828 Mr Sedgewick: Justice John Sedgwick of St Oswald's parish, recorded as dead 4 July 1699: *North Country Diaries*, SS 124, p. 147.

829 Margaret, daughter of Richard Neil, under-sheriff of Durham 12 April, baptised in the catherdral: *Durham Cathedral Registers*, p. 10.

830 George Kirby, Treasurer to Bishop Cosin's household: *Cosin Corr.* II, pp. 228, 245, 247, 327.

the next year, which he hath promised. For I tell him I will not abate anything but require &c according to your bargain. And I think the barn hath cost 06£ & upward (as Mr Wrench who received your bill yesterday told me) the last year. I viewed it before it was repayred; it was in decay.

For Dr Turner I thank you: & will write to him so soon as I heare he is made master.[831] I am glad your bills are passed: & that you are well.[832] But feavers & physitians I never heard of before, though Mr Wrench had a letter from you. Whatsoever becomes of Shadwell, have good regard to your health. My service to Sir R. Gayer & his Lady & to my Lady Rich, at their coming. I am huge glad of what you write concerning their health.

Now for Bough Church. I much marvail that you could not foresee that when the church was once up (God send it) that I meant unless I could get a combination for afternoon sermons (for < > it is too near the cathedrall for forenoon sermons) too bigg affresh for maintenance. There are other parishes in this countrey (as Chester & Lanchester endowed with 10£ apeice which stand in more need of maintenance and at Chester many tithes are now to be sold, which by the Oxford Act /for uniting churches\ may be given to the curat there.[833] He who sells hath promised me favour if I will buy any: and I intend to move the parishioners, & to give money with them, if they will give. I intend to preach there on Sunday (as I oft do) & some gentlemen tell me they will meet me at dinner. But they little think what proposall I will make to them /provided it exceeds not 500£\ and that is, I'le tell you, to give a 10th part of what < > shall be bestowed & to beg of them besides. I hope to do good by this: & be out of debt by Martinmass, if God lend me life so long. Now after all this, by that saying Dr Durell //sticks not to contribute his 5£ but rather towards the better endowment of some church etc. I think I may venture to set down the Dr 5£ for Bough Church: but you answer nothing for yourselfe, but that the Dean speaketh reason. If you please you may tell him what I wrote about Chester which it is like will better please him than that of Bough Church did. And to tell you my mind freely, I do intend to uphold the

831 Turner: L. **124**.

832 May refer to Shadwell, L. **85** above.

833 Probably 'An Act for uniting churches in cities and towns corporate', 17 Charles II 1665, c. 3, which dealt with the uniting of small churches and giving the income to only one curate: *Statutes of the Realm*, V, *1625–80*, London 1819, pp. 576–7.

begging trade for the church, (if I find it successful) as long as I live. I have a subscription on foot (& some money I have received) amongst such gentlemen, (I know 50) that have been scholars at Houghton School, for building a schoolm{aste}rs. house, at least additional buildings to the school. But you will wonder perhaps at another work// in which I have already spent some money (& if I want not money, I hope to finish it this summer) & that is to make a bowling green in the coney garth by the garden < > in the place where the pond was, which I have filled up, (it being too near the house & I having three besides.) This I have been solicited unto by many gentlemen, & I have told them I am content to do it at myne own charge, provided they will submitt to these conditions, to pay 4d for every oath /sworn in it by them\ & a tenth part of their clean winnings (for who knows some may play the fool & lose 10£) & this they promise. If I do this, the Hospitall people shall have the keeping of it, & all advantage for their further maintenance which may do them some good. So God bless us in all our honest endeavours. To his Protection I commend you & remain

Sir

Your most affectionate servant

G.D.

Hath John his book yet & is it placed to my account?[834] & how much cometh all to for him? For I will make him pay again: & he & I are just upon clearing. God be praised.

what < > shall: 'they' erased.

127 **3 December 1670**

T. 44.237

G.D. to W.S. from Houghton

Houghton. Dec. 3. 1670.

Mr Dean;

I this day received yours at Durham (where I had not time {to} return an answer) and into what perplexity it putteth me, you may easily ghess. But I hope my brother's condition is not so bad as Mr Harvey reported it to be.[835] For I cannot imagine that either he or his wife would conceal it from me: though it be two months since I heard

834 John: G.D.'s brother John.

835 Mr Harvey: unidentified.

from him. About a year & halfe since he had a sore ague, a double tertian.[836] But he afterwards gott his strength again. I advised him to a course of physick: & he said he would enter into it. But I cannot say whether he did so. In the spring he sent me word his health was not good. But since never complained: so that I thought he was well. The truth is I beleve the air he liveth in is not good. And I have advised him to remove to Lincoln for sometime for the air sake to recover his health & if you would please to advise him to the same, I should take it for a great favoer from you. He often complaineth of agues with his children, one of which dyed about September last; & 2 or 3 more had agues then. If you please to write, direct it to him at West-Rasin, to be left at the Antilope in Lincoln, by Grantham Post.

I am sorry for your sorrow & God comfort us both. I am glad Sir Robt. Gayer & his relations are so well. God continue their health. The </pulpit\> cloath of St Pauls was of damask red & purple, & hung a little over the desk /onely\ with a gold fringe. I liked it better than the usuall city fashion of putting the pulpit into a petty-coat: besides it is not /so\ chargable: & I study thrift in the case.

This day I read in my Lords letter to Mr Stapylton, that the King had promised him the bestowing of the next prebend of Durham that shall fall by Praerogative: this my Lord bad him to tell me as my concernment: & he hath told it to everybody as well as to me, & I may well tell it to you.[837] There is much talk of Dr Wood for Lichfield: but I know not what to beleeve of it.[838] But I hear that severall have made sute or said so at least for his Prebend here, if he prevail there. Which I am sure I have never done: nor do I, I thank God, set my mind on preferments. But //this I thought good to tell you if you knew it not before, as Mr Flower saith, he & Sir Andrew Henley did. I was told that Mr Godolphin was like to succeed Col. Legg in the bed-chamber.[839] I wish it may be so. I wish you health & comfort after your sorrow, & so commend you to Gods protection and remain

Your most affectionate servant

G.D.

---

836 A double tertian: a fever recurring on the second day.

837 See Introduction, pp. 20–21.

838 Lichfield was vacant because the bishop, John Hacket, Wood's great enemy, died 28 October 1670. Wood succeeded him 9 June 1670: *ODNB*.

839 William Legg(e), Groom of the Bed Chamber to Charles I and Charles II. Died 13 October 1670: *ODNB*; *Cosin Corr.* II, p. 257. Sidney Godolphin was already nominated 12 September 1668: *ODNB*.

The money I had of my brother I have paid him again & all accounts between us are even.//

</pulpit\>: 'altar' erased.

128 **2 May 1671**
T. 44.255
G.D. to W.S. from Houghton

Houghton May 2 1671.

Mr Dean;

I should be glad you would tell me you are well. I now send you this letter, which perhaps may give you some trouble in my business, & perhaps not, as you will perceive.

Yesterday I had a letter from my Lord dated Apr. 27. In it he tells me that that day it cost him two twenty shillings peices to enter two caveats in the two Principall Secretaryes office, & to engage the secretarys themselves in the matter, about the promise the King made my Lord, to give the next Prebend of Durham that by promotion should fall in his majesties guift to me /G.D.\ (so he writeth) and if Dr Wood be made a Bishop it is requisite, saith my Lord, that I /G.D.\ should have somebody there to follow the seals.[840] Mr Flower writeth to the same purpose, & saith he found </one\> at my Lord Arlington's office looking after Dr Woods living.[841]

But I do not see it certayn, that Dr Wood shall be made a Bishop; nor secondly that if he be, he shall leave his Prebend /and\ 3. If both these bee, yet the Prebend I think is not voyd till his consecration or homage.

But if the two former happen, I must crave your help. For I like not to make a journey to London at adventure because 1. I am not sent for by my Lord. 2. I think (if all things happen well) it is yet too soon. 3. If things go amiss, I shall be laughed at. I crave yr. assistance, & advice to Mr Flower, whom I think I must employ if things succeed, for he is a good trudgover, & acquainted, I think, at both the Secretaryes office: And also to furnish him with money if need require: also to draw up a certificate for me, & to sign it, & get it signed by my Lord /& Mr Dean\ & others, B{isho}ps or whom you please that know me, & also a petition in my name, for I suppose, all things pass by petition before

840 Underlined in the manuscript. Theoretically the king had this nomination because he had appointed Wood to a bishopric.

841 Henry Bennet (1618–85), first Lord Arlington, Keeper of the Privy Purse at the Restoration. Secretary of State 1662–74. Probably the most important politician at this time: *ODNB*.

the Secretarys. But as I said, I think, this is not to be done unless & untill the Bishoprick be obtained, & the prebend quitt. But if < > these /be\ needfull, upon /the bare\ nomination to a B{isho}prick (as I think they are not) I must desire you to help in them; if Dr Wood happen to be nominated & if his majesty will make good his gracious promise to my Lord. Our brother Ralph Bl{ackiston} useth to say, let us love one another, & do for one another & sometimes go for one another. I beleeve my Lord of Canterbury (if it were needful) would not refuse to sign a certificate for me, as he did 10 years since: nor my Lord of York.[842] I think also Dr Thrisscross would not onely do the same, but also stir in it, if he was desired. I must /not\ conceal from you that all things considered, there is hardly a better /prebend\ in the church of Durham than this I speak of: but this between you and me. //And so I commend you to Gods protection & rest, Sir

Your most affectionate servant

G.D.

My service to Sir Ro. Gayer & the Ladyes when you see them.//

129 **12 May 1671**
T. 44.257
G.D. to W.S. from Houghton

Houghton. May 12. 1671.

Mr Dean,

By the Tuesday Post I received your letter for which I thank you. I perceive the two first stiles are yet to be climbed over. For Dr Wood is not yet B{isho}p. & when he is, he will be still for the Prebend.[843] The Lord Keeper Williams, when he was Bp. of Lincoln, retained a Prebend in the same church;[844] and it was said, the Psalm which by the statutes of that Church that Prebendary was to say daily, was Dixi custodiam: by the same token an < > old expectant Prebendary, who rose no higher, said daily the next psalm expectans expectavi.[845] I will not

842 Gilbert Sheldon was still Archbishop of Canterbury. Richard Sterne (1595/6–1683) was Archbishop of York 1664–83: *ODNB*.

843 Wood retained the eleventh prebend whilst bishop: Mussett, p. 87.

844 John Williams (1582–1650), whilst Bishop of Lincoln 1621–41, was a prebendary and precentor of Lincoln from 1613 to 1642: CCED, person ID 43875; *ODNB*.

845 Dixi custodiam: Psalm 39.1. 'I said, I will take heed to my ways, that I sin not with my tongue: I will keep my mouth with a bridle, while the wicked is before me' (AV). Expectans expectavi: Psalm 40.1. 'I waited patiently for the Lord: and he inclined unto me, and heard my cry' (AV).

much trouble my head with difficultyes that are like to arise: those Prebends are not for me which will not come without haling & plucking. God grant, I may give him an account for what I have: and if I have no Prebend, I have none to answer for. I must needs acknowledg my Lord of Canterbury's kindness, whose promise is as large as I could anyways reasonable expect /& larger than I can deserve\. And if you think good you may say, so with the tender of my duty. I am building walls & chambers & I have provided /& wrought\ most of the materialls for a new chapel. But I long for harvest, that I may be enabled to pay for them. I am persuaded that if I should succeed Dr Wood, his houses would cost me more than they will cost either him or another: but I would < > not have him know /I say\ so much: least I should be thought to have as large a mind as a B{isho}p. With my humble service to you, I thank you, & remain

Sir,

Your most affectionate servant,

G.D.

My service to Dr Fr. Turner, mentioned in your letter: and to the generous old gentleman his father, if he be in town.[846]

130 **23 May 1671**

T. 44.262

G.D. to W.S. from Houghton

Houghton. May 23. 1671.

Mr Dean;

I hope I need not move you to move my Lord of Canterbury, who you said would do any thing for me but oppose the Duke.[847] I am ready to beleive his Highness doth acquiesce: but I hear, not onely Dr Durell, but also that Dr Grey or his friends solicite for the Prebend, which perhaps may not fall. I think Dr Woods prebend is better worth than 200£, & Dr Durell worth 120£, & Dr Greys 80£ besides wages.[848] So that if a man might choose, it was easy to say, which he would take. I think I have most need, having spent farre more in this countrey, than I have gotten; being indebted 300£, though I hope I have corn on the ground to pay for halfe of it: I have been here 9 years; & what service I have done my Lord & his diocese, let others say: for I love not

846 L. **124**.

847 Duke of York, later James II.

848 John Durell held the fourth stall, Robert Grey the eighth: Mussett, pp. 37, 66.

arguing for my selfe in such cases, though these things do a little tempt me to it. But the thoughts of preferrment never yet broke my sleep; nor is it like to do it now

I had a letter on Sunday from Stoke from Mr London, who tells me Sir Robt. Gayer hath been more like to die than live of a feaver; but is now well recovered, & means to be at London this week.[849] I pray present my service to him & to his Lady & God make them than[k]full.

I hear from my Lord, that Sir Andrew Henley is very solicitous in my behalfe; for which I am much engaged to him.

I think this day month (the morrow after Trinity Sunday), I shall go towards Barwick with the Chancellor for my Lord's visitation.[850] With my service & thanks I commend you to Gods protection & rest.

Sir

Your affectionate servant.

G.D.

131 **29 May 1671**

T. 44.263

G.D. to W.S. from Houghton

Houghton. May 29. 1671

Mr Dean,

Yesterday I received the news of Dr Woods advancement, & of his retaining the Prebend in commendam.[851] I do not much concern my selfe in it: but I am right glad that I went not to London about it, as some of my friends would have had me: oh! how I should have {been} laughed at! I have answered my Lord, who sent me this news, that I am as good as I was before, being in the mans case who lost 200£ by wooll, for want of sheep. But I most earnestly pray you, that you would make my acknowledgement to my Lord of Canterbury, for his Graces favour & furtherance: for I understand both by my Lord & Mr Flower how much I am engaged to his Grace. The lack of these things affects not me so much as they </would\> some others. I think I had best to send to /my\ old friend my Lord Wood, to condole for this /his\ heavey burden: perhaps he will give me a Prebend at Litchfield

849 Mr London: unidentified.

850 Barwick: Berwick.

851 Wood held the eleventh stall until 1692 (Mussett, p. 87). He had a dispensation of 8 August 1671 from residence in Durham: DCM, DCD/B/AA/4, p. 162. The phrase *in commendam* was especially used where a bishop held a benefice as well as his bishopric: Walker, *Oxford Companion to Law*, p. 246.

/where my grandfather was born\:[852] for when his wife went from hence, & asked what I would have to her husband, I gave her in charge to secure the next good Prebend at Litchfield for me. I beleeve I must be his curat here to preach his commendam courses. In the meantime (to be serious) because I cannot build at his house, I'le build at home. Excuse all trouble: you know who said it, let us love one another & do for one another.[853] I am

Sir

Yr. obliged servant,

G.D.

</would\>: 'do' erased.

132 **7 July 1671**

T. 92.20

G.D. to W.S. from Houghton

Houghton. July. 7. 1671.

Mr Dean;

Even so it is, neither better nor worse, our great bell is cracked with ringing at a yeomans funerall. And most of the parish are of opinion it will be sent with less cost to London, than to York. Now it may be, though you are dean of a church with one bell, you may have acquaintance with some that have good skill in bell-mettall. For though we intend to send old Michael Robinson of East Rainton the Churchwarden, whom you know, with it;[854] yet none of us have acquaintance with a skilfull man, who may agree with the bell-founder: and the parish hope you may have some acquaintance with such a man. If you can do us any good, pray let me know soon: for if you cannot I know not who can. I must further acquaint< > you /with\ a great countrey grievance. For I declaring there was but one bell in Pauls, a man cryed out cheating, saying he thought always there had been a main power of bells there: & said expressly the countrey was cheated, who, to his certain knowledg, paid Poll-money for at least twenty years together at a penny a head: & could they not, said he, buy bells with the money.[855] I have been at Barwick lately in my Lords visitation with the Chancellor. But I cannot tell you any news

852 My grandfather ...: Possibly G.D.'s grandfather Hales.
853 Let us love one another: I John 4.7; also L. **128**.
854 One of the 'Twenty Four' in 1660: DCRO, EP/Ho 168, f. 170.
855 Paul's: St Paul's.

either from thence or from hence. The foundation of my chapell was laid the day I went, & the work goeth well on. And the two new rooms I built, are covered (with lead) & finished without. This maketh me more beggarlike than I was before. I have bought no cloaths for a great while, but a single pair of breeches of about King Rufus's price.[856] Is your house in hand? The church? Or what great work are you about? For Wrench called here on Tuesday & said Mr Dean said you was so oversett with work, that he was afraid it would kill you. And he, good man, never asked with what works. And lest I should further trouble you, I rest

Sir,

Yr. most humble servant.

G.D.

aquaint< > you: 'tance with' erased.

133 **24 November 1671**
T. 44.277
G.D. to W.S. from Houghton

Houghton. Nov. 24. 1671.

Mr Dean;

I wrote to you by the Tuesdays Post, & that day I received yours, which, had it come a little sooner, might have saved the trouble which mine will give you. I have satisfyed Mr Wrench that you have the bill of exchange. I did not know that you had been in Suffolk: & I am sorry for your loss of your friends there.

I was yesterday at Durham & one proffered to me & to Dr Basire & Mr Wrench a petition for Mris Webb to you for more maintenance, & told me the Justices would subscribe it in her name /& desired us to do so,\ but I answered I would not, for I thought the contents were not true for though she was /poor & sickly\ I said, she had not 4 children to maintayn, nor so much as one, as I thought; for her youngest was about 18 & lately had left the mother & was gone to service & was never yet baptized,[857] and I thought the justices did not well to promote a petition for maintenance of a lusty infidell Hussy.

But indeed you must do something with the rest of your Brethren for Bough Church. I have the subscription of seaven Prebendarys for

856 King Rufus's price: J. Stow, *The Annales of England*, London 1600, f. 178, describes how William Rufus spurned a pair of hose costing 3s but accepted a worse pair costing 13s 4d.

857 Mrs Webb: unidentified.

5£ & Dr Dalton & he of Carlisle or Bristow[858] (by what name or title soever) have promised to subscribe & you & Dr Durell are absent, & I'ld to Dr Neil to morrow, & there is the whole number. I have agreed for setting up the battle round about the church & chancell, & finishing all the stone work (steeple & flagging excepted) for 130£ but it will cost 250£ in lead.[859] My service to Sir R. Gayer &c. I do not see that I am concerned in the bishoprick of Bristow, though you seem to think so. Secundum usum Litchfield.[860]

//As I told you before, < > quoth Father Palmer. It is best in such cases, at most to stand fair: and if it cometh it need not be feared:[861] if it come not, it may be sleighted with a generous neglect. But I must /now\ go to lay the 4 walks in my orchard. And when I am there, I shall think of the Duke of Northfolk, who when he was faced by Q.Eliz. for affecting the Q. & crown of Scotland answered, that when he was in his great bowling alley at Norwich (the best in England saith Tho. Fuller), he {deserved} the kingdom of Scotland: & so much at this time for Prebends.//[862]

Sir

Your most affectionate servant,

G.D.

134 **18 December 1671**

T. 44.281

G.D. to W.S. from Durham

Durham Castle. Dec. 18. 1671.

Mr Dean;

Yesterday I received yours in this place (for I supplyed the </course\> of my Lord elect of Bristow) & this day ill weather &

858 Guy Carleton, Dean of Carlisle, 1660–72, and canon of the twelfth stall in Durham cathedral 1660–85, was nominated to Bristol (Bristow) 1 December 1671. He kept his Durham prebend *in commendam*: *ODNB*; Mussett, p. 94.

859 Battle = battlements.

860 Secundum usum = according to the use. Underlined in the original. Sancroft had probably suggested that he might obtain Carleton's prebend: LL. **132**, **144**.

861 Father Palmer: unidentified.

862 Thomas Fuller: L. **16**. For the project that Thomas Howard would marry Mary, Queen of Scots: *ODNB* under Howard, fourth Duke of Norfolk (1538–72). This also gives William Camden, *The Historie of the most renowned and victorious princesse Elizabeth, late Queen of England …*, London 1635, I, p. 130 as the origin of the story, but figuring a tennis court rather than a bowling alley.

indisposition keep me in this place.[863] Wrench was with me when I received it, & when I shewed it to < >him, oh how he kicked & flung! Send tankards to me, quoth he;[864] I promise you if you bring any to me I'ld give it you back again; said I, then I shall have them both. But do what I can, I must stay till he write to you, & have your answer: & I am like to do that, for Christmas is at hand, & I cannot go to Newcastle in hast & there is no goldsmith here. In the mean time I ghess at your meaning, & must thank you. But I say your arms must be set on.[865] And so much for tankards.

I have spoken with Mr Cradock & he is sorry he understood not Mistress Webb's case better before.[866] </But I had\> told them as much almost as you now write. I think nothing more will be done in it. But if any paper came to your hands, you can lay it by.

I read with pleasure what you write of Fressingfield vicarage, & Immanuel Chapell. But I would fayn know how you settle those fee farm rents. I ghess it must be upon trustees. I love a man that loveth the church as well as his own flesh & blood. And I am of opinion that we priests that have no wives, ought to look upon the church & poor as our next heirs. And truly I could think well of myselfe, if I could be assured that I have profited the living church, as much as I have bettered the materiall & dead church, by my means /or\ money. But when I think of that burden that was laid when I was made Priest (till no place be left either for viciousness of life, or error in doctrine) fearfulness & trembling take hold upon me; & in this thing God be mercifull to me & to all priests.

For the other thing you mention, vadat sicut vadit.[867] I beleive I am as little concerned for it, as any that expected it upon lesse grounds. Though, I hold it the best Preb{end} in this church. There now belong to this church 3 B{isho}ps & as many Deans: the metropolitan hath not many more of his province.[868]

---

863 For Bishop of Bristol see previous letter.

864 This section is unclear but it seems that W.S. has sent two tankards, perhaps one for Wrench and one for G.D., and the arms of W.S. are to be engraved on them: see also L. **135**.

865 arms: of W.S. 'Ar. On a chevron between three crosses formée gules as many doves of the first': B. Burke, *The General Armory of England, Scotland, Ireland and Wales*, London 1884.

866 Thomas Cradock, Attorney General to Bishop Cosin, *Cosin Corr.* II, p. 232; *North Country Diaries*, SS 124, p. 123.

867 vadat sicut vadit = Let it go as it goes.

868 The Bishops were Carleton (Bristol) and Wood (Coventry and Lichfield); the Deans, Neile (Ripon), Smith (Carlisle), Sancroft (St Paul's). The Metropolitan was the Archbishop of York.

In the spring it will be 7 years since I saw London, & 10 since I was in mine own countrey. And if I can I would gladly see my friends in both places: but I think, if I should, I must make but little stay in either place. For my Lords affairs, aswell as mine own would urge my return. And so God keep us all.

Your most affectionate servant,

Geo. Davenport.

My humble service to Sir Robt. Gayer, when you see them or write to him.

</course\>: 'place' erased; </But I had\>: 'For I' erased.

135 **26 July 1672**
T. 43.21
G.D. to W.S. from Houghton

Houghton Jul. 26. 1672.

Mr Dean;

Since I saw you I neither received any letter from London nor have I received any from thence. I thank God I have my health well, & I should be glad to hear that my friends have their health. I suppose Sir Andrew Henley may be marryed before this:[869] & I was told on Sunday last by my Lady Mary Heveningham at Tinmouth Castle (where her husband your countreyman is prisoner)[870] that Sir William Rich is marryed to my Lord of Alesbury's daughter:[871] I pray let me know from you whether it be so. I pray present my service to Sir Robt. Gayer & his Lady & my Lady Rich when you see them. Wrench swallowed the Tankard; but hee made many good morows, as much as it holdeth </go\> downs. So I was defeated. Wood hath paid 20£ before hand towards this years tithes at Heighinton & given his bond for 20£ more. Dr Smith is in Residence.[872] I seldom see Durham: but I went the other day to see him, because he is to go away the beginning of the next week. My brother John met me at Newark, as we came from London & I have been in hopes of seeing him

---

869 He married his second wife on 20 May 1672: *HPC*, II, p. 523.

870 Sir William Heveningham of Ketteringham, Norfolk, was imprisoned for his part in the death of Charles I. His wife was Mary, daughter of John Carey, fifth Baron Hunsdon. The *ODNB* says he was imprisoned in Windsor.

871 Sir William Rich, son and heir of Sir Thomas Rich, married Lady Anne Bruce, daughter of Robert, Earl of Ailesbury on 28 May: *HPC*, III, p. 330.

872 Thomas Smith, canon of the first stall: Mussett, p. 14; for his presence: DCM, DCD/B/AA/4, p. 171.

here. But he saith harvest will hinder him. He is well. Mr Dean saith my Lord of Canterbury hath gotten the gout which his Dr prayed for. I hope it will do him good. I am sorry to hear of Mr Thorndyke's death.[873] I pray present my service to all that enquire after me, if any do. And so I commend you to God's protection and remain

Sir

Your most humble servant.

G.D.

{I} had like to have forgotten the *..*(as many in such cases do:) *...*I pay it to Mr Wrench.

</go|>: 'good' erased.

136 **21 July 1673**
R. 100, f. 169
G.D. to W.S. from Houghton

Houghton. Jul. 21. 1673.

Mr Dean;

In the first place, I must pay you fifteen shillings, upon our Johns account for so much paid by you to Mr John Duke.[874] I also owe you three pounds for 3 dormants fetcht out of your house in the College, & now dormant in the roof of the Bough-Church. Both these summs I will pay to Mr Wrench so soon as I have money: but I am about 10£ out of purse already; </though\> 80£ in subscriptions is due to me. This church is now all covered with roof & boards, & the battlements I hope will be finished this week: and then {hope} for 200£ to buy lead of which summ 50£ or therabouts is due for lead sold 20 years since from the church, by a bond. So I have dispatcht the church, in one sense. In the next place, I returned from my journey a month since; & left all my friends, God be thanked, in good health. I wrote not to you since that time, partly because I forgott, & partly because Mr Wrench said he thought you was in Suffolk. Thirdly, I desire to hear of your health; & whether your house be yet habitable. For if ever I come to London (as I think I shall not) in[875] intend to lie there. For lodgings /& meat\ are dear in other places there. So said Ralph Blackiston, when he sent me his horses for 6 weekes.[876]

873 Herbert Thorndike, died 11 July 1672: above, L. **18**.
874 John Duke: unidentified.
875 Sic.
876 Above, L. **78**.

Nextly, in my journey I saw Dr Samways, & Mr /Dean\ Holdsworth & Dr Neil, who hath the best Deanery in England (for spurrs I mean) if he could get in it. But my Lord of York opposeth him, unless he will take institution from him.[877] I think Mr Holdsworth will shortly come & see me: but he & Sir Joseph Cradock have brewed a new suit about his jurisdiction, as he telleth me.[878] I also saw the Dean at Lincoln at Lincoln.[879] I'le warrant you ten questions passed betwixt us, before he knew me (& yet I have not altered my band) and I was too proud to tell him my name, till he called my face to remembrance. Now I come home; & here Mr Mansiur[880] & Mr Forder remember their service to you, and I am in good health God be praised: but we fear a wet harvest, though we have no hopes of sheeving corn for 5 weeks.[881] Lastly, I pray let me know how Sir Robt. Gayer doth, & whether he still talketh of France & Spain, & how the good Ladyes are, with my service to them all. And so commending you to God's protection, I am

Your faithfull servant,

G.D.

</though\>: 'but' erased.

137 **4 May 1674**

R. 101, f. 36r/v

G.D. to W.S. from Houghton

Houghton May 4 1674.

Sir,

.... 30 I received this morning. And as I am glad of your return & *...* to health so I am sorry for your late sickness, of which I assure you, I did not {hear an}y thing till of late, Sir Robt. Gayer in his letter, acquainted me with it. For before *...* sent me word, from Mr Dean of Lincoln, that you was not detained for wan*...*. I make this Apology for myselfe, & for my not writing to you before. But *...* I know where to find you, I take the first occasion I can.

---

877 Peter Samwaies: L. **10**; Thomas Holdsworth, Dean of Middleham: L. **3**; John Neil, Dean of Ripon, L. **89**; My Lord of York: Richard Sterne: L. **128**.

878 Sir Joseph Cradock, father of Thomas, the Attorney General to Bishop Cosin, was knighted in 1661: *Stapylton Corr.*, p. 249. The jurisdiction concerned the status of Middleham as exempt: above, L. **57**.

879 Sic. Dean at Lincoln: Michael Honeywood: L. **30**.

880 Name uncertain, person unidentified.

881 Mr Forder: chapel clerk in Bishop Cosin's household: L. **137**.

For your building at St Paul's, God send the good work prosperity.[882] I hope you have a good stock of money by you. I am in the mire about Bough-Church (but if it was to do < > again I would do it) having expended 320£ about it, & received but 220£, & am yet in debt for it 54£ & yet neither window glazed, nor steeple higher than the church. But when God sends us a Bishop[883] (which is the next point to be considered) I will shame him, if he helpeth me not : & that, if I have money is easily done, by doing it myselfe. But I have subscriptions for above 70£.

It is constantly said here the Bishop of Oxford will be Bishop of Durham:[884] and some /have\ said he hath confessed he hath his majestys promise for it. If this be so, here is work for you. Mr Forder hath been with me full two years, & he desireth to be entertained by the next B{isho}p in his former places, Clerk of the Chapel & Chaffer of the wax.[885] Now I must earnestly entreat you to move in his behalfe: and if you cannot do it to the B{isho}p himselfe, I am sure you may speak to my Ld. of Canterbury, & desire him to move in his cause & I verily beleeve he will do so much for him. And if you think it convenient, to give him my duty, & say it is my request to his Grace, I shall be content to own it. But that as you see cause. </Mr Forder\> sent by Mr Johnson of Washingtons letter to Mr Edw{ar}d Johnson in this matter: & he hath promised all the assistance he can make.[886] I doubt not but you will assist all you can in this affair, if there be shortly a B{isho}p.

Mr Ra. Blackiston hath been here with me since Nov. 24, but I think he will shortly go to Ryton being very well: he giveth especiall charge that his service be presented to you.

You put yourselfe to a needless trouble in Apologizing about Mr

---

882 The actual building of the new cathedral did not begin until 1675, the preparation of the site and agreement on the design having taken nine years: J. Lang, *The Rebuilding of St Paul's after the Great Fire of London*, Oxford 1956, pp. 27–75.

883 John Cosin died in January 1672 but his successor was not appointed until two years later.

884 Nathaniel Crewe (1633–1721), Bishop of Oxford 1671–74, elected to Durham 18 August 1674. He had requested the bishopric. There was opposition and rumour of simony: *ODNB*.

885 L. **136**.

886 Henry Johnson, rector of Washington, Durham, 1662 until his death in 1683: *Al. Cant.*

Dobsons business.[887] I could not but write to you, at his instance: but I told him I thought you would not write back to the Chapter. They have bound him in a bond of 100£ to reside at his living at Michaelmas or to resign it: & that made him more eager for this, where there is good house. Mr Thompson of Merrington gott Heighington; though he was lately marryed to his maid, a poor woman's daughter.[888] Mrs Wood would fain continue your tenant: for she meaneth to live there.[889]

Wrench went to Bolden on Easter Eve, & cannot find the way back. He doth not use to keep such long residence: & if I be not deceived, he is to preach on Sunday his course.

Lastly, this is to let you understand I have not been very well of late. I gott cold a month since riding to Durham about 5 of the clock {p. 2} in the morning, & that caused a great defluxion of rheum, *...* & cough: but I think I have almost mastered it. I ca *...* coughing or spitting (as the Duke of Buckingham made *...* about K{ing} Richard 3d, as witnesseth Jo. Stow).[890] and in the *..* horn topp. But one thing I had almost forgotten, is your ho{use} completed & done? or what is wanting ? I have 1000 y{ards of wall} about the coneygarth & courtyard to set up this year if I may: being *..* much retarded by the ill ways which will not let us fetch coals for lime.

My service to Sir Robt. Gayer & the Ladyes when you either see them, *...* send to them. And so God have you in in[891] keeping.

Your affectionate servant,

Geo. Davenport.

</Mr Forder\>: 'He' erased.

---

887 Probably Lancelot Dobson, G.D.'s curate formerly at Houghton. Son of George Dobson, gent., of Brancepeth. Vicar of Ellingham 1665–92, Chillingham 1679–92. He seems to have lived in Chillingham. He was involved in legal quarrels over Ellingham: *Al.Cant.*; Ramsey, 'Records of Houghton-le-Spring', p. 686; Northumberland County History Committee, *History of Northumberland*, 15 vols, Newcastle 1893–1940, II, 258–61.

888 James Thompson, vicar of Merrington, Durham, 1660–73, of Heighington until his death in 1684: *Al. Cant.*

889 Mrs Wood: perhaps the wife or widow of Mr Wood, the tenant of Heighington tithes.

890 John Stow (1525–1605): *ODNB*. In *Annales or a general Chronicle of England begun by John Stow: continued and augmented with matters foraigne and domestique, ancient and moderne, unto the end of this present yeare 1631 by Edmund Howes gent.*, London 1631, p. 462, a discussion between the Duke of Buckingham and a bishop concerning the king (Richard III) in which the duke comments on the difficulty of understanding the latter's interrupted speech 'your often breathing and sodaine stopping in your communication …'.

891 Sic.

138 **27 July 1674**
R. 100, f. 171
G.D. to W.S. from Durham

Durham. Jul. 27. 1674.

Mr Dean;

I had a letter from you at your return from Suffolk: but not any since that. I wrote to you soon after, & desired you to endeavour to obtain Mr Forder his chapell clerks place under the next Bishop: & then there was discourse of a Bishop soon to be nominated &/so\ there is now. But there has been so much talk of it & so long the people now say they will beleeve it untill the Bandleleers (so it is named) come down.[892] I have been this day at Relly: where the tenants desire abatement of rent; there I mean that rent 28£. I answered I saw no cause for it: & they, I think, are satisfyed with that answer. But then dilapidations there. The kitchen is like to fall, the sparrs are so bad; & it is thatched. A toofall lets in rain, & it is slated, & the sparrs are too weak for the slates, & the side piece too weak also. I have spoken to Mr Wrench to procure < > wood of the Dean (he is now at Barwick /& returns within 2 days\) & I think a tunn or little more will do it. This was my mornings work: for I preached yesterday for Mr Wrench, who was to preach for Dr Durell; & now stays to dine with the dean of Carlisle, who having ended his residence, is returning.[893] For your own health, I should be glad to hear of it: (I thank God I have mine well now; & complain not of shortness of breath) some say here you are well; & my kinswoman saith when she was with you, she thought you looked better than she ever knew, & that you was fatt, which I do not beleeve.[894] I beleeve Mr Stapylton & Mr Neil will see you: & I doubt not you will be ready to help them if you can. They are miserably wronged here by false reports. I pray present my service to Sir Robert Gayer & the Ladyes when you see them. And so commending you to God's protection. I rest

Your most affectionate servant,

G.D.

My Landlord Wrenches service to you: & Mr Dean of Carlisles.

892 Bandleleers: perhaps Scots usage, for flags or pennons: *A Dictionary of the Older Scottish Tongue*, 12 vols, London 1937–2000, under bandeliers.

893 Thomas Smith, Dean of Carlisle 1671–84: above, L. **135**.

894 My kinswoman: may be Mrs Mary Hales, mentioned in G.D.'s will.

139 **29 January 1675**
R. 100, f. 170
G.D. to W.S. from Houghton

Houghton. Jan. 29.1674.

Mr Dean;

I was yesterday at Durham, & dined with Mr Dean, who preached in the Cathedrall last Sunday, & is well, & saith he hath lost no strength.[895] Mr Wrench saith he received your letter; & bad me tell you, that he should have more money for you: but said not how much.[896] But he & I differ in one point; he saith (& so he told Mr Holdsworth) that he must look to the letting of the corps for this year. I told him I thought he mistook you: forasmuch as you resigned since Michaelmass.[897] He alleged out of your letter, that you write the tenants must face about, & look to another landlord. This doubt you must clear, for he hath already refused to pay Mris Webb any more. Mr Holdsworth was with the Dean: for I went with him. But of the Prebendarys I think he saw only Mr Wrench. I suppose he is now with you. You know you have a trunk with Mr Wrench; & in it a gown, hatt, & capp; & what also I know not. Dr Neil is as well as he hath been this 7 years: as Dr Cartwright saith who saw him since he was dead at London.[898] I am exceeding glad of what you write concerning Sir Robt. Gayer: to whom I pray my service when you see him, & to the good Ladyes. I pray you if you see Dr Beaumont, forgett not my questions: for I would gladly be satisfyed in them.[899] And if you bee in Lambeth Chapell within a month, I desire you to tell me whether the wainscoat roofe, which is flatt & painted have any mouldings upon it. My chapell roofe is done with wainscoat as that is: & the workmen & I are not yet agreed whether mouldings (to draw it in pannells) will make it more beautifull. I am sure it will make it more costly: and < > the wood work on the inside I think will cost me 100£, at which you will wonder.

895 Dean Sudbury had been ill: DCM, Treasurer's Books, DCD/L/BB/37, p. 10 (a Chapter meeting in the Dean's bedchamber 16 December 1674).

896 Wrench had received some dividend for Sancroft: DCM, DCD/L/BB/36, p. 22.

897 Sancroft had resigned his prebend by 23 October 1674 and was succeeded by Thomas Holdsworth who was installed 1 June 1675 and held it to 1681: Mussett, p. 71; DCM, DCD/L/BB/37, p. 35.

898 Thomas Cartwright, canon of the fifth stall of Durham cathedral, 1672–86: Mussett, p. 45. Neil's death must have been rumoured.

899 Joseph Beaumont (1616–99), Master of Peterhouse in 1663 and from 1674 to 1699 Regius Professor of Divinity: *ODNB*.

But </the chapell\> is allowed by those that see it, to be better than the chapell at Durham Castle. It maketh me poor: but doth not make me repent. I have provided an organ for it. I'le //this Post// acquaint my brother with what you < > write of Mr Welsted. Northallerton is in the gift of the dean & chapter of Durham.[900] And so in hast I am Sir

Your most affectionate & humble servant,

G.D.

</chapel\>: 'it' erased.

140 **3 July 1675**
T. 42.165
G.D. to W.S. from Houghton

Houghton. July. 3. 1675.

Mr Dean;

There is one Mr Sherwood, my tenant in Leicestershire who hath promised me to pay his rent (which I think will about 28£) at any place in London I shall appoint about Lammas next.[901] And I think I had best to appoint it to be paid to your nephew, Mr Wm. Sancroft in Freemans Yard neer the Royall Exchange[902] (that /as\ I remember is the place) & then I suppose I may receive the like summe here from Mr Wrench upon your account. If this may be done, I pray, give ordere to your nephew to receive the summe that shall be brought (& I hope it will be brought to him) and if it may not be done, I desire I may know from you /that I may find another convenience\.
Mr Holdsworth went last Monday to Middleham, having continued at Durham since his installation. But I ghess he may return the next week, when it is said, my Lord of Durham will be in the countrey. Both he & Mr Dean tell me that Sir Andrew Henley is dead: for which I am very sorry.[903] I should be glad to hear that Sir Robt. Gayer & all that family & my Lady Rich, are well. Thank God I have my health well: & am almost perswaded to go as far as York to see my Lord's Grace, when the Bishop cometh down: for I reckon we must go as

---

900 It was vacant and disputed: DCM, DCD/B/AA/4, ff. 220–21, April–June 1675.
901 G.D. had inherited lands in Bushby and Wigston, Leics. Lammas was 1 August.
902 William Sancroft was steward to Sancroft, responsible for selling his manuscripts to Tanner, hence their modern presence in the Bodleian Library: *ODNB*.
903 Sir Andrew Henley died 17 May 1675: *HPC*, II, p. 523. Robert, his son by his first wife, succeeded.

farr as the Tese:[904] & York is but a days journey beyond it. My chapell is now fully finished & a good organ errected in it, & reasonably well furnished with altar cloaths & cushions. And I hope before Michaelmass to finish all the outwalls of the house, which I have or shall make all new;[905] & then I trust I shall give over all building whatsoever (unless I build a tenant's house upon Howden Hill.) And it is time; for I have been a builder full ten years: & am almost glutted yea and almost burst too. Are you yet gotten into your Deanery House? & is St Paul's begun? We chose Knights of the Shire last week. Coll. Tempest & Mr Vane (eldest son of Sir Henry) & the /latter\ dyed two days after of the small pox having marryed his cosin Germane (Sir Tho. Lyddalls daughter) about a month before.[906] Sir James Clavering stood at the same time, & I voted for him & Tempest, but Vane gott the second place. And so much for our Countrey news. I find /in\ the Gazet the Church of Westminster have lost their candlesticks (I heard they were the gift of our Dean) and their Basin. And so much at this time (for my messenger stayeth)

From

Sir,

Yr. most obliged servant.

G.D.

141 3 September 1675

R. 100, f. 172

G.D. to W.S. from Houghton

Houghton. Sept. 3. 1675.

Mr Dean;

This morning between the hours of eight & nine the buildings of G.D. were finished: for then the wallers put an end to the long wall encompassing the coneygarth & all the house. All which wall of 750

904 Traditionally the Bishop of Durham was greeted by his clergy on entering his bishopric for the first time, at the River Tees.

905 Michaelmas: 29 September.

906 This was the first county election, opposed by Cosin while he lived.The candidates were John Tempest (who had supported the enfranchisement of the County against Cosin), who polled 1034 votes, Thomas Vane of Raby Castle, who polled 856 votes, and Sir James Clavering of Axwell, baronet, who polled 747 votes: *HPC*, I, pp. 225–6; JohnTempest (c. 1623–97) was only son to Sir Thomas Tempest of The Ile: *HPC*, III, p. 534. Vane died 25 June; in May he had married Frances, daughter of Sir Thomas Liddle of Ravensworth: *HPC*, III, pp. 622–3. Vane was succeeded as MP by his brother Christopher: ibid., p. 622.

yards in length & 4 yards high I have built with good lime & stone from the ground & hope, God willing, the next month to plant the coney garth with apple trees; the one halfe of the wall being already planted with good fruit trees. And so much for that. But first my Lord of Durham came hither 3 weeks since to see it: & was something loving in its praise. I have expected Mr Wrench this way every day this week: but I am told he is not very well, & complains of a pain in his stomach; with which, its said, he seems the more affected, because his brother died of such a distemper. God preserve him. But I hear he goeth abroad. And now to the matter in hand. I received yours of Jul.10. & with sorrow read what you write of the death of my two good friends.[907] Of the unhopefullness of their heirs, I have heard by others: and that troubleth me more than the death of their parents. God mend all. My friend in Leicestershire wrote me word a month since, that he had written to his brother at London to pay 20£ to your nephew for my use, which he hoped he would do. But if he failed to do it, he assureth me that at or before Michaelmass he /himself\ will pay it & something more to him, < > being to be at London at that time, with a drove of cattell. If I live till Michaelmass, I have, I trust </right money enough to\> pay all my debts. And then I may adventure 10£ in hanging my dining room, & buy me new cloaths. This countrey affordeth no news. I hear you are busy about the Quire of St Pauls. God send it all perfected. Mr Holdsworth is at Myddleham. Mr Turner My Lords chaplain </was\> here two or three days & preached for me:[908] & so he did at Newcastle before the Judges to admiration. He doth all things exceeding well, for a man of his inches. My Lord hath been at Newcastle & Sir Ralph Delavales 3 days & returned to Durham last night.[909] He tells me he findeth the castles of Durham & Aukland beyond the reports of others, & his own expectation. Dr Durell was expected the last night: & my Lady Gerard very speedily. Mr Dean kept his bed again 4 or 5 days a fortnight since, for his legg: but it is well again, & he hath since been at Aukland.[910] Severall men, they say,

---

907 One must have been Sir Andrew Henley (L. **140**) The other may have been the second Lady Rich who died this year: GEC, *Baronetage*, III, p. 180; *HPC*, III, p. 329. The heirs were Sir Robert Henley (1655–81) (*HPC*, II, p. 525), who was encumbered by his father's debts, and Sir William Rich: Introduction, p. 23.

908 Mr Turner: L. **66**.

909 Sir Ralph Delaval (1622–91), of Hartley and Seaton Delaval, Northumberland, first baronet, only son and heir of Robert, who had died in 1623: *ODNB* under Delaval family; Ramsey, 'Records of Houghton-le-Spring', p. 681.

910 For Sudbury's health: L. **139**.

stand upon his leggs: that is, cannot be advanced a stepp higher, so long as his leggs are in their way. But enough. God help us all. I am

Your humble servant,

G.D.

him, < >being: 'himself' erased; </was\>: 'hath been' erased.

142 **9 October 1675**

R. 100, f. 173

G.D. to W.S. from Houghton

Houghton. Octob. 9. 1675.

Mr Dean;

Yours of Sept.14. I received Sept. 19. by the same token, that Sir Robert Gayer came hither within an hour after. He stayd Saturday night and Sunday & on Munday I went with him to Richmond.

According to your order; I received the 25£.01s. 08d of Mr Wrench, which I meant not to have done till I /had\ heard what money was paid to you by my correspondent, who promised faithfully to pay it about Michaelmass & what he payeth short, I will make up. But I must tell you /two days since\ Mr Turner in a manner urged it /upon me\ because he is miserably overgone in the yellow jaundice, and the most yellow person I ever beheld.[911] Dr Wilson is dayly twice with him: he is not sick, & doth come down into the parler everyday.[912] But I conceive he is in great danger. I was with him Tuesday, Wednesday, & Thursday: & promised to be with him on Tuesday next. He hath made his will, and desireth a generall acquittance from you, which I assured him you would readily send. Though of late years all accounts passed between you two onely. His friends are most desirous of this: & though I write this without /his or\ their knowledg, I do desire you to send it by the first post, for the satisfaction of them all. Pray for him: & if I find him worse I will send you word.

I will say no more of my business: for so soon as you receive any money, I shall hear from my friend; & what remaineth unpaid, I will take order to send you. Mr Holdsworth is at Myddleham. Mr Forder presenteth his service to you. Commending you to Gods protection, I am Sir

Your most faithfull servant,

G.D.

911 'he': Wrench.

912 Dr Wilson: apparently a London physician who treated Bishop Cosin's daughter, Anne, wife of Denis Granville: *Stapylton Corr.*, p. 210.

143 **19 October 1675**
R. 100, f. 174
G.D. to W.S. from Durham

Durham. Oct. 19. 1675.

Mr Dean; I write this from Mr Wrench's house, to whom I came this day to deliver your release; & to visit him. He is as he was, I cannot say better or worse, saving that his flesh falleth away. He was twice abroad the last week in Dr Smiths garden & in Mr Deans. Mr Dean of Myddleham, who walketh by me as I scribble, remembers his service to you, and bids me say, he wisheth /you\ your deed at London.[913] I would gladly hear that my money is paid to your nephew; of which you say nothing, which makes me beleeve it is not. I cannot send you the account from Mr Wrench at this time; because he is but just gotten out of bed, & it will be too long to transcribe /nor can I now so much as ask for it\. But so soon as I can gett it, I will send it to you. I am Sir

Your most humble servant,
G.D.

Mr Wrench commends him to your hearty prayers.

{*Below this as follows*}

579	584
552. 05. 00	552. 05. 00
26. 15. 00	31. 05. 00

144 **29 October 1675**
R. 101, f. 38r
G.D. to W.S. from Durham

Durham Oct. 29 1675.

Mr Dean;

On Friday last I sent a letter to you, & in it inclosed Mr Wrenchs account which I transcribed and examined. And then I thought he was rather //better// than worse. But since he grew weaker; and on Tuesday night about eleven of the clock (when we little suspected, about an hour or two before) it pleased to God to put a period to his life. And yesterday being St Simon & Jude's Day we buryed him in the

913 Thomas Holdsworth: L. **57**.

Cathedrall.[914] He hath left a sorrowful widow whom he made sole executrix of his will.[915] I have lost the best friend I had in this countrey: but the will of God be done.

I hope you find the account exact, & every way perfect. And I pray you if you do so to signify so much to Mistress Wrench or to me.[916] Your nephew sent me word that he had received 20£ upon my account. So that now I owe you 05£. 01s.08d being the remainder of 25£ 01s. 08d. which I received of Mr Wrench to make his account even with you. And very glad I am that you sent the release, which I delivered to him a week before his death. I will find some oportunity to send his 5£ to you. I hear Mr Knightley is (a kinsman of my Lords) is to have his Prebend.[917] And report (but I know not upon what ground) sayth Mr Turner is to have his living. To him I write by this Post: the true value being rather under 120£ per annum than above. God keep us. To his protection I commend you, and am Sir

Your most affectionate servant

Geo. Davenport.

I hope Sir Robt. Gayer gott well home.

145 **18 March 1676**

R. 101, f. 37r

G.D. to W.S. from Houghton

Houghton. Mar. 18. 1675.

Mr Dean,

I received yours of Febr. 29. Whether Mr Holdsworth be at Durham now or not, I cannot tell, but think, he may be for his living against Easter. But I heard he was there about a fortnight since.[918] What

---

914 St Simon and St Jude's day: 28 October. The cathedral records give his death 26 October and burial as here: DCM, DCD/L/BB/37, p. 34; *Durham Cathedral Registers*, p. 97.

915 No will found.

916 Residual money sent to Wrench's widow Anne, née Baddeley: DCM, DCD/L/BB/37, p. 157; L. **146**.

917 Richard Knightley succeeded to the sixth stall in Durham cathedral on Wrench's death in 1675 but held it only until the following year, when he received the seventh stall, which he retained until his death in 1695. The relationship, if any, to the bishop is not clear, but they had been friends for many years: Mussett, pp. 53, 60; C.E. Whiting, *Nathaniel Lord Crewe, Bishop of Durham (1674–1721), and his Diocese*, London 1940, pp. 13, 25, 85, 142.

918 He was due to be in residence from 7 April: DCM, DCD/B/AA/4, f. 229.

you mean by money in his hands I know not.[919] But I remember that about 6 months since I received a letter from you, as I was by his dore & when I had hastily read it, I showed it to him: & by a letter he shewed me from you after, I thought I did amiss in showing my letter to him. I am apt to think I shall never see London again; & the rather because I have no business there. The truth is, I like home so well, that when I am in my codling walk (which is 220 yards in length) I can pity poor Deans & say alas for the diligent overseer of St Pauls works. But I am angry, when I think of those wretches who conclude that we live in the Podex of the land.[920] God be thanked, I have my health reasonably well; and I rather impair in my flesh than add to it. I can walk five miles at a heat, in the walk I now mentioned. But I cannot abide to clime a hill. I grow into years too; being now in the 45th year of mine age. I wonder that you can forbear to say in your letters how St Pauls works go on: when I cannot forbear to tell you of such a triffle as planting an orchard, or making a codling hedge the longest in the north say some. I wish that pious work may be finished: for my part I am fayn to let Bow Church stand for the present, having no money to go on forward with it, & being about 100£ out of purse. But my Lord of Durham promised to assist me: & I hope he will do so at his return. Sir I have no more to trouble you with at present; but commending you to Gods protection & myselfe to your prayers. I am

Yr. most affectionate & faithfull servant

G.D.

146 **1 July 1676**

T. 92.19

G.D. to W.S. from Houghton

Houghton. July 1. 1676.

Good Mr Dean,

Mr Wharton of the lead mines came to see me this morning & telleth me he heareth that Sir Robt. Henley the younger hath run a footman through with his sword.[921] For Gods sake be so

---

919 Money due from Holdsworth to Sancroft: DCM, DCD/L/BB/37, pp. 135, 137.

920 Podex = rump.

921 Sir Robert Henley the younger: the elder son of Sir Andrew (died 1675) and Mary (née Gayer): *VCH, Hants*, IV, p. 36. Humphrey Wharton obtained a lease of lead mines for three lives from Cosin and had been granted a lease of the Stanhope and Wolsingham lead mines whilst the see was vacant but the king later revoked it: *CSP, Dom. 1673–5*, p. 353; *HPC*, III, pp. 696–7.

kind as to let me know what the business is: for it perplexeth me sore: and I have written this day to Sir Robt. Gayer about it. I hope the son of such a mother cannot so greatly miscarry.

I have not heard of you for a long time, save by my Lord of Durham's chaplain, Mr Turner: who hath promised (by the way) to preach at the consecration of my chapell: for my Lord of Durham told me at his coming down, that he is resolved to consecrate it. And my Lord of Bristow (who is 3 miles off with his daughter) tells me he meaneth to come also:[922] & my Lord of Litchfield is daily expected:[923] so that it is commonly said I am like to see 3 Bishops at a time in this house. And so much for Bishops.

The dean of Carlisle I hear is come to begin his Residence having buryed the Lady Fletcher.[924] The dean of Middleham, I hear, is at his deanery. My Lord beginneth his visitation a fortnight since for Northumberland, & intendeth to consecrate Berwick Church & after the assizes to visit the Dean & Chapter & this county.

I have my health well, God be thanked: & grow no fatter. We expect daily a bell-founder to cast our great bell, & have some hopes to have two more bells, or one, added to them, if the people will be piously disposed. I < > would gladly hear how your work goeth on at St Pauls. When the wall is a yard high (& surely it is now higher) you have a right to my Lords legacy of 100£.[925] And so with my humble service to you I am

Sir

Your most obliged servant,

G.D.

{*In small writing in another hand:* James Richmond.}

I < > would: 'find' erased.

922 Guy Carleton: L. **42**.

923 Thomas Wood: L. **78**.

924 Catherine, Lady Fletcher, widow of Sir Henry Fletcher of Cockermouth, baronet, who died fighting for the king in 1645. In about 1655 she married Thomas Smith, her chaplain and tutor to her son. Smith became prebendary of the fourth stall of Durham cathedral and Dean of Carlisle (from 1671). She died on 16 April 1676. He then married Anne, the widow of Richard Wrench (née Baddeley), soon after 4 November 1676: GEC, *Baronetage*, II, p. 83; *ODNB*, under Smith, Thomas (1614–1702).

925 *Cosin Corr.* II, p. 297; Cosin's will specifies five yards.

147 **15 September 1676**

R. 101, f. 39r

G.D. to W.S. from Houghton

Houghton: Sept. 15 . 1676.

Mr Dean;

I received yours of July the 11th long since. I have learned since that time that Sir Ro. Henley's business happened at the sessions at Dorchester after Easter:[926] & that all is well. For which I am very glad.

I likewise rejoyce to hear that St Pauls work goeth on so well. God grant that it may be well finished. On Sunday Sept. 3 my Lord of Durham consecrated my chapell here & Mr Turner preached. The Bishop of Bristoll /(Ld. of Litchfield fayled)| & Mr Dean of Durham & Mr Dean of Carlisle & knights & gentlemen & the quire of Durham & who not present. And we made a shift to dine 400 people & lived upon scrapps that were left for a whole week after. In the afternoon my Lord confirmed at the church about 500 persons. And now we are at church, give me leave to tell you, that we have a fortnight since cast our great bell, which cost 41£ & made new frames /(price 30£)\ for five bells (having but 3 formerly) & have now agreed to have two other bells lesser (the steeple will not hold larger) and they are to cost 72£.[927] And because we cannot tax the parish </for the new bells\> we are resolved to begg up the money if we can; & I am to give 10£ and I take the boldness to ask, whether you for your old affection to the parish will give anything.

I presume you may have heard of Mris Basire's death.[928] She was buryed July 27. And now I must tell you that Dr Basire is farr from being well, having the jaundise (but it is hoped they are going) scurvy, stone, griping in his belly, & timpany (but that also as it soon came, so it abateth; and his Drs. greatly mistrust him.[929] I was with him on Munday, & all day yesterday at his desire, & am to go again to morrow. Pray for him, which is his desire to all his friends. Yesterday in the afternoon he sent to the Cathedrall to be prayed for there.

Richmonds bond I have safe. But I never see him in Jayle: but out of

926 L. **146**.

927 *Durham Parish Books*, SS 84, p. 339.

928 Frances Basire, née Corbett, married Dr Isaac Basire (1607–76) who died 12 October: *ODNB*, under Basire, Isaac.

929 timpany: = swelling of the abdomen: *OED*.

< > it I have /often.\ I am out of hopes of getting anything from him unless it rain money. And I do not perceive that your action hurteth him. But I should be glad to see him now & sufficient assurance. No more at present, but commending you to God's protection & myselfe to your prayers.

I am, Sir,

Yr. most affectionate servant

G.D.

</for the new bells\>: 'it' erased.

148 **13 March 1677**

T. 40.75

G.D. to W.S. from Houghton

Houghton Mar. 13. 1676.

Mr Dean;

Now that your work is over, and for fear we should forget one another & having many questions to ask, I trouble you with this. I would know how you have your health; & how your work at St Pauls advanceth; and how Sir Robt. Gayer & his Lady and all his children (I know not how many he hath) are. Again; know you of any man who meditateth a second edition of Mr Somners Saxon Lexicon?[930] For most of them were burnt in Mr Dugdale's lodging, when London was burnt and the author intended a new edition. A dozen years since I sent him some observations I had made upon his Lexicon, by Dr Casaubon:[931] and he returned me a letter of thanks & said he would improve them, for correction in some parts & alteration in others of his Lexicon: and desired my continuance therein. I have lately made many more: and perhaps some of them might be usefull, if a second edition was intended. The chiefe desire of them is, to shew many of those old words are still in use in some parts of England especially here; or that from those words, others not much unlike them are derived, & still used by us.

Furthermore I have a nephew (of mine own name) who is a curat at Ropwell about two miles from Chelmsford, and a priest.[932] He

930 William Somner (1598–1669), *Dictionarium Saxonico-Latino-Anglicum*, 1659. A second edition appeared in 1701: *ODNB*.

931 Meric Casaubon (1599–1671): L. **34**.

932 George, son of G.D.'s brother Stephen, a scholar financed by Cosin, obtained his B.A. from Peterhouse in 1672/3 and M.A. in 1676. He became rector of Steeple, Essex, in 1678: *Al. Cant.*; Hoskins, *The Midland Peasant*, p. 309; L. **110**.

commenced Master of Arts of Peterhouse (where he was my Lord's first scholar) the last commencement. But that I may hide nothing from you, he left the College 3 years since, upon a scandalous report made upon him. But his tutor /Mr Clark\, was with me & telleth me he was grievously wronged & that the whore & her mother (for that was the business) did both acquit him and that another scholar took the child and kept it:[933] but he was so foolish as to leave the college upon that report. This his tutor assured me for truth: & the last commencement (that being his year) the college gave him his grace & /he\ took his degree. Now I would entreat you if you see Dr Beaumont, to ask him about this matter. And also, if you could tell how, to help him to some better place. For I hear he preacheth twice a day for 20£ a year & findeth himselfe victualls: and for his better maintenance keepeth a small school. I can do him no good here: and I have a very diligent curat (Mr Alcock born at Gateside) with whom I would not part.[934] I am very confident that he was wronged: but if he was not (as God forbid) I am loath he should be cast off for ever. [935] I have my health, God be thanked, well. But I have not been at Durham since Jan. 11. The weather was either cold, or the ways foule. On the first of this moneth I saw dust in the high-way in the fields.[936] But for eight days together /afterwards\ we had a sharp east wind, which ended in snow: and now we are in expectation of a < > flood. Mr Ralph Blackiston was buryed at Ryton Jan. 30.[937] I helped to carry him to his grave. I hear his living is given to one Dr Cave, whose two books I have seen.[938] I wish he come and live here. Do you do anything in your convocation? I should be glad to hear you are in good health: for I think I shall never /have\ any business at London to bring me there; and so by consequence, never see you more, unless I make a journey on purpose. But let us pray for one another. My brother was well, a while since. But I can never tempt him hither; he puts off from spring

933 John Clark from Houghton School, elected Fellow 1666–77. Rector of Stathern, Leics., 1675–90. *Al. Cant.*

934 John Alcock: Ramsey, 'Records of Houghton-le-Spring', p. 687; *Al. Cant.*

935 Sic.

936 The winter of 1676–7 was extremely cold and 'frost fairs' were held on the River Thames.

937 Blackiston, Cosin's brother-in-law: *Cosin Corr.* II, p. 27 and n.

938 William Cave (1637–1713), Chaplain to Charles II. A close friend of Thomas Comber, Dean of Durham from 1691. He produced many works of Church History and was noted for his thorough research and clarity of style: *ODNB*.

to summer: and from summer to spring: and saith riding is tedious to him: but hee would fayn hear, that Mr Welsteds 50£ is ready for him. I pray present my service to Sir Robt. Gayer and his Lady, when you see them. And so begging your excuse for this trouble, I commend you to God's protection, and am

Sir

Your most obliged servant,

G.D.

a < > flood: 'mighty' erased.

No further letters of George Davenport are known to survive from 1677. He died unexpectedly on 6 July 1677, after a short illness, and was buried in the chancel of Houghton church.

APPENDIX I

George Davenport's Catalogue

The Rud Catalogue numbers are given in square brackets. The notes in smaller print are from the information given by Dr Doyle and Mr Piper in the search room of Archives and Special Collections in Palace Green Library, Durham. The approximate date of the manuscript and Davenport signatures or marks of ownership (noted as GD) are given.

T. 88, f. 72r

Catalogus librorum MSS. In bibliotheca Geo. Davenport.

1. Origenis homiliae in Genesim, Exodum, Leviticum, Jesum Nave, Judices, Regna, Esaiam, Jeremiam & Ezechielem. Lat. [V.I.1.]
   {s. xii2, English perhaps Cisterician, with note of contents by GD f. 1*}
2. Petri Lombardi glossa in librum Psalmorum. Liber pulcherimus. [V.I.4.]
   {s. xii3/4. From Durham priory. GD 1663.}
3. Petri Lombardi libri quatuor sententiarum. [V.I.5.]
   {s. xii ex. From Durham priory. GD 1663.}
4. Eiusdem Lombardi libri 4. Sentensiarum. Imperfecte. [V.I.6.]
   {s. xiii med. Written in France. GD 1664.}
5. Breviarium (ut videtur) ad usum Sarum. Liber permagnus. [V.I.3.]
   {s. xv. For use in Norwich diocese.}
6. Breviarium (ut videtur) mutilatum. [V.I.2.]
   {s. xv med. From Hutton Rudby.}
7. 1. Rogeri de Waltham Canonici Londinensis. Compendium morale de dictis & factis exemplaribus antiquorum.
   2. S. Augustini Exhortatio ad comitem Julianum.
   3. S. Augustinus de Conversione.
   4. S. Augustini tractatus ad Religiosos.
   5. S. Augustini Epistola ad Cyrillum de /laude\ Jeronymi.
   6. Cyrilli Epistola ad Augustinum de transitu Jeronymi. [V.I.7.]
   {s. xv med. GD 1670 and list of contents.}
8. 1. S. Anselmus, de similitudinibus.
   2. S. Anselmus, de concordia prescientia & praedestinationis, & gratiae Dei cum libero Arbitrio.

3. S. Augustinus de Libero Arbitrio.
4. S. Augustinus de verbis Domini secundum quatuor Evangelistas.
5. S. Augustinus de verbis Apostoli. [V.I.8.]
{s. xiv. From Durham priory. GD 1663.}

1. S. Augustini homeliae 124 in S. Johannem Evangelistam.
2. Methodius Episcopus de principio saeculi & regnis gentium, & fine saeculorum.
3. S. Augustini meditationes de spiritu sancto. [V.II.3.]
{s. xv med. GD 1670.}

f. 72v

10. 1. S. Ephrem Diaconi Edisseni libri sexti.
2. Tractatus ex homeliis S. Gregorii.
3. Eusebii Emeseni Exhortatores homeliae octe.
4. S. Cesarii Episcopi Arelatensis sermones tres.
5. S. Augustinus de tribus habitaculis caelesti, terrestri, & infernali.
{Actually Patrick, Bishop of Dublin 1074–84.}
6. Hugo de S. Victore (vel potius Aelredus Rievallensis) de duodecim abusionibus claustri.
{Actually Hugh of Fouillton.}
7. De natura apis pagina unica anglice.
{Richard Rolle, one of only two known copies.}
8. De negligentia, concupiscentia et nequitia.
9. De recordatione donorum Dei de recordatione passionis Christi, de modo contemplandi Deum. De amore erga Deum de septem peccatis mortalibus & de remediis contra ea. [V.I.12.]
{s. xv med. GD 1664.}

11. 1. S. Aelredi Abbatis Rievallensis sermones viginti & septem.
2. Magistri Achardi de S. Victore sermone de lectione evangelica. Ductus est Jesus in desertum. [V.I.11.]
{s. xii/xiii English, Cistercian after 1167. GD 1660 ex dono R viri Tim. Thurscross, notes by GD.}

12. Odonis Abbatis sermones 201. [V.II.8.]
{s. xiii med; Odo of Cheriton, Peter of Rheims etc.; from Durham priory. GD 1664, ex dono … Nicolai Frevil 1664. Notes by GD.}

13. Johannis Mandevile militis liber peregrinationis. Ad * * varia prosa & versa [V.III.7.]?
{s. xv ex. Rud ascribed this to Davenport.}

14. Eiusdem Johannis Mandevile peregrinatio. Gallice. [V. I.10.]
{s. xv in. GD 1664, notes.}

15. Livre du government des Rois & des Princes par frere Giles de Rome de l'ordre du Augustine. [V.I.9.]
{with Chaucer, Hymn to the Blessed Virgin. s. xiv ex. GD 1670.}

16. John Lidgate monk of Bury of the life of the Virgin Mary four books

to King Henry the fifth in verse. [V.II.16.]
{GD 1664. 'Perlegi' by him at f. 90v.}

17. John Lidgate of the destruction of Thebs translated & the life of St Margaret in verse: and the life of St Alexis of St Mary Magdalene in prose. [V.II.14.]
{s. xv med. GD 1664 and notes by him.}
18. Jeffrey Chaucers five books of Troilus and Chreseide & Cupids letter to lovers. [V.II.13.]
{s. xv med. GD 1664.}
19. Thomas Hoccleve his complaint. Fabula de quadam Imperatrice Romana in verse, eiusdem moralizatio in prose. His ars sciendi mori and fabula de quadam muliera mala in verse. [V.III.9.]
{1421–26, written by Hoccleve. GD 1664; 'perlegi' 1666.}
20. Boetius his five books of Philosophical comfort translated into verse. [V.II.15.]
{Trans. by John Walton. s. xv. GD 1664.}

f. 73r

21. Boetius de Consolatione Philosophiae cum commentario. [V.II.11.]
{s. xiv ex. GD 1664, with his notes.}
22. Gulielmi Parisiensis Episcopi summa de septem vitiis. [V.II.7.]
{s. xiv med. GD 1663.}
23. Liber Metrice sermone Gallico. Desideraturum principium & finis. [V.II.17]
{Chanson de geste. s. xiii/2. Northern France but in England mid s. xiv.}
24. Glossa ordinaria & interlinearis in librum Numerorum. [V.II.1.]
{s. xii/2. From Durham priory. A Puiset volume. GD 1662.}
25. 1. S. Bernardi Sermones 86 in canticum canticorum.
{GD 1662.}
    2. Speculum Exemplare in quinque partibus.
    3. Rabbi Samuelis Epistola de Messiae adventu.
    4. Origenis homeliae 26 in Jesum Nave.
    5. Johannis Wiltoni (monachi Westmonasteriensis) Horologium sapientiae. [V.I.13.]
26. 1. Petri Aureoli compendium sensus literalis totius S. Scripturae.
    2. Index locorum S. Scripturae expositorum in operibus S. Augustini, S. Hieronymi, S. Gregorii, Origenis, Haymonis, Hugonis de S. Victore, Bedae & Hieronymi. [V.II.4.]
{s. xiv ex / xv in. GD 1664.}
27. 1. Libri triginta & quatuor de bello Trojano ut videtur primum & ultimum folium desiderantur.
{s. xv in. G. Colonna, On the Destruction of Troy. From Norwich priory. GD 1664.}
    2. Turpinus Archiepiscopus Rhemensis de Gestis Regis Caroli.

3. Calixtus Papa de inventione corporis Turpini Archiepiscopi & martyris.
4. Calixtus Papa de translatione corporis S. Jacobi.
5. Leonis Papae epistola de translatione S. Jacobi.
6. Calixtus Papa de miraculis sancti Jacobi.
7. Aristotoles de Physinomia.
8. Aristotoles de morte. [V.II.12.]

28. Liber sextus Decretalium Bonifacii octavi. [V.III.4.]
{s. xiii–xiv. From Durham priory. GD 1663.}

29. Sermones in Evangelia & epistolas Dominical{es}. Per totum annum nec non in plurimis festis. [V.III.2.]
{s. xiii1/2. GD 1662.}

f. 73v

30. 1. Speculum Amicitiae.
2. Speculum Humilitatis
3. Casiodorus de Anima.
4. S. Augustinus de spiritu & anima.
5. Robert Grosthead de veneno.
6. Hugonis de S. Victore Didascalicon.
7. Tractatus de anima & eius potentiis.
8. 24 Propositiones Philosophorum de essentis divina.
9. Tractatus de septem noctibus.
10. Liber Bestiarum, avium, arborum etc.
11. Victoria Jesus Christi contra Anti- Christum.
12. Libellus de quatuor virtutibus cardinalibus.
13. Concordia Evangelistae Lucae cum quibusdam figuris veteris Testamenti primum oratione soluta, deinde versu. [V.II.5.]
{Separate pieces joined early. Thomas Lawson, monk of Durham, former owner. GD 1663.}

31. 1. Bonaventures meditations of the life of Christ.
2. The Meditations of Bonaventure translated by Walter Hilton. [V.III.8.?]
{s. xv in. GD 1664.}

32. 1. Doctrina cordis, or the doctrine of the heart in seaven chapters, written as is supposed by Robt. Grosthead Bishop of Lincoln.
2. A Letter of Religious Governaunce sent to a Religious Woman.
3. A Letter sent to a Religious woman of the twelve fruits of the holy Ghost in twelve chapters by the same Author. [V.III.24.]
{s. xv med. From an East Anglian nunnery. GD 1664, 'perlegi'.}

33. 1. Constitutiones Clementinae editae a Clemente quinto in Concilio Viennensi.
2. Nonnulla eiusdem farinas. [V.III.3.]
{From Durham priory. GD 1663.}

34. Anonymi Quaestiones in Theologia Scholastica. [V.II.9.]
{From St Augustine's Canterbury. GD 1664.}

35. 1. Judgment of Urines * *.
2. Tractatus de Sphera.
3. Physicall Receipts.
4. Grammaticalia. [V.III.10.]
{GD 1663.}

f. 74r

36. 1. Purveanse of the feste for the Kynge at home with the Lord Spenser with Receipts to make dishes.
2. Gode Medycines of gode leches.
3. Nomina herbarum iuxta alphabetum.
4. Medicamina, carmina, unguenta etc. [V.III.11.]
{All xv in.}

37. 1. Quaedam notabilia quae continentur in libro qui vocatur fasciculus morum ex scriptione Thomae Elyphaunt 1477.
2. Sermones de Tempore. A letter that Our Lord sent to diverse places to keep /Sunday.\
3. A sermon on Deum time et mandata eius observa.
4. Excommunications & cursings.
5. The Lord's Prayer, Ave Maria, Crede, ten commandments, seaven deadly sins, seaven sacraments etc.
6. An exhortation to be made by a curett to his parochines.
7. Oratio pro statu S. matris ecclesiae or bidding of prayer in English.
8. De Baptismo, sponsalibus, & visitatione infermorum.
9. Confessio generalis die Paschae in English. [V.IV.2.]
{GD 'Donum Johannis Tempest armigerii'. Also from him to Davenport are 38 [V.III.17.], 44 [V.IV.5.] and 54.2 [V.IV.9.]. Of the Ile or Old Durham.}

38. Martyrologium per anni circulum. [V.III.17.]
{Usuard. Perhaps from Lincolnshire. From Tempest. Had belonged to John Heath whose daughter married Tempest.}

39. Sermons upon the Gospels for the four Sundays in Advent, the six Sundays in Lent & Easter Day. [V.IV.3.]
{s. xv med.}

40. 1. The Life & Martyrdome with the translation and invention of the glorious spouse of Christe saynt Barbara.
{By Jan van Wackerzde.}
2. The miracles of the same glorious virgyne. [V.IV.4.]

41. The Golden Rose drawen outt of the true love of God, by Richard Hampole. [V.IV.6.]
{s. xv med. GD 1664; 'perlegi Nov. 15 1665.'}

42. 1. Sermones de spiritu s{ancto}, de novo sacerdotio, de Beata Maria, de nativitate Christi etc.

2. Petrus Blesensis de duodecim utilitatibus tribulationum.
3. Opusculum vitae & passionis Christi eiusque genetricis Mariae ex revelationibus B. Brigittae ex compilatum & compendiosa legenda eiusdem. [V.IV.16.]

f. 74V

4. A letter to religious susters.
5. Novem Virtutes quas Dominus cuidam viro sancto ore suo revelavit.
6. Quatuor novissimorum liber quem plerique cordiale appellant. [V.III.16.]

{s. xv–xvi. Connections with Sion. Note by GD of contents.}

43. 1. Ysidorii Yspalensis Episcopi Etymologiarum libri viginti ad Braulionem Ep.
2. Etymologiarum liber juxta alphabetum in Isidorus saepissime citatum. [V.III.20.]

{s. xiii med. From Bury St Edmunds. GD 1664.}

44. Statuta Edvardi Tertii Regis Angliae Gallice. [V.IV.5.]

{Gift from Tempest. Notes by GD.}

45. Manuale ad usum sarum i.e. officium Baptismi ordo ad facienda sponsalia, ordo ad visitandum infirmum, vigiliae mortuorum, ordo officii sepulturae. [V.III.21.]

{s. xiv ex. Notes by GD.}

46. 1. Visio Turkilli de stystede in Essexia.
2. Albertani Causidici Brissiensis Tractatus dicendi & tacendi.
3. Ejusdem consolationis et consiliis liber.
4. Ejusdem liber de dilectione Dei proximi & aliarum rerum. [V.III.22.]

{Various parts s. xiv in; xiv/xv. Written in England. GD 1664.}

46 [sic] 1. Laurentii Dunelmensis monachi uponosticon, Apologia, orationes * * de morte amici. Oratione soluta in versu. [V.III.1.]

{s. xii. Probably written in Durham priory. GD 1570, gift from Nicholas Freville of Hardwick.}

48 [sic] The New Testament translated into English by John Wiccleve as it is supposed. [V.V.1.]

{s. xiv ex / xv in. GD 1666. At present missing (stolen).}

49. Biblia minimis characteribus (ut fertur) Jacobi Quarti Scotorum Regis. [V.V.17.]

{s. xiii. Gift to GD from James Mickleton, 1669, to whom it had come from the Hall family of Consett, into which he had married.}

50. Biblia itidem minisculis characteribus.[V.V.18.]

{s. xiii med. GD. A gift from his friend George Barkas, gent., 1665.}

51. 1. Anti Claudianus Alani de * * poema.
2. Alanus de planctu naturae in metro et prosa.

3. Galffredi Vinesalfe poetria nova principium, Papa stupor mundi.
4. Ricardi Alngervile de Bury Episcopus Dunelmensii, Philobiblon. [V.V.2.]
{s. xv med. Notes by GD.}

52. 1. Of the planets, golden table, mans urine & its colours.
2. De urinis et earum coloribus et circulis. [V.IV.7.]
{s. xv med. Davenport may have joined these. GD 1654.}

f. 75r

53. Anonymi liber Homeliarum sive sermonum continet folia 288. [V.V.3.]
{s. xiii. English Mendicant, then Bury St Edmunds before 1378. GD 1664.}

54. 1. Liber de tribus magis.
2. Nonnihil de S. Hilda virgine. [V.IV.9.]
{s. xv English. Various owners then gift from Tempest. GD 1664.}

55. 1. Varia de matrimonio, Symoniae Baptismo &c.
2. Statuta synodalia. [V.V.7.]
{s. xiv med. GD notes.}

56. 1. Origenes in Canticum Canticorum.
2. S. Bernardi scala Humulitatis.
3. S. Bernardus de libero Arbitrio. [V.V.8.]
{s. xii. GD notes.}

57. 1. Destinaria, destinyes from nativityes.
2. Physicall Receipts.
3. The Substance of urines, the colour, the regiones & the contentis that longeth to the dome of urines.
4. Of the four complexions.
5. Rules of Phisnomy. [V.V.13.]
{s. xv ex, English. GD notes.}

58. 1. De S. Maria virgine varia.
2. Officium, canonizatio & miracula Johannis de Brydlington.
3. Notabilis Expostio super Psalmum Quinquagesimum.
4. De Privilegiis quatuor sabbatorum quadragesimae, trium Dominicarum & sextae feriae.
5. De modo legendi in ecclesia Dei.
6. De institutione quatuor temporum varia. [V.V.19.]
{s. xvi. Bridlington priory. GD 1654.}

59. Anonymus de misericordia, cordis munditia, pace, patientia, generali judicio, poenis inferni, gloria Paradisi, obedientia, et paupertate. [V.V.14.]
{s. xiv/xv. Chapter list by GD.}

60. 1. The sawter of mercy compyled by Sir John Cressever Bacheler of ______ on Good Friday 1495.
2. The meditation of the Life & Passion of Jhesu Christ made by

the devoute brother Jordan of the Order of Seynt Austine. [V.V.12.]
{s. xv/xvi. Notes by GD.}

61. Rosarium B. Mariae virginis & de duobus modis dicendi illud & psalterium gloriosae virginis. [V.III.23.]
62. Hymni de Sanctis et in Dominicis cum notulis. [V.V.6.]
{s. xi–xiii. From Christ church Canterbury, then Durham priory. Evidence of local Durham owners. GD notes.}

f. 75v

63. Psalterium de passione Christi cum figuris. [V.V.16.]
{Printed 1485. Stolen from Cosin's library in s. xviii. Now Bodleian Library Arch Bod. G. f 16. GD 1648.}
64. Calendarium. Quindecim 00. Ad laudes tam nonam, completorium, orations, salutations, septem psalmi poenitentiales, commendationes animarum. Psalmus de passione Domini. Psalterium abbreviatum a B. Jeronymo. [V.V.5.]
{s. xv med. 1663 GD.}

Dr Doyle draws attention to the fact that the above list does not include the Cosin manuscripts listed below:

[V.III.12] E. de Evesham, Quadrilogus of Beckett, s. xiv, from St Alban's. Had been Leonard Pilkington's (canon of the seventh stall in Durham, 1567–99). G Davenport 1570.
[V.III.15] Jacobus de Cessoli, De scaccararum ludo, s. xiv med. Contents list by GD.
[V.III.18] Franciscan tracts on poverty, s. xiv, not before 1323. G Davenport 1670 and notes.
[V.III.19] Ranulph Higden, Polychronicon, extracts, s. xv in.
[V.V.9] Misc. in Latin, English and French. Notes by GD.
[V.V.15] Meditations s. xiii–xv. Of mixed origins. Davenport.

These make up the seventy manuscripts recorded on Davenport's tombstone in Houghton church.

APPENDIX II

Will of George Davenport 1677[1]

In the name of God Amen. I George Davenport, Clerk, Rector of Houghton le Spring in the County Palatine of Durham, being in good health of body, and of sound and perfect memory, do make this my last will and testament. First, and principally, I commend my soul into the hands of Almighty God. My body I bequeath to the earth to be buryed in the chancell of Houghton aforesaid, if it shall please God to call me in any place within this county of Durham. And for my lands and worldly goods I give them as followeth. I give to my kinswoman Mistress Mary Hales an annuity or rent charge of ten pounds to be paid out of my lands in Bushby by quarterly payments for and during her naturall life. And if I do not make her a deed for the same I desire and expect that my brother John should make such a deed to her.

I give to my brother John Davenport Rector of West Rasen in the county of Lincoln all my lands in Bushby and Wigston in the county of Leicester, and all writings and evidences concerning the same, to have and to hold to him and his heirs for ever. And I desire him to have a care in the education of the children of Elizabeth daughter to my brother Steven. I give to my brother Steven Davenport twenty pounds: and I forgive him all summs of money which he oweth me. And I give to his wife my little silver tankard. I give to my brother Johns wife my diamond ring. I give to Richard son of my brother John my largest silver tankard. I give to the poor of Wigston, where I was born, twenty pounds to be added to the poor stock there. I give to the poor of this parish of Houghton fourty pounds to be added to their stock and ten pounds to be distributed among them at my buryall or soon after. Furthermore it is my will, that if I live not to endow the late built hospitall at Houghton with lands or other revenues of ten pounds (or therabouts) yearly value, then my executor shall pay to the

1 DUL, Durham Probate Records 1/1677/D2/1–2; 1/1677/D2/3–4, copy.

Governors of Kepyar School and almshouse the sum of one hundred and sixty pounds, to purchase lands or a yearly rent charge of ten pounds for the maintenance of three poor people: which three people I will may be chosen by the said Governors, with the advice of the Rector of Houghton, out of the poor inhabitants of the said parish of Houghton. I give to my servant George Gregson five pounds, and all my apparell for wearing as well wollen as linnen. I give to every one of my servants which shall be dwelling in my family at the time of my decease fourty shillings: also I give to Ralph Robinson, parish clerk fourty shillings. I give to my nephew George Davenport clerk, son to my brother Steven one hundred pounds. All papers or books of mine owne writing I give to my brother John. All the rest of my estate reall and personall I give and bequeath to my nephew John Davenport son of my brother Steven, which said John I appoint sole executor of this my last will and testament, willing him to pay all my debts, and to discharge my funerall expences, which I would not should exceed twenty marks at the most. And I forbid all preaching at my funerall. And in witness that I ordain this to be my last will and testament I do hereunto set my hand and seal this </seaven\>teenth day of September in the year of our Lord one thousand six hundred seaventy and six.

Sealed and published in the presence of us.

John Alcock — Geo. Davenport
Richard Foorder — {with seal}.

</seaven\>: over eight, erased.

APPENDIX III

Inventory of George Davenport 1677[1]

A true and perfect Inventory of the goods and chattles of Mr George Davenport Rector of Houghton in the Spring in the County of Durham late deceased taken & prized the seventh day of July in the yeare of Our Lord God 1677 by us whose names are here underwritten.

	£ s d
Imp. His purse	10 00 00
Item in the Kitching one payer of Rackes, three speels, foure paire of tongus, four fires hovells, two Reiking crooks, three Iron potts, one Jacke, one paire of Crankes, one warming pan and other small iron things in the Citching, five skeels, one churne, one dozen and a halfe of trenchers with other small wooden vessells, two tables, one cawell, foure furmes, one case of Pistolls & harnesse, two paire of limses, one frying pan, one dreeping pan, two tubbs, two chists and one payre of barrs.	4 18 08
The maids chamber	
Item one bedstead & bedding, two chists & two straw skepps	20 15 00
The milke house	
Item one brase lead, one brase tapp, ten milch bouls, three treyes, eight earthen potts, one table, one candle box and one tubb.	1 05 00
The Pantry	
Item eighteene pewter disshes, three douzen and foure plates, two dozen of spoons, two case of knives, one dresser table, one spence ? with other small earthen vessels, one black jacke, two pewther and foure lattin candlestickes, one	

1 DUL, Durham Probate Records, 1/1677/D2/5.
A glossary is provided at the end of this appendix.

silver tankard, one silver salt, one silver sugar Box, one silver mustard box, three silver spoons. One silver tumbler and one taster of silver. 10 00 00

The Hall

Item three tables, eleven chaires, one long form, three carpetts one dish, twenty foure scutchins and six small pictures and a paire of Barrs. 03 01 08

The Parler

Item seven thrum chares, seven chishons, two tables, one Carpett, three paper picturs, & one old picture. 02 14 06

Item In the Inner Parler One bedsteed & bedding, foure low leather chaires,one truncke, Six scutchions, two winder Curtins
& a Rod, nine Dozen of Napkins, ten table cloaths,
Ten pillowvers, twenty paire of sheets & two & a halfe,
Eight twoells, two side board cloaths, one paire of barrs. 14 04 06

The Little Chamber

Item One Bedsteed and curteins, one Rugge, one payre of blancketts, one bolster, one Pillowver, one Dressing Cubbard, one winder curtin and rodds. 01 06 08

The Dineing Roome

Item Twelve thrum worke chaires, eleven pictures, two scutchings, one mappe, two tables & one carpett, one paire of Barrs. 10 00 00

The Reed Chamber

Item One bedsteed with bedding, hangings about the roome one window Curting and Rod, one little table, one Carpett, one Chaire, twelve scuthions & one picture. 02 10 00

The Men's Chamber

Item two Beddsteads and furnitory 01 10 00

The Greene Chamber

Item one Beddstead, with furnitory, hangings about the Roome, five thrum worke chaires, two trunkes, one table, foure scutchings, foure paper pictures, two winder curtings, one Rod & one paire of Barrs. 06 13 00

The Waine Scott Chamber

Item one Bedsteed with furnitory, one little case of drawers, Two Chares, one little table and carpett, two wall Watches, Seven little pictures, three window curtings, two Rodds, one close stool & one paire of Barrs. 02 02 00

The Tower

Item one Bedsteed and Bedding two little tables and shelves in the studdy, pannells and other lieces of wood in the Chamber above and one paire of Barrs.	02 02 00
The Chapple.	
Item one Organ, two Candlesticks & six Cushions, One Comon prayer booke.	25 00 00
The Seller	
Item sixteene douzen of glasse bottles, one douzen of stone Bottles, seven Hogsheads, three Teartes, foure halfe Barrells, seven Ancres, five paire of garm trees, foure locks.	02 18 00
Item The Cropp of Corne growing one the grounds	70 00 00
The Bakehouse	
Item one chese presse, one frame for casting of lead, one trevett, one cole Rake, one fire forke, one cover for a lead, one wooden trough, one drier in the kill, and two wooden trowes more.	00 13 04
The Stable	
Item two wooden Arkes, two Bridles and Saddles	00 15 00
Item Plough geere and wane geere, heckes & Railes with other loose wood within the yeard with manner, coales, lyme, rough stones, hewen stones and slates.	17 10 00
The Barne	
Item Wheat, Straw and Hay, winnowing cloath, one Screen, two Pecks with some straw in the stack yeard, and oates in the granerey and in the Priest's Chamber.	11 00 00
Item thirteene horses, mares and foales	44 00 00
Item six oxen, eleven cowes, one paire of stotts, one steere, one whie, one calfe and foure swine & a Bull	70 01 08

John Shadfoorth
Ralph Robinson
Richard Foorder
Ralph Robinson

His Library Apprized by us whose names are underwritten	£ s d
The Summ is	100 00 00

H.Johnson Rector de Washington
John Alcock Curatus de Houghton

£ s d
435 19 00

Glossary

Ark wooden chest.
Ancres buckles?
Black jack leather jug or tankard for ale.
Cawell large tub.
Chishions cushions.
Crankes iron hooks set in a frame and used for toasting bread.
Furme wooden backless seat.
Furnitory appropriate parts or tools.
Garm yarn?
Heckes racks.
Jacke e.g. a jack for turning a spit.
Lattin mixed metal, yellow.
Lead brewing vessel.
Limses tubs.
Manner manure.
Peck measure for dry goods (¼ bushel).
Pillowver pillow case.
Recking hooks iron hooks for holding a pot over a fire.
Skeel wooden bucket.
Skepps wicker or wooden basket.
Skutchins cushions.
Speels spindles?
Steere young ox.
Stott young castrated ox or heifer.
Taster small shallow cup of silver, for tasting wine.
Thrum (chair) woven, e.g. rush, seat.
Trencher flat wooden plate.
Trevett stand for a pot, placed over a fire.
Trowes troughs.
Troyes pair of weighing scales.
Trunckle low bed pushed under a higher bed.
Wane large, two wheeled cart.
Whie heifer up to the age of three years or until calved.

APPENDIX IV

Dilapidation Document for Houghton le Spring on Davenport's entry into his living 19 June 1665

T. 144.151

Whereas a cause of Delapidacions hath byn instituted by me George Davenport, clerk, Rector of the Parish Church of Houghton le Springe in the Diocese of Durham in the Arches Court of Canterbury against the right worshipful William Sancroft Dr. in Divinity, Deane of the Cathedral Church of St Paul London and late Rector of Houghton aforesaid. In which since the judge of the said court hath condemned the said Dr Sancroft to pay unto mee the said George Davenport the summe of one hundred pounds for his part and proportion towards the Reparacions of the decayes and dilapidations of the parsonage house and other buildings belonging to the said rectory, and of the Chancell of the said church. Now I the said George Davenport doe hereby acknowledge that I /have\ had & received of & from the said William Sancroft the said summe of One hundred pounds for /and\ in full Payment and in satisfaction of his part towards the reparacions of the dilapidacions and decayes afore mentioned. And I doe hereby acquit release and discharge the said William Sancroft his Executors and Administrators thereof and of and from all other or further claimes or demands from him or them for or concerning the said decayes and dilapidations. In witnes whereof I have hereunto sett my hand and seale. This nineteenth day of June. Anno Domini 1665.

Geo. Davenport

Sealed & delivered
In the presence of
Ric. Baddeley
R.Wrench

APPENDIX V

Churchwardens' Accounts of Houghton le Spring 1667[1]

An inventorie of all the moveable goods now remaineing and belonging to the parish church of Houghton in the Springes as the same was given in the 10th of April 1667 by the churchwardens of the s{ai}de parish.

In the custodie of Mr Dobson
Two bookes of Sewell and Harding
Two Register books
Erasmus Paraphrase
A book of Homilies
The Kings works in folio
A Booke for Registering the names
of Strange Ministers
In the Custodie of the Church wardens
Two Chalices or cups of silver
With two covers of silver to them
Two large peuder fflaggons
One lesser peuder fflaggon
One peuder plate for bread
Two Runlets[2] for wine
Two suplices
A Carpett Cloath for the table
A Cushing for the Pulpitt
A White damaske cloath for the table
A large Church Bible in folio printed..
A Communion Table

---

1 DCRO, EP/Ho 168.
2 Runlets = casks.

Two Service books of the last edition
One for the Clerke
Ten Firdale[3] formes
A large arke of oake
A large cubord in the vesturie
A great iron a loake
A Table of the 10 Commandments
The King's Armes
The Table of marriages
A Litany Deske
In the Custodie of the Sexton
A Hacke[4]
A Spade
A Shovell

---

3 Firdale = fir wood =pine.
4 Hacke = pick axe or muck fork.

APPENDIX VI

Books Referred to in the Letters

Only books mentioned in the text of the letters are included; books solely referred to in notes are omitted. The reference is to the number of the letter in this collection. All details of the books are contained in the notes to the letters; nothing is repeated below.

Bacon, F., Lord Verulam, *Historia naturalis et experimentalis ad condendam philosophiam sive phoenomena universi; Historia vitae et mortis*. L. **23**.
Boate, A., *The character of a trulie vertuous and pious Woman as it hath been acted by Mistris Margaret Dungan*, London 1654. L. **9**.
Castell, E., *Lexicon*. L. **20**. *Lexicon*, which accompanied Walton's Polyglot Bible, London 1658 and later. LL. **29**, **30**, **101**, **116**, **118**, **119**, **121**, **123**, **124**.
Ciaconius, A., *Vitae et regestae pontificum necnon s.r.e. cardinalium*, Vol. I, Rome 1601. L. **38**.
Conciliorum omnium generalium et provincialium collectio regia, 37 vols, Paris 1644. L. **18**.
Cosin, J., *A Scholastical History of the Canon of Holy Scripture*, London 1657. LL. **19**, **31**.
Cosin, J., *Historia Transubstantiationis Papalis*, 1656. L. **31**.
Dee, J., *A true and faithful relation of what passed for many years between Dr Jn Dee … and some spirits*, published by M. Casaubon, 1659. L. **34**.
Drusius, J., L. **23**.
Dugdale, W., *Monasticon Anglicanum*, London 1655. L. **43**.
Florio, G., *Vocabulario Italiano e Inglese. A Dictionary Italian and English*, London 1659, with additions by G. Torriano. L. **35**.
Fuller, T., *Church History*, London 1655. L. **17**.
Fuller, T., *History of the Worthies of England*, London 1662. L. **20**.
Fuller, T., ed., *Abel Redivivus*, 1651. L. **42**.
Gell, R., *Essay towards the Amendation of the last English Translation of the Bible*, 1659. L. **35**.

Grotius, H., various works. L. **20**.
Hammond, H., *Account of Mr Daniel Cawdrey's Triplex Diatribe concerning superstition*, London 1654, 1655. L. **5**.
Harrington, J., *A brief View of the State of the Church of England as it stood in Queen Elizabeth's and King James' reign to the year 1608*, 1653. L. **42**.
Heylin, P., *Examen historicum*, 1658. L. **32**.
Irvine, A., *A dialogue between A and B, two plain country Gentlemen, concerning the times*. L. **59**.
Isaacson, H., *An exact narrative of the life and death of Lancelot Andrewes*, London 1650/51. L. **42**.
Knatchbull, N., *Animadversiones in libros Novi Testamenti*, 1659. L. **35**.
L'Estrange, H., *The Alliance of Divine Offices*, 1659. L. **35**.
Mason, F., *De ministero Anglicano*, 1625. LL. **15, 17, 20**.
Mede, J., *Works*, 1648, with *Life*. L. **9**.
Parker, Mr, unidentified book. L. **34**.
Plutarch, *Lives*, and *Moralia*. L. **38**.
Sancroft, W., *Lex Ignea*. L. **102**.
Sanderson, W., *A Compleat History of the Life and Raigne of King Charles*, London 1658. L. **30**.
Somner, W., *Dictionerium*, L. **148**.
Spelman, H., *Concilia*, 1639. L. **19**.
Statute Books, unidentified. LL. **19, 37**.
Stokes, D., *Paraphratical Explication of the Prophecies of Habakkuk*, Oxford 1646. L. **25**.
Stow, J., *Annales*, 1631. L. **137**.
Taylor, J., *Cases of Conscience*, Part I, 1655. L. **4**.
Thorndike, H., *An Epilogue to the Tragedy of the Church of England*, 1659. L. **34**.
Tooker (Tucker), W., unspecified volume. L. **44**.
Vicecomes, J., *Observationum ecclesiasticarum*, Vol. IV. L. **49**. (DUL Catalogue of Cosin's Library, D. 432)
Walton, B., *Polyglot Bible*, 6 vols, London 1653–7. LL. **5, 18, 29, 30, 119**.

BIBLIOGRAPHY

Unprinted Sources

Durham Cathedral Muniments at 5 The College, Durham
DCD/B/AA/4, Chapter act books
DCD/L/BB/27–39, Treasurer's books
DCD/LP 22/211, Loose papers

Durham County Record Office
EP/Ho 168
EP/Pi 53

Durham University Library, Archives
Cosin Letter Books 1B
Durham Probate Records 1/1677/D2/1–8 (will and inventory of GD)
Halmole Court Books DCD, DHC/1/1
Sharpe MS 167, Bishop Cosin's Survey 1662

Kew, The National Archives
PCC Wills, with name and date in footnotes here

Leicester Record Office
DE 1139/2–3 (Ringrose transcripts)
Wigston Magna parish register

Lincolnshire Record Office
West Rasen parish register

London, British Library
Additional MS 4292
Additional MS 30478. *Anthems & services in use in Durham Cathedral, by various composers of 16th and 17th centuries* (belonged in 1664 to George Davenport)
Harleian MSS 3783, 3784, 3785, 3786
Sloane MS 813

Oxford, Bodleian Library
Rawlinson MSS, Letters 100, 101
Tanner MSS 40, 42, 43, 44, 45, 47, 48, 49, 52, 55, 92, 144, 145, 149, 150, 155, 314

Warwickshire Record Office
Exhall (Coventry) parish register

Printed Sources

Abbott, W.C., *The Writings and Speeches of Oliver Cromwell*, 4 vols, Cambridge (Mass.) 1937.

Acts and Ordinances of the Interregnum, 1640–1660, ed. C.H. Firth and R.S. Rait, 3 vols, London 1911.

Ambler, R.W., *Churches, Chapels and the Parish Communities of Lincolnshire 1660–1900*, History of Lincolnshire 9, Lincoln 2000.

Aylmer, G.E., and Cant, R., *A History of York Minster*, Oxford 1977.

Balfour, J., ed., *The Scots Peerage*, 9 vols, Edinburgh 1911.

The Baptismal, Marriage and Burial Registers of the Cathedral Church of Christ and Blessed Mary the Virgin at Durham, 1609–1896, transcribed and annotated by E.A. White, Harleian Society (1897).

Barnes, H., 'On Quarter Sessions Orders Relating to the Plague in County Durham in 1665', *Archaeologia Aeliana* 15 (1892), pp. 18–22.

Bendall, S., Brooke, C., and Collinson, P., *A History of Emmanuel College, Cambridge*, Woodbridge 1999.

Best, G.F.A., *Temporal Pillars: Queen Anne's Bounty, the Ecclesiastical Commissioners and the Church of England*, Cambridge 1964.

Bibby, R., *A Survey of a Northumbrian Castle, Village and Church*, Newcastle 1973.

Bosher, R.S., *The Making of the Restoration Settlement: The Influence of the Laudians (1649–1662)*, London 1951.

Brickstock, R., *Durham Castle: Fortress, Palace, College*, Durham 2007.

Broughton, J., *All Saints, Wigston Magna*, Wigston 1999.

Broughton, J., *The Old Church – a History of St Wistan's Church, Wigston Magna*, Wigston Magna (Leics.) 2000.

Brown, F., Driver, S.R., and Briggs, C.A., *Hebrew and English Lexicon with an appendix containing Biblical Aramaic*, Peabody (Mass.) 1906.

Burke, B., *The General Armory of England, Scotland, Ireland and Wales*, London 1884, repr. 1967.

Cambridge History of the Bible, 3 vols, Cambridge 1963–70.

Carr, R.E., *The History of the Carr Family of Dunston Hill, County Durham*, 3 vols, London 1893–9.

Cases in the Court of Arches, 1660–1913, ed. J. Houston, British Record Society 85 (1972).

Chandaman, C.D., *The English Public Revenue, 1660–1688*, Oxford 1975.

Church Wardens Accounts of Pittington and other Parishes in the Diocese of Durham from 1580–1700, ed. J. Barmby, 5584 (1888).

Clark, G., *The Oxford History of England, 10: The Later Stuarts, 1660–1714*, 2nd edn, Oxford 1955, repr. 1992.

Cokayne, G.E., *Complete Baronetage*, 6 vols, London 1900–09, repr. 1983.

Cokayne, G.E., *The Complete Peerage of England, Scotland, Ireland, Great Britain and the United Kingdom, extant, extinct or dormant*, 14 vols in 15, London 1910–1998.

Cookson, G., *Sunderland: Building a City*, London 2010.

Cosin, J., *The Correspondence of John Cosin … together with other papers illustrative of his life and times*, 2 vols, ed. G. Ornsby, SS 52 (1869), SS 55 (1870).

Cosin, J., *The Works of the Right Reverend Father in God John Cosin …*, 5 vols, Oxford 1893–5.

Crawford-Hodgson, J., 'A Survey of the Churches in the Archdeaconry of Northumberland, temp. Charles II', *Archaeologia Aeliana*, 2nd ser., 17 (1895), pp. 244–62.

Creighton, C., *The History of Epidemics in Britain*, 2 vols, Cambridge 1891–4.

Cuming, G.J., ed., *The Durham Book*, Westport (Conn.) 1961, repr. 1979.

Curzon, L.B., *Dictionary of Law*, London 1979.

Darnell, W.N., *The Life and Correspondence of Isaac Basire*, London 1831.

Davies, G., *The Early Stuarts, 1603–1660*, 2nd edn, Oxford 1959, repr. 1992.

A Dictionary of the Older Scottish Tongue, 12 vols, London 1937–2000.

Dictionnaire de Biographie Française, 18 vols, Paris 1933 onwards.

Dimock Fletcher, W.G., *Leicestershire Pedigrees and Royal Descents*, Leicester 1887.

Doyle, A.I., 'The Cosin Manuscripts and George Davenport', *The Book Collector* 53/1 (Spring 2004) pp. 32–45.

Doyle, A.I., 'John Cosin (1595–1672) as a Library-Maker', *The Book Collector* 40/3 (1991), pp. 335–57.

D'Oyly, G., *The Life of William Sancroft, Archbishop of Canterbury*, 2 vols, London 1821.

Dugdale, W., *Monasticon Anglicanum*, London 1655.

Dumble, W., 'The Durham Lilburnes and the English Revolution', in Marcombe, ed., *The Last Principality*, pp. 226–52.

Durston, C., *Cromwell's Major Generals: Godly Government during the English Revolution*, Manchester 2001.

Evelyn, J., *The Diary of John Evelyn*, ed. E.S. De Beer, 6 vols, Oxford 1955.

Field, J., *Durham Cathedral, Light of the North*, London 2006.

Firth, C.H., *The Last Years of the Protectorate, 1656–8*, 2 vols, London 1909.

Fletcher, W.G.D., *Leicester Pedigrees and Royal Descents*, Leicester 1887.

Fordyce, W., *The History and Antiquities of the County Palatine of Durham*, 2 vols, Newcastle 1857.

Foster, J., *Alumni Oxonienses, 1500–1714*, 4 vols, Oxford 1891.

Freeman, J., 'The Distribution and Use of Ecclesiastical Patronage in the Diocese of Durham, 1558–1640', in Marcombe, ed., *The Last Principality*, pp. 152–75.

Fryde, E.B., Greenway D.E., Porter S., and Roy, I., eds, *Handbook of British Chronology*, 3rd edn, London 1986.

Gee, H., 'The Correspondence of George Davenport, sometime Rector of Houghton-le-Spring', *Archaeologia Aeliana*, 3rd ser., 9 (1913), pp. 1–10.

Gee, H., 'The Derwentdale Plot, 1663', *Transactions of the Royal Historical Society*, 3rd ser., 11 (1917), pp. 125–42.

Granville, D., *The Remains of Denis Granville, Dean of Durham*, ed. G. Ornsby, SS 47 (1865).

Granville, R., *The Life of the Honourable and Very Reverend Denis Granville, DD*, Exeter 1902.

Green, A., Parkinson, E., and Spufford, M., *County Durham Hearth Tax Assessment, Lady Day 1666*, Index Library 119, British Record Society 2006.

Green, I.M., *The Re-establishment of the Church of England, 1660–1663*, Oxford 1978.

Heal, F., and Holmes, C., *The Gentry in England and Wales, 1500–1700*, London 1994.

Hennessy, G., *Novum Repertorium Ecclesiasticum Parochiale Londinense, or, London Diocesan Clergy Succession from the Earliest Times to the Year 1898*, London 1898.

Highet, T.P., *Early History of the Davenports of Davenport*, Chetham Society, 3rd ser., 9 (1960).

The History of Parliament. The House of Commons 1660–1690, 3 vols, ed. B.D. Henning, London 1983.

Hoskins, W.G., *The Midland Peasant: a Study of a Leicestershire Village*, London 1957.

Howell, R., *Newcastle upon Tyne and the Puritan Revolution. A Study of the Civil War in the North of England*, Oxford 1967.

Hutchinson, W., *The History and Antiquities of the County Palatine of Durham*, 3 vols, Newcastle 1785–94.

Hutton, R., *The Restoration: a Political and Religious History of England and Wales, 1658–1667*, Oxford 1998.

James, M., *Family, Lineage and Civil Society: a Study of Society, Politics and Mentality in the Durham Region, 1500–1640*, Oxford 1974.

Journals of the House of Lords, beginning anno decimo octavo Caroli secundi 1666, vol. XII, *1666–75*, London 1771.

Lang, J., *The Rebuilding of St Paul's after the Great Fire of London*, Oxford 1956.

Lehmberg, S.E., *Cathedrals under Siege, 1600–1700*, Philadelphia 1996.

Le Neve, J., *Fasti ecclesiae anglicanae, 1541–1857*, various edns, 12 vols, London 1969 onwards.

Litten, J., *The English Way of Death*, London 1991.

Livermore, H.V., *A New History of Portugal*, Cambridge 1966.

Luther, M., *Works, I: Lectures on Genesis 1–5*, ed. J. Pelikan, St Louis 1958.

Mackenzie, E., and Ross, D., *An Historical, Topographical and Descriptive View of the County Palatine of Durham*, 3 vols, Newcastle 1834.

Maland, D., *Europe in the Seventeenth Century*, London 1966.

Manning, O., and Bray, W., *The History and Antiquities of the County of Surrey*, 3 vols, 1809–14, repr. Wakefield 1974.

Marcombe, D., ed., *The Last Principality: Politics, Religion and Society in the Bishopric of Durham, 1494–1660*, Nottingham 1987.

Matthews, A.G., *Calamy Revised being a Revision of Edmund Calamy's Account of the Ministers & Others Ejected and Silenced, 1660–2*, Oxford 1934.

Matthews, A.G., *Walker Revised being a Revision of John Walker's Sufferings of the Clergy during the Grand Rebellion, 1642–60*, Oxford 1948.

M'Call, H.B., *The Early History of Bedale in the North Riding of Yorkshire*, London 1907.

McConica, J., *The History of the University of Oxford, III: The Collegeiate University*, Oxford 1986.

Miscellanea, ed. J. Raine, SS 37 (1861).

Miscellanea, ed. C. Talbot, Catholic Record Society 53 (1960).

Morgan, V., *A History of the University of Cambridge, II: 1546–1750*, Cambridge 2004.

Mussett, P., *List of Deans and Major Canons of Durham, 1541–1900*, Durham 1974.

Newcourt, W., *London: an Exact Delineation of the Cities of London and Westminster and the Suburbs thereof, together with the Borough of Southwark*, London 1905.

Nichols, J., *The History and Antiquities of the County of Leicester*, 4 vols in 8 parts, London 1795–1811, repr. Wakefield 1971.

North Country Diaries, ed. J.C. Hodgson, SS 118 (1910), 124 (1915).

Northumberland County History Committee, *A History of Northumberland*, 15 vols, Newcastle 1893–1940.

O'Day, R., *The English Clergy: the Emergence and Consolidation of a Profession, 1558–1642*, Leicester 1979.

Orde, A., 'Ecclesiastical Estate Management in County Durham in the Eighteenth Century', *Northern History* 45 (2008), pp. 159–71.

Osmond, P.H., *A Life of John Cosin, Bishop of Durham 1660–1672*, London and Oxford 1913.

Oxford Dictionary of the Christian Church, ed. F.L. Cross and E.A. Livingstone, 3rd edn, Oxford 1997.

Oxford English Dictionary, ed. J.A.H. Murray et al., 13 vols, Oxford 1933.

Packer, J.W., *The Transformation of Anglicanism*, Manchester 1969.

Parkinson, E., *The Establishment of the Hearth Tax, 1662–66*, List and Index Society, Special Series, 43 (2008).

Pearl, V., *London and the Outbreak of the Puritan Revolution: City, Government and National Politics, 1625–43*, Oxford 1961.

Plomer, H.R., *A Dictionary of the Booksellers and Printers who were at work in England, Scotland and Ireland from 1641 to 1667*, Bibliographical Society, London 1907.

Plomer, H.R., *A Dictionary of Booksellers and Printers who were at work in England, Scotland and Ireland from 1668 to 1725*, Bibliographical Society, London 1922.

Pollard, W., and Redgrave, G.R., *A Short-Title Catalogue of the Books printed in England, Scotland and Ireland, 1475–1640*, 2nd edn, 3 vols, London 1986–91.

Power, M., 'Shadwell: the Development of a London Suburban Community in the Seventeenth Century', *The London Journal* 4/1 (1978), pp. 28–46.

Protestation Returns 1641/2, Lincolnshire, transcribed by W.F. Webster, Nottingham 1984.

Purdue, A.W., *Merchants and Gentry in North East England, 1650–1830. The Carrs and the Ellisons*, Sunderland 1999.

Quentin, H., *Jean-Dominique Mansi et les grandes collections conciliares*, Paris 1900.

Raine, R., *The Statutes of the Cathedral Church of York*, Leeds 1900.

Ramsey, R.W., 'Kepier Grammar School, Houghton-le-Spring and its Library', *Archaeologia Aeliana*, 3rd ser., 3 (1907), pp. 306–33.

Ramsey, R.W., 'Records of Houghton-le-Spring', *English Historical Review* 20, (no. 80, 1905), pp. 673–692.

Raymond, J., ed., *News, Newspapers and Society in Early Modern Britain*, London and Portland (Or.) 1999.

Records of the Committee for Compounding etc., with Delinquent Royalists in Durham and Northumberland during the Civil War (1643–1660), ed. R. Welford, SS 111 (1905).

Register of Admissions to the Honorable Society of the Middle Temple, I: 1501–1781, compiled by H.A.C. Sturgess et al., London 1949.

Rushford, F.H., *Houghton le Spring. A History*, Durham 1951.

Shaw, W.A., and Burtchaell, G.D., *The Knights of England*, 2 vols, London 1906.

Shrewsbury, J.F.D., *A History of Bubonic Plague in the British Isles*, Cambridge 1971.

Spurr, J., *The Restoration Church of England, 1646–1689*, Newhaven 1991.

Stapylton, M., *Northumbrian Documents of the Seventeenth and Eighteenth Centuries, comprising the Register of the Estates of Roman Catholics in Northumberland and the Correspondence of Miles Stapylton*, ed. C. Hodgson, SS 131 (1918).

Statutes and Ordinances of the Interregnum, 3 vols, 1642–66, London 1911.

Statutes of the Cathedral Church of Durham, with Other Documents relating to its Foundation and Endowment by King Henry the eighth and Queen Mary, ed. A.H. Thompson, SS 143 (1929).

Statutes of the Realm, 9 vols in 10, London 1810–22.

Stow, J., *The Annales of England*, London 1600.

Stow, J., *Annales or a general Chronicle of England begun by John Stow: continued and augmented with matters foreign and domestique, ancient and modern, unto the end of this present year 1631 by Edmund Howes, gent.*, London 1631.

Surtees, R., *The History and Antiquities of the County Palatine of Durham*, 4 vols, London 1816–40.

Tanner, N.P., *Decrees of the Ecumenical Councils*, 2 vols, Washington (DC) 1990.

Tillbrook, M., 'Arminianism and Society in County Durham, 1617–1642', in Marcombe, ed., *The Last Principality*, pp. 202–6.

Toy, R., *The Parish Church of St Michael and All Angels, Houghton le Spring – an Account of its History and Significance*, Durham 2000.

A Transcript of the Registers of the Worshipful Company of Stationers, 1640–1708AD, II, *1655–1675*, London 1913.

Twigg, J., *The University of Cambridge and the English Revolution*, Woodbridge 1990.

Tyacke, N., *Anti-Calvinists: the Rise of English Arminianism c. 1590–1640*, Oxford 1987.

Valor ecclesiasticus temp. Henry VIII auctoritate regia institutus, 6 vols, London 1810.

Venn, J.A., *Alumni Cantabrigienses*, 4 vols, Cambridge 1922–7.

Venning, T., *Cromwellian Foreign Policy*, Basingstoke 1995.

Victoria History of the Counties of England as follows:

Berkshire, ed. P.H. Ditchfield and W. Page, 4 vols, London 1906–27.

Buckinghamshire, ed. W. Page, 4 vols, London 1905–28.

Durham, ed. W. Page, 3 vols, London 1905–28.

Gloucestershire, ed. W. Page et al., 11 vols, London 1907 onwards.

Hampshire and the Isle of Wight, ed. W. Page, 5 vols, London 1900–14.

Leicestershire, ed. W. Page et al., 5 vols, London 1907 onwards.

Surrey, ed. H.E. Malden et al., 5 vols, London 1902–14.

York, City of, ed. W. Page and P.M. Tillott, London 1961.

York, County of, ed. W. Page, 3 vols, London 1907–25.

York: East Riding, ed. W. Page and K.J. Allison, 8 vols, London 1969–2008.

York: North Riding, ed. W. Page, 3 vols, London 1914–25.

Walker, D.M., *Oxford Companion to Law*, Oxford 1980.

Walker, E.C., *William Dell, Master Puritan*, Cambridge 1970.

Western, J.R., *The English Militia in the Eighteenth Century: the Story of a Political Issue, 1660–1802*, London 1965.

Whiting, C.E., 'The Great Plot of 1663', *Durham University Journal* 22 (1920), pp. 155–67.

Whiting, C.E., *Nathaniel Lord Crewe, Bishop of Durham (1674–1721), and his Diocese*, London 1940.

Williams, J.B., *A History of English Journalism to the Foundation of the Gazette*, London 1908.

Williamson, P.A., Taylor, S.J., Mears, N., and Raffe, A., eds, *British State Prayers, Fasts, Thanksgivings and Days of Prayer, 1540–1950s*, Church of England Record Society, forthcoming.

Williamson, P.A., Taylor, S.J., Mears, N., and Raffe, A., *The British Nation and Divine Providence, 1540–2003*, in preparation.

Wing, D., *Short Title Catalogue of Books Printed in England, Scotland, Ireland, Wales and British America, and English Books Printed in Other Countries, 1641–1700*, (Vol I 2nd ed), 4 vols 1980–98, New York.

Wright, J., *The English Dialect Dictionary*, 6 vols, London 1898–1905.

INDEX OF PERSONS

There may be more than one reference per page. Alternative spellings are given in brackets for ease of retrieval, from *ODNB* etc. Dates are given only when needed for identification.

INDEX OF PLACES

INDEX OF SUBJECTS